THE AMERICAN ALPINE JOURNAL

2017

[Front Cover] Brette Harrington warms her hands during a free attempt on Great Sail Peak on Baffin Island (see p.171). *Joshua Lavigne* [This page] Jasmin Fauteux on the first pitch of La Fourchette Sternale Droite, Nipissis River area, Québec, during the first ascent (see p.168). *Maarten van Haeren*

2017   VOLUME 59 ISSUE 91

CONTENTS

Photo] Zach Harrison finishes up the leaning corner on the first pitch of Valhalla (5.12-), Insomnia Canyon, Arizona (see p.116). *Blake McCord*

CLIMBS & EXPEDITIONS

The American Alpine Journal, 710 Tenth St. Suite 100, Golden, Colorado 80401
Telephone: (303) 384-0110 E-mail: aaj@americanalpineclub.org
www.publications.americanalpineclub.org

ISSN: 0065-6925
ISBN: 978-1-933056-96-8
ISBN: (hardcover edition): 978-1-933056-98-2

[Photo] Flying over the Cirque of the Unclimbables in Canada's Northwest Territories (see p.76). *Mark Smiley*

FRIENDS OF THE AAJ

[Photo] **Marc-André Leclerc** during the first free ascent of the route Titanic on Torre Egger (see p.222). A week earlier, Leclerc had soloed the peak. *Austin Siadak*

2016 GREAT RANGES FELLOWSHIP

[EIGER]

Anonymous (2)
Brooks-Matthews Foundation
Yvon & Malinda Chouinard
Kevin Duncan
Timothy Forbes

Clark L. Gerhardt Jr.
Robert Hyman & Deb Atwood
Lou Kasischke
Ryan Maitland
Craig McKibben & Sarah Merner

Mark & Teresa Richey
Carey Roberts
Cody J Smith
Doug & Maggie Walker

[ALPAMAYO]

Alpenglow Foundation
Edmund and Betsy Cabot
Foundation
Jim Edwards & Michelle Mass
Chuck & Lisa Fleischman
Charlotte Fox
Eiichi Fukushima
Gerald E. Gallwas

Rocky Henderson
Mark Kroese
Phil Lakin Jr.
David Landman
George H. Lowe III
Garry Menzel
Miriam Nelson
Naoe Sakashita

Richard Salisbury
Steve & Paula Mae Schwartz
Bill & Barbara Straka
Duncan Stuart
Steven J. Swenson & Ann Dalton
Larry True & Linda Brown

[ROBSON]

Lisa Abbott
Jon Anderson
Vaclav E. Benes
Gordon A. Benner, M.D.
Audrey Borisov
Tanya Bradby & Martin Slovacek
Jim Collins
The Duckworth Family
Phil Duff
Ken Ehrhart
Dan A. Emmett
Philip Erard
Christopher Flory

Bruce Franks
James & Franziska Garrett
David V. Goeddel
Wayne & Cynthia Griffin
Richard E. Hoffman, M.D.
Scott Holder
Thomas F. Hornbein, M.D.
Thomas C. Janson
Cristin Julian
Paul Lego
Randy Luskey
Anthony & Carolyn Mansfield
Danny McCracken

Peter & Kathleen Metcalf
Matt Ochs
John A. Rehmer
Wolf Riehle
David Riggs
Darcy Ryan
Lauren Sigman
Oliver Stauffer
Theodore P. Streibert
Joshua Swidler
Geoffrey C. Tabin, M.D.
Jack Tracy

[TEEWINOT]

Anonymous
Jonah Adelman
Warren Adelman
Mark Aiston
Glen Anders
Santiago Arteaga
James Balog
Arthur Barnes
Gail Bates
Doug & Sandy Beall
Sumit Bhardwaj
Craig & Kathy Blockwick
Marty Brigham
Paul Brunner & Coleen
    Curry
Deanne Buck
Thomas C. Burch
William A. Burd
Mitch Campbell
R.J. Campbell
Jay Cassell
Dan Cohen
Jeffrey Cohen
Kevin Cooney
John Costello
Frederick P. Couper
Beckie & Dave Covill
Matt & Charlotte
    Culberson
Brittany Cupp
John Davidge & Deborah
    Lott
Elizabeth & Joseph
    Davidson
Scott Davis
Walter P. Dembitsky, M.D.
Stan & Judy Dempsey

Kit DesLauriers
Ed Diffendal
John Donlou
Richard & Martha Draves
Jesse Dwyer
Charles Eilers
Stuart H. Ellison
Terrence J. English
Drew Fink
Chas Fisher
Keith Fleischman
Philip Francis
James A. Frank
Jim Frush
Ken & Rebecca Gart
Neil Gehrels
Marilyn Geninatti
Michael & Kristin Gibbons
Bill Givens
Charles Goldman
Robert Hall
James Halle
Aaron Hammond
Andre Haroche
Roger Hartl
Leslie Hassen
Ryan Hill
Scot T. Hillman
Mark K. Hingston
Michael Hodges
Marley & Jennifer Hodgson
Todd Hoffman
James Holmes
Alex Intermill
Steve & Michelle Jones
Diane Kearns
Arthur Kearns

William Kilpatrick, M.D.
Joel G. Kinney
Erik Lambert
Jon Leavitt
Michael L. Lederer
William E. Long
Evan T. Lukow
Chris Lynch
Brent V. Manning
Edwards Matthews
George McCown
Dan McCoy
Brad McQueen
Scott Milliman
Barrett Morgan
Halsted "Hacksaw" Morris
Paul Morrow
Mie Nakane
Kit Natland
Nathan Nicholas
Vanessa O'Brien
Sean Obrien
Bob Palais
John Parsons
Adam & Merritt Patridge
Charles Peck
Brian Peters
Will Philips
Mark Powers
Phil Powers
Louis Reichardt
John D. Reppy
Jim Rickards
Michael Riley
David Robertson
Joel P. Robinson
Arthur Rock

John Rudolph
Jeffrey L. Rueppel
David Ryon, M.D.
Vik Sahney
Brian Salomaki
Jeb Sanford
Janet Schlindwein
Mark Schoening
Kristiann Schoening
Stephen Schofield
Raymond VJ Schrag
Stephen Scofield
George Shaw
John Sirois
George N. Smith
Brian Sohn
Katherine Song
Rob & Jennifer Stephenson
Bob Street
John Sykes
Jack & Pat Tackle
Crystal Tan
Steve & Krista Howard
David Thoenen
Erwin Thomet
Ben Toews
John Townsend
Dieter H. von Hennig
Jeff S. Wagener, M.D.
Mark D. Wilford
Rich Wilsey
Doug Wilson
Todd Winzenried
Jason Wolfe
Fred Wolfe
Keegan Young
Rob Ziegler

THE AMERICAN ALPINE JOURNAL

EXECUTIVE EDITOR
Dougald MacDonald

SENIOR EDITOR
Lindsay Griffin

ASSOCIATE EDITORS
Andy Anderson, Geoff Hornby,
Chris Kalman, Erik Rieger

ART DIRECTOR
David Boersma

CONTRIBUTING EDITORS
James Benoit, *In Memoriam*
David Stevenson, *Book Reviews*

ILLUSTRATIONS AND MAPS
Martin Gamache, Craig Muderlak, Drew
Thayer

PROOFREADERS
Allison Albright, Whitney Clark, Alison
Criscitiello, Rolando Garibotti, Clark
Gerhardt, Damien Gildea, Vanessa
Logsdon, Bruce Normand, Eric Rueth,
Katie Sauter

INDEXERS
Ralph Ferrara, Eve Tallman

TRANSLATORS
Claude Gardien, Sergio Martin de Santos,
Oh Young-hoon, Simone Sturm

REGIONAL CONTACTS
Steve Gruhn, Mark Westman, *Alaska*;
Sevi Bohorquez, Sergio Ramirez Carrascal,
Peru; Luis Pardo, *Colombia*; Damien Gildea,
Antarctica; Rolando Garibotti, Marcelo Scanu,
Argentina-Chile; Alex von Ungern, *Bolivia*;
Geoff Hornby, *Middle East*; Harish Kapadia,
Nandini Purandare, *India*; Rodolphe Popier,
Richard Salisbury, *Nepal*; Tamotsu Nakamura,
Hiroshi Hagiwara, *Japan*; Peter Jensen-Choi,
Oh Young-hoon, *Korea*; Elena Dmitrenko, Anna
Piunova, *Russia, Tajikistan, and Kyrgyzstan*;
Xia Zhongming, *China*

ADVISORY BOARD
Whitney Clark, Alison Criscitiello, Kelly
Cordes, Damien Gildea, Colin Haley, Mark
Jenkins, Chris Weidner, Graham Zimmerman

WITH HEARTFELT THANKS TO...
Christine Blackmon, Alex Catlin,
Martin Gamache, David Jones, Craig
Muderlak, Connie Self, and our hundreds
of generous donors, authors, and
photographers

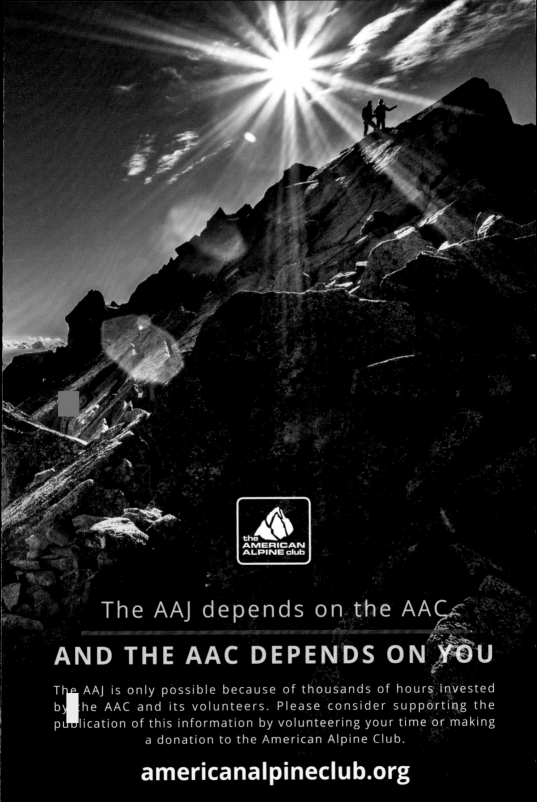

The AAJ depends on the AAC

AND THE AAC DEPENDS ON YOU

The AAJ is only possible because of thousands of hours invested by the AAC and its volunteers. Please consider supporting the publication of this information by volunteering your time or making a donation to the American Alpine Club.

americanalpineclub.org

[Photo] Nick Bullock headed toward the steepest section of the north buttress of Nyanchen Tanglha Southeast. *Paul Ramsden*

THE WRONG VALLEY

CLIMBING A HIDDEN WALL ON A 7,000-METER PEAK IN TIBET

PAUL RAMSDEN

The strange thing about climbing new routes in China and Tibet is that once you're lucky enough to complete a few successful expeditions you suddenly start receiving the *Japanese Alpine News*. One day it pops through the letterbox and then just keeps on coming. It's a great record of the peaks of this region and the limited climbing there. The *JAN* also acts as a chronicle of the activities of the great Tibet explorer Tamotsu "Tom" Nakamura.

While perusing the latest edition in the loo/research office several years ago, I was struck by Tom's photos of the four 7,000-meter Nyanchen Tanglha peaks. About 90 kilometers to the northwest of Lhasa, these are the highest peaks in the mountain chain of the same name (also spelled Nyainqentanglha and other variations), running west to east, in parallel with the Himalaya. From the nearby road, the potential looks minimal, but Tom's pictures from the northeast showed a large north wall falling from the 7,000-meter summits, with a particularly striking arête at the northwest end. A plan started to formulate!

Wanting to go to Tibet is very different from actually getting there. First of all, the China Tibet Mountaineering Association (CTMA) is not easy to contact. Email addresses exist, but getting a response is a different matter. Once in contact, the granting of permits is based on the local political situation. If the locals in that area have been kicking off against the authorities, then you will never get a permit. If you do get a permit, the situation may change weekly, leading to last-minute cancellations. Ever since Mick Fowler and I made the first ascent of Manamcho in the East Nyanchen Tanglha Range, in 2007, we'd been applying for permits for other peaks in Tibet for eight years, to no avail. Suddenly the CTMA agreed that a permit would be possible. A week before we were to fly to Lhasa, the CTMA announced they couldn't email the entry pass, so we would have to collect it in China before proceeding to Tibet. More hassle and expensive flight changes. On the subject of Tibet, lets just say it's not cheap.

I had been climbing with Mick Fowler off and on for the last 15 years—and for my last four expeditions—but this new objective was over 7,000 meters, a bit high for the now-sexagenarian Fowler, so I had to shop around for a new partner. Now, this is not an easy decision, as a climbing partner for such routes needs to be just the right person, yet the pool of people interested in technical climbing on Himalayan peaks is actually not that big, for some reason.

[Top] The Nyanchen Tanglha group from the north. The 2016 Bullock-Ramsden route (1,600m) climbed the shaded face of the left-most summit, Nyanchen Tanglha Southeast (7,046m). No other routes have been climbed from this side on these 7,000-meter peaks. [Bottom] The climbers descended by the east ridge (left skyline), rappelled the steepest cliff to the saddle, and then dropped down the south side (opposite) into an unfamiliar valley. *Expedition Photos*

I'd first met Nick Bullock in Namche Bazaar, many years ago. At the time he seemed like a wild, intense, scary character, but when I popped over to visit him in North Wales last year, he was cat-sitting while writing his second book, an altogether calmer person. Clearly the last 12 years of living out of the back of his van had been good for him. In the end, we got on really well, never a cross word between us, just a steady stream of mild mutual verbal abuse, just the way I like a team to behave.

Tibet had changed a lot since my last visit, nine years earlier. Lhasa was about five times bigger, with high-rise buildings everywhere. The Tibetans have been swamped with ethnic Chinese settlers. The road network is totally overloaded with vehicles, though I was pleased to see that many of them are now electric, which improves the air quality a lot.

Outside of Lhasa, all the small towns have grown considerably, with extensive Chinese development everywhere. It's only when you get into the remote villages and farms that things look pretty much as they always have, except for the satellite dishes and mobile phones. It's quite a surprise when a yak herder whips out his iPhone 6 and demonstrates that he has a 3G signal, just an hour's walk from base camp.

Acclimatization requirements meant we'd have to spend a long time on the very short journey to base camp. Lhasa is at 3,700 meters, and we spent two nights there after flying in. We then drove for half a day to Damshung, at 4,200 meters, and spent two nights there. Then we drove for one hour and spent a night at the road head, at 4,700 meters, in the local headman's house, then walked for four hours to base camp with packhorses. In all, it took us six days to travel to base camp—a journey that required only six hours on our way out.

WE ARRIVED IN the mountains in bad weather, and there was much confusion over which valley we should walk into. The maps of the area are quite poor and location names very confused. The locals warned us that we were approaching the mountain from the wrong side, as it was too steep to climb from that valley—that sounded brilliant!

They also warned us the area was infested with bears that would "bite you in the face." Nick's reaction to this news was a real picture—he and Greg Boswell had famously been attacked by a grizzly in Canada one year before. I thought he might refuse to go on. In the end, we saw nothing bigger than a mouse.

At base camp we didn't have the usual cook and tea boy (we couldn't afford them in Tibet), so it was just the two of us for a month—pretty intense with someone you don't know that well. At this stage we still didn't even know if we were in the right valley, so there was a bit of tension in the air. But camp was in a pretty location, and we soon felt right at home and ready to explore. It's likely we were the first Westerners ever to enter this valley.

Our original plan had been to climb the north buttress of Nyanchen Tanglha's main summit, the farthest up the valley, which looked just brilliant in Tom's pictures. However, as we walked below the face of the lowest and easternmost 7,000-meter peak along the ridge, Nyanchen Tanglha Southeast (7,046m, a.k.a. Nyanchen Tanglha IV), we realized it had a recessed north face whose steep lower half was not visible from anywhere other than directly beneath it. I'd seen a hint of this on Google Earth, but as we edged into position the clouds cleared to reveal the sort of route you always dream about finding. We were speechless.

The 1,600-meter face was very steep in the first half before giving way a bit and forming an impressive arête. The lower headwall looked problematic: steep rock with what appeared to be a thin veneer of ice—it looked like it might go, but only just. If that veneer turned out to be just a bit of powder snow from the last storm, then we would have big problems. Hardly able to contain our excitement, we headed back down to base camp to prepare ourselves for the main event.

OUR FIRST ATTEMPT on the route is best forgotten. We camped under the face, it dumped snow, the tent nearly blew away, and we retreated. We needed to let the mountain slough some snow for a few days, so returned to base camp and waited. Reading, making bread, eating enormous meals, debates on whether to take a toothbrush—all the usual stuff. Soon bored, I insisted conditions must be suitable, or as good as they were going to get, so we set off for our second attempt.

Camped once again under the face in perfect weather, we saw a lot less snow on the face than before. We decided the direct start looked a bit thin in the first rock band, and there is nothing more dispiriting than failing on the first pitch of a 1,600-meter wall. A gully to the left offered more ice, and we could see a traverse back into the center of the face a bit higher up. Avoiding the regular spindrift sloughs coming down the center would be an added bonus.

[Left] The Nyanchen Tanglha peaks, 90 kilometers northwest of Lhasa, are the high points of the 750-kilometer range of the same name. *Google Maps* [Right] Nick Bullock at base camp. *Paul Ramsden*

I always enjoy the walk up to the foot of a big climb. As the perspective changes, the face rears up alarmingly, but as the lower pitches become visible in more detail, suddenly the whole thing looks more manageable. I suppose it's burying your head in the sand, but I really try to think about such a big route as one pitch at a time. Deal with what's in front of you and worry about the rest later. It's just as well the first pitches appeared manageable, because, amazingly, the foot of the face was the first time that Nick and I had ever tied on a rope together.

We soon discovered we were unlikely to find any easy-going névé on this trip. The snow was deep, really deep, and the only ice was found when things steepened up and the powder had sloughed off. That first day, working our way up the lower slopes, was really hard work, with seemingly never-ending post-holing as we climbed toward our planned bivy ledge, below the steepening rock bands.

Before the climb I'd stipulated to Nick that "slow and heavy," not light and fast, was the way to succeed on big new routes in the Himalaya, and that we'd stop whenever we got to a really good camp spot, even early in the day. But the snow arête I'd been aiming for turned out to be knife-sharp, with rocks just below the surface. It eventually produced two semi-reclining sitting ledges—grim! With us perched on separate ledges, there was no way to put up the tent, so I just wrapped myself in the fabric, pulled on the duvet jacket, and tried to melt some water with the wind constantly blowing the stove out. Nick was not impressed with the promised Ramsden Five-Star Bivy.

As the sun came up, we could see the good weather had vanished and we were back to the usual Nyanchen Tanglha cloud and precipitation. But the night really had not been that bad. After some breakfast, we were ready to get stuck into the technical ground above. A very steep rock band crossed the full width of the face, and in most places it was too steep for ice. But in the center was a thin veneer of white covering the rock. Today we would find out if this was unclimbable powder snow or reasonable ice.

We traversed diagonally up and rightward, aiming for steep runnels and the elusive ice. Indeed, much of what had looked like ice from below turned out to be powder snow stuck under overhangs, with a thin, delaminated snow crust on the vertical rock. Luckily, a series of shallow runnels did hold some goodish ice. It often wasn't thick enough to take a full ice screw,

[Above] **Paul Ramsden engaged in the crux runnels of "goodish" ice, the key to breaching the steepest rock band on the north buttress of Nyanchen Tanglha** Southeast. *Nick Bullock*

but if you dug around on the adjacent rock, bits of rock gear were available.

Slowly we worked up some very absorbing pitches, occasionally hauling sacks. The climbing was excellent; Nick thought it reminded him of the upper part of the Colton-MacIntyre on the Grandes Jorasses. When the groove line ended, Nick was forced to climb a steep rock wall, uncovering a series of flakes beneath the snowy veneer that allowed for good but scary hooking, a fine lead.

Then we were through the rock band and looking for somewhere to camp. Determined to have better night's sleep, I announced it was time to test my latest version of the snow hammock, a large rectangle of sturdy fabric that you attach to the face with ice screws and fill with snow to create a ledge. My mother-in-law had sewn a new, stronger version than

[Top] Working left to the crest of the buttress on day three of the climb. [Bottom] The author looks pleased with his mother-in-law's sewing. *Nick Bullock*

the one I'd tried before; it worked brilliantly and we ended up with a nearly flat tent site in a truly ridiculous position. It had been a tough day, though, and we woke pretty exhausted. From this point we had two options: either follow the crest of the buttress or the more mixed ground on the right. Concerns about avalanche potential on some of the snowfields and the feasibility of the rock bands to the right meant the crest of the buttress was clearly the best option.

Traversing leftward, we hit the crest and climbed an arête in a wild position. We decided to make day three a short one and stopped as soon as we could find another good spot for the snow hammock. In the evening we had great views of huge Nam Tso Lake to the north—we literally could see moisture being sucked off the surface, ready to dump on us. The lake is so big (about half the size of Rhode Island) that even though it was roughly 20 kilometers away, our route felt a bit like a sea cliff.

As the crest of the buttress became less technical, the snow just got deeper and deeper, which, combined with the altitude, made for some lung-busting pitches. Our fourth camp was good, but that night it started to dump snow, and at 6,700 meters you suddenly start to realize the seriousness of your position. Retreat down the line would be difficult, due to lack of ice for V-thread anchors, and we didn't have enough of a rack to abseil on rock all the way. Upward to the summit and, hopefully, down an easier ridge was the best option, but we worried about avalanches with all the new snow.

Dawn brought more snow and cloud. Postholing upward, we made the summit about midday. It was the third ascent of the peak—the first was in 1995, from the south—and my first time over 7,000 meters. We both were knackered. The clouds blocked any view, so after a quick selfie I was keen to get off.

I was pretty sure our best option was to descend the east ridge until it terminated in a huge cliff, at which point we could abseil the north side on Abalakov ice anchors before regaining the ridge at a col. From there it looked like an easy walk down to the valley and base camp. Dense fog turned the relatively easy but quite complicated east ridge into a real navigational challenge. After falling into three bergschrunds, I decided to call it quits for the day. The tent fit quite nicely into the last hole I had made.

There was little food left, it dumped snow all night, and we didn't actually know where we were, due to the dense cloud, so it wasn't the best night ever. In the morning, we stayed put for a few hours until visibility improved. At this stage avalanches were our main concern, but there wasn't actually anything we could do about it. There was no Plan B at this stage.

Fortunately, the cloud cleared and let us identify our precise location, allowing us to continue. The east ridge terminated in a large vertical face, but I was able to find a rappel line down the north side to a point where we could get back onto the ridge. We continued to the col without incident. From here we had planned to descend to the north, toward our base camp. However, now it was clear that the southern slope was easier and safer, even if it did descend into an unknown valley. We had no map, but it was a no-brainer, really, and it got us safely down to the moraine without incident.

The next day we stumbled down over a purgatory of loose boulders and soft, muddy moraine. No tracks, no sign that

[Above] Paul Ramsden leads the way down the east ridge. The two had hoped to continue down to the north, back to their high camp, but after a day and a half on the ridge, with significant avalanche risk, they realized their only option was to head down the opposite side of the mountain. *Nick Bullock*

anyone had ever been there before. Not a day I'd care to repeat. To our great and pleasant surprise, however, the valley opened onto grassy slopes just above the small hamlet where our liaison officer was staying with the village headman. They were somewhat amazed to see us— even more amazed to hear that we had summited. After all, we had gone up the wrong valley.

SUMMARY: First ascent of the north buttress of Nyanchen Tanglha Southeast (7,046m), by Nick Bullock and Paul Ramsden (both U.K.), October 2–9, 2016. The route gained 1,600m and was graded ED+; they descended by the east ridge and south face. This was the third ascent of the peak and the first climb on the north side of the Nyanchen Tanglha group.

ABOUT THE AUTHOR: *Paul Ramsden, 47, is based in Nottingham, England. He wrote about the first ascent of Gave Ding in Nepal, with Mick Fowler, in AAJ 2016.*

JAM BAND

FREE CLIMBING IN BAFFIN ISLAND'S STEWART VALLEY

MATTEO DELLA BORDELLA

Istill remember when I first saw the *Asgard Jamming* film. It was 2009, in Lecco, a presentation by Nico Favresse and Sean Villanueva. For me it was revolutionary: These guys were climbing in great style on an amazing wall in a beautiful and remote place—Baffin Island—and, incredibly, they were having a lot of fun, laughing and playing musical instruments.

In the environment where I grew up, under the influence of the Ragni di Lecco (the historic "Lecco Spiders" climbing group) in northern Italy, alpinism and expeditions have always been very serious business. In their movies or lectures, the great alpinists tended to emphasize the suffering and drama of their climbs—there was never any space for jokes. *Asgard Jamming* opened my eyes. The Belgians were risking their lives and tackling "impossible" challenges, but they didn't rattle on about numbers or danger. Their amazing images did the talking for them. This became my ideal of the "perfect" expedition—the adventure I would like to live.

Since then I've been lucky to climb in many places around the world: Patagonia, the Karakoram, the Himalaya, Greenland, Mexico. Over time I began to realize that every expedition could be "perfect" as long as it had three equally important ingredients: 1) a beautiful wall to free climb; 2) an experience beyond the technical challenge of climbing, taking me out of my comfort zone; and 3) a group of compatible friends—strong, determined, but also a lot of fun.

As I thought over my options for 2016, after many hours of browsing the Internet, it seemed that Baffin Island, and more precisely the remote Stewart Valley, would be the ideal place for my next expedition. When I proposed this idea to my friends Luca Schiera and Matteo "Giga" De Zaiacomo, they accepted without question. Like me, Luca and Giga are members of the new generation of Ragni di Lecco. In the past few years, Luca has been one of my best partners for serious adventures, and I knew I could trust him 100 percent. Giga was only 22 years old, but the three of us had already done a major expedition together, attempting a new route on Bhagirathi IV in India.

And then came a huge stroke of good fortune. Since that inspiring lecture in 2009, I had stayed in touch with Nico and Sean; we'd even done some climbs together in Italy. Now I learned that they also planned to climb in the Stewart Valley in the summer of 2016. "What do you think of joining forces and going together?" Nico asked me. The answer was obvious!

[Photo] **Matteo De Zaiacomo climbing pitch 10 of Coconut Connection, the first all-free route up the west-northwest face of Great Sail Peak.** *Sean Villanueva*

Nico and Sean played on a higher level than us, but we shared the same goal and the same expedition philosophy, and we liked each other. There was only one problem: I couldn't play any musical instrument! For the Italian team, Giga could play violin and Luca played guitar, but I would have to add learning an instrument to my "to do" list. I opted for the Jew's harp, thinking it might be the simplest to learn.

WE ARRIVED IN Clyde River, Nunavut, on June 3. The temperature was exactly 0°C, and it looked like full winter—the land was completely white and frozen. We needed only one day to organize our gear, and on June 5 we were ready to start our 180-kilometer ski tour to the Stewart Valley, towing sledges behind us.

When you ski over the frozen sea, pulling a sledge for 30 to 35 kilometers a day, the perception of time is relative: Sometimes you get caught in your thoughts and ski for a couple of hours without even realizing it; other times you keep looking at your watch and the time never moves. In the last few months I'd been completely dedicated to climbing—and learning to play the Jew's harp—and did not do any specific training for skiing. I struggled to keep up with the others and began setting intermediate goals, never looking at my watch until I had reached them. Given 24 hours of daylight, we chose to wake in early afternoon, start skiing in the evening, and keep going until 3, 4, or 5 a.m.; it was easier to slide over the frozen snow with the lower temperatures at night. Our daily routine was interrupted only by playing music, which seemed to happen pretty much everywhere and anytime!

After six days we reached our first destination: the Walker Arm of Sam Ford Fjord. Here we also found the food and gear stash that a local guy had carried in a few days in advance by snowmobile. Given that we planned a 60-day expedition, we opted for this solution instead of a completely "fair means" expedition. Maybe if we were stronger we could have brought everything on our sledges. There is always room for improvement.

After all those days moving only horizontally, the sight of the huge rock faces of Walker Citadel, Beluga Spire, and Polar Sun Spire suddenly awakened our dormant climbers' instinct. And though our main goal was to climb in the Stewart Valley, we felt like having an appetizer. On June 13 we divided in two parties and went for alpine-style ascents of the northwest side of Walker Citadel, well to the right of all the existing routes, including the two that Nico, Sean, and their partners had climbed two summers earlier (*AAJ 2015*). My first contact with the rock didn't meet expectations—the granite was not great, with many loose blocks. After an initial hard section, the line Giga and I chose got easier and easier. We started simul-climbing and ended up on an easy ridge. At that point the weather worsened, with high winds. We were about 200 meters from the end of the ridge, and since the remaining climb didn't look great and we had no idea how to descend from the summit, we decided to head down immediately, following the line of the ridge. We arrived back at base camp about 24 hours after starting, with mixed feelings about rock climbing on Baffin Island.

A few hours later, Luca, Nico, and Sean also returned to base camp. Their line had proved to be better, and despite the weather they pushed on to the summit of Walker

[Above] **After six days of skiing with sleds, the team arrives in Sam Ford Fjord, eager to climb. The most prominent sunlit wall is the north face of Kiguti.** *Sean Villanueva*

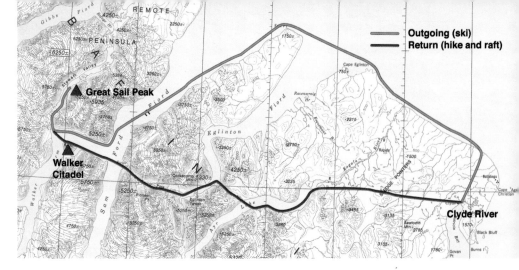

Great Sail Peak

Walker
Citadel

Clyde River

Outgoing (ski)
Return (hike and raft)

Citadel, after a 1,000-meter, 5.12a first ascent. They descended a snow couloir on the south side of the mountain and circled back to camp, 32 hours after leaving, tired but happy.

After a couple of days of recovery, we began our move into the Stewart Valley. Our next camp was about 12 kilometers away, and ferrying all the food and the equipment required multiple trips; luckily, the lake that fills much of the Stewart Valley was still well frozen, so we could use our sledges to pull the bags across the ice. Here the rock looked better and the walls were steeper. This valley was going to be our home for an entire month, and I couldn't wait to put my hands on the rock.

[Map] Green line: The full team's route to Stewart Valley. Red line: The Italians' overland return to Clyde River. [Photo] Northwest buttress of Walker Citadel. (1) Down the Slope Without a Ski. (2) E Poi Boh. *Luca Schiera*

ALTHOUGH THERE WERE several amazing rock faces nearby, we all agreed that the huge west side of Great Sail Peak was the most attractive, and that our goal should be the first free ascent of this 1,000-meter-plus wall. We thought it would be cool to do it as a team of five, in big-wall style, climbing together and playing music along the way. Given my poor performances with the Jew's harp, I'd been asked to sing during our daily concerts, and I fell back on well-known Italian songs like "Bella Ciao," the WW II resistance tune, or "Fratelli d'Italia," the Italian national anthem.

We spent a couple of days climbing and fixing the first part of the wall, mostly following the 1998 American route, with some variations, in changeable and quite cold weather. Seven pitches up, we reached the enormous ledge system that crosses the face. We had found some real climbing—up to 7a+/b—but compared with what we saw above it felt like a warmup. The face already had two routes: the American route Rum, Sodomy, and the Lash (Catto-Child-Lowe-Ogden-Synnott-Wiltsie, 1998) and the Russian route Rubicon (Davy-Klenov-Odintsov-Rozov-Ruchkin, 2002). For us, it was not really important where those two lines went; they were both impressive lines, but opened in a very different style from ours. [*Both routes were completed in the spring, when very cold temperatures more or less mandate traditional aid climbing. Few parties had explored the summertime climbing potential in Baffin's eastern fjords*

[Above] **Nico Favresse chilling in the portaledge.**
Sean Villanueva [Right] **Sean Villanueva leads pitch
21 of Coconut Connection.** *Matteo De Zaiacomo*

*until 2014, when separate Belgian-American and
Canadian teams made numerous and rapid free
ascents in Sam Ford Fjord.*] We were looking for
a good line where redpointing the hardest pitches
might be required. A discontinuous crack system
just 15 meters right of the Russian route seemed to
offer a promising start.

After the first pitch, which followed a
65-meter splitter crack, we got directly into the
business. For four days, we alternated teams as
we moved upward. Since we could count on 24
hours of daylight, we could climb through the
night. Some pitches were opened with a mix of
free and aid climbing, often on micro-nuts and
Peckers, but we never felt the need to place bolts.
On the fifth day, Sean and Nico redpointed the
three hardest pitches (about 5.12d). Since we had
climbed about 350 meters above the big ledge
and didn't have any more rope to fix, we decided
it was time to leave the comfort of the ledge and
start life in the portaledges.

Snow started to fall, but luckily we were
hanging under the steeper part of the wall, so
the wind-blown snow barely touched us. On day
seven the weather remained bad and we relaxed,
recovered, and played some music. Nico was
working on a new tune:

> *Matteo was climbing all night long
> Then Giga was climbing all night long
> Then Luca was climbing all night long*

[Top] Matteo Della Bordella climbing pitch 18 of Coconut Connection. The free route linked portions of both original aid routes on the wall plus about 300 meters of new ground. *Luca Schiera* [Bottom] By mid-July, summer had arrived at the 71st parallel—but just barely. As they began their return journey toward Clyde River, the Italians paddled packrafts through the slush covering the Stewart Valley's big lake. *Sean Villanueva*

Then Sean was climbing all night long
Then I was climbing all night long.
Weeeee have climbed...
We have climbed Great Sail Peak!

During the storm, we discussed what to do next. Since the line we were following ended in a blank, overhanging wall, the logical solution was to traverse left to the Russian route, which followed an obvious system of dihedrals and cracks. Our plan was to launch a summit bid as soon as the weather improved.

In the afternoon of the eighth day on the wall, we left our portaledge camp. The climbing on the upper wall was simply amazing. We followed the Russian route for seven or eight pitches, with some free variations. Free climbing near the top of such a huge wall, under the midnight sun, felt like living in a parallel universe. After climbing all night, at 5 a.m. on the fourth of July, my 32nd birthday, we all stood on the summit of Great Sail Peak, having completed the Coconut Connection (1,050m, 5.12d). What a birthday present!

AFTER WE'D RAPPELLED the route back to the big ledge, we realized that we still had three days of food and stable weather. Soon we were discussing what may sound like a crazy plan: Why don't we split in two teams and try to climb the wall again, by another two new routes? Two big corner systems, in the center and on the left of the wall, were still untouched, and both seemed to have continuous crack systems that would favor fast, alpine-style progression.

On July 7, Luca and I started to climb the big corner system on the left, following nice cracks, with several offwidths and chimneys. On what might be the crux pitch, I tried to avoid a wide section—bigger than a number six cam—by laybacking. I slipped and fell until I was caught by a tipped-out number six. The rope snagged a flake, and when I came to a stop I was staring at the exposed white soul of the rope. Spicy times! Fortunately, I found a smarter solution to redpoint this pitch.

The weather was deteriorating, but Luca and I decided to keep climbing and rush toward the top, before the conditions could become even worse. On the morning of July 8, we found ourselves again on the summit of Great Sail Peak, only four days after our first visit—this time wrapped in clouds and fog. We rappelled the Coconut Connection and returned to find Giga at the ledge camp, 24 hours after we'd left him. Giga had dislocated his shoulder near the top of Coconut Connection and had been forced to wait while we climbed.

Meanwhile, Nico and Sean had found a king line in the central corner, with mostly continuous, Yosemite-style cracks. One hundred meters below the summit, the storm forced them to improvise a bivy and wait for better conditions. After about eight hours of shivering, their patience paid off and the sunshine came back, allowing them to free the last, crucial link of their 700-meter 5.12a climb: a 30-meter unprotectable slab. Thirty-six hours after leaving, they too were back on the big ledge.

Our food was all gone. Now it really was time to descend to base camp.

THE WALLS OPPOSITE Great Sail Peak have several features between 400 and 700 meters high, many of them still unclimbed. We felt we couldn't leave without checking out this side of the valley, so Luca and Nico went for a new route on Copier Pinnacle, the pyramid just in front of our base camp, while Sean and I went for a rounded, dome-like wall that we baptized the Tree of Wisdom. Both routes followed obvious crack systems, with several offwidth sections. High

[Left] The west-northwest face of Great Sail Peak, showing the three Belgian-Italian routes from 2016. See p.171 for a photo of all routes on the face, including the 2016 Canadian-American climbs. (1) Mascalzone Latino. (2) The Northwest Passage. (3) Coconut Connection. *Luca Schiera* [Right] Hiking past Ayr Lake on day five of the trek back to Clyde River. *Luca Schiera*

THE CLIMBS

WALKER ARM

Walker Citadel: Down the Slope Without a Ski (1,000m, 5.12a). Left side of northwest buttress. Descent by snow couloir on south side. Favresse-Schiera-Villanueva, June 14-15

Walker Citadel: E Poi Boh, attempt on northwest buttress (800m, 5.11d) De Zaiacomo–Della Bordella, June 14

STEWART VALLEY

Great Sail Peak, Coconut Connection (1,050m, 5.12d). Free link-up including sections of Rum, Sodomy, and the Lash (1998), Rubicon (2002), and about 300 meters of new terrain. Climbed capsule-style, with every pitch led free by at least one climber. Entire team, June 22–July 4

Great Sail Peak, Mascalzone Latino (600m plus easy ridge, 5.12b A0 pendulum). Della Bordella–Schiera, July 7-8

Great Sail Peak, The Northwest Passage (700m, 5.12a). Favresse-Villanueva, July 7-8

The Tree of Wisdom, The Seed of Madness (600m, 5.11c A0 pendulum). Della Bordella–Villanueva, July 13-14

Copier Pinnacle, 24 Hour Round Trip Camp to Camp (600m, 5.11d). Southeast prow of the formation. Favresse-Schiera, July 13-14

The Citadel, Catacomb (900m, 5.12a). Offwidth and chimney system just left of Arctic Monkeys (McAleese-Thomas-Turner, 2010) on "Welshman's Peak," the far right side of the Citadel. Favresse-Villanueva, July 25

All climbs and attempts were done without bolts.

on our route, the mountain played a little joke on Sean and me when the crack system we'd been following for 500 meters ended in a desperate blank slab, just 20 meters shy of the summit. Since we weren't carrying a bolt kit, our only option was to rappel for 120 meters, swing to the left to reach a parallel chimney system and follow this to the top.

After almost 50 days together, the full band played a last concert in the Stewart Valley. Nico and Sean, of course, were our undisputed leaders, but I like to think that during all this time the Italian players also learned something about music and were a little less out of tune. Our songs echoed from Great Sail and the surrounding walls, and apart from rabbits, mice, and maybe polar bears, the only creatures listening were a Canadian-American trio who had arrived in the valley soon after us and were now working on their own new routes on Great Sail Peak. (*See p.171 for their full report.*)

Summer had arrived at the 71st parallel; the snow had given way to grass and the ice to open water. Our plan was for the three Ragni di Lecco to head back to Clyde River by a more direct path, cutting overland; we would alternate navigation by packraft with hiking on foot. Nico and Sean would wait at least another week for the arrival of the French sailboat Maewan, aboard which they would continue toward the famed Northwest Passage. Before leaving the Stewart Valley, they opened an impressive and intimidating route on the Citadel, which they described as the hardest wide climb they had ever done: "a feast of wet and mossy slots, chimneys, and offwidths—a masterpiece for any wide-crack addict with a slight love for masochism." I

was glad I was not with them—it sounded like a nightmare.

After a quick start toward Clyde River in perfect weather, we three Italians waited out a storm at Walker Arm for three days and then reached Eglington Fjord two days later. We decided to take a day off to scramble to the top of Eglington Tower and enjoy the beautiful panorama. But soon after this climb, almost simultaneously, my left knee and Giga's left ankle both started hurting really badly—it was clear we were suffering from too much walking with heavy bags. With more than 100 kilometers still to go before reaching Clyde River, we hoped to rely our packrafts and move mostly over water, but while dragging the boats over ice both Giga and Luca's rafts were shredded. Now we were forced to stumble across the tundra in clouds of mosquitoes. When I hit the concrete road in Clyde River, eight days after leaving Walker Arm, my knee locked up completely. Luca had to carry my backpack for the last kilometer into the village.

We'd free-climbed big walls, I was definitely far out of my comfort zone, and my friends had been everything I'd hoped. Maybe this really was the perfect expedition. As the saying goes, "It doesn't always have to be fun to be fun!"

SUMMARY: First ascents in Walker Arm and the Stewart Valley of Baffin Island, Nunavut, Canada, including the first free ascent of the ca 1,050-meter west-northwest face of Great Sail Peak, by Matteo Della Bordella, Matteo De Zaiacomo, and Luca Schiera (Italy) and Nicolas Favresse and Sean Villanueva O'Driscoll (Belgium), June-July 2016. See "The Climbs" for descriptions of all routes. Additional route-line photos may be found at the AAJ website.

ABOUT THE AUTHOR: *Born in 1984, Matteo Della Bordella lives in Varese, Italy, and has been a member of the Ragni di Lecco since 2006. In February 2017, he and two other Ragni climbers completed the first ascent of the east face of Cerro Murallón in Patagonia (see p.66).*

THE LINE

THIRD TIME LUCKY ON KYZYL ASKER'S PRIZED ICE ROUTE

INES PAPERT

We spend the night half-sitting, half-standing, one butt cheek each, hanging from the anchor. We are freezing and our bivy sack keeps sliding down our bodies; it's impossible to zip it completely, and snow keeps blowing in through a hole at the top.

It had started to snow toward the end of the day, like it always did, eventually turning into hail. The snow began looking for the fastest way down the wall—this was the spindrift I knew all too well from Kyzyl Asker. When the storm eased, Luka Lindič and I kept climbing late into the night. We had found our bivy site, such as it was, on a nearly vertical wall.

Despite the shivering and discomfort, I feel content. We are only about 100 meters shy of the peak. After two previous expeditions to Kyzyl Asker, success is close at hand. We just have to make it to morning. And this is not the first time I have survived a long night on Kyzyl Asker.

Kyzyl Asker, the "Red Soldier," is a 5,842-meter fortress of red granite straddling the frontier between Kyrgyzstan and China. My first expedition here was inspired by a photo of the peak and the line—soon to become The Line—shared by the German mountaineer Robert Steiner. I was incredibly excited after seeing that photo. The line immediately draws the eye, a perfect formation of water ice on a high mountain, like I had never seen before.

The line faces southeast, which is the reason water ice can be seen at such a high altitude. But the southeastern exposure also significantly increases the difficulty and complexity of climbing the route. In summer the sun is too hot, melting the ice and making the entire climb too dangerous. Later in the season you have a very high chance of getting caught in a snowstorm, and getting in and out of the mountains can be impossible.

Wolfgang Russegger (Austria), Thomas Senf (Germany), and I planned our first expedition in the fall of 2010, hoping to find colder, safer conditions; no

[Photos] The line of Lost in China on the southeast face of Kyzyl Asker. Several other routes ascend the granite buttresses to the right. The marked box delineates the area shown in the full photo on the facing page, where the two climbers (circled) are starting up the final third of the huge ice ribbon. *Rocker*

other team had arrived so late in the year. At least five expeditions had made their way toward the southeast face of Kyzyl Asker, starting in 1998, and several attempts had been made on the big ice line in the summer or early fall. But warm weather and snowfall had caused each to fail.

When we arrived in Kyrgyzstan, we discovered our plan wasn't foolproof. Early-winter snowfall had made the road from Naryn into the mountains impassable. Was our first expedition to the Red Soldier destined to end in the capital city of Bishkek?

We decided on the only—yet very expensive—option: a helicopter to base camp. Finding a safe weather window for the flight ended up being nearly as difficult as climbing the wall. Finally we made it into the mountains and placed an advanced base camp 30 minutes below the face. After a first attempt and a horrible bivouac, we retreated and waited 10 days before we could try again. On October 19, the three of us climbed the first 900 meters of the wall. The climbing was very difficult (up to M8), and our luck was bad. Three hundred meters below the top, we endured another terrible bivy, with heavy snowfall, high winds, very cold temperatures, and a stove that didn't work. In the morning we were forced down again.

In 2011, we also tried to approach the mountain from Kyrgyzstan, this time in September, hoping the roads would be clear. Wolfgang Russegger was back for another try, along with Charly Fritzer (also Kurz, Franz Walter, son, Emanuel, would camp. Emanuel found to be a great adventure, endless frustration. To from this side, you have nearly 120 kilometers. 4,000 meters. Just before down in swampy terrain for several days. At the managed to free it, our gear to camp, but we from Austria). Wolfgang and my 11-year-old accompany us to base the entire experience but for me it provided approach the mountains to ride a heavy truck for Base camp is at nearly camp, the truck bogged and could not be moved last minute the driver allowing us to move all still faced a 16-kilometer trek, over a 5,200-meter pass, to reach advanced base.

> **Two expeditions to Kyzyl Asker with no success—this was a hard pill for me to swallow.**

My son and his two companions left for home, and the real effort began. My two climbing partners were sick, and it took us 10 days to move everything to advanced base. Finally, on September 12, we were ready for an attempt. We climbed rapidly to 5,300 meters, the only decent bivy site on the route, and planned to wait there as ice fell through the heat of the day. But Charly was very sick, showing signs of cerebral edema, and we quickly made the decision to descend.

I was close to despair. But at least I was able to convince Wolfgang to try a new route on the Great Walls of China, a huge line of east-facing cliffs, rising to 5,000 meters, very near Kyzyl Asker. We called our line Quantum of Solace, a beautiful, 600-meter climb but only a small consolation.

Two expeditions to Kyzyl Asker and no success—this was a hard pill for me to swallow. I made a promise to myself: Only when I found the right partner would I make another attempt. Maybe a two-person team would be quicker and therefore more suitable for this route? I carried a picture of the mountain in my pocket and often thought about how it might be climbed, the strategy and logistics that might overcome such complex problems.

But I didn't want to make this wall the story of my life. In the following years I ventured to other corners of the world. I was able to make the first ascent of a 6,719-meter mountain in Nepal, Likhu Chuli I, and the fifth ascent—nearly all free—of Riders on the Storm on Torre

[Left] A stuck truck delayed the team's arrival at base camp by several days in 2011. *Franz Walter*
[Right] A horrible bivouac 300 meters below the top ended the second attempt in 2010. *Thomas Senf*

Central in Patagonia. I did first ascents of ice and mixed routes and big walls all over—the Alps, Scotland, Norway, and Canada. Still, I had yet to find a line as perfect as the one on Kyzyl Asker.

My friends would call me someone who never gives up, who is willing to fight to reach a goal. But as far as Kyzyl Asker was concerned, I found myself hoping another team would succeed. An Alaskan climber, Samuel Johnson, made two attempts, in 2012 and 2015, both ending with the same sudden storms and spindrift that had battered our climbs.

In the meantime, a Belgian and French team opened a new door to Kyzyl Asker. In 2013, they approached from the Chinese side and climbed the big rock buttress to the right of the ice line. We hadn't explored this option because the image resolution on Google Earth in 2010 and 2011 was still very poor, and it was impossible to recognize any roads or other infrastructure in this part of China. Several years later, things looked very different. Though more expensive, approaching through western China has massive advantages over coming through Kyrgyzstan. The roads into the mountains are lower, providing the opportunity to leave later in the season, and the gradual gain in elevation makes for better acclimatization. Yet, from the end of the road, it is only a day and a half of walking to base camp.

Suddenly my desire for Kyzyl Asker is back. I speak to my friend Luka Lindič about the line, and it quickly becomes clear that he is just as enthusiastic about the project as I am. I had met Luka several years earlier at a meeting in Chamonix organized by Arc'teryx, our common sponsor, and we made plans to climb together someday. I knew Luka would be a great partner. His tremendous skills, as well as his sincerity and reliability, are traits I truly treasure. Two weeks before we leave for China, Luka and I climb the north face of Triglav in his home country of Slovenia, and this is enough to confirm that our approach to climbing and life in general are the same.

We are accompanied to base camp in China by Rocker, a Chinese climber and photographer who acts as our guide through the difficulties of language, culture, and navigation in this vast country. Without him we would be lost.

For a warmup and acclimatization, Luka and I repeat a 650-meter route on the Great Walls of China. Border Control had first been climbed by Guy Robertson and Ed Tresidder, during their second visit to the area. On September 21, Luka and I are able to free the climb at WI5 M7.

Nine days later we are ready for Kyzyl Asker. We leave advanced base at 5 a.m. The day begins cold but very clear, with stars above. Luka and I simul-climb the first few hundred meters in the dark. We know we have to make progress quickly before the predicted weather

[Above] **The cramped bivouac on the final attempt. Fortunately, the day dawned clear.** *Luka Lindič*

window closes and we have to retreat—or get stuck in a snowstorm. When we begin belaying, we stretch the ropes to full length and beyond, gaining height quickly. Soon the sun touches the upper face of the mountain, but it is still too cold to melt the ice. Luka is leading above me, out of sight around a corner, when suddenly I hear a piercing scream. But it is a yell of excitement, not of fear. I'm not sure what is going on—surely he is nowhere near the summit! As I follow the pitch I see what has prompted Luka's howl of joy: Perfect ice lies before us, leading all the way toward the summit ridge. Neither Luka nor I had ever seen such superb ice at this altitude. In 2010 these same pitches had taken much, much longer. This time they seem almost easy. The only burden is our heavy backpack—the person following must carry the pack with everything we'll need for a bivy.

In late afternoon a thunderstorm sweeps over the mountain, sending hail rattling down the gully. It is impossible to climb for a few minutes. Thankfully, the spectacle is soon over, and Luka barely hesitates. He pushes hard up a couple of difficult mixed pitches to get as close to the summit ridge as he can. I can feel the altitude with the heavy pack on my shoulders.

Around 10 p.m., two pitches below the ridge, we decide it is too cold to continue. After some searching, we find a spot for a bivouac. Two hours of chopping with our ice axes creates a seat for a short night, half hanging from the anchor. We are protected from the wind but far from comfortable, with spindrift filtering into the bivy sack. Luka says it's one of the toughest bivouacs he's ever had. I have experienced nights like this before on Kyzyl Asker.

We stay put until around 10 a.m., after the first rays of sunlight help us warm up. Once on the final ridge, we untie from our ropes and leave them and the pack behind, making our way to the peak. Luka gives me a wink and lets me lead: "After all your hardships on the mountain, this is how it should be." I climb the last meters to the cornice, speechless with happiness. Luka arrives and I can see the joy in his face too. It is only noon.

We are aware of the short weather window and so we quickly rappel the route. We are back at ABC at 7 p.m., just before a massive thunderstorm sweeps over the mountain, sending spindrift avalanches down the face. Our climb could not have lasted an hour longer.

SUMMARY: First ascent of Lost in China (1,200m, ED WI5+ M6) on the southeast face of Kyzyl Asker (5,842m), in the Western Kokshaal-Too, September 30–October 1, 2016, by Luka Lindič (Slovenia) and Ines Papert (Germany). During acclimatization, the two made the first free ascent of Border Control (650m, ED WI5 M7, Robertson-Tresidder, 2004) to the summit of Great Walls of China.

ABOUT THE AUTHOR: *Born in 1974, Ines Papert was a four-time ice climbing world champion in the early 2000s before focusing on difficult ice and mixed climbs and new routes in the mountains. She lives in southern Germany. Papert says she has replaced that photo of Kyzyl Asker in her pocket with a new photo—another mountain she and Lindič hope to climb.*

Translated from German by Simone Sturm.

[Photo] Beautiful climbing in the main gully on Kyzyl Asker. "Perfect ice lies before us, leading all the way to the summit ridge. *Ines Papert*

TWO CLIMBS ALONE

SOLO ON ROBSON'S EMPEROR FACE AND TORRE EGGER

MARC-ANDRÉ LECLERC

{ AS TOLD TO CHRIS KALMAN · ART BY CRAIG MUDERLAK }

Over the past couple of years, I've done a handful of ascents that various climbing luminaries have described as "cutting edge." For those who don't know me, it may seem these climbs were somewhat out of left field. But the truth is, I've been climbing a long, long time. I started in a gym when I was nine years old. By 11, I was scrambling low fifth class in the mountains of the Pacific Northwest. I was doing alpine routes at 14 and started free soloing in earnest (5.10) at 15. I'm 24 now, which many people think is rather young for the kinds of alpine solos I am doing. And yet I've been preparing for this for 15 years—nearly two-thirds of my life. Everything I've done thus far—even just learning how to distribute my weight on steep vegetation and moss-covered fourth class—has led up to this.

In 2016, I did two climbs, in particular, that seemed to cause a stir. One was the first solo ascent of Mt. Robson's Emperor Face, which I climbed during a short weather window in April. The second was the first winter solo of Torre Egger in Patagonia. I did many other climbs in 2016 that were meaningful to me (*see pages 158, 166, 171, and 223*), but somehow Robson and Egger stand out.

MT. ROBSON

THE TRUTH IS, I hadn't intended to solo the Emperor Face last April—at least, not initially. April was more or less reserved for climbing with Luka Lindič (Slovenia). We spent the first two weeks of that month climbing in the Valley of the Ten Peaks, in Banff National Park, and we accomplished some very nice climbs after the weather shut us down on our main objective. Our next big goal was one of the harder routes on Robson—the Haley-House, for example— but we just ran out of time. Luka had to attend to other things. I had talked a lot with Jon Walsh about the Emperor Face, and he had mentioned that Infinite Patience would be a good option to solo. I tucked this away in the back of my head, in case the opportunity ever arose.

Of course, I'd wanted to climb the Emperor Face ever since I first saw a photo of Robson when I was about ten years old. All last winter and spring in the Rockies, I checked the weather forecast for Robson compulsively. It's a really difficult mountain to get in good condition. Even when Luka and I were in the Valley of the Ten Peaks, it wasn't in. It just so happened that when we got out of Ten Peaks following our last new route, I looked at the weather and saw the window. Right then and there, I realized: *This is it.*

First, I wanted to make sure I was in proper shape, mentally and physically, to tackle the route. So I decided to solo Andromeda Strain on Mt. Andromeda. I had personal history with Andromeda, which had shut me down in 2014 when I tried to solo the Shooting Gallery. At that time, I had never alpine climbed in the Rockies and had no idea how hard it was. I ended up having a very scary experience, bivying in -35°C weather and getting frostbite. I ended up having to climb a desperate, unroped 30 meters, smashing the rock apart with my tools and hooking the leftovers, before I could finally get an anchor and bail. At that time, I realized, I was not ready for soloing there at all.

Every subsequent climb I did in the Rockies was a learning experience. The Greenwood-Locke on Temple, the Stanley Headwall routes, the climbs in the Valley of the Ten Peaks—all of them taught me so much about the Rockies' very particular style, the angles of the rock, the consistency of the snow. By the end of my trip with Luka, we were really in a rhythm: Find a hook, get your tool in a crack, brush, brush, brush the snow, brush it with your tool, brush it with your hand, blow on it, look at it, get a pick, repeat. By our last climb together, we definitely felt like we knew what we were doing. So I felt comfortable attempting to solo the Strain. And this time on Andromeda, on April 14, I felt completely safe and in control—everything was really clicking. I decided I would give Robson a try.

After Andromeda, I hitchhiked into town and made arrangements to catch a bus up to Robson the next day. The weather window was super short, so I knew I had to go as soon as possible, before freezing levels shot up.

From the start, even on the approach, I was deeply into the experience. Sometimes in the mountains, I'm just thinking about the climb, listening to tunes, my head may be in a different place. But on Robson it was somehow different. I had never been to the mountain before, and I just wanted to take everything in. I was super into all the colors and the little critters that were waking up for springtime. The mountain has such a strong aura. It was like taking psychedelics or

[Above] The Emperor Face of Mt. Robson, in right center, rises about 7,500 feet above Berg Lake to the 12,972-foot summit. *Craig Muderlak* [Previous page] Marc-André Leclerc at sunset on the summit of Robson, after his solo ascent of the Emperor Face. *Marc-André Leclerc*

something, where you find a clarity that is out of reach in day-to-day life. That night I slept in the open on moraine at the base of the Emperor Face and woke to a glow on the eastern horizon.

As on the Strain, the climbing went very well. There were some hard sections, like the initial ice pillar and a snow mushroom that I had to tunnel through high on the route—probably the crux—but by and large I felt very solid the whole time. It seemed like every time I brushed away the snow, there was a web of thin cracks beneath where I could hammer the pick of my tool, making for very safe and secure climbing. I carried a tag line (which I used to haul my pack twice), and I knew I could bail at almost any moment. In the end, I just never needed to.

I have been asked how fast I was, but I honestly cannot say how many hours the Emperor Face took to climb. I began when I felt ready and I reached the top at sundown.

On the summit I realized my feet were too knotted up and painful to start down right away. I had brought an emergency bivy sack, so I decided to just dig a trench and wait it out for a little bit. I took off my boots and tried to let my feet recover. I made some soup and boiled water to put in my Dromedary. I put the Drom under my hip, since that was where I was losing the most heat, and then I actually fell asleep for a while. When I woke up, I decided to rewarm the water. But my headlamp had died, and I ended up spilling the water all over my bivy sack. I knew right then that it was time to go. I fought to get fresh batteries into the headlamp, forced my frozen boots back onto my feet, packed up the rime-covered bivy sack, and started a cold descent.

As soon as I started down, I found that old familiar rhythm and my world shrank to a six-foot bubble of light, the V-threader, and the rappels. And then it got really awesome. The sun was starting to come up on the other side of the mountain, and Robson's prominence is super huge so its shadow just went on forever. As the sun lit up the world around me, I knew I was in the clear. There was still some tedium to deal with, but I knew I was going to make it out, and I really relaxed into the moment and enjoyed the whole descent.

TORRE EGGER

WHEN THE FIRST thoughts of soloing in the Torres entered my mind at the age of 21, Egger was what fanned the flames of my imagination. It was, at the time, the only peak in the Torre group that hadn't been soloed, which made it somehow more mysterious than the others. Later on, when the notion of soloing in the Torres began to manifest physically, and I soloed the Corkscrew on Cerro Torre (February 2015) and Tomahawk and Exocet on Aguja Standhardt (September 2015), I began to realize that I might actually possess the skill set to make the Egger solo happen. It was the first one I thought of and the last one I did.

Colin Haley and I had talked about the idea of soloing Egger. Then, in January 2016, during the austral summer, Haley became the first person to do it. But neither of us—and nobody else to my knowledge—had ever talked about soloing it in winter. I hadn't thought about it myself until I was standing beneath Egger after soloing Standhardt and I began to see the line I might follow. I had to be there in person to even conceive of it as a possibility. Staring up at it that day, I became convinced I would have to try it.

On my first attempt, on September 12, 2016, I started up the east face following a dike and corner on the Martin-O'Neill Link-up (2002). This involved some M6 mixed climbing and an A2 self-belayed pitch in a corner. I slept on the hanging glacier beneath Punta Herron, then

[Above] Torre Egger is the center of the three most prominent peaks shown here, between Cerro Torre and Aguja Standhardt. Leclerc's solo ascent reached the pocket glacier low on Torre Egger and then continued up the shadowed face directly to the summit. *Craig Muderlak*

followed the line of the peak's first winter ascent (Arnold-Senf-Siegrist, 2010), moving leftward up a groove system to join Titanic (Cominelli-Giarolli-Nadali-Orlandi-Sarchi, 1987), halfway up the tower. I continued up Titanic all the way to a small ledge about 200 meters below the summit, where I made my second exposed bivouac. By early the next morning I was out of fuel and food, and it began to snow. I was forced to bail, and I rappelled in heavy snow and spindrift. The descent was a bit stressful at first, but in the end it went smoothly in spite of everything.

Four days later, I set out to try Egger again. This time, I started up an easy ice gully directly beneath the seracs under Punta Herron. I had vowed never to climb beneath a serac, but in this case I made an exception. The several hours it saved me made the entire climb feel more safe and practical, and in the cold darkness of the morning it felt like an acceptable level of risk. During the climb, I free soloed up to M5 and 5.10, which was well within my comfort zone, and I daisy soloed two short sections on the Titanic headwall. This time the weather cooperated, and the decision to climb the direct line beneath the serac paid off—I reached the summit largely without event. The descent went smoothly as well, and all of a sudden I was back on the ground,

hiking toward El Chaltén. The entire trip from my high camp to the summit and back took only 21 hours.

After I returned to town, my high from the climb seemed to remain in the mountains. I have often felt a letdown for a couple of days after what seemed like a really important ascent. In the case of Egger, after all the energy I had put into conceptualizing it and convincing myself it was possible, it turned out not to be that hard, technically. The hardest part, retrospectively, was imagining the climb in the first place.

I've been left with almost more satisfaction from my first try, when I had to rappel in a storm. I had always told people, "If you're high up on Egger and the weather changes, and you're by yourself, you're doomed." When I woke up that morning and it was snowing heavily, I was like, *Oh shit, this is actually happening!* As I started rapping, I felt super intimidated, but right in the midst of the situation I had most feared, I just started to draw on all of the experience I'd been building, the systems and know-how in the mountains. I had purposely gone out and climbed by myself in bad weather—a lot—just to build experience. And in the end, it was fine.

I actually feel that I've gotten somewhat less risky in the past few years. The most dangerous climb I ever did was when I soloed Cerro Torre, when I was 21. After that I sort of had a moment where I said, *OK, that was a really cool climb, and I'm proud of it, and I think it made sense at that stage in my life, but I don't think I want to expose myself again to that level of risk.* I feel like that climb could be the boldness high point of my life, actually, when you take into account the ratio of danger versus experience level.

During the weeks following the Egger climb, many people congratulated me on my "groundbreaking" achievement. But lately I find myself thinking that maybe the only reason my climbs seem so significant is because I'm one of the few people in my generation trying these kinds of things. With very few exceptions, most kids my age don't go to the mountains at all. It just makes me wonder: If more people were going to the mountains, would climbing have progressed at a different rate? Are these climbs even that hard or am I just the only one trying them?

SUMMARY: First solo ascent of the Emperor Face of Mt. Robson (3,954m) in Canada, via Infinite Patience (ca 2,250m, VI WI5 M5, Blanchard-Dumerac-Pellet, 2002), April 17, 2016. Descent by the west face and Emperor Ridge. First solo winter ascent of Torre Egger in Argentina, via a link-up of routes concluding with Titanic (ca 950m, 5.10 A1 80°), September 17, 2016.

ABOUT THE AUTHOR: *Born in 1992, Marc-André Leclerc was raised in the Fraser Valley of British Columbia, Canada, and now calls Squamish home. Chris Kalman, an AAJ associate editor, interviewed Leclerc for this article in October 2016.*

MYSTICAL REALM

A REMOTE BIG WALL IN THE RAMPARTS OF BRITISH COLUMBIA

TIM MCALLISTER

Halfway up the ten-pitch headwall, at yet another hanging belay, Tony looked at me with a grin. "Normally I climb with someone first, you know, *before* venturing out on a big climb like this."

It's true: We had never roped up before. I'm also 20 years Tony's senior; I used to climb with his dad. Tony and I had worked together for a few weeks in Oman, humping seismic cables around the Jebel mountains. Still, it was a leap of faith when he texted me: "Interested in climbing Postern with me? The macdaddy of unclimbed walls!... If you already have plans maybe you should bail on them…lol…you will be pretty psyched on this wall."

I had taken some photos of the elusive Postern Mountain the winter before, on a wildlife-study flight with Parks Canada, and I had offered to share them with Tony. I remember being blown away by the sweeping buttresses and walls that make up the 2,944-meter peak's northwest aspect. Alpine rock has always been my favorite part of the climbing spectrum,

[Above] Postern Mountain (2,944m) in winter. (1) Catto-Hesse (2001). (2) Mystical Realm (2016). *Tim McAllister*

and I have enjoyed putting up new lines in many of the remote ranges in British Columbia. But I had never made a journey into the Ramparts.

I knew that Tony and Jason Ammerlaan had attempted the northwest side of the peak two years before. Halfway up the ultra-steep headwall, the top in their sights, a hand injury had sent them packing without the reward of the summit. I bumped into Tony on the touristy streets of Jasper while they were on their way home. His eyes were wild as he told the story of their attempt. Although he was reticent to specify exactly where they'd climbed, I surmised it was Postern.

Last August, a rare solid weather forecast had Tony scrambling for partners. After the recent birth of his son, Jason had declined the invitation. Tony must have spun through his digital Rolodex a few times before he texted me.

Two days later we met in a parking lot in Jasper National Park that smelled of horses and bug spray. We danced the familiar jig of racking up for a five-day

[Photo] Tony McLane beginning the sixth pitch of Postern's headwall, near the high point on his 2014 attempt with Jason Ammerlaan. *Tim McAllister*

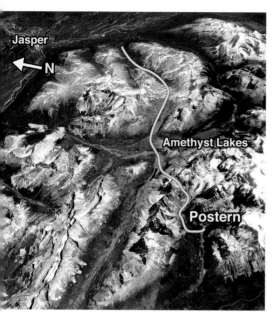

[Top] The climbers hiked 25 kilometers up Portal Creek to Amethyst Lakes. *Google Earth* [Bottom] Next day they hiked over the Bastion-Drawbridge col and 800 meters down the other side, then around the right side of Postern to reach its northwest face. They descended the southeast ridge (left skyline). *Tim McAllister*

adventure. Bolt kit? More like pins. Jumars? A Grigri will do. Crampons? A single ultralight ice axe should be sufficient. Before we knew it, we were ready.

WHAT MAKES THE Rampart Group very unusual in the Canadian Rockies is that the peaks are formed of solid, blocky quartzite instead of the typical shattered limestone. It takes a solid day or more to get to the base of these mountains, and few climbers make the arduous hike. Among the 37 peaks that make up this range, only 16 new routes were recorded in the past 40 years. Most notable was the Lowe-Hannibal Route on Mt. Geikie (ca 3,270m), climbed in August 1979—part of George Lowe's *grand cours* hat trick (Mt. Alberta and Twins Tower being the others). Honky Tonquin (VI+ 5.10 A3)—another outstanding line on the north face of Geikie— was climbed by Scott Simper and the late Seth Shaw over nine days in 1996 and is still unrepeated. Our planned route up Postern Mountain lay in the next valley to the west, in British Columbia, stepping up the remoteness another notch.

Twenty-five or so kilometers of mostly pleasant hiking had us sleeping under the stars on a pretty little grass bench perched above Amethyst Lakes. In the morning we stashed our big packs under a quartzite boulder and marched up to the Bastion-Drawbridge Col, which separates Alberta and British Columbia. From there we could see the profile of Postern and the descent we hoped to take, down the steep wall separating Postern from Casemate Mountain to its southeast. It looked like a lot of hiking, climbing, and rappelling.

We dropped about 800 meters to the valley floor and picked up a rope, hammer, and some pins that Tony and Jason had stashed two years prior. After a desperate (for me) boulder-to-boulder leap across Geikie Creek, we hiked downstream and made dinner. We guessed there would be no water for a couple of days, so we guzzled and then filled two liters each to carry. At about 6 p.m., we started up the arduous scree cone toward the foot of the northwest face. The dark, 1,000-meter wall loomed as we slowly made our way to the toe of the northwest buttress, which forms the left side of a narrow amphitheater, and which Mark Hesse and John Catto had climbed in 2001 in an impressive four-day ascent. Tony's mellow vibe allowed me to bury my doubts as we started gearing up. But not for long.

Before I had my shoes on, Tony disappeared around the corner and started up the near vertical buttress, following ramps and crack systems, soloing terrain on which I would have enjoyed a rope and a belay. I yelled up, expressing my concern, but he assured me it was no big deal and added that we had about 400 meters to solo before we roped up. Great. I sucked it up and followed him, with what felt like gray matter leaking into my eyes but was really only sweat. I did ask for the rope once, as I really didn't want to die, and was grateful when it slithered down to me.

The shadows grew long as we meandered up the buttress. I finally caught up with Tony as he flaked the rope and switched on his headlamp in preparation for a couple of steeper pitches. My pack tugged at my back as the beam of my headlamp narrowed my reality to the small circle of light in front of me. It was hard to appreciate the good crack climbing and solid rock after such a long day, but I tried.

At a big ledge system, we unroped and traversed right for 20 meters, away from the Hesse and Catto line and directly underneath the headwall. At a semi-flat spot under an overhang, we silently shuffled a few big rocks, blew up our sleeping pads, tucked ourselves in beneath the one lightweight sleeping bag we carried, and passed out. We were right on schedule.

0600 CAME FAST. We brewed instant coffee, scrambled out right on the huge ledge, put on our rock shoes, and for breakfast did a little more soloing up to the base of the true headwall. The sky to the north bore strings of cirrus clouds, silky and foreboding. Fresh wind lifted the roar of the rowdy creek into the amphitheater, disturbing the stillness. Neither of us mentioned these changes. We were where we were.

A pitch below the imposing orange headwall, we made a belay and Tony climbed around a corner and disappeared. I paid out a bunch of rope, and after what seemed like a long time he yelled, "Secure!" To my surprise, he now was about 15 meters below me, with no gear between us. He had downclimbed a vertical wall into a traverse that I wasn't interested in soloing—I ended up down-aiding, pulling on gear as I descended. On the ledge beside Tony, my eyes scanned upward to trace the only viable weakness, a line of thin cracks, roofs, and bulges.

Tony led up the dihedral, and it looked hard right away. Clean and compact, the orange quartzite was streaked with white and black horizontal bands. Thin cracks provided good gear and jams. Face holds were in short supply, but bomber. Everything was overhanging—like nothing either of us had ever seen on an alpine climb. When I joined Tony at the belay on the second pitch, still huffing and puffing after pulling on the last few pieces of gear, he mentioned that Jason had onsighted this pitch during their attempt. It felt like 5.12 to me.

Apparently, this was the easy part. The climbing soon got harder, and we slowed. On some of the pitches I jugged with the Grigri and a prusik, while Tony hauled the packs with two Micro Traxions. We climbed six pitches of sustained, hard 5.11, with some tricky aid sections. Tony pounded beaks and knifeblades to patch together discontinuous cracks. This took us to a small ledge—Tony and Jason's high point. I couldn't imagine rappelling from here and hiking all the way out. A wave of gratitude for their efforts washed over me. Still, I silently hoped the climbing would get easier. It didn't.

We shuffled left for five meters to the only obvious weakness that split the upper headwall. Tony shot me the "want to take over?" look, but I thought it made sense for the monkey 20 years younger to keep on keeping on. The name of this game was to get to the top of the wall before dark. The thought of hanging in my harness all night thwarted any desire I might have had for the sharp end.

Tony battled hard through roofs and changing corners, employing technical trickery to free as much as possible. But the unrelenting compact rock and difficult (or absent) protection forced him to stand in slings from time to time. Whatever it took. As the wind intensified and the sky darkened, our outrageousness exposure and isolation truly sunk in.

Nearing the end of the headwall, after three more long pitches, the rope slithered in fits and starts through the Grigri as Tony led on. He was out of sight and silent. Finally I heard him scream, "Secure!" He was 50 meters out. The 6mm tag line hung three meters out in space. I hadn't seen him in an hour.

I was just taking him off belay when I heard him yell something else that was stolen by the wind. I hesitated and then yelled back for clarity. More chopped half words. I kept him on belay, and after a pause the rope began to move. Finally I caught "secure!" again. Jugging the impressively steep pitch was challenging, and I took huge swings due to the lack of directionals after Tony's abundant back-cleaning. As I slid my prusik up the taut rope, I could only hope the cord wasn't running over a sharp edge.

Lost in my personal battle, I still marveled at the beauty of our position.

[Photo] The author stares down some mandatory strenuous free climbing during a traverse on the fourth pitch. *Tony McLane*

We weren't desperate or miserable or cold. We were doing exactly what we'd come for. Pulling around another small roof, I saw Tony's Cheshire grin as he leaned over the rim, with his chalk bag protecting the rope from a nasty razor slot at his feet. He was standing on top of the headwall.

AFTER THE TYPICAL, awkward high-five-to-hug combo, we took a moment to absorb our position. My sweat from jugging cooled as the last light to the west faded behind worrying clouds. We untied and scrambled over ledges, looking to find a bivy sheltered from the wind. A snow patch provided much-needed water. We settled on a large slab and fashioned a tarp shelter. Strong winds buffeted the tarp all night and, like a married couple, we fought over our small mummy bag.

Dawn broke cool and windy—but still no rain. The views of the upper Fraser River and the steep black buttresses of the south face of Mt. Geikie were spectacular. I tried to make out Mt. Robson to the north, but it was obscured in the murk. I radioed Jasper Dispatch to let them know we were fine. My friend Gord, warm in his dispatch seat, told us nonchalantly that he had just seen the final Tragically Hip concert in Ontario. It felt like we were in a different realm.

We made our way back onto the northwest buttress for the final three long pitches of the Catto-Hesse Route—superb 5.10d on perfect quartzite. The thin cracks were technical, and route-finding was tricky. We summited in midmorning under gray and windy skies and started immediately down the ridge to the southeast, the line Rex Gibson and Ernie Niederer had followed in 1927 for the peak's first ascent.

The ridge was longer than expected and loose in places. As I followed Tony around a gendarme, a block the size of a mini-fridge pulled out like a cash register from under my feet and crashed a thousand feet down a horrendous gully. My feet cut loose but my hands gripped a solid ledge. I almost puked with fear. A couple of raps to avoid steep downclimbing plunked us on the broad col between Postern and Casemate.

From the col, we downclimbed a lower-angle face to the east, toward Geikie Creek, patching together a labyrinth of ledges and grassy patches. An hour later we began six or seven 60-meter rappels to reach a small, steep pocket glacier. We hacked away at the hard gray with our one tool to chip steps—trying not to blow it. Our efforts felt pathetic, comical—but the consequences of being so far out there were real.

Back at Geikie Creek, I chose to wade across this time instead of making the huge leap across the boulders. As I searched for a suitable location, Tony made the jump and grabbed my stashed poles to ease my crossing. We choked down a couple of bars and started the thousand-meter grind up to the col, and then back down to our original bivy site, on the eastern side of the Ramparts. The next morning we woke, wet and weary, to fresh snow on the ground. Our climb was only the third ascent of Postern Mountain, and, in our opinion, a timely progression of style and grade. Elated, we shouldered our packs for the last time and slogged toward Jasper. A giant grizzly scat filled with purple berries pointed the way down the snowy trail.

SUMMARY: First ascent of Mystical Realm (1,000m, 5.11d A2) on the northwest face of Postern Mountain (2,944m) in British Columbia, Canada, by Tim McAllister and Tony McLane, August 18–22, 2016 (round trip from trailhead). The climb shared the first 300m and final 200m of the Catto-Hesse Route (2001) on the northwest buttress.

ABOUT THE AUTHOR: *Tim McAllister lives near Invermere, British Columbia, in the shadow of the Bugaboos. He works full-time as an IFMGA guide and is always plotting new routes on obscure cliffs in his backyard.*

[Photo] Tim McAllister follows pitch nine, way, way above the headwaters of the Fraser River. "I couldn't imagine rappelling from Tony and Jason's high point and hiking all the way out." *Tony McLane*

METROPHOBIA

TOTAL IMMERSION IN SOUTHERN GREENLAND

JÉRÔME SULLIVAN

Once planted in my head, Silvan's project grew relentlessly in my thoughts, from a seed to a blossoming tree, shaded by strong moments of doubt, a clash between the desire to live fully and the need for self-preservation. What alpinist has not known nights of insomnia before a serious climb? Silvan's project awoke this demonic conflict within me.

Silvan Schüpbach and Christian "Laddy" Ledergerber had already approached one committing climb in Greenland by kayak, in 2014, paddling for seven days and walking two more to reach the Shark's Tooth, whose 900-meter northeast face they climbed all free. This had seemed to me a perfect adventure, far from the routine of work and daily life. This time, he wanted to push things even further. The idea was to kayak 170 kilometers, each way, through the fjords of southern Greenland and then climb an enigmatic pillar of stone more than 2,000 meters high. The few accounts of climbing on Apostelen Tommelfinger (the Apostle's Thumb) described rock ranging from good to absolutely horrid. It seemed the southwest face had never been climbed. During a climb of Ulamertorsuaq, about 40 kilometers to the southeast, Silvan had taken a photo of the Tommelfinger's headwall. It looked steep and imposing. The photo watered the seedling in my mind, its vines tangling into both hemispheres.

Every previous team visiting this area had been dropped off by helicopter. Our plan was to approach "by fair means." Initially I regarded this concept with skepticism. Is not the very idea of fairness subjective? Was this term not a media creation for something that simply should be inherent to the concept of an expedition?

During the weeks before our departure, I felt in turns confident that this would be a great adventure and afraid I wouldn't be prepared. Would the paddling revive the shoulder injury I had acquired while falling into a crevasse on the Hielo Continental in Patagonia two years earlier? Would the rock be unstable and dangerous? In the *AAJ* I read about a team that had bailed

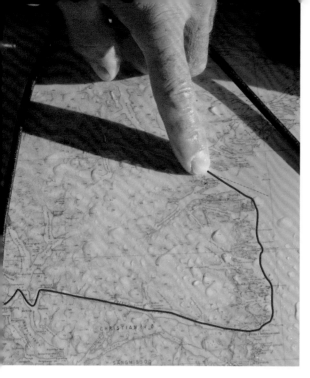

just below the summit of Apostelen Tommelfinger after rockfall broke the foot of one of the climbers while he lay in a portaledge. Five years later, he returned and climbed half the wall again, only to discover that a huge pillar they had climbed previously was now detached and half missing (*AAJ 2009*).

A few personal factors were also somewhat alarming: I had never kayaked, and two members of our team of five were total strangers.

To live a year like a wolf or a hundred like a sheep, I thought, pushing away the undercurrents of doubt. I sent a message to Sylvan that now strikes me as a ridiculous attempt at self-persuasion: "Not much time to train but really motivated for the project. Not worried for the kayaking. The wall is where the real challenge lies."

[Previous page] **Arriving below Apostelen Tommelfinger after a week of paddling.** [Above] **The seven-day kayaking approach covered 170 kilometers, some of it across open ocean.** *Silvan Schüpbach*

ANTOINE MOINEVILLE, MY companion on many faraway adventures, and I decided to train on the small Lac de Passy, down-valley from Chamonix, when we could spare time away from guiding. We borrowed a fiberglass slalom kayak and a river kayak—completely different from the sea kayaks we would use in Greenland—and loaded them into the car. The big puddle of a lake was lined with girls in bikinis and wailing children splashing in the shallows. The water was smooth and warm, reflecting Mont Blanc and its satellites. No swell, no wind, no freezing water, no heavy loads, no hours on end of intense paddling—it was like a walk in the park to train for a Himalayan ascent.

A couple of weeks later, our team of five—Silvan, Laddy, and Fabio Lupo (the Swiss guys) and me and Antoine (the Frenchies)—met in the small fishing town of Nanortalik, near the southern tip of Greenland. Laddy, the most experienced sea kayaker, was our captain. Fabio was new to big walls and expeditions but had been very serious in his preparation, with many miles of kayaking. Antoine also had kayaking experience from his youth. I was the duckling—my kayaking odometer showing a total of five kilometers. Before leaving town we met up with a local kayaker to get some tips on tides and currents. "In this 3°C water you have five minutes to get out, then you're fish bait!" His deep laughter threatened to open the Pandora's box in my mind, into which I had stuffed my aquatic worries.

We caught a lift by boat to the fishing village of Aappilattoq. There, we packed the kayaks with our climbing gear, reduced to the strict minimum (a double rack, four 60-meter half ropes, a tag line, and food). We brought a fishing rod in hopes of supplementing our basic menu of polenta, pasta, and porridge. Our Swiss cheese sponsor had given us 25 kilograms of their finest, which fit perfectly into the triangular ends of the kayaks. Soups and bars were lodged in the empty spaces between cams and other gear.

Launching the kayaks, we paddled straight east, headed for the sea. The first passage

[Above] The kayaking could be calm and even tedious or it could be suddenly life-threatening—sometimes in the same day. *Silvan Schüpbach*

would be Prins Christian Sund, a fjord that extended about 70 kilometers and would take us three interminable days to traverse. I struggled to keep up with my companions. By the second day I had pain from my little toenail to the extremity of my earlobe. The scale of the walls enclosing the fjord gave me the depressing impression that our velocity was that of snail. I decided to stay close to the shore, where smaller details like patterns in the rock or clumps of floating seaweed would enhance the impression of speed, tricking my brain into ephemeral satisfaction. At various times during the first 20 kilometers, I suggested stopping to climb one of the impressive walls we passed. My companions laughed as if I'd meant this as a joke. The rhythm of our days was tuned to the turning of the tides, as we tried, without much success, to use the currents to our favor.

The whole fair-means concept was taking on another color, as I began to understand that I had seriously underestimated the approach. Not only was the commitment greatly increased, but the physical and mental toll of kayaking would make the climbing more difficult too. Instead of getting fat at base camp, we were burning calories and seriously digging into our reserves of motivation and energy. It was clear to me that we would arrive at the foot of the wall exhausted.

The real kayaking had yet to start. In order to reach Lidenow Fjord, where Apostelen Tommelfinger rose from the northern shore, we had to turn to the north along the deeply incised coastline and cross committing open bays and fjords, where dry land would be far from reach. The winds were usually from the northwest—we would be paddling straight into them. Our frail vessels rocked up and down in the swell, my four companions appearing and disappearing from view in turn. Black fangs of rock jutted from the ocean, contrasting with vivid blue icebergs. The swell reflected off rock and ice, creating wild water. The sound of cracking ice and thunderous waves made for a dreadful atmosphere.

"Raft up!" shouted Laddy. We converged in the middle of a broad bay to form a stable, multi-hull raft. "We have to paddle faster and get out of here," our captain said. "If the wind picks up any more we're fucked! We need to move quickly and find a sheltered cove for the night." Our island of safety broke up and we paddled with renewed urgency. Then, moments

[Top] Climbing toward the 100-meter serac wall guarding the route. "Had we not just paddled for seven days, I would have turned around immediately." [Bottom] The second bivy. Packing portaledges wasn't an option in kayaks. *Silvan Schüpbach*

before we finally reached the far side of the bay, the smooth, rubbery back of a whale broke the water before me, cracking my deep bubble of concentration. Seabirds glided around a zebra-striped rock buttress. Life! I felt my lungs inflate with the salt-suffused air, the parched skin of my face relax, and the grip on my paddle loosen. I opened to the place and time, body and mind distilling into sea spray and wind. I was where I wanted to be.

WHEN WE TURNED the corner into Lindenow Fjord and headed back to the west, the water calmed and more mind-numbing paddling began. The landing for Apostelens Tommelfinger was still more than 30 kilometers away. Every morning was punctuated by Laddy's motivating war cry: "Paddle, paddle, paddle!!!" I didn't know whether to laugh or knock him out with my paddle. I had developed tendinitis in my fingers from gripping the paddle's shaft, and my posterior seemed to have molded to the shape of the plastic seat. My companions, for whom I had thought this must be a pleasure cruise, also expressed pain and discomfort—which was quite heartening to me. When we stopped every night there was a moment of peace and respite—until the mosquitos came out. The only fish we could catch was the ulk (a.k.a. scorpion fish), a monstrous-looking creature with bulging eyes and four rows of teeth that tasted as foul as it looked.

As the fjord narrowed, excitement replaced our fatigue. A shallow bay opened to pastures of green, spotted with huge golden boulders and myriad colorful flowers. Streams gushed from the dark blue glacier above, coiling through the finely ground sand of the beach. The Tommelfinger loomed behind, its jagged spires shooting toward the sky. I leaped into the water, gleeful that I would not touch a kayak again for ten days.

We packed away our dry suits and emptied the boats. We had little time to rest from the fatigue of our journey. The next day we shuttled gear and food toward the foot of the wall, taking some time to scope a line. One major obstacle quickly became apparent: To access the most interesting section of the wall, and the part that seemingly had the best rock, we had to surmount a terrifying hanging glacier. There seemed to be nearly constant icefall from this 100-meter barrier. Had we not just paddled for seven days, I would have turned around immediately, judging the risks to be too high. After long deliberation we decided to scale the glacier on its extreme right side. Above this, 700 meters of steep rock steps and hanging glaciers would finally lead to the real climbing, a 1,000-meter missile of granite rocketing toward the stars.

Russian roulette is a game you try not to play too often in a long climbing career. That morning I felt like the chamber of the gun had too many bullets. We reached the foot of the glacier with dark thoughts and the desire to get it over with quickly. After a pitch of dirt, rocks, and ice, threatening to fall apart at any moment, Silvan geared up for the second pitch, a 40-meter overhang of compact white ice. Our four ice screws were meager protection for such an obstacle, but Silvan is a master. Antoine, Fabio, and I waited with the haul bags, hiding from falling ice in a small cavern while Silvan and Laddy climbed.

[Above] **Fabio Lupo leading one of the first pitches on the headwall above the upper glacier.** *Christian Ledergerber*

Click, click, click…. This time, happily, the game went our way. Above the ice plateau, a massive belly of monolithic rock arched upward. We laboriously carried the bags toward our line, observing impact craters in the snow. From time to time a whistling sound signaled an incoming rock, and we ran in circles like terrorized rabbits, as we had no idea where the rocks were coming from.

The climb began next day with wet chimneys and mossy cracks. It was actually quite enjoyable and we gained elevation quickly. Climbing on such slippery terrain is like dancing with an egg balanced on your head—much delicacy and caution are required. The clock was ticking and we adopted a ballistic strategy. We divided into two teams: one to lead and belay, and another to jug and haul the bags behind.

Above the highest snowfield were few ledges, and we had no way to carry portaledges in the kayaks. Our second bivy, sleeping in suspended hammocks, brought to mind the famous black and white photo of Royal Robbins on El Cap's North America Wall. We twisted and turned all night as sounds of falling ice filled our dreams. The next morning dense mist clotted the mountain, filling the air with brisk humidity. The clouds swished in and out, giving us glimpses of the endless glacier extending to the westward. The hanging glacier, now far below us, spewed out seemingly impossible quantities of deep blue ice. The whole mountain shook and trembled. We joked about the metro passing below: "Last stop, Apostlen Tommelfinger!"

It was a good reminder that we weren't stuck in Paris or Basel, waiting for the subway to carry us to work. *Metro, work, sleep, metro, work, sleep.* We feared the falling seracs, but worse was the fear of being trapped in a life where every day resembles the next. The anxiety of facing the absurdity of this world stripped of the freedom to choose our own path, a life devoid of authenticity, where desire, love, and passion are luxuries. Here we were afraid, but we were living a life we'd chosen!

After four days of climbing, we reached a big ledge two-thirds of the way up the tower. The mist dissipated slowly and, although we were soaked to the bone, it appeared the summit was within reach. That night we had a long discussion about strategy. It was obvious we should attempt a fast push to the summit and back, but we wondered if we should rest for a day to maximize our chances. The discussion was long, and each of us took part, examining the pros and cons. The weather seemed to be stable, and finally we decided to rest.

Then, as we settled in the sleeping bags, Laddy suddenly exclaimed, "Let's go for it tomorrow!" In unison we all instantly agreed.

The next day was full of exciting climbing: ice-choked chimneys where the only possible anchor was a body belay atop a chockstone; exposed slabs connecting cracks; golden sun-burnt granite. As we rose above the surrounding peaks, we could see unfamiliar walls and glaciers cascading down from the continental plateau. The fjord's dark blue twinkled with pieces of ice reflecting the sun. As we topped out, frosty clouds engulfed the mountain in a deep gray cape, but still we lingered on the western summit of Apostelen Tommelfinger, savoring our success along with some of the delicious Swiss cheese. We wanted to stretch out this moment, to stay forever. But eventually we finished the cheese and slowly lowered into the clouds.

The next day the wall was covered in ice and unclimbable. We all congratulated Laddy on his sixth sense—our planned rest day would have cost us the summit! But now we had spent five humid nights on the wall, and my sleeping bag was an amorphous mass of soggy down. I felt like a gutter dog. Thirty-something rappels were necessary to reach the glacier. We had been quick enough that we could allow ourselves the luxury of two days' rest before sitting in the kayaks again. I could already hear the war cries: "Paddle, paddle, PADDLE!!!" *Fucking fair means.*

OUR BODIES WERE worn out from two weeks of nonstop effort. Though I had learned much about kayaking and I could now keep up with the group, the 40-kilometer open-sea crossing between the Lindenow and Prins Christian Sund fjords promised another struggle for survival. One day after leaving our comfortable base camp, we faced a decision whether to commit to a 15-kilometer crossing of an open bay. The shore would be far from reach, and the wind was even stronger than on the way in, whipping salt spray into our faces and pushing us out toward the infinite horizon. A two-meter swell was capped with white froth, and the storm dug at its sides, making the waves dangerously steep. But the desire to put the danger behind us outweighed these concerns, and we decided to make a run for it.

After just a few minutes of paddling I realized a corner of my spray skirt had slipped off and water had gotten inside my kayak. A terrible mistake! The boat tipped dangerously, the water inside obliterating all balance and steering. I capsized three times in half an hour. For 15 minutes my kayak was completely immersed. Our attempts to pump out the water were abandoned as incoming waves filled the hull much quicker than I could pump. Laddy tugged me through the icebergs toward shore. *You have five minutes to get out, then you're fish bait!* On shore, trembling and blue-lipped, I was wrapped in a survival blanket and given warm water. It took many hours of shivering in a damp sleeping bag before I was warm enough to consider starting again.

Four more days of kayaking lay ahead, and naturally I was filled with apprehension. Although we

> We feared the falling seracs, but worse was the fear of being trapped in a life where every day resembles the next. Here we were afraid, but we were living a life we'd chosen!

had finished the most exposed part of the voyage, the northern wind stayed strong until the end, propelling us toward the finish but also making the navigation more demanding.

We arrived back at Aappilattoq 21 days after leaving. It seemed like so much more. Time had dilated, like Dali's melting watches. The outside world had progressively and unconsciously faded from our minds. "Fair means" had been the cornerstone of our trip, and the game we played had pushed me to my limits. Yet the term still seemed insufficient compared with what we had lived through. The notion of fairness implies a standard, a rule, which seems totally contradictory to the freedom implied in mountaineering. Our approach and style had not been about rules but about letting go, leaving the constraints and shackles of daily lives in our wake. We'd been immersed in a dreamy world where the absurdity of worldly needs was replaced by something much more basic. Such an immersion takes time...and distance.

SUMMARY: First ascent of Metrophobia (1,700m, 7a A2+ 120° ice) on the southwest face of the ca 2,100m western summit of Apostelen Tommelfinger (a.k.a. Tiningnertok), by Christian Ledergerber, Fabio Lupo, Antoine Moineville, Silvan Schüpbach, and Jérôme Sullivan, July 29–August 4, 2016.

ABOUT THE AUTHOR: *Born in Los Angeles in 1983, Jérôme Sullivan moved to Bordeaux, France, as a child, giving him an early taste for traveling and exploration. He works as a mountain guide in Chamonix.*

[Top] The author after capsizing three times in half an hour. *Christian Ledergerber* [Bottom] The line of Metrophobia to the west summit of Apostelen Tommelfinger. The main peak, first climbed in 1975, via the south pillar, is out of picture to the right. *Silvan Schüpbach*

THE GOLDEN AGE

TWENTY-ONE NEW ROUTES
IN THE SIERRA IN A SINGLE SEASON

VITALIY MUSIYENKO

[Photo] **Austin Siadak savors the alpenglow after a new route on Mt. Whitney.** *Vitaliy Musiyenko*

Time stands still as the warm rays of the setting sun illuminate the surrounding ridgelines. As the lush meadows a thousand feet below gradually succumb to darkness, a south-facing fence of jagged High Sierra giants jets out of the earth, glowing gold.

In the midst of the moment, the split fingernails, burning muscles, and cut-up limbs are forgotten. Even the smoke from a nearby fire has cleared, allowing us to put off the mysterious descent we still have to complete before night falls. Captured by the dramatic view from the top of Eagle Scout Creek Dome, my friend Brian Prince and I make no effort to move. Are we dreaming?

Across the deep valley is the south face of Hamilton Dome and surrounding spires. We've seen no record of any climbing activity on these 500- to 1,500-foot walls, which appear to

be made of good rock. It seems as if we've discovered a Shangri-la of alpine rock climbing. The potential for adventurous first ascents within the few square miles that surround us is enormous.

This is my third trip into the Valhalla region of the High Sierra and was supposed to be my last long approach of the busy season—my friends and I have already completed about ten new routes. Blessed with the ability to ruin a perfect moment, I stand up and throw my hands in the air: "One day, Simba, all of this will be yours," I joke to Brian, sweeping my arm dramatically across the valley before us. "But for now, let's figure out how to get down."

Less than a week later, we return and make six first ascents—all grade IV—in as many days. With so many new routes to climb, it feels like it should be 1915, not the summer of 2015.

MANY PEOPLE WOULD be surprised to hear there are large unclimbed walls with high-quality rock in a well-known, fair-weather mountain range like the Sierra Nevada. Three years ago I was one of them, but the last few seasons have proven otherwise.

My improbable journey into the wild began in late October 1986, near the Chernobyl nuclear reactor, only a few month after the catastrophic accident. To the world, it is known as one of the worst nuclear disasters in history. For me, it's the reason why most of my preteen youth was spent going from one medical facility to another in constant search of treatments for various complications. After my mother moved our family of two to the United States, it wasn't easy to force change onto an overweight, asthmatic teen. But I joined the high school football team, where I learned about discipline, hard work, and dedication. A few years later, I was more than 100 pounds lighter. The qualities I learned on the football field later helped me earn a degree and a job as a registered nurse. With the job came new friends and a newfound hobby of hiking peaks near Lake Tahoe.

In December 2009, I learned to use crampons and, soon after, a winter climb of Mt. Whitney's Mountaineer's Route changed the course of my life. I joined an online climbing forum.

"Where are the unclimbed peaks in California?" I asked.

The only productive response I recall was, "Start rock climbing."

People on the Internet wouldn't reveal the hidden gems of the Sierra, but after bagging close to 50 peaks during my first season in the mountains, I felt confident enough to attempt Denali in 2011 and then test my growing skills in the Cordillera Blanca and Patagonia. However, I would return home with buyer's remorse, wondering why I hadn't spent my vacation exploring the local mountains instead. I now realized I could climb as many peaks in a 27-hour car-to-car push in California as I had in a seven-week trip to Peru. The climbing in the contiguous United States won't earn you a Piolet d'Or, but personally I enjoy the stable weather, lack of bureaucracy, and temperatures in which one can actually free climb. I love the challenge of finding a place no one has revealed in written or online reports, and finding such places only half a day's drive away makes the Sierra that much more appealing.

In 2012, I began shifting my focus toward first ascents, after a few guys invited me on an attempt of an unclimbed 1,000-foot tower in the Castle Rocks area of Sequoia National Park. With some beginner's luck, we sent and had the honor to name it the Fortress. Fifth-class bushwhacking, lichen-infested cracks, and getting stung by over a dozen yellow jackets aren't moments I'd want to relive, but they still evoke a big smile each time I reminisce.

My friends and I later climbed some new routes in the Tokopah Valley, a scenic area with 800-foot domes of solid granite. There we learned to be creative and draw our own history up a nearly blank canvas. Gaining confidence and the necessary skills was a gradual process, and finding a challenge was never a problem.

In 2014, I started a direct line splitting the 2,000-foot Bubbs Creek Wall in Kings Canyon National Park. At the time the wall had only one free route, the crux of which was a full grade harder than I could redpoint. But nothing makes one want to improve quicker than an ambitious goal, and by the end of the summer the new route was complete. With 18 pitches, 13 of which were 5.11 or harder, the Emperor (V 5.12a) became one of the most sustained free climbs in the range when I finally redpointed it in 2015.

About a month later, I found myself climbing a new, almost entirely free route on the mythical Angel Wings. Moving over varied terrain, I was gazing over unknown ridgelines into the future. Being surrounded by such beauty reminded me that the joy of the mountains was not in chasing difficulty, but in finding freedom. That season, in 2015, alongside various

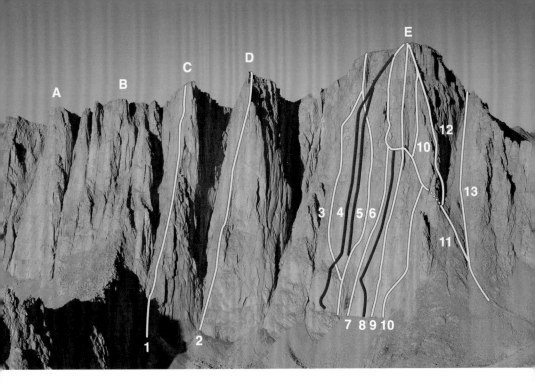

[Above] The east face of the Mt. Whitney group, with the 2016 routes in red. (A) Aiguille Extra. (B) Third Needle. (C) Crooks Peak (Day Needle). (1) Beckey Route. (D) Keeler Needle. (2) Harding Route. (E) Mt. Whitney. (3) If At First. (4) Inyo Face. (5) The Uncertainty Principle. (6) Left Wing Extremist. (7) Direct East Face. (8) Happy to Be Here. (9) Hairline. (10) Great Book. (11) East Face. (12) Sunshine-Peewee (East Buttress). (13) Mountaineer's Route. All lines approximate. *John Scurlock*

friends, I completed 17 new routes and first free ascents.

Unfortunately, it took the passing of a dear friend to lead me even deeper into exploring the Sierra. Edward Lau was a dedicated climber who passed away unexpectedly. He and I had climbed together often and spent a lot of time dreaming of the limitless possibilities for the future. One of his goals for the year was to recover from an injured knee so we could go somewhere remote and attempt a new route, which would have been a first for Ed. His premature departure was a sad reminder that, even for the fittest and healthiest, the next day is never guaranteed. For someone born in the aftermath of a nuclear disaster, this rang especially true for me. I wanted to be in the mountains more than I wanted to trade my time on Earth for money, so before the summer of 2016 I decided to quit the job I'd held for seven years and spend most of my time in the place I adore the most—the Sierra Nevada.

IN LATE JUNE, my extended vacation began with ascents of two potentially new routes on the Gambler's Special (12,927') and a formation we named the Dark Tower (*see Climbs and Expeditions*). The day after one of these climbs, dropping 7,000 feet during the hike out, I was exhausted. But along with my morning coffee, I picked up a permit for the Mt. Whitney zone. I already had plans to climb with Austin Siadak, a traveling photographer with as much enthusiasm for the mountains as me, so I decided to roll the dice and texted him a proposition.

"Hey, want to attempt a new route on Mt. Whitney?" The next day we drove up to the trailhead. Armed with several overlays of what had been done on Whitney's 1,600-foot east face, we headed to the base to have a look at the possibilities. I was especially drawn to the blank space between Left Wing Extremist (V 5.11-, Rowell-Wilson) and If At First (V 5.10+), which was climbed by Seth Dilles and Michael Strassman after six epic attempts and a bivouac during the first ascent.

Patagonian winds followed us up the granite wall, where we felt as small and vulnerable as a lone ship on the ocean. Bailing from high up with our 100-foot, 5mm tagline would have been difficult even in perfect weather, so luckily we didn't have to. At the end of the day, we had completed a new, mostly independent, all-free route, onsight, with no fixed gear left behind. We called our line the Inyo Face (2,200' of climbing, V 5.11), as the east face of Whitney marks the western edge of the Inyo County. In addition, a photo of the winter winds blowing snow from the top of Whitney had hung above my bed since the winter of 2010, when I climbed the peak for the first time—it had been in my face for years.

There was another intriguing crack system parallel to the one we'd just climbed, so I returned three weeks later with Adam Ferro. Since meeting Adam in Patagonia a few years ago, we've joined forces every year for a trip into the Sierra, with a focus on enjoying the mountains, not enduring them. Together we are on a lucky roll, and every new route we've found has been as enjoyable as many established classics.

Cameron Burns and Steve Porcella had attempted the crack system I had in mind in 1991, but altitude sickness forced them to retreat two pitches above the approach pedestal.

Completing a climb started by two prolific explorers of the range felt like an honor. The new route matched the style of the Inyo Face, albeit slightly more difficult and sustained. With Cameron and Steve's help, we named it the Uncertainty Principle (V 5.11/5.10 R), as the outcome felt uncertain from the bottom of the climb until nearly 14,000 feet, where Adam onsighted the crux and we joined terrain I had climbed with Austin a few weeks prior.

Two quality new lines on one of California's most iconic peaks would be enough for anyone, and maybe we were pushing our luck. But the elegant prow splitting the wall between Hairline (V 5.10 A3)

[Left] The northwest side of Mt. Gardiner (12,907', left), showing the new routes from July 2016. (1) Polemonium (1,500', IV 5.10-) on the "Golden Bear Tower." (2) Vermillion Pt. 1 (1,300', IV 5.11-R/X). *Vitaliy Musiyenko* and the Direct East Face (IV 5.10c) looked like a great challenge to tackle with my good friend Brian Prince, who had returned from working in Alaska just in time for another Sierra binge. Though the proposed line looked clean, we found loose, run-out climbing on flaky rock, with just a few decent pitches. Neither of us would recommend the route. We named the line Happy To Be Here (V 5.11-), a very sarcastic reference, yet the sunshine and the views from the summit were as glorious as ever. Whitney was the first peak I ever climbed in the High Sierra, and revisiting it by three new routes in one season was an incredible experience.

EARLIER THAT SPRING, Daniel Jeffcoach and I had made a moderate, long first ascent on Happy Dome in Kings Canyon, an enjoyable climb with exhilarating views of the High Sierra. Especially intriguing to me were two big, northwest-facing walls that dominated the skyline to the east. Mt. Gardiner (12,907') features a pair of needlelike buttresses with a snow couloir separating them down the middle. The big face on Mt. Clarence King (12,905'), to the north, looked like a perfect pyramid, elegant yet intimidating—almost as large as the northwest face of Half Dome, but very deep in the backcountry. There was no history of previous ascents up either face.

In early July, after my first trip into the Whitney cirque, I spent a week exploring these intriguing formations with my friend Chaz Langelier, an infectious disease specialist at UCSF. The day after marching in for 15 miles, we climbed a direct line up the middle of Clarence King's 1,500-foot face. The biggest surprise was finding ancient bail anchors until approximately halfway up. From what I could tell, the unknown climbers likely rappelled with a single rope and were in a hurry—one of the anchors was an eight-foot sling with the knot jammed in a constriction. Who were they? Who knows? Even with the Internet and other resources, the physical evidence of some past ascents and attempts can only fuel our imagination. It would be a boring world if all the questions had answers.

[Right] Chaz Langelier on the summit ridge of Mt. Gardiner, completing the new route Polemonium. *Vitaliy Musiyenko*

[Above] The northwest side of Mt. Clarence King (12,905'). The Dreamer (V 5.11) follows the prominent gray streak to the foot of the headwall, then climbs directly to the summit. Chaz Langelier and Vitaliy Musiyenko found bail anchors up to about the halfway point on the 1,500-foot face, but their line from July 2016 is likely the first complete route. [Below] "Brian Prince enjoying the finer things in life in our favorite range." *Vitaliy Musiyenko*

The line of anchors ended before an overhang where the rock noticeably deteriorated in quality. Instead of trying to climb through the kitty litter rock above, I executed a delicate traverse, pulling off loose blocks and finding hidden openings for protection as I went. Another wild overhang took us to a series of enjoyable, high-quality crack systems that brought us directly to the summit in five more pitches. We named the climb the Dreamer (V 5.11). Finding such a large, likely unclimbed wall in 2016 just half a day's drive from home keeps me dreaming of even bigger, steeper peaks tucked into scenic backcountry locations.

The next day Chaz and I hiked over to the Gardiner Basin, then around to the valley below Gardiner Pass, setting camp at 11,500 feet near another stunning lake. In the glow of the setting sun, the needle-like central buttress of Mt. Gardiner assumed the profile of a standing bear—at least according to Chaz. In the morning, we started climbing at the toe and followed a direct line of cracks straight to the exposed summit.

"If Fred Beckey climbed this wall long ago, it would be a North American classic," Chaz said as we relaxed on the summit.

"Without a doubt."

After taking in the gorgeous scenery, descending a knife-edge ridge, and bathing in an ice-cold pool near camp, I too suddenly noticed the tower's resemblance to a bear. We dubbed the central buttress the Golden Bear Tower and our route the Polemonium (IV 5.10a), after all the beautiful purple flowers growing from cracks along our line.

The following day, we climbed the other, slightly shorter of the peak's two prominent buttresses, which packed sustained difficulties and exciting climbing. The highlights included a memorable traverse above a flake I dubbed the Impaler, a dislodged rock that exploded within a meter of my head, and the mental and physical crux coming 30 feet above a ledge, protected by gear I wouldn't trust to hold body weight on an aid climb. Knowing that we were midway up a wall, with no cell phone reception, 15 miles from the road, was great motivation to send. A wild sequence up in-cut crimps guarded the high point of the buttress, completing Vermillion Pt. 1 (IV 5.11- R/X).

THOUGH EVERY TRIP into the wilderness is unique, the outing I anticipated most last summer was a return to the Tehipite Valley, a place that feels lost in time. Imagine Yosemite Valley but requiring more than 20 miles of hiking from the nearest trailhead—no roads, crowds, or opportunity for quick rescue. A wild place with poison oak, rattlesnakes the size of anacondas, the last grizzly bear in the state of California, uncontacted Native American tribes, and dinosaurs. Well, some of those things anyway. Tehipite only sees a team of climbers every couple of years. Daniel Jeffcoach and I planned to return for a rematch with the largest unclimbed wall we have ever encountered.

Daniel and I met on the climb of the Fortress, which was both of our first first ascent. Daniel was once close to becoming a pro snowboarder, before deciding annual concussions and broken bones were not for him, and he switched his focus to starting a family. A father of two with a full-time teaching job, one of his biggest passions is finding new rock climbs, mainly in Sequoia and Kings Canyon National Parks, a place that is like his second home. And he's not keeping his finds a secret—he created *sekiclimbing.com* to supply free climbing beta to anyone with a taste for backcountry adventure.

The wall we hoped to climb was another two miles upstream from the fairly well-known Tehipite Dome and an the opposite side of the Middle Fork of the Kings River. We gave the wall our best effort in 2015, but after two days and 1,600' of climbing, we were only two-thirds of the way up and out of time. During the 22-mile hike back to the trailhead, carrying crushing

[Top] Brian Prince climbing on the Watsi Wall, high above the Tehipite Valley. The wall is 22 miles up the canyon from the trailhead. [Bottom left] Fishing in the Middle Fork of the King River, below the Watsi Wall. The approximate line of Infinity Pool (21 pitches, VI 5.11+ R A2+) is shown. [Bottom right] The descent from the Watsi Wall followed a spectacular canyon that likely had never been traveled before. *Vitaliy Musiyenko*

50-pound packs, we wondered what we could have done differently. Allowing more time and bringing Brian Prince into the mix turned out to be the solution. With a bigger team, we'd be able to stay positive and divide the mentally taxing leads, as well as the labor of cooking freshly caught fish down in camp.

With an earlier start and knowledge of the lower terrain, we managed to climb three pitches above our previous high point by the end of our first day on the wall. We found a sloping ledge big enough for the three of us to spend the night sitting up. Above us was a blank overhang, which didn't look possible without a bolt ladder. But killing the impossible

[Above] The author scatters ashes of Edward Lau from the summit of Mt. Hitchcock after another new route. Lau's death at a young age inpsired Musiyenko to make the most of his summer in the Sierra. *Adam Ferro*

was not in our plans. The next morning, to our surprise, some sketchy aid with a slim rack of thin gear got us past the overhang. From there, we free climbed another 700 feet all the way to the elusive summit. The descent was a great adventure of its own, making our way down a beautiful canyon with dreamy pools for cooling off. We named the formation the Watsi Wall, after the Mono people's word for "Lost," and the 21-pitch route the Infinity Pool (VI 5.11+ R A2+).

As I had after new climbs all summer, I scattered some of Ed Lau's ashes on top, remembering all the positive qualities my friend possessed, many of which I am still trying to adopt. It was Ed's seventh summit of the summer and his ninth first ascent. The wind spread his unforgettable spirit over the infinite landscape of the western Sierra.

As the summer came to a close, I had made about 30 trips into the mountains, completed 21 new routes, and hiked countless miles. (*See Climbs and Expeditions for more route descriptions.*) Yet the year's highlight was not a new route but a first solo of the full Evolution Crest traverse—a grade VI climb that traverses over 20 thirteeners. By distance it doubles the size of the full Palisade Traverse, and the first team, in 2008, needed eight days to complete it. For me it took three monster days and allowed me to explore my limits—and the vast Sierra—like nothing I'd ever done.

It was the opportunity to push my mental and physical boundaries in an incredible setting that got me hooked on climbing, but it's the friendships I've formed and the endless opportunities to see new places that keep me going back to the mountains. Exploring the High Sierra has brought me an intimate connection to things that have been hiding deep within me— all the imperfections and weaknesses but also positive attributes and strength. For the first time in my life, I feel like I'm exercising my creativity close to its potential.

For reasons like these, it is important not to take wilderness for granted, as the future is not guaranteed for anyone or anything, especially in an era of rapid climate change and a time when small changes to current laws could completely alter access and funding for our public lands. The coming generations should have their chance to see the wild corners of the Sierra in the same ways that earlier explorers did. In the same ways that I have.

Finding new places to explore is much harder than it used to be, but for those who claim the golden age has long passed, I will say this: The fact that in one summer a person could climb more virgin Sierra rock than the height of Mt. Everest above sea level demonstrates that—as long as we protect our wild lands—the future of exploration is bright.

About the Author: *Vitaliy Musiyenko is a 30-year-old registered nurse. After his extended vacation, he found a new job in an emergency medicine department close to the mountains of the Sierra Nevada.*

EL VALOR DEL MIEDO

THE FIRST ASCENT OF CERRO MURALLÓN'S EAST FACE

MATTEO DELLA BORDELLA

The idea of attempting Cerro Murallón came to us way back in 2010, even before my first trip to Patagonia. Matteo "Berna" Bernasconi and I both were looking for a big adventure. We were not afraid of failing, just wanting to live the full Patagonian experience.

Berna and I are part of the "new" generation of Ragni di Lecco, an invitation-only alpine club based out of Lecco, Italy. The history of Ragni climbers' accomplishments in Patagonia is long. Wearing the "red sweater," the symbol of the Ragni group, is a source of endless motivation; we try to follow in the footsteps of the great alpinists who preceded us.

At one point, Berna and I sat down with two old heroes from this storied group: Mario Conti, who made the first ascent of Cerro Torre in 1974, and Carlo Aldè, who climbed the first technical route up Cerro Murallón in 1984. They enlightened us with a few ideas for these mythical mountains. When they finished talking, I couldn't wait to see Patagonia with my own eyes.

Two mountains caught our attention: Torre Egger, with its still unclimbed west face, and Cerro Murallón, which to us offered an ideal combination of isolation and beautiful unclimbed walls. Murallón sounded too complicated for two guys with little expedition experience. We opted first for Torre Egger and spent about 160 days in Patagonia over three years to climb this mountain. Torre Egger was a very hard school that allowed no mistakes, but we learned a lot of things: about expeditions, big-wall climbing, organization, and mental strength.

After completing this huge adventure, in 2013, Berna and I took different paths for a few years. I looked for new challenges in alpinism, in Patagonia, Greenland, and other places around the world, while he dedicated himself to his job as a mountain guide.

In January 2016, also after a three-year saga, I made the first repeat, and first ever ascent in alpine style, of the East Pillar of Fitz Roy, a route opened in 1976 by Ragni members Casimiro Ferrari and Vittorio Meles. On this climb, I relied on an exceptional partner, David Bacci, also from the Ragni group. Later that season, David and I managed a short reconnaissance trip to see Cerro Murallón firsthand. Despite being only 100km from Cerro Torre, the difficult approach and isolation made Murallón radically different from the mountains of the Chaltén massif. For such an expedition, three climbers seemed ideal. So, the circle closed: I asked Berna if he still was interested, and he answered enthusiastically.

[Photo] **David Bacci leads a delicate mixed pitch just above the bivouac during the first ascent of the east face of Cerro Murallón.** *Matteo Della Bordella*

[Left] The east face of Cerro Murallón, showing the line of El Valor del Miedo (2017) and the team's bivy site on the route. Circle marks the Ragni (Italian) climbers' high point in 1984. The northeast arête, climbed by the Ragni team in 1984, is on the right. *Matteo Della Bordella* [Right] The author welcomes the sun, high on the east face, with the Upsala Glacier and Lago Argentino behind. *Matteo Bernasconi*

David, Berna, and I met in El Calafate on January 10, 2017. The weather this season was dramatic, with continuous low pressure for a month and a half. But our morale was high. With a month's food, we set off by boat to Estancia Cristina, at the northern end of Lago Argentino. From there we moved all of our food and equipment by Jeep to Refugio Upsala, and then started shuttling loads on foot to Refugio Pascale. This small box of iron and wood was our home for four weeks.

By January 15 we had everything we needed at Refugio Pascale and started waiting for a window—at least one good enough to hike to the base of the wall and choose our line. The waiting game went on for several days…and then weeks. Luckily there were a few boulders around, so we could have fun and keep fit. Every two days we would call a friend in Italy for the forecast and he would tell us, "For the next five days: bad weather with strong winds and precipitation." I had learned from past experience, especially on Torre Egger, that climbing these mountains is a matter of patience. Toward the end of January, things started to look different: a possible window in the first week of February.

On February 1, we hiked toward the north side of Cerro Murallón with a week of food and all our gear. We had only been able to see the mountains for one day in the previous three weeks, so we had no idea of the conditions. We were open to many options. Trying to free the northeast ridge, opened by Ragni climbers in 1984, was really appealing. For difficulty, the northwest face, a sheer 900m rock wall, had only one existing route, climbed by Stefan Glowacz and Robert Jasper in 2005, and might offer other options. On the other hand, the unclimbed east face had all the ingredients for a great adventure.

We set up advanced base camp one and a half hours from the foot of Cerro Murallón, in what we thought was a sheltered spot; nevertheless, while we were putting up our tent, strong wind broke a pole and ripped the fabric. After waiting here for a day and a half, we decided to head up to the wall at about 3 p.m. on February 3. We had received a positive but not very reliable forecast for the following two days. Since we had barely seen Cerro Murallón during our whole expedition, we made a blind choice about what line to attempt. I love rock climbing, but the conditions suggested this was not the time. The mixed climbing on the east face was a more appealing option. We knew Bruno Sourzac and Laurence Monnoyeur had attempted the center of the face in 1999, climbing approximately two-thirds way up the wall, with difficulties to M5 A2 90°, before retreating in a storm. However, we were unsure of their exact line. [*Editor's note: Another attempt on the east face occurred in 1984, when, before attempting the northeast ridge, Ragni climbers Carlo Aldè, Fabio Lenti, and Paolo Vitali climbed about halfway up the east wall, reaching the central snowfield below the steeper headwall. Casimiro Ferrari then insisted they abandon the east face to focus on their original objective, and the trio used up their last sunny day for two months to retrieve their gear and move it to the northeast ridge.*]

There were many question marks concerning the approach, the line, and what would happen if good weather focused the warmth of the sun onto the ice. We would need to be fast, bringing only the essentials for climbing a 1,000-meter face, including food for a day and a half and ultra-light sleeping bags and half-mattresses.

That night we bivied on the glacier below Cerro Murallón amid an eerie atmosphere. There was no wind, but the mountain remained hidden by dense fog. When the alarm rang at 3:30 a.m., the fog lingered. Disappointed, we stayed in our sleeping bags. But at 5 a.m. the fog suddenly disappeared: Our long-awaited window had come!

We hurried to start hiking toward the east face. Eventually, with first light, we had the chance to quickly study the wall and choose a possible line. We aimed for what looked like a couloir with good ice, eventually leading to a snowy shoulder where we could assess the upper wall.

At 7:30 a.m., David starting leading the first of six pitches in a long block, following an ice runnel, while Berna and I followed with the backpacks. His final two pitches, leading to

THE RAGNI IN PATAGONIA

THE RAGNI DI LECCO group was founded in 1946, in Lecco, Italy. The name Ragni, or "spiders," refers to a time when Tita Piaz saw Gigi Vitali climbing in Grigna, in the early years of the group, and his movements were so elegant that Piaz said, "He climbs like a spider!" To join the Ragni, you need to be nominated by three members, your résumé has to be approved by a technical committee, and two-thirds of the members at a special meeting have to vote in your favor. There were about 100 members at the end of 2016.

The Ragni began sponsoring international expeditions in the mid-1950s. Among the first was Walter Bonatti and Carlo Mauri's trip to Patagonia in 1958, during which they made the first attempt on Cerro Torre's west side and traversed the Adela group. Along with Folco Doro Altán and René Eggman, they also did first ascent of Cerro Mariano Moreno. Over the six decades since then, the Ragni have been responsible for some of Patagonia's most significant climbs.

1956: First ascent of Monte Sarmiento, Tierra del Fuego

1958: Bonatti-Mauri climbs in El Chaltén massif

1966: Monte Buckland, Tierra del Fuego

1970: New high point on west face of Cerro Torre, 250 meters below top

1974: First ascent of Cerro Torre, by west face (the Ragni Route)

1976: First ascent of east pillar of Fitz Roy

1984: Northeast arête of Cerro Murallón

1986: New routes on Aguja Poincenot's west face, the south face of the Central Tower of Paine, and Monte Sarmiento (celebrating the Ragni group's 40th anniversary)

1988: First ascent of Cerro Riso Patrón and first winter traverse of Hielo Patagonico Sur

1989: First winter ascent of Monte San Valentin, by a new route

1992: New route on north tower of Paine

2006: North face of San Lorenzo

2008: Northwest face of Piergiorgio

2013: West face of Torre Egger

Thanks to Matteo Della Bordella, Rolando Garibotti, and Pataclimb.com

[Above] Unable to find the easy walk down, the climbers rappelled the south face under huge seracs. They estimated they would need three or four rappels but instead made ten. *David Bacci*

the snowy shoulder, proved to be steep and sustained, with a few overhanging sections. The ice was good, since the goulotte was still in the shade. However, at noon, when we arrived at the shoulder, we were greeted by powerful sunshine, and looking up we could see many of the ice runnels melting, with snow and rock debris falling down the wall. David and Berna proposed to wait for the shade of afternoon, but I knew that losing four hours might be crucial, especially given the nature of the season so far. So, despite less than ideal conditions, I proposed to lead straight up, the section of the wall that looked to be most sheltered from falling rock and ice.

Prior to this, I had not led an ice pitch in three years, and I had never done a true mixed climb. *No time like the present!* Little by little, I found my way up through soft snow, rock, and a little ice. Sometimes I climbed with ice tools, other times I preferred to just grab the holds with my hands—and I had to admit I was having a lot of fun! After three 60-meter pitches, the sun had left the wall. I could see the next pitch was going to be a perfectly vertical ice runnel, so I turned over the lead to Berna, who is more confident on this kind of terrain. We were making steady progress.

Berna led the next 300 meters until we arrived under the final headwall, approximately 200 meters tall. The route-finding had been a bit tricky and it was getting late. After a 60-meter traverse left, we sighted a line through the upper wall and prepared a snowy bivy ledge. Unfortunately, after dinner, an unexpected avalanche hit the ledge, leaving us under 20cm of fresh snow. Berna's inflatable mattress was flattened. Thankfully, most of the slide rushed past our exposed position.

We woke on February 5 at first light. Clouds thickening on the horizon blocked the sun. We could feel the first gusts of Patagonian wind. David took the first pitch above the bivy. The headwall looked more difficult than anything in the 800 meters below us. The weather continued to worsen, but we soon reached the base of the final 40-meter pitch. David gave it his all, fighting his way up through delicate dry tooling and aid moves. Berna and I shouted and cheered as the wind blew stronger and stronger. At 1 p.m. we all reached the top of the wall. The air was filled with blowing snow.

A hard decision awaited: How to get down? We could either rappel 1,000 meters down the wall we had just climbed, with little gear, or attempt to descend the unfamiliar southwest side of Murallón. Rolando Garibotti, who followed this route with Silvo Karo to make the only known ascent of Cerro Murallón's western and highest peak, in 2003, had told us this would be mostly walking, so we chose this option. After about 300 meters of easy hiking, we reached the east summit of Cerro Murallón and then headed across the plateau, looking for the way down. We soon found ourselves wandering around giant seracs. Although Rolo had written of this route that "a cow could do it," three men couldn't find the way! We weren't the first to

[Above] Cerro Murallón (left) from the Upsala Glacier. The east face is in the sun. The 2017 route up the east face and the 1984 ascent of the northeast arête both topped out on the east summit (farthest right). The 2017 team rappeled the wall at far left, under the seracs. At right, the highest peak is Cerro Don Bosco. *Rolando Garibotti*

experience this situation. In 1984, after climbing the northeast buttress to the east summit (which they believed to be the highest point), Carlo Aldè, Casimiro Ferrari, and Paolo Vitali also attempted this descent; however, after a day of wandering through a labyrinth of seracs and a fall into a crevasse, they felt there was no way out and decided to rappel their route.

As evening arrived, we consider a shivering bivy in a snow hole, but then a quick opening in the clouds allowed us to see the Cono Glacier, far below us to the left. We decided to rappel to the south, down a big serac, to reach the glacier. What we thought would be three or four rappels turned into ten. Once on the glacier, we found a terrible maze of crevasses. At 10:30 p.m., exhausted, wet, and with almost no food, we stumbled across two huge rocks in the middle of the glacier, offering some respite from the storm. It was the best gift we could imagine.

On February 6, we split our last energy bar for breakfast and started a long day of hiking. Our tent was still 25 kilometers away on the far side of the mountain. The Cono Glacier's poor condition forced us up and down mountains of ice, and then, once in the moraine, through huge piles of unstable blocks. Our situation improved once we reached the Upsala Glacier, and we finally reached our advanced camp again after a 13-hour day, three days after leaving.

In seven years of trips to Patagonia, Cerro Murallón was my wildest adventure by far. The world felt far away, and I felt small and exposed to the power of nature. I'm looking forward to more expeditions like this, where the climbing, though most important, is still only one of many aspects forming a complete adventure.

SUMMARY: First ascent of the east face of Cerro Murallón, to the east summit (ca 2,770m), by El Valor del Miedo (1,000m, M6 A2 90°+), by David Bacci, Matteo Bernasconi, and Matteo Della Bordella, February 4–6, 2017.

ABOUT THE AUTHOR: *Born in 1984, Matteo Della Bordella lives in Varese, Italy, and has been a member of the Ragni di Lecco since 2006. Since 2010 he has made annual visits to Patagonia, where his climbs include a "fair means" ascent of Cerro Torre's southeast ridge.*

VISIONS

LOOKING BACK, LOOKING AHEAD

JEFF LOWE

Climbing has been the hub of my life, with spokes of interest radiating in all directions, like a magnetic field. Asked by the editor to write a short piece for this journal regarding the future of climbing, I foolishly accepted. I was honored and humbled, and thought it would be an opportunity to voice some ideas that have been gestating for some time. These days I'm experiencing energy at the DNA level, at the energy/mass/energy/mass vortex. One moment I'm in my entropic physical reality and the next I'm in a timeless space of boundless awareness. My thinking has become very nonlinear. One thought connects to a hundred, which in turn explode exponentially. It's difficult to communicate in this state, where time has no meaning. But deadlines are real in corporeal existence.

It's so great to still be alive with this beautiful planet and to look back over 60 years of the evolution of ascent. All those years ago, climbing in America was truly a fringe activity. My father, Ralph, introduced each of his eight kids to climbing. Dad was a nature lover, lover of different cultures, navy pilot, war hero, lawyer, rancher, hiker, climber, skier, and friend of the high and low. Born into a Mormon family, he was an early convert to atheism and science. He was also something of an animal whisperer. At various times and in various combinations we kept a three-legged bobcat, many dogs, skunks, squirrels, rats, cats, foxes, wolves, a badger, horses, mountain lions, a caiman that grew to four feet, an eight-foot boa constrictor, rattlesnakes for milking, a snapping turtle, and Bruno the black bear, who weighed about 500 pounds.

I was six in 1957 when Dad took Mike, who is five years older than me, Greg, 18 months older, and me on a 40-mile drive south from our home in Ogden, Utah, to Pete's Rock on Salt Lake City's east bench. Harold Goodro was there with several other Wasatch Mountain Club people, bouldering and doing short top-rope climbs. Harold was an accomplished mountaineer and a first-rate rock climber. (In 1949, in mountain boots, he led a climb in Big Cottonwood Canyon now rated 5.10c.) That day we three young brothers were encouraged to attempt any boulder problem we wanted or dared to, even the high ones. We were never told, "That one's too hard, you're too young." Dad and Harold gave us the freedom to judge for ourselves, guided by a natural fear of falling and only pushing harder and higher at our own individual tempos, motivated by curiosity and joy in stretching our bodies and minds in intimate discovery of the rock. More succinctly, we learned how much *fun* climbing could be. Maybe these early experiences helped the Lowe brothers avoid serious injuries during the six decades since then.

In August 1958, dad took us up the Exum Ridge of the Grand Teton. It was a perfect introduction to real mountains. Back home, we joined the local climbing club, Steinfells, took part in practice belay sessions, classes in first aid and mountain rescue, and advanced free and

[Photo] **Ralph Lowe belaying sons Mike, Greg, and Jeff on an early climb. "We were never told, 'That one's too hard, you're too young.' Dad gave us the freedom to judge for ourselves."** *Lowe Collection*

aid climbing seminars with leading climbers such as Royal Robbins, Chuck Pratt, Layton Kor, and Yvon Chouinard. Of all of them, Chouinard had the biggest impact on me.

Out of a pure love of adventure and a thirst to drink our fill of the climbers' Kool-Aid, we became knowledgeable in the history, traditions, styles, techniques, and tools of ascent. In the winter of 1963, three new titles appeared on dad's bookshelf, and each strongly impacted and informed my life from that time forward. Heinrich Harrer's classic *The White Spider* sparked my climber's imagination. *The Agony and the Ecstasy*, Irving Stone's evocatively characterized biographical novel of Michelangelo, drew me into a world of inspired talent, dedication, hard work, emotional surrender and sacrifice, required to produce the greatest art. The third book, lighter reading and more thrilling to my young emotions, was Toni Sailer's account of his road to sweeping the gold medals in the alpine ski events at the 1956 Winter Olympics in Cortina, Italy. That summer, Greg and I either bouldered or climbed on 72 consecutive days of our school vacation. I was hooked for life.

When Royal Robbins led the first climb of the Salathé Wall on El Capitan, it brought my attention to the differing qualities inherent in sieging a climb with fixed ropes versus lightweight alpine style. Our inclination leaned strongly toward Royal's view: Alpine style was much better. The very next fall, when Robbins, Chouinard, Chuck Pratt, and Tom Frost climbed El Cap's North America Wall, and we later read about their nine-day adventure in *Summit* magazine, our minds burst open with possibilities.

If you look into a crevasse as you try to step over it, you're likely to plunge in. But if you focus on where you want to go, there is no problem.

By the mid- to late '60s, Mike was guiding for Exum in the Tetons and making first winter climbs there with a small cast of Salt Lake City climbers, including my cousin George Lowe. At that time, although I was happy and doing well in ski racing, along with free climbing new routes up to 5.11 and making first ascents of grade V walls, I started to question my priorities. I loved the dance of arcing through race gates, knees sucking up the bumps, but I didn't really enjoy competing with others or the too frequent displays of ego, whether triumphant or quashed.

After making the fourth ascent of the North America Wall (with Don Peterson in 1970), I gave up the regimented path of ski racing to follow my climbing passions on the untouched walls of Zion, the Wind Rivers, the Black Canyon, Sawtooths, Sierra Nevada, and the mountain ranges of Western Canada. In the Canadian Rockies, in 1970, my cousin George introduced me to my first climb with an Eiger-like north face as we made the first complete ascent of Mt. Temple's 4,500-foot-high north ridge. I was transported back to the emotions I'd felt while reading *The White Spider*.

So began a period of a few years during which, each winter, I learned how to deal with deep cold, heavy snow, and avalanche hazard, instructing Colorado Outward Bound courses for fun while saving enough money for seven months of low-budget adventure. Walls in Yosemite and Zion toned us technically and physically in spring. The North Cascades, Tetons, Wyoming, Nevada, and Colorado mountains kept us busy in June and July, then it was north to the

[Above left] **Jeff Lowe in March 2017, at work on this essay, at home in Colorado.** *Connie Self* [Above right] **Lowe in 1994 on the ground-breaking Octopussy (WI6 M8) in East Vail, Colorado, a climb that sparked a worldwide revolution in mixed climbing.** *Brad Johnson*

Bugaboos and Canadian Rockies for big alpine climbs in late summer, more Colorado free climbing and Zion big walls in September—and a lot of cragging in our spare time. Eventually I made my way to other ranges: to the Mont Blanc massif in Europe, the Cordillera Blanca in Peru, and to the Karakoram and Himalaya.

Inspired by miserable experiences while hiking, skiing, and climbing with heavy loads in external-frame packs, Greg designed and sewed the first sophisticated internal-frame pack. Soon, quite often, Mike and I would join Greg in our family's basement hobby room, which was a de facto prototype and production facility for what would become Lowe Alpine Systems. Greg developed the constant-angle curve for passive and spring-loaded camming devices, the first rigid-floor, single-point hanging tent, and then came tubular ice protection, ice tools with changeable picks and adzes, single-wall tents, and more. Our heads were full of endless ideas for equipment, dreams of impossible climbs, and the gear that would be required to climb them in alpine style.

Since then, almost every "impossible" vision has materialized. It's humbling and gratifying to be part of all that, and it's hard to imagine what the next 60 years will bring in climbing. But I hope it will reflect the following considerations.

Planet Earth is our host. We depend on her for everything we have. And climbers are increasingly recognizing their responsibility to the planet as primary consumers and users of vertical landscapes. As climbers we gain a unique and valuable perspective from above and outside of civilization. I hope this will engender greater activism among all climbing tribes: acting locally and banding together regionally and nationally for activism based on soft love, respect, wonder, gratitude, celebration of others, humility, and humor.

Not only is our well-being tied to the condition of the planet, we as individuals also learn the most about ourselves by adapting ourselves to its challenges—through intimate acquaintance with all of its natural laws and forces, both known and yet to be discovered; all of its colors, textures, sights, sounds, smells and tastes; all of its miraculous plants and creatures; and the fantastic pulsating, vibratory balance of the whole entirety. This planet is perfectly designed as a classroom for humans. The dimensions and living architecture of the mountains, polar ice caps, rivers, oceans, jungles, and forests are perfect for extracting every last ounce of effort and creativity from those who approach them alone or in a small group, with fair means, lightly equipped. Add too much technology, too many people, or constrained thinking, however, and true adventure is soon beaten into submission. As outdoor adventurers, we live our lives loving ease and yet searching for difficulty. The rhythm of that contrast is the heartbeat of our being.

Finally, I would say this: You can live a life based in fear, and you'll get more of what you're afraid of, or you can base your life in love, and anything is possible. As a young mountain guide in the 1970s, I observed some clients on glaciers hesitating at the moment they began to make a long step across a crevasse; they would look down and begin to fall in. I learned in those moments to give a strong tug on the rope to help them across. I call it the crevasse theory: If you look into the crevasse as you try to step over it, you're likely to plunge in. But if you focus on where you want to go, there is no problem. As Carlos Castaneda has written, you must follow the "path with a heart." Put another way: Place your confidence in your dreams, not in your nightmares.

ABOUT THE AUTHOR: *Born in 1950, Jeff Lowe lives in Colorado. The 2014 film* Jeff Lowe's Metanoia *(jeffloweclimber.com) tells the story of his influential climbs and progressive neurological illness. The 2017 AAJ is dedicated to Lowe in recognition of his vision, courage, and determination.*

THE CIRQUE

FAR FROM UNCLIMBABLE, THESE PEAKS
AND WALLS HAVE LURED CLIMBERS FOR
MORE THAN 65 YEARS. AND THERE'S
MUCH MORE TO DO.

PAT GOODMAN

[Photo] **The Cirque of the Unclimbables under a late-summer auorora borealis.** *Ben Ditto*

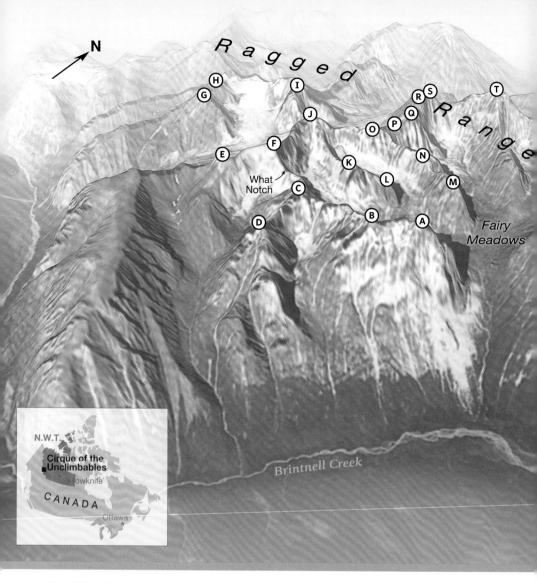

[Above] The Cirque is usually approached by a floatplane to Glacier Lake (lower right) and a stiff hike to Fairy Meadows. Scale varies in this perspective view. The horizontal distance between Glacier Lake and Lotus Flower Tower is about 4.2 miles (6.7km). *Martin Gamache / Art of the Mappable*

Is OK? Is OK?" The heavily accented voice crackled in the worn headset protecting my ears from the rattle-hum of the floatplane as we circled through dark clouds obscuring the peaks below. Judging from the firm grip on my knee, Spanish climber Eneko Pou was not enjoying the turbulence as we bounced through the sky, hoping to find landable conditions on Glacier Lake, airstrip for the legendary Cirque of the Unclimbables in the Northwest Territories.

Eneko and his brother Iker were heading in to attempt the second ascent of the Great Canadian Knife (VI 5.13b) on the stunning southeast face of Mt. Proboscis. It was the summer of 2000 and the weather, like many seasons before and many after, had been a bit temperamental. I had just spent a few weeks in the Cirque, hoping to climb the famed Lotus Flower Tower. Warren LaFave, bush pilot and owner of Kluane Air and the Inconnu Lodge, had picked up me and my climbing partner a few days before, but now he'd decided he needed an English-speaking "co-pilot" for the touchy

Cirque of the Unclimbables

(A) Mt. Harrison Smith
(B) Middle Cathedral Peak
(C) Pentadactyl Spires
(D) Echelon Spires
(E) Mt. Contact
(F) Proboscis
(G) Mt. Peacock
(H) Kleinspitze
(I) Higher Polymer
(J) Mt. Meringue
(K) Bustle Tower
(L) Terrace Tower
(M) East Huey Spire
(N) Middle and West Huey
(O) Phenocryst
(P) Tara Tower
(Q) Lotus Flower Tower
(R) Tathagata
(S) Parrot Beak Peak
(T) Mt. Sir James MacBrien
(U) Trident Peak
(V) Crescent Peak

Glacier Lake

conditions that day, so he pulled me from the lavish confines of his lodge and jammed me in the back of the plane for what turned out to be a pretty wild ride.

Incessant drizzle held hostage any view of the mountains above Glacier Lake as we taxied to shore. The Pou brothers brushed off the rowdy landing with grace as we pulled hundreds of pounds of gear from the plane. Soon a part in the clouds revealed the towering monoliths a few miles away. ¡*Venga ya. Venga hombre!* Not even the fog of mosquitoes could conceal the warmth of their smiles.

Whether approached by aircraft or overland, these intensely remote peaks foster a profound sense of adventure long before the rack leaves your pack. The Cirque of the Unclimbables (which is actually several cirques) is simply magical. The glacially carved walls and lush alpine meadows are similar in grandeur to those of Yosemite Valley. It's perhaps no coincidence that the mighty walls of both venues were once called "unclimbable," but now offer some of the most astounding rock climbs in the world.

EXPLORATION

THE LOGAN MOUNTAINS have attracted intrepid adventurers since the 1870s, when the Cassiar gold rush inspired the daring to travel by boat up the South Nahanni River in search of fortune. The Nahanni originates in the Mackenzie Mountains, the far northern extension of the Rockies, and winds south along the border of the Yukon and Northwest territories, passing close to the northern and eastern ramparts of the Logan Mountains before joining the Liard River some 350 miles to the south.

In the early 1930s the ostentatious oil and uranium tycoon Harry Snyder took advantage of the revolutionary floatplane to make the first recorded forays into the northern Logans; for a time, the intimidating batholitic intrusions in this area were known as the Snyder Mountains, but the name didn't stick. Ultimately they became known as the Ragged Range, a subrange of the Logan Mountains, which in turn is a subrange of the Mackenzie Mountains. Nearby Mt. Ida, named after Snyder's wife, and Brintnell Creek (which feeds Glacier Lake), named after his pilot, still hold their original names.

Climbers began exploring the area in 1952, when the Yale Logan Expedition, a party of six led by Dudley W. Bolyard, flew in to Glacier Lake (then known as Brintnell Lake) and made the first ascents of West Cathedral Peak and half a dozen peaks south of the Cirque, including Mt. Ida and Die Eisspitze. Bolyard's 1953 *Canadian Alpine Journal* article described "unlimited

PROBOSCIS: THE ORIGINAL ROUTE

BY JIM MCCARTHY

"PICK AN OBJECTIVE that you feel will contribute something to the development of American climbing, gather the strongest group of technical climbers available to do the job, and the AAC will back the venture." This was the invitation offered by the Council of the American Alpine Club as part of a program of vigorous encouragement of modern technical climbing in North America.

Picking the objective was perhaps easiest. Yvon Chouinard's lead article in the 1963 *American Alpine Journal* suggested that, as most of the classic lines in Yosemite Valley had already been completed, the climbers, trained in the most demanding area in the country, should turn to the challenging routes in the high mountains. The Logan Mountains in the Northwest Territories of Canada offered both huge rock walls and an extremely remote location. One particular part of the area had even been given the intriguing name of "Cirque of the Unclimbables." We would go to the Logan Mountains.

We [Layton Kor, Richard McCracken, Royal Robbins, and I] decided to convene in Boulder, Colorado, make our final preparations there, and head north. When I arrived in mid-July, the first difficulty soon presented itself. Although we had counted on making the trip to Watson Lake, Yukon Territory, in two vehicles, one was clearly too decrepit to make the trip. We faced the unpleasant and chancy proposition of crowding the four of us into the interior of my aged Volkswagen sedan, piling 700 pounds of gear on the roof rack, and hoping for the best. We finally got started on the evening of July 21, shock absorbers fully compressed and tail pipes dragging. After a nightmarish interlude of enforced immobility, sleeplessness, and incipient mechanical breakdown, we creaked into Watson Lake four days later.

The next morning found us flying north in a BC-Yukon Air Service de Havilland Beaver....

ON AUGUST 3...in clearing weather after a bad night and a stormy morning, we quickly sorted our gear and made last-minute decisions about what items of personal equipment to take.... We worked in two teams. While one leader climbed and his teammate belayed, the other team would haul equipment, food, and water on fixed lines using Jümar prusik handles. Royal and Dick drew the first half of the wall, where Layton and I would haul. As the wall steepened, the crack, which was so encouraging from below, got worse and worse. Clouds appeared and the temperature dropped. Forced to considerable ingenuity in placing pitons that would hold his weight, and slowed by the cold, Royal made haste slowly. When he finally decided to belay in slings and bring Dick up, we noticed that it was getting late. By the time I had arrived, everyone was preparing to bivouac in slings, one above the other, like pictures on the wall.... It snowed continually that night, but the wall was too steep to catch it.

When morning finally came, we were only too eager to get climbing. Royal led off, but as the crack got worse and worse, his progress became slower and slower. At the end of the 150-foot line he placed a bolt and brought us up. The crack was still shallow on the next lead and Dick had to tie

[Bottom] The 1963 ascent of Proboscis' 2,000-foot southeast face brought advancd big-wall techniques from Yosemite Valley to the Northwest Territories, making possible one of the first grade VI rock climbs in a remote wilderness setting. *Robbins Collection* [Above right] A carabiner from the 1963 ascent, discovered on Proboscis during a climb in 2010. *Emily Stifler Wolfe*

off every piton. It was still relatively early in the long subarctic day, and a strong wind cleared the sky temporarily. Hanging in my slings, watching Dick's colorful blue figure struggle high above our heads on the overhanging wall, I felt very much at peace. Then I noticed Royal nodding while he belayed. The warmth of the sun was putting us all to sleep.

Dick struggled on and finally reached the ledges we had expected to get to the first night, and soon we saw that they would have offered only a very uncomfortable bivouac at best. Layton started up a chimney. It was the first time that our feet had been out of slings in more than thirty hours. Climbing at top speed, Layton finally managed to reach some ledges below yet another overhanging section of the wall. After assiduous digging and scraping, we were able to enjoy the utmost in bivouac living that night—lying down.

It stormed most of the night, but we were protected by the overhanging wall above. Layton led off [next morning], and, finding the crack receptive, he quickly ran out the full length of rope. On the next pitch the second piton pulled out. Without much help from friction, I was unable to stop the fall before my left hand had been pulled rather messily through carabiners.... The difficult direct-aid leads gradually gave way to mixed fifth- and sixth-class climbing. One final lead of fifth class brought us to the top at eight p.m....

We placed 251 pitons and two expansion bolts, spent three days on the wall, and had three bivouacs. We feel that this is one of the most difficult *technical* rock climbs ever done under remote alpine conditions, as well as one of the most elegantly direct routes that one can hope to climb.

This story is excerpted from an article first published in AAJ 1964.

possibilities of virgin mountains rivaling the Alps and Cascades in grandeur and difficulty."

This inspired Arnold Wexler, a research engineer from New York who helped pioneer the idea of dynamic belaying and made the first ascent of nearly 50 Canadian mountains, to plan his own trip to the area. In 1955, after an aerial recon piloted by the famed George Dalziel, Wexler and his team decided to explore a cirque of granite peaks towering to the northwest of Glacier Lake. Upon closer inspection, Wexler declared most of the peaks "unclimbable," thus giving the Cirque its lyrical and enticing name. Nevertheless, he and his team completed the first ascent of Mt. Sir James MacBrien (the highest peak in the cirque, at 9,051 feet, and second-highest peak in the Northwest Territories, after Thunder Mountain). They also climbed Middle Cathedral Peak, Pentadactyl Spires, and the Echelon Spires, as well as a few other significant summits.

In 1960, a team led by the dauntless William "Bill" Buckingham followed Wexler's path to the Logans. Buckingham, a Wyoming mathematician and avid Tetons climber, would go on to make more than 50 first ascents in the Logan Range and create skillfully drawn maps and trip reports that continue to inspire climbers. Undoubtedly intrigued by Wexler's proclamation of a "Cirque of the Unclimbables," Buckingham and his team made this the focal point of a month-long visit, during which they named and climbed nearly every substantial summit in the area by way of clever and circuitous fourth- and easy fifth-class routes. Perhaps their greatest achievement was the first ascent of Mt. Proboscis. Described by Buckingham in *AAJ 1961* as "rising like the dorsal fin of some great prehistoric beast," Proboscis hosts a proud 2,000-foot wall on the southeast face and has one of the toughest summits in the Logans. The 1960 south ridge route (IV 5.7 A2) remains a challenging endeavor to this day.

Buckingham's reference to "a mountain

sheared in half" inspired the immensely talented climbers Layton Kor, Jim McCarthy, Dick McCracken, and Royal Robbins to pay Proboscis a visit in August 1963. Backed by the American Alpine Club, the team established the Original Route (VI 5.8 A4) up the southeast face, proving these massive walls were, in fact, quite climbable (*see AAJ 1964 excerpt on the previous page*).

The next peak that lured climbers to the cirque was the soaring 2,000-foot pillar that Buckingham named Lotus Flower Tower after climbing it by way of the connecting ridge between Parrot Beak and Phenocryst. Lotus Flower's southeast-facing wall was impressively featured and lined with cracks, and Jim McCarthy returned for an attempt in August 1968 with Sandy Bill and Tom Frost. Over three days, the men followed a great line with flawless crack climbing, with an evening of entertainment (for two of the team) in which a bivouac hammock disintegrated. ("The sound of parting seams was drowned by Jim's cry of anguish," Bill wrote in the *AAJ*.) Their route was graded V 5.9 A1 and subsequently became one of Steck and Roper's "Fifty Classic Climbs of North America"—today it remains one of the most sought-after alpine objectives in North America.

Sandy Bill returned in 1973 with Joe Bridges, Laura Brant, James McCartney, and Galen Rowell to make the first ascents of Bustle Tower, via the west ridge (IV 5.9 A1), and Terrace Tower, via the northeast corner (III 5.6). They also made an impressive effort on the large southeast face of Parrot Beak, the last big unclimbed wall in the Cirque. (The wall was not climbed until 1981, when Canadians Perry Beckham, Scott Flavelle, Dave Lane, and Phil Hein finished the job.) More influential than the 1973 team's climbs was Rowell's brilliant photography and subsequent writing, which exposed the area to an international audience and ushered in an era of unprecedented popularity.

THE MODERN ERA

IN ONE SINGLE year, 1977, the number of recorded routes in the Cirque more than doubled. A big group of Austrian climbers came away with several substantial ascents. Gustav Ammerer, Karl Kosa, and Erwin Weilguny made the first ascent of the northeast face of Proboscis (V 5.9 A2). Erich Lackner, Kosa, and Weilguny climbed the southwest wall on Flattop (IV 5.7 A1). Hilda and Rudi Lindner did the first ascent of Middle Huey Spire's south face (IV 5.9 A3) and also Phenocryst's big south buttress (IV 5.7 A1). Meanwhile, Belgian climbers Jacques Collaer, Renzo Lorenzi, and Jacques Ramouillet established a route up the largest section of wall on Bustle Tower's south face (VI 5.10 A1).

That same year, American climbers Steve Levin, Mark Robinson, and Sandy Stewart made the first free ascent of the 1968 south face route on Lotus Flower Tower (V 5.10+), creating a big-wall free climb accessible to many climbers—in an extraordinary location. This team also noted and removed large amounts of trash from both the route and the campsites in Fairy Meadows.

By the end of the 1980s, most of the big features in the Cirque had been climbed, and the next logical step was to start picking the plums between the older routes, with a focus primarily on free climbing. "The best rock climbers of the nineties are even more divided than those of my era in the sixties and seventies," wrote Galen Rowell in *AAJ 1993*. "However, today's antagonists are far less likely to be operating in the same arena. One discrete group trains almost exclusively for competition, while another pursues adventure on ultimate rock walls." Rowell persuaded Todd Skinner and Paul Piana to try to merge the two approaches in a free attempt on the southeast face of Proboscis in 1992. Their goal was the world's most continuously difficult alpine free climb.

[Photo] David Fay moving up the spectacular 1968 route on Lotus Flower Tower's south face. The rock is peppered with knobs, making for enjoyable free climbing. *John Collis*

[Above left] Wilderness beauty en route to the Cirque. *Ben Ditto* [Top right] Scott Adamson checks out the bouldering around Fairy Meadows, with Mt. Harrison Smith behind. *Chad Copeland* [Bottom right] Most climbers choose to fly to Glacier Lake. *Ben Ditto* [Next page] A glimpse of the untapped climbing potential between Mt. Ida and Mt. Sidney Dobson. This video scene is about four air miles south of Glacier Lake. *Tom Zychowski (see AAJ website for video link)*

Todd and Paul completed the first ascent of the Great Canadian Knife (VI 5.13b) after weeks of navigating through a sea of feldspar crystals and cracks; their line is outrageous when compared with older routes that follow naturally protected cracks—it follows a bolt-protected arête for nearly half its length. Two years later, Scott Cosgrove, Jeff Jackson, and Kurt Smith added another free route to this mighty wall, Yukon Tears (VI 5.12c). Although it follows a more natural line than Piana and Skinner's route, it too required a good deal of bolt-protected climbing.

As the new millennium began, however, climbers still found plenty of new routes and first free ascents without extensive bolting. In August 2001, Jonny Copp brought his legendary stoke to the Cirque, and he and Josh Wharton established Pecking Order (V+ 5.11 R) on the southeast face of Parrot Beak with only two bolts. They also managed the first free ascent of Via Costa Brava (VI 5.12 R) on Proboscis, onsight in nine hours, and a base-to-summit speed record on the Lotus Flower Tower of 4 hours 26 minutes. Timmy O'Neill joined Copp on Bustle Tower to make the first free ascent of Club International (V 5.11b), and Brooke Andrews joined him for the first ascent of Don't Get Piggy (V+ 5.12a), a significant variation to Club International.

Several other impressive first free ascents fell that same year, thanks to the efforts of Yan Mongrain and Jay Knower, who opened the White Tower (III 5.11) and Light in August (IV 5.12-) on Terrace Tower. Mark Reeves and Steve Sinfield established the Hustler (V 5.10- R) on Phenocryst Spire that same season. Clearly, the Cirque still had solid offerings for the skilled and willing: The combined bolt count of every free route established that year was below that of Fitzcarraldo, a controversial and paradoxical German route put up just a few years earlier.

In the 1990s, German climber Kurt Albert had begun practicing what he perceived as a new twist on the alpine ideal of "fair means," by recanting motorized support while traveling into remote climbing venues. In July 1995, Albert partnered with Stefan Glowacz, Gerd Heidorn, and Leo Reitzner, parked their rental car at Flat Lakes, near the Tungsten Mine in Yukon Territory, then paddled canoes down the Little and South Nahanni rivers to the confluence of Brintnell Creek for approximately 80 miles, before setting off on another 13 miles of rugged foot travel. Their exit strategy would be to follow the overland path back to the South Nahanni River, where they would paddle another 250 miles to reach the Liard River. While in the Cirque, they established Fitzcarraldo (V 5.12b) on the north pillar of Mt. Harrison Smith, thus becoming the first group of modern climbers to eschew air support to open a big-wall route in the Cirque of the Unclimbables. Yet their loads included many pounds of bolts—they placed 50 on the 16-pitch route.

The approach by river and land has gained some popularity and offers guaranteed adventure in case the weather limits climbing. In 2013, Tim Emmett and Sean Leary hatched an ambitious plan: They adopted the river and hike approach, but upped the ante by using stand-up paddleboards. After visiting the nearby Vampire Peaks and wingsuiting off Vampire Spire, they wanted to climb the Lotus Flower Tower and wingsuit off that one as well, but they had to settle for an impromptu skydive into the Cirque from the skids of a helicopter that happened to be in the area for geology work.

In recent years, all-female teams have begun having a significant impact in the Cirque. In 2009, German climbers Ines Papert and Lisi Steurer established Power of Silence (IV 5.13a) on Middle Huey Spire—this effort stands out to me as especially profound, partly because it's a fairly obvious crack line that went unclimbed for decades and also because the pair sent a route at this grade in the Cirque with only a handful of bolts. Papert and Steurer went on to make the first free ascent of Riders on the Storm (IV 5.12d) on East Huey Spire. In 2010, Lorna Illingworth, Madaleine Sorkin, and Emily Stifler established Women at Work (VI 5.12 R), a significant variation to the Via Costa Brava on Proboscis (itself a variation to the 1963 Original Route, climbed in 1992 by Spanish climbers Jose Maria Cadina and Joaquin Olmo at VI 5.11 A1). Women at Work recently has been the preferred free line on the wall.

CLIMBING POTENTIAL

THE CIRQUE OF the Unclimbables is not climbed out. The southeast faces of Tara Tower and Tathagata both appear to offer clean granite and have no recorded free routes. Phenocryst's big south buttress (IV 5.7 A1) begs to free climbed, and Mt. Contact has only one recorded route, Piton Karmik (VI 5.10b A3), established in 2001 by Thierry Bionda, Denis Burdet, and Antonin Guenat; Contact's big, clean southeast face would be all the rage if not for its towering neighbor Proboscis.

In the right conditions—and for the right climbers—the Cirque could be a gold mine for ridge traverses and summit linkups. The most obvious traverse would start up the northeast face of Proboscis then ramble north along knife-edge ridges connecting Flat Top, Mt. Meringue, Phenocryst, Tara Tower, Lotus Flower Tower, Tathagata, and Parrot Beak, and eventually end on the summit of Sir James MacBrien.

This would cover about five miles, with more than 4,500 feet of vertical gain, and would require at least 10 new pitches on uncharted terrain.

Not far southwest of the Cirque, the area between Mt. Ida (scene of the first recorded climbs in the Ragged Range) and Mt. Sidney Dobson offers an incredible amount of unexplored vertical terrain. Though the walls of the this zone are not as extensive as those in the Cirque, they are not dissimilar in quality and height—and undoubtedly offer more solitude.

The boulders of the Cirque might deserve a visit in themselves. In the summer of 2000, I flew in with a certain boulderer known as Verm, and our supplies included a few crash pads as well as a haul bag full of beer; we finished all the beer, but a few of the boulder problems were left unopened.

LOGISTICS

AFTER ALL THE buzzing activity of the 1980s and '90s, the Cirque was looking a bit disheveled. In August 2000, the Alpine Club of Canada, American Alpine Club, and the Inconnu Lodge hosted the Cirque Project to remove piles of abandoned rubbish and install a much-needed pit toilet in Fairy Meadows, base camp for the Cirque. Bolt-protected sport climbs had begun to pepper many of the Meadows' enormous boulders, and loads of old tat and a few erroneous sport climbs were removed at this time.

In June 2009 the Cirque came under the protection of Nahanni National Park Reserve, which now includes the Ragged Range and nearby Vampire Peaks, making Nahanni the third-largest national park in Canada. The park service has since updated the pit toilet in Fairy Meadows and redirected and vastly improved the approach trail from Glacier Lake.

Climbers tend to visit the Cirque for a few weeks in August, which historically offers the most stable weather. The bugs have abated a bit and you still get 18-plus hours of daylight. That said, climbers have visited the Cirque as early as June and as late as October. The bugs can be horrible in July, and snowpack can be an issue, but 24 hours of daylight is a real bonus. September offers a nearly bug-free experience and a solid opportunity to see the aurora borealis, but the days are cold and quite short, plus the season can end abruptly when snow starts to fall.

If you only have a few weeks to visit the Cirque, with no desire for extra discomfort, I suggest air support. Kluane Airways has been flying people into the Ragged Range for more than 20 years. Warren LaFave, the owner, loves the character climbers bring to his world-class

fishing and recreational resort, the Inconnu Lodge. Accommodations at the Inconnu upon return from the mountains are generally included with the flight cost—this place is nearly as awe-inspiring as the Cirque. The lodge is about 87 air miles from the Cirque, which means an hour of airtime to Glacier Lake. The trail from the lake to Fairy Meadows climbs about 1,500 feet and takes most heavily loaded folks four to six hours. Helicopter charters eliminate most of the hiking, but the flights are expensive; contact Kluane Airways for pricing and availability: 1-250-860- 4187; info@kluaneairways.com; kluaneairways.com.

If you have a flexible schedule and a strong affinity for adventure, you can access the Cirque via the Little (class IV) and South Nahanni rivers (class II). Most people use canoes or kayaks, but I have jammed three people and gear into a single 10-foot raft with great success. The float trip takes four to six days and will require another day or so of hiking from the river to Glacier Lake, then up to the cirque (12-plus miles). Once finished climbing, you can take a floatplane from Glacier Lake (recommended) or continue paddling down the South Nahanni River (class III) for three to six more days.

Nahanni National Park Reserve requires visitors to the Cirque to check in and out and buy a permit; in 2017, the fee was $147.20/person (CDN). To register for a backcountry permit, email nahanni.info@pc.gc.ca or phone 1-867-695-3151.

Fairy Meadows is home to whistle pigs and ground squirrels that will ravage your food if you leave it out. Glacier Lake is frequented by bears, and Fairy Meadows is not that far for them to wander, so plan accordingly (hang food/trash and keep a clean campsite). The mosquitoes are ravenous, especially by the lake; head nets and bug spray will help keep you sane. You might want to filter your water to avoid what Yukoners call "the beaver fever."

It's essential to practice "leave no trace" in this beautiful place. There is a pit toilet—use it! Stay on established trails, try not to create new campsites, and, although some folks burn trash, I strongly advise against this practice. For the love of all things special, pack it out.

ABOUT THE AUTHOR: *Pat Goodman, 39, has made nine trips to the Ragged Range, including two visits to the Cirque of the Unclimbables. He lives in Fayetteville, West Virginia.*

[Below] The magical Cirque, spanning from Mt. Harrison Smith (far left) past Proboscis (center left) and Lotus Flower Tower to Mt. Sir James MacBrien (center right). *Gary Bremner / gbpcreative.ca*

[Photo] Graham Zimmerman pauses to take in the view during the descent from Celeno Peak in Alaska's University Range after the first ascent of the west face (see p.148). *Chris Wright*

CLIMBS & EXPEDITIONS

REPORTS GENERALLY ARE arranged geographically, from north to south, and from west to east, within a country or region. Unless noted, all reports are from the 2016 calendar year. We encourage climbers to submit notable ascents for future editions (**email us at** *aaj@americanalpineclub. org*). The complete *AAJ* database, from 1929 to present, can be searched at *publications. americanalpineclub.org*. Online reports frequently contain additional text, photos, maps, and topos—look for these symbols indicating additional resources at the website:

FULL-LENGTH REPORT	ADDITIONAL PHOTOS	MAPS OR TOPOS	VIDEO OR MULTIMEDIA

UNITED STATES

[Above] The north face of South Hozomeen Mountain (8,003'), deep in Washington's North Cascades. The two-day first ascent gained the prominent right trending ramp in the center of the face and followed it to the ridgeline, then took the Southwest Route back left to the top. *John Scurlock*

WASHINGTON / NORTH CASCADES

SOUTH HOZOMEEN MOUNTAIN, NORTH FACE

On August 13 and 14, Rolf Larson and I made the first ascent of the intimidating north face of South Hozomeen Mountain (8,003'). This rarely climbed peak is among the steepest in the Lower 48. We'd gawked at it from neighboring North Hozomeen three years prior, speculating that a massive, slanting dihedral feature might yield a feasible route. [*Larson and Wehrly completed the first ascent of the Zorro Face (west face) of North Hozomeen in late August 2013; see AAJ 2014.*]

Our all-free, 13-pitch line (15 pitches to the summit) begins directly beneath the overhanging summit, travels three pitches more or less straight up to gain the dihedral, and then grinds up the right-hand facet of this giant corner for 10 more pitches to reach the summit ridge. The last two pitches to the top belong to the Southwest Route, pioneered by Fred Beckey and crew during the impressive first ascent of the peak in 1947.

The pitches on the face were all 5.7 to 5.9, with a long stretch of 4th class in the middle (some simul-climbing), plus two mid-5th class pitches on the Beckey route to the top. The first three pitches were quite solid and a lot of fun. However, the remaining pitches, while moderate in technical difficulty, do not offer straightforward climbing—careful route-finding and hold selection were mandatory. We'd hoped the giant dihedral would hold a nice crack system, but the feature was generally comprised of very rotten and decomposing rock, or filled with copious humus. Some of our 60m "moderate" leads took over 1.5 hours, with abundant loose flakes, rotten and flaring cracks, and infrequent and mostly ornamental gear.

After 11 pitches of hyper-vigilant climbing, we shiver-bivied on a sloping ledge perched on the exposed right margin of the dihedral, a couple of thousand feet above the basin. The next morning we dispatched a tenuous and traversing crux pitch to regain the big corner, then a relatively nice pitch to the ridge crest, where we joined the Southwest Route to the summit. We placed no bolts and used only two pins to supplement our 11th-pitch belay and bivy anchor. The descent of the Southwest Route was complex and time-consuming.

We feel fortunate to have solved—and survived—this problem. Unfortunately, we can't really recommend the route, although it might appeal to those aspiring to exercise their risk-management skills. 📷

— ERIC WEHRLY

FALLEN ANGEL PEAK, ACT LIKE YOU'RE HAVING FUN!

IN MID-SEPTEMBER, ERIC Wehrly and I snagged a new and aesthetic line within a day's "walk" from the road in the North Cascades. It was my first rock FA in the range and a chance to learn from Eric, who has many first ascents to his name.

We parked near the measuring station on the west fork of Newhalem Creek and followed the creek to a junction where we turned west. We followed this drainage up into an alpine basin beneath the north aspect of Fallen Angel (ca 6,840'). On the approach we encountered just about every terrain obstacle the Cascades' subalpine zones have to offer, perhaps even meriting a "New Wave" bushwhack rating. A physical, but not mental, respite from the eight-hour approach was offered by a sustained and exposed stretch of moss-coated, fifth-class chimney climbing, which granted passage through the lower cliff bands.

The climb itself was great. After 100' or so of easy soloing, we climbed eight roped pitches to the summit. The rock was quite solid and clean, even on the junky-looking first pitch, requiring only sporadic, to-be-expected alpine gardening. The harder technical climbing followed high-quality crack systems up bright gneiss.

[Above] The north side of Fallen Angel Peak, showing the line of Act Like You're Having Fun! (8 pitches, 5.10+). The route follows good cracks to reach the prominent Grim Reaper Arête. *Eric Wehrly*

Swapping leads, I drew the spectacular crux pitch (5.10+), which follows a striking arête that we named the Scythe, in reference to Cascades climber (and Fallen Angel first ascensionist) John Roper's original name for the north-northeast-facing prow that defines this side of the peak: the Grim Reaper Arête. On this pitch I avoided a belayer-slayer block, which Eric inadvertently trundled while following. Unfortunately, this marred our otherwise pure ascent as Eric weighted the rope to avoid a crushed foot. The final ridge to the summit afforded views of the area's devil-themed peaks and other peaks of the North Cascades.

We descended the south face via four 35m rappels, then followed fourth-class ledges east to a notch in the ridge. We returned to our camp on the slabs beneath the route at 4 p.m., and, knowing the descent to the car would require a lot of daylight and luck, we spent a beautiful night in the alpine, recounting the day over beers. Despite our best efforts to learn from our

[Above] Eric Wehrly searches for well-anchored turf as he navigates mossy gully systems and steep, bushy slopes on the approach to Fallen Angel Peak. *Chris Mutzel*

route-finding mistakes on the way in, it took us nearly nine hours to descend the six miles back to the car. We had to jokingly remind each other to smile in any photos that were taken. Thus the name: Act Like You're Having Fun! (1,000', III 5.10+).

— CHRIS MUTZEL

M&M WALL, GOLDEN AGE

In the summer of 2014 I had the privilege of joining Blake Herrington and Max Tepfer to establish a new line on the mysterious M&M Wall (a.k.a. Supercave Wall). This impressive, 1,000' south-facing wall is two miles north of the famous Liberty Bell massif. The 11-pitch route we climbed that summer, the Tiger, featured beautiful climbing on flawless granite (*AAJ 2015*).

Over the following two years I would often return to the images I had snapped of the cliff, dreaming of the possibility of another line, linking features up the steep swath of stone to the left of the Tiger. In the spring of 2016, I returned with a highly motivated Tom Wright and established Golden Age over two weekends in May and June. Taking advantage of spring snow in the approach gully and a straightforward 4th-class ledge system leading to the top, we opted for a top-down

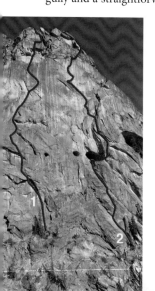

approach. Some large trundles and epic top-rope sends were realized, but progress was slowed by intermittent bursts of precipitation and regularly scheduled union breaks. On the final ascent day, a coin toss determined the order of leads, and both climbers freed every pitch.

Golden Age (IV 5.12b) features sustained 5.11 climbing with one pitch of 5.12. All belays are bolted, and there is excellent protection throughout the climb. The name is a response to the pundits claiming that the golden age of climbing has passed. With the explosion of difficult multi-pitch free climbs being established throughout North America over the last decade, we would have to say we are still living in the golden age. 📷 🔍

— COLIN MOORHEAD, *CANADA*

[Left] The M&M Wall (a.k.a. Supercave Wall) near Washington Pass. (1) Golden Age (IV 5.12b, Moorhead-Wright, 2016). (2) The Tiger (IV 5.12b, Herrington-Mooorhead-Tepfer, 2014). Other routes exist farther right. *Colin Moorhead*

LIBERTY BELL, A SLAVE TO LIBERTY

IN EARLY AUGUST, Mikey Schaefer completed a difficult new route on Liberty Bell. A Slave to Liberty (450m, 11 pitches, 5.13-) climbs the first three pitches of Freedom or Death (5.10, 5.11, 5.11), then steps right to join Thin Red Line just before its third-pitch anchor. From there the route climbs eight new pitches (four of which are 5.12), with the crux 5.13 slab on pitch eight.

Parts of this line had previously been attempted aid-solo by Darin Berdinka, but the route remained incomplete. In 2015, Schaefer rope-soloed to the base of the crux pitch and then returned over several weeks to suss and equip the best line, before forest fires forced him to abandon the project for the season. He returned in July 2016 and pioneered the final few pitches to the top through a series of roofs. After several days of equipping and top-roping, he made a one-day free ascent on August 6, leading every pitch with the support of Shanjean Lee. 🔍

– ANDY ANDERSON, *WITH INFORMATION FROM MOUNTAIN PROJECT*

DARRINGTON, ILLUSION WALL, THE EPIC TAIL OF SIR NORBERT

IN LATE 2015, Chris Hagen, Matt Leslie, Jeremy Luscher, and Alan Semrau finished a three-year project to climb a mostly trad route up the Illusion Wall, in the Squire Creek area of Darrington. The Epic Tail of Sir Norbert (IV 5.10+) follows the prow of the wall to its highest point. The line, named after Hagen's dog, has only 12 protection bolts over 10 pitches and 1,500' of climbing. 📄 📷 🔍

– *INFORMATION PROVIDED BY* CHRIS HAGEN

DRAGONTAIL PEAK, ICELINE BLING

ON APRIL 3, Craig Pope, my wife Priti Wright, and I climbed a new ice route on the north face of Dragontail Peak, a direct line up the north buttress that we dubbed Iceline Bling (250m, WI5 M4). This is an alternate start to the classic Triple Couloirs (WI3 M3), depositing the climber at the top of the first couloir; it's also a worthy line on its own, though it may not form consistently each year. Iceline Bling begins just left of the toe of the north buttress. Two pitches of WI4 and some easy snow took us to the crux (WI5 M4), which Craig led up a thinly iced slab to a short column. More easy snow (climber's left) brought us to the Triple Couloirs, where one can continue upward or downclimb to Colchuck Lake as we did. 📷

– JEFF WRIGHT

[Above] **Craig Pope leads the crux pitch on Iceline Bling (250m, WI5 M4). The route tackles a direct line up the north buttress of Dragontail Peak. It may not form consistently every year.** *Jeff Wright*

[Above left] The west face of Mt. Stuart, showing the full line of King Kong, a.k.a. Joe Puryear Memorial Route (IV 5.11+). *Sol Wertkin* [Above right] Sol Wertkin on the crux 5.11+ splitter of King Kong. *Mahting Productions*

KING KONG
THE JOE PURYEAR MEMORIAL ROUTE ON MT. STUART

BY SOL WERTKIN

DURING THE FIRST ascent of Gorillas in the Mist on the west face of Mt. Stuart, in 2009, Jens Holsten, Blake Herrington and I endured an unplanned bivy high on the mountain in stormy conditions. The next day, after summiting and making it back to the trailhead, we ran into friends Joe Puryear and Max Hasson, who were on their way to rescue us after my wife woke up that morning in an empty bed and sounded the alarm. When Joe died the following October while attempting a new route on Labuche Kang in Tibet, I made the decision to complete a direct finish in his honor. Joe often talked about the great influence that Mt. Stuart, a peak visible from his childhood home, had on his climbing career.

I made numerous attempts at the direct line up the west face. In August 2011, Jens Holsten, Mark Westman, and I traversed left after the first four pitches of Gorillas in the Mist and climbed two pitches of new ground, aiming for a headwall with an aesthetic splitter crack. However, we ran out of daylight and finished more easily to the left (Gorillas Direct, 5.10+).

Over the following years, I kept working on the "direct direct" finish, but the difficulty of reaching the headwall pitches and the necessity of cleaning the cracks delayed a full ascent. In early September, Tyree Johnson and I finally completed the 60m headwall crack, but not before I took an 8m whipper from the last move. A week later I returned with Jon Gleason and was able to climb the crack clean.

King Kong likely holds the hardest pitch of rock climbing on Mt. Stuart, and a complete ascent to the summit will likely be the longest climb in the range. With the short days of September we did not complete the line to the summit, descending the west ridge from atop the 900' wall.

SUMMARY: First ascent of King Kong (IV 5.11+) on the west face of Mt. Stuart, adding a difficult two-pitch finish to Gorillas in the Mist (IV 5.11-, Herrington-Holsten-Wertkin, 2009) and Gorillas Direct (5.10+, Holsten-Wertkin-Westman, 2011), September 9, 2016.

OREGON

HOOD RIVER VALLEY, EAST FORK CRAGS, PETE'S PILE, BELLY DANCER TRAVERSE

CLIMBERS TEND TO snort when I suggest we visit my favorite crag. The slur "Pete's Pile" was first hurled at this dirty, lichen-encrusted collection of basalt columns back in the late 1980s, when it was being developed by a scruffy ski patroller of that name. But my motto is that if you can't be with the rock you love, love the rock you're with. In the mid '90s, when I was the crag's primary developer, I led a doomed movement to rename it Pete's Pillars. After all, the view across the East Fork of the Hood River to nearby Mt. Hood is stunning, the air crisp and cool even on a hot summer's morning, and the rock solid enough for my non-particular taste. Best of all, under all that grunge are loads of virgin cracks, just waiting for a sturdy brush and a strong arm to set them free.

[Above] John Inglis follows the first horizontal pitch of the eight-pitch Belly Dancer Traverse. *John Harlin III*

The cliff is only 200 feet high, more and less, so even after a decade as the AAJ's editor, I never thought of my beloved Pete's as being AAJ-worthy—she simply wasn't tall enough. Then, some 20 years after first brushing Pete's flanks, I had an epiphany. My fair crag might be short in stature, but she's wide in girth. Would her full belly yield to my lustful embrace?

John Inglis and I first teamed up to go sideways in 2014. We launched vertically at the left outside edge of a black wall that's closed to climbing due to rare plants (the "closed" signs have now rotted). This took us to an obvious horizontal weakness at about 80 feet that we called the Belly Band. From there we moved leftward for four roughly 80-foot pitches, until we reached a vertical route named K9 Shanghai, about halfway across the traverse. Out of time, we lowered to the ground. We returned some months later and climbed up K9 Shanghai to complete the rest of the traverse, finishing on top. Each half took us four to five hours.

We then attempted to combine the two halves, expecting them to yield faster with familiarity. They didn't, spitting us off again at the halfway point. Inglis was not available for my next attempt, which fared no better. Finally, in June 2016, Inglis and I teamed up again for an all-day effort. We finished at dusk some nine hours after launching.

The route takes so much time because leader and follower must climb equally cautiously. All the protectable cracks rise straight up between columns, which means that if the leader falls while rounding a pillar, he pendulums backward, potentially slamming hard into one or more column walls. (We clipped a few existing bolts but placed none of our own.) If the following climber falls just after removing a piece of gear, he faces his own slam-dance pendulum in reverse. We brushed only on lead and only when hand or footholds didn't otherwise reveal themselves. You'll find the line nearly as dirty now as when we began, and almost as adventurous (we did knock off a few dangerous blocks).

The vitals: one upward pitch to reach the Belly Band, then eight pitches sideways (about 600 feet). The route reveals itself as you go—on each attempt we took exactly the same line of weakness, varying from 60 to 80 feet off the ground. Each pitch is short in distance (70–80 feet) but long in effort. Half the pitches went at 5.9; the other half at 5.10. Belly Dancer Traverse: 5.10+ PG-13.

– JOHN HARLIN III

[Above] **Alex Parker starting the crux pitch of the Pencil, a previously unclimbed ice feature above the Eliot Glacier on Mt. Hood.** *Jacob Oram*

MT. HOOD, THE PENCIL

ON JANUARY 28, 2017, Tim Bemrich, Jacob Oram, and I made the first ascent of a feature long known to climbers as the Pencil: a steep, very narrow ice line on the north face of Mt. Hood, between the North Face Gully routes and the Eliot Headwall.

We approached via the standard slog up the south side to the Hogsback, from which we soloed the Devil's Kitchen Headwall by headlamp, putting us on the summit for sunrise. From there, we descended the Sunshine Route to the shoulder above Snow Dome, where we roped up and crossed the upper Eliot Glacier to the bottom of the route.

We were happy to find solid sticks leading up to an obvious horn with a sling that had been left during a previous attempt on the line. The crux second pitch took us through a series of steep sections on variable, mostly thin ice, with the occasional rock move, for nearly 60m of WI3/3+. The third pitch had a very quick section of secure WI3- right off the anchor that gradually mellowed into a snowfield with good névé. This took us to the top of the ridge in a 60m-plus rope stretcher, where a very short but quality pitch of WI3 brought us onto the Cathedral Spire snowfield. We simulclimbed to the top of Cathedral Spire, then downclimbed to reach the notch above the Ravine. From here we joined the North Face Right Gully route to reach the summit for the second time that day.

— ALEX PARKER

BROAD DOME, ATLANTIS WALL, SIERRA SWASHBUCKLE

DURING THE FIRST week of August, Julian Kuettner and I completed a new line up the Atlantis Wall, on the south face of Broad Dome in the Sonora Pass area. The Atlantis Wall sits above the middle of Donnell Reservoir, approximately 15 miles from the town of Strawberry. From the parking area, you must hump all your kit and grog to the dam, then hoist your boat (a canoe, in our case) over a large gate and lower it to the water, before getting in and paddling across the reservoir about three-quarters of a mile.

[Left] **Tied in? Check. Harness doubled back? Check. Life jacket? John Greer about to start the first pitch of Sierra Swashbuckle (IV 5.11 C1), complete with aquatic safety gear. During the week the climbers worked on the route, the water level dropped 20 meters.** *Julian Kuettner*

After studying photos of the face, we had decided on a few lines that seemed promising. The best of these began in a giant left-facing corner chimney, then went through a series of changing corners, and ended in a gully system below the summit. Our route began right above the water. After securing the boat, I placed the first few pieces and tenuously started the first pitch while wearing my life vest. This pitch ended about 10m up on a sloping ledge at the base of a steep, undulating corner. By the end of the trip, this first pitch had grown to approximately 30m as the water level dropped.

Over the next week, we pushed the route up the wall, the low altitude and direct sunlight turning us into melted pools of wax on the verge of heatstroke. After 10 pitches we topped out and spent the night on top before rappelling the route. We really wanted to free the whole route but only had time to go back and clean the amazing second pitch. On Sunday morning, our last day of the trip, we both managed to redpoint this pitch. We both felt that the few other pitches that required aid will go free with a little more time and cleaning. We named the route Sierra Swashbuckle (10 pitches, 5.11 C1). [*Editor's note: The Atlantis Wall (ca 1,000') now has six known Grade IV or V routes. This trip was supported by an AAC Live Your Dream grant.*]

– JOHN GREER

FLATIRON BUTTE, MULTIPLE NEW ROUTES

OVER THREE DAYS in early July, Jonathan Schaffer and I established four new lines on the prominent east face of Flatiron Butte, located to the north of Yosemite National Park in the Hoover Wilderness. All routes were free-climbed ground-up, in a single push, and each is about 900' in length. To the best of our knowledge, only two of the 24 pitches we climbed

[Below] The east face of Flatiron Butte. (1) Golden Triangle (5.10, Evans-Nicodemi, 2016). (2) Triple Beam Dream (5.11+, Fasoldt-Schaffer, 2016). (3) Straight Flush (5.11+, Fasoldt-Schaffer, 2016). (4) Et Tu, Brute!/Brutus of Wyde Memorial Route (5.9+ A2, Binder-Harris-Holland-Hove, 2001; 5.11a, Musiyenko-Taylor, 2014). (5) Notorious RBG (5.11+, Fasoldt-Schaffer, 2016). (6) Throat Yogurt (5.11-, Fasoldt-Schaffer, 2016). (7) Parasitic Nematode (5.10+, Musiyenko-Taylor, 2014). (8) Northeast Ridge (Beckey-Nolting, 1981). *Pete Fasoldt*

had ever seen human passage; no gear was left behind on any route. (*Descriptions of these four routes, from 5.11- to 5.11+, are at the AAJ website.*)

In early August I returned to the Butte with Mike Pennings. After a repeat of Brutus of Wyde (2001, freed in 2014), we set our sights on a north-facing rock feature set back southwest from Flatiron's summit ridge. The feature, upon which we bestowed the name Red Square, is quite evident during the descent. We climbed a line left of center, through some bad rock and up grovelly terrain for three pitches. Savory Chicken (100m, 5.11) may not be worth a repeat, but potential for other climbs exists on the face. The next day we climbed a route on Flatiron's lower-angle northwest face. Bodie Mike's Barbecue climbs 5.9 choss for a few pitches to gain the summit ridge. 🖻 🗐

– PETE FASOLDT

FLATIRON BUTTE, GOLDEN TRIANGLE

ON JUNE 24, Damien Nicodemi and I climbed a new route on the east face of Flatiron Butte. Our route begins in a left-facing corner beneath the obvious pine tree on the left side of the face. We climbed the path of least resistance, primarily following corner systems, many of which ended up being vegetated. Every pitch was freed by at least one of us. In the few instances where the leader had to hang on gear in order to remove vegetation from the cracks, the follower was able to free the pitch. Golden Triangle (1,500', III/IV 5.10) features good rock quality interrupted by brief sections of loose rock on wandering ledges, but we believe with some traffic this route will clean up quite nicely. Cruxes are found on the third and sixth pitches. We left no permanent protection or anchors on the climb. 🖻

– RYAN EVANS

INCREDIBLE HULK, LENTICULAR GYRATIONS

ON SEPTEMBER 5, Jeff Gicklhorn, Patrick O'Donnell, and I free climbed a new route on the Incredible Hulk. Jeff and I had envisioned this route in 2014, and we took two calendar years to equip it, making many short weekend trips spread out over three seasons. Various setbacks occurred over this long project, including broken drill bits, hail and rain storms, and some ground-up questing that left us far out from our protection with no bolt kit. The crux pitch caused significant headaches, as it required the most bolts and was 1,000' up the wall.

At the risk of not completing the climb in 2016, Patrick O'Donnell was invited along for our free attempt. On September 5, Patrick and I freed the entire route, either on lead or top-rope, with Jeff freeing all but the last two pitches. Each person led three pitches.

Lenticular Gyrations (1,100', III 5.12c) shares approximately 60' with other climbs, but opens up over 1,000' of new terrain, with the crux eighth lead being one of the steepest pitches on the Hulk. The route is mostly varied crack climbing on excellent rock. We placed two bolts at each anchor, and seven of the route's ten protection bolts are found on the crux pitch.

As part of this project, Jeff and I also freed a new start variation to Tradewinds, climbing the first two pitches of Lenticular Gyrations, then connecting into Tradewinds at its third anchor. This variation offers a better warmup and higher quality climbing than the original start to Tradewinds. 🖻 🔍

– AARON CASSEBEER

INCREDIBLE HULK, WIND SHEAR

JUST WHEN WE thought the Hulk had been pretty much tapped out of quality long, independent lines, Peter Croft visually pieced together a wild and improbable series of features that hugged the steep arête dividing Airstream and Positive Vibrations—we were hooked and the fun began.

Peter, Andy Puhvel, and I established the core of the new route during a couple of outings in the summer of 2014 and thought it was a done deal. But a stunning blank arête that could add a spectacular independent finish lured us back in the summer of 2016. The arête pitch (5.11+) proved to be one of the best pitches on the Hulk and a fitting finale. With the addition of two new 5.11 pitches near the start, we finally completed Wind Shear (14 pitches, 5.12) on July 31.

– DAVE NETTLE

CALIFORNIA / YOSEMITE NATIONAL PARK

MT. WATKINS, TEABAG WISDOM

AFTER RUNNING INTO Bruce Morris, who did two new routes on the east face of Mt. Watkins, in a local climbing gym and hearing all his praise for this infrequently visited corner of Yosemite Valley, I decided to check the east face for myself. Chris Kolpp and I first repeated Golden Dawn (IV 5.10d), which Bruce and Urmas Franosch had put up in the 1980s, and then attempted a new route starting a few hundred feet below and to the east.

From the base the line seemed intimidating, as multiple overhangs guarded the summit and between these was plenty of blank slab, yet we could see dikes, intermittent cracks, and other features that inspired hope. We started before dawn and ran out of light halfway up the wall. Determined to go back, we added a few hand-drilled bolts on the way down, by headlamp, before climbing out via the gully that we had rappelled to reach the base. Returning to our cars after 4 a.m., we were dehydrated and delirious, yet excited about a fine adventure. While making hot drinks, we had a good laugh at the messages we discovered on our

[Right] **Chris Kolpp during the first ascent of Teabag Wisdom on the east face of Mt. Watkins.** *Vitaliy Musiyenko*

[Above] **Mt. Watkins from the southeast. The ca 2,400-foot south face is far left. (1) Teabag Wisdom (IV 5.11a) . (2) New Life (IV 5.10) on "Harding Tower." Yasoo Dome is on the far right.** *xRez Studio*

teabags: "Patience is the companion of wisdom" and "Wisdom doesn't necessarily come with age. Sometimes age just shows up all by itself."

We had to return three times in order to drill rappel anchors, complete the first ascent, and make an in-a-day free ascent. Teabag Wisdom (1,350', IV 5.11a) features perfect granite and varied climbing that will put a smile on your face. Many claim to be enlightened while climbing—Chris and I get our wisdom from teabags. "One day you'll just be a memory for some people, do your best to be a good one." 📷 🔍

– VITALIY MUSIYENKO

TENAYA CANYON, HARDING TOWER, NEW LIFE

DEEP IN TENAYA Canyon is a slabby dome hidden by Mt. Watkins to the west and Yasoo Dome to the east. In late September, with no knowledge of any previously established climbs on the formation or the best way to approach, Mark Westman and I hiked to the top from the Olmsted Point parking lot in Tuolumne Meadows. We reached the base by descending a gully on the formation's east side, with a few rappels to overcome a steep drop-off.

After getting over the initial overhang on the dome, we climbed about seven varied pitches, most of which had huge runouts on solid face and slab climbing. (Because it was a very long route and we were trying to finish in a day, we did not place any bolts, but the route could become a very fun moderate with the addition of some fixed pro.) We unroped on the big ledge two-thirds of the way up and scrambled west to an attractive crack system I had spied while climbing on Mt. Watkins. After five more pitches we got to the summit.

We named the formation Harding Tower and our route New Life (2,000', IV 5.10), as that's what it felt like for Mark on his first long climb after recently overcoming a cancer. The name also holds truth for aspiring adventure climbers—not all the plums have been picked, even in Yosemite Valley. 📷

– VITALIY MUSIYENKO

DAWN WALL, RAPID SECOND ASCENT

ON NOVEMBER 21, Adam Ondra from the Czech Republic completed the second free ascent of the Dawn Wall (VI 5.14d), the 32-pitch El Capitan route generally regarded as the world's hardest big-wall free climb. The route on El Cap's southeast face, freed by Tommy Caldwell and Kevin Jorgeson over a 19-day push ending in January 2015 (concluding nearly seven years of work by Caldwell and later Jorgeson) took Ondra eight days on his final push. Ondra's arrival garnered worldwide attention, as his intentions were pre-announced and because many wondered how his sport climbing, bouldering, and competition skills would translate to the mythic walls of Yosemite during his first visit. [*Ondra wrote a feature article about climbing the world's first 9b+ (5.15c), the route Change in Norway, for AAJ 2013.*]

[Above] **Adam Ondra celebrates after redpointing the most difficult pitches of the Dawn Wall. He had tried the crux 14th pitch eight times the previous day.** *Heinz Zak*

After arriving in Yosemite in October, Ondra quickly set to work. In a nod to traditional Valley style, he went ground-up on the Dawn Wall, using a mix of free and aid tactics to fix lines up the route. After several weeks of rehearsing the pitches, with a brief interlude for an onsight attempt on the Nose (VI 5.14a) with his father, Ondra began his free push from the ground on November 14.

After climbing the first 13 pitches over two days and resting the third, he made eight unsuccessful attempts to redpoint the 14th pitch on November 17. The following day he sent both pitch 14 and pitch 15, the two hardest pitches on the route, in a single afternoon. Ondra felt the second of these traversing pitches was 5.14c (graded 5.14d on the first ascent); he also upgraded pitch 10 from 5.14a to 5.14b.

On November 19, his sixth day on the route, he redpointed two 5.14 pitches and four of 5.13 to reach the top of Wino Tower. Ondra followed the Loop Pitch variation on pitch 16 (5.14a), avoiding the famous sideways dyno that only Jorgeson has redpointed during a free ascent of the route.

After waiting out a storm atop Wino Tower, Ondra climbed the 12 remaining, relatively moderate (up to 5.13a) pitches and reached the summit of El Cap on the afternoon of November 21.

"Hats off to Tommy and Kevin, who believed that the whole climb was possible," Ondra said in an update published by Black Diamond before the final push. "I have the advantage that I know that the climb is possible and that helps me to keep the faith that I might be able to do it as well. I am humbled and impressed by what Tommy and Kevin did!"

— ANDY ANDERSON, *WITH INFORMATION FROM ERIC BISSELL AND PUBLISHED REPORTS*

YOSEMITE OVERVIEW

DURING WHAT WAS likely a record-breaking summer for park visitation, three-hour traffic jams edged slowly in a counterclockwise loop around the Valley floor while El Capitan's mostly empty walls flickered through the exhaust and idle air of 102° July days. At the time, it seemed difficult to imagine that roughly a dozen of the world's best rock climbers would descend on Yosemite a few months later with the goals of repeating some of El Capitan's most difficult free routes.

[Above] Eric Bissell engages the tiered roof crux on pitch five of Mr. Midwest (13 pitches, 5.13b) on El Capitan during the first free ascent, with Cameron King. *Drew Smith*

Before the Sierra snow returned in earnest last autumn after years of drought, Jacopo Larcher (Italy) and Barbara Zangerl (Austria) made the third free ascent of Zodiac (5.13d), Jorg Verhoeven (Netherlands) made the second free ascent of the Dihedral Wall (5.14a), Sébastien Berthe (Belgium) made the second ascent of the Free Heart Route (5.13b V10), and Adam Ondra (Czech) completed the second ascent of the Dawn Wall (5.14d, *see previous report*). Perhaps most unusually, Pete Whittaker (U.K.) managed to rope-solo the Freerider (5.12d/5.13a), all free in a day. As the dust settled toward the end of November, Larcher said in an interview on the Planet Mountain website, "I'm sure that the real free climbing boom in Yosemite is only just about to begin."

Though the headlines focused on last autumn's exploits, climbers living in Yosemite and its surrounding communities established new routes around the park throughout the year. In May, Cameron King and Eric Bissell finished the first free ascent of Mr. Midwest (13 pitches, 5.13b) on the textured west face of El Cap. After three months of weekends and 10 days on the wall, Kevin DeWeese and Steve Bosque established Hail to the Chief (11 pitches, 5.9 A3) on Lower Cathedral Spire, named for President Obama's Yosemite visit that occurred while the two were working on the route. In October, Brandon Adams and Tito Krull plucked the final dihedral line from the center of Liberty Cap with their first ascent of Stiff Upper Lip (10 pitches, 5.9 A3+).

Speed climbing saw its milestones last season as well. In mid-June, Scott Bennett and Brad Gobright linked three El Cap routes in a day, climbing Zodiac, the Nose and Lurking Fear in 23 hours 10 minutes. Theirs was the third El Cap triple in a day, and the first to complete this particular combination. Multiple women closed in on a sub-24 solo ascent of the Nose on El Cap, and on August 5 local climbing guide Miranda Oakley started up the route at 5:30 a.m. and topped out in quiet darkness 21 hours 50 minutes later, achieving the first female solo NIAD.

In October, two large routes with small sections of aid, the Misty Wall near Yosemite Falls and the West Face of Sentinel, saw complete free ascents via short variations to their original routes. Under the tutelage of John Long, the routes were group efforts of rebolting, cleaning, and projecting before being redpointed by Jon Cardwell and Marcus Garcia on the Misty Wall Direct (5.13), and Kevin Jorgeson and Ben Rueck on Sentinel's West Face (5.13).

— ERIC BISSELL

CREST JEWELS
SIX LONG NEW ROUTES ON THE WHEELER CREST

BY RICHARD SHORE

IN THE FALL of 2015, I began exploring the expansive Wheeler Crest, repeating a few of the classic routes with friends. We became entranced with the wildness of the place: long approaches, no trails, no crowds, just the occasional bighorn sheep, peregrine falcon, or golden eagle to keep us company. Those early efforts opened our eyes to the vast scale of the Crest and its mind-blowing potential for new routes.

On December 14, 2015, Myles Moser and Amy Ness started a line up the steep southeast buttress of Wells Peak. They climbed through an intimidating black diorite band before reaching the excellent granite above, and then rappelled to the ground. A few days later, on December 18, I joined the duo for the summit push. We quickly regained their previous high point and swapped leads through the virgin terrain above. The sun exposure on this subalpine tower was surreal—climbing in T-shirts on a forecasted 41°F winter day? Then shade hit the route and we recognized why there was still snow on the ground. The route ended on the peak's prominent southern subsummit, from which we rappelled the line of ascent. We called our climb Forbidden Fruit (IV 5.11).

[Above] **Tony Lewis negotiates a tricky traverse on pitch sixth of Super Grey Pinnacle (IV 5.10).** *Richard Shore*

Snow kept us out of the Wheeler Crest until the following April. Then, taking advantage of the short prime season (longer, cooler days and, most importantly, running water), we ventured deeper into the canyons. Our efforts focused on the Grey Band, a series of pinnacles hidden behind the well-documented routes in Mayfield Canyon.

On April 5, Myles and I made the painful uphill approach to the most prominent tower in the Grey Band, the unimaginatively named Big Grey Pinnacle. This 1,000' tower was already home to two vintage routes on its eastern side, and we were aiming for a new line up its featured southeast face. After scrambling up a blocky orange buttress at the base, we found four continuously challenging pitches (5.10+, 5.11-, 5.12, 5.10-). Racing the fading afternoon light, we continued up a rope length of moderate cracks and run-out face to the shoulder of the tower, and then a polished 5.9+ corner to the top. I dropped our only headlamp and the extra webbing high on the route, and rappelling into the darkness became infinitely more interesting. Staggering back to camp hours later, bloodied and bruised, we had been treated to a Bighorn Beatdown (IV 5.12).

On April 19, Natalie Brechtel and I hiked back up into the Grey Band with intentions of climbing the Lost Pink Tower. Sandwiched between gray spires, this 700-foot peak of magnificent pink granite was not only "lost," but also completely neglected by climbers for decades. Our proposed line was obvious: a long, blocky ramp that led up and right from the base to the solitary weakness in the center of the wall: a left-facing corner system with two

[Above] Part of the Wheeler Crest, showing (A) the top of Lost Pink Tower, (B) Cobbler's Bench, and (C) Super Grey Pinnacle. None of these walls had been climbed before 2016. (1) Rattler (IV 5.11 R). (2) Super Grey Pinnacle (IV 5.10+). *Richard Shore*

pitches of stemming and jamming (5.9+). The virgin summit was soon deflowered, and the Love Line (III 5.10+) had been conceived.

On April 23, Tony Lewis and I made the three-hour slog up into the Grey Band once again, with eyes fixated on the unclimbed 1,200-foot pinnacle hidden behind Cobbler's Bench Tower. We started up the toe of the pinnacle's east buttress, and four pitches up to 5.10 brought us to a ledge. Exhausted from hand-drilling many bolts, we fixed a few ropes and scrambled back down to camp for the evening.

The next morning we woke to dark skies and a building storm. We quickly ascended the ropes to our high point and tackled the short face crux (5.10+). It was snowing steadily at this point, but we quickly decided to push onward. On top of the untrodden summit, we snapped a few photos and rapidly descended the route by rappel in whiteout conditions. Sticking to the Grey Band theme, we named our new tower the Super Grey Pinnacle (IV 5.10+).

While climbing this route, I spotted a continuous crack system on the north face of Big Grey Pinnacle, a few hundred feet right of the original 1976 Rowell-Belden east face route. It was still holding snow and an attempt would have to wait until autumn, after the scorching summer heat in Bishop had subsided.

It was still quite warm on September 16, and Johnny Karagozian and I hiked up to the base of Big Grey Pinnacle at night to avoid the sun and the infamous "buzztails" that guard the approaches to these towers. We were treated to spectacular alpenglow at sunrise, and much to our delight the climb quickly went into a shady respite for the day. The route provided us with eight pitches of interesting and physical climbing—mostly 5.8 and 5.9 in grubby chimneys and flares, but also an exposed 5.10 arête halfway up and a clean finger-to-hand splitter above. The peaceful day was only occasionally interrupted by the shrill cry of a curious and acrobatic avian, and our new route was named in his honor: the Peregrine Pillar (IV 5.10).

Over two weekends in early October, Tony Lewis, Andrew Soleman, and I returned to the Wheeler Crest and one of the last unclimbed monolithic features in the area, the southeast buttress of the Cobbler's Bench Tower. Three pitches of moderate cracks and face climbing led to the bulk of the route, a highly featured yet technical slab up the ever-narrowing buttress. We climbed six pitches before running out of steam on our first attempt.

A week later we returned and reclimbed the lower pitches, hoping the difficulty above would ease off. We kept to a minimalist ethic while taking a serpentine path up the steep face, hand-drilling protection bolts from stances and utilizing natural anchors whenever possible. The result was a fantastic, sustained, and committing climb, with only two fixed belays over 1,100 vertical feet and some healthy runouts on most of the nine pitches. A bit shaken from the heady climb, we were elated to cool our nerves on the summit. After descending the gully between the Cobbler's Bench and Super Grey Pinnacle, we left a bighorn sheep's skull at the base as a reminder to future parties of the wild beauty and serious nature of climbing on the Wheeler Crest. Watch your step, because you might get bit by the Rattler (IV 5.11 R). 📷 📄

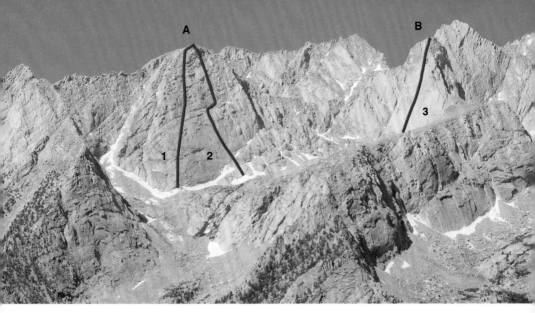

THE CLEAVER, DARK TOWER, AND GAMBLER'S SPECIAL, NEW ROUTES AND FIRST FREE ASCENT

In June, Brian Prince, Alaina Robertson, and I set up a camp below the northeast face of the Gambler's Special and Dark Tower to celebrate Alaina's birthday with some exploratory climbing. The Dark Tower is a subsummit of the Cleaver (13,382'), and we named it after finding no previous record or signs of ascent. Roland's Journey (1,000', III 5.9) started from toe of the main buttress and tackled the middle part of the steep red headwall.

After climbing the Dark Tower, Alaina Robertson and I completed a long, fun and engaging climb on the northeast face of the Gambler's Special. This peak, which is unnamed on most maps, rises along a ridgeline about a quarter mile southeast of the Cleaver. We found no evidence of previous climbs, only evidence of the plane crash for which it is named (the plane was en route to Vegas). Ghostriders in the Sky (2,000', IV+ 5.10 PG-13) starts near three prominent cracks on the eastern part of the face and goes up mostly clean, flaring crack systems with a memorable overhang about three or four pitches up. The harder sections featured adequate protection, but the more moderate terrain was run-out and exciting.

[Above] The northeast side of (A) Gambler's Special and (B) Dark Tower, southeast of the Cleaver. (1) Ghostriders in the Sky. (2) Wait and Bleed. (3) Roland's Journey. [Right] Shaun Reed savors a cool 5.11 flake and crack system on the Butcher (IV 5.12) on the southeast face of the Cleaver. *Vitaliy Musiyenko*

I returned to the area about a month later with Shaun Reed, who had completed a new route on the southeast face of the Cleaver with another friend in 2015 and now wanted to free it. The Butcher (850', IV 5.12) features sustained and enjoyable cracks, with the crux being a wild 5.12 overhang near the middle of the wall. After several attempts, we managed to free the crux with barely enough daylight to finish the route. This climb is a must-do for those who enjoy difficult cracks. [*The new route is just to the left of Chronic Harmonic (IV 5.11+), which Reed and Nate Ricklin put up in 2014; see AAJ 2016.*]

We then set our sights on a wide system on the western side of the Gambler's Special, which turned out to be more of an adventure than a great rock climb. After encountering mostly garbage rock, we were happy that at least the line topped out on the main summit. We called the route Wait and Bleed (1,600', IV 5.10- PG13). 📷

— VITALIY MUSIYENKO

CALIFORNIA / KINGS CANYON NATIONAL PARK

HAPPY DOME, MEN IN HEAT

A FEW YEARS ago, Daniel Jeffcoach and I spotted an unnamed and apparently unclimbed formation above North Dome. The approach starts from the Road's End parking lot, and to our surprise it took no longer than three to four hours to reach the base. With great views and great climbing, Men in Heat (1,800', IV 5.8 R) follows perfect granite from bottom to top, consisting mostly of run-out face climbing that connects cool features. Aside from a bolted anchor, there is no other fixed hardware. It would be nice to add a few bolts to make this climb a safer outing for people uncomfortable with major runouts on 5.7 and 5.8.

— VITALIY MUSIYENKO

NORTH SENTINEL, NEW ROUTES

THE NORTH SENTINEL is a tooth-shaped granite face on the north side of Kings Canyon, across from North Dome and below Grand Sentinel. With a straightforward approach, we were surprised it had not seen any previous attention from climbers. Over the course of 2016, I had the pleasure to visit it three times with various partners. We climbed three independent routes and one variation, all of which follow nice crack systems on quality rock.

Brian Prince, Daniel Jeffcoach, Brandon Thau, and I first climbed FML Crack (750', IV 5.11 C1), which could also be called the Thank God Crack by those into the wide. After an approach pitch, it follows a single crack system, the crux of which is a burly OW that requires a number 5 and a number 6 cam.

Brian, Chaz Langalier, Caitlin Taylor, and I then tackled the major dihedral on the eastern aspect of the formation, calling it

[Left] Daniel Jeffcoach on the "approach pitch" to the first ascent of FML Crack on North Sentinel. *Vitaliy Musiyenko*

Eddie's Chimney (III 5.10+). The route looked more intimidating than it was—we found clean cracks of all sizes, sustained in the 5.9 to mid-5.10 range. After topping out we made two 60m rappels partway down the dihedral and then climbed a line to the right that we dubbed Eddie's Crack (200', 5.11c). It is the best all-natural finger to hands crack (no pin scars) I have come across in the wild. Brian and I split it in two leads, but it could be climbed in one epic 70m pitch.

[Above] **North Sentinel in Kings Canyon. (1) Eddie's Chimney. (2) Eddie's Crack. (3) FML Crack. (4) Chasing the Wind.** *Vitaliy Musiyenko*

Daniel and Adam Sheppard had begun Chasing the Wind (800', III 5.10) but aborted their attempt after four pitches, due to an incoming storm. A few weeks later, Caitlin and I finished the line to the pointy summit, adding another three pitches. This route makes for a fast and easy descent of the formation with two 60m ropes. 📷

— VITALIY MUSIYENKO

BOYDEN CAVE WALL, MAGIC MOUNTAIN MARBLE MAJESTY

WHEN YOU'RE DRIVING to Kings Canyon, there are some giant marble buttresses on the left side of the road, but you have to cross the Kings River to get to them. In the case of Boyden Cave Wall, near the popular Boyden Cavern in Giant Sequoia National Monument, I was pleased to find a southeast-facing expanse of climbable marble on the road side of the river, away from the tourists.

On October 2, Neal Harder and I completed Magic Mountain Marble Majesty (8 pitches, 5.11a), the first route on the Boyden Cave Wall. This route ascends over 1,000' of solid and uniquely featured marble, with bolts and some traditional protection, climbing features rarely found in California, more akin to those found on European limestone. Chris LaBounty and I had established the first half of this route in 2014, but a fire kept the area closed until 2016.

The recommended rack includes a single set of cams from small to number three, plus extras from 0.5 to 1. The route is set up for double-rope rappels from the top of the seventh pitch; we downclimbed the relatively low-angle eighth pitch. The road into the area is generally open from May until mid-November. 📷

— BRANDON THAU

[Right] **The Boyden Cave Wall in Giant Sequoia National Monument, showing the eight-pitch Magic Mountain Marble Majesty, completed by Neal Harder and Brandon Thau in October 2016.** *Brandon Thau*

MORO ROCK, MODERN GUILT, FIRST FREE ASCENT

SEVERAL YEARS AGO, Tom Ruddy climbed an independent, direct line up the striking west face of Moro Rock, with hopes of completing an all-free ascent in the future. After several years of work, he had freed most of the route but moved away before putting it all together. On April 4, Brian Prince and I completed the all-free ascent of Moro Rock's most difficult full-length route, with each of the 10 pitches being redpointed ground-up in a day. Modern Guilt (1,000', IV 5.12) features incredible climbing and is sustained in the 5.10 to 5.11 range. No pitch could be called a one-move wonder, as most of them keep you engaged from the beginning to end. The route is mostly bolt-protected, but a single set of cams and some small offset nuts will be needed. Bring your best edging skills and a cool head, and prepare for one of the most fun difficult routes in the state. 📷

– VITALIY MUSIYENKO

CASTLE ROCKS, NEW ROUTE AND FIRST FREE ASCENT

ON JUNE 5, Neal Harder, Chris LaBounty, and I established the Surge (1,000', 5.8) on the east face of the Fortress, in the Castle Rocks area. Our route follows face and flake features to the right of the only other established route, the Siege (*AAJ 2013*). We found the face climbing to be surprisingly moderate and very similar to that on Middle Cathedral in Yosemite Valley. The route has five 60m pitches, with an additional 300' of scrambling to attain the summit tower. Bolted belays and the occasional lead bolt supplement natural protection. The recommended approach is to follow the ridgeline dividing the Fin from the Fortress and then descend the steep rock gully on the west side and contouring around to the base.

The following day, we freed the A0 section of Golden Axe (1,000', 5.12), a route on the south face of the Ax formation that the three of us first climbed at 5.11 A0 (*AAJ 2007*). This was the second known ascent of the route.

This trip marked the last new route established by Chris LaBounty before his untimely death in the Dolomites from a wingsuit BASE accident. Neal and I were very fortunate to have experienced this beautiful and peaceful place with him as the last of our long list of Sierra backcountry trips as a team.

– BRANDON THAU

MT. HITCHCOCK AND ARCTIC LAKE WALL, NEW ROUTES

IN LATE JULY, Adam Ferro and I hiked over the Whitney-Russell col and set up camp by a small tarn 500' below Arctic Lake. From there we approached the long northeast face of Mt. Hitchcock, which consists of many subpeaks and attractive buttresses, few of which have seen any attention. We completed two great crack climbs here.

Starlight Dihedral (1,600', IV/V 5.11) follows a good line with multiple dihedrals in the lower part of the wall, linked to a prominent corner system by a very run-out but moderate slab. Welcome to Krackizstan (1,600', IV/V 5.11a) climbs a much less obvious wall that appeared clean and continuous when seen from our descent of Starlight Dihedral. The route follows awesome cracks from bottom to the top. Both routes are in a stunning setting with quality climbing and deserve traffic. One of them has already been repeated by a motivated Bay

[Above left] New lines on the western summit of the Arctic Lake Wall (from left to right): Arctic Beast (5.11c), Too Much Fun (5.10), and Chillin' the Most (5.10-). It's believed there are several more routes on this face, but their exact position is not known. *Damien Nicodemi* [Above right] Brian Prince leads through one of the overhangs on Arctic Beast (5.11c). *Vitaliy Musiyenko*

Area couple—in a single weekend!

Adam and I also climbed the second prominent corner and crack system from the eastern edge of the main Arctic Lake Wall. Too Much Fun (550', III 5.10) follows high-quality moderate cracks to the ridge, which we scrambled to the summit.

Brian Prince and I returned to the Arctic Lake Wall about a month later to tackle a direct line pulling several of the giant roofs closer to the middle of the formation. After getting stormed off on the first attempt, we completed Arctic Beast (700', III 5.11c).

— VITALIY MUSIYENKO

ARCTIC LAKE WALL, CHILLIN' THE MOST

ON JULY 18, Ryan Evans and I climbed what we believe to be a new route on the southeast-facing Arctic Lake Wall, to the west of Mt. Russell. The route begins in highly featured orange rock and surmounts a short roof before gaining a ledge at the base of a large, white dihedral approximately 200' up. The dihedral looked too difficult to protect with natural gear, so the route traverses right and continues up a less prominent dihedral, eventually gaining a splitter crack that leads to the summit ridge. Two fun pitches on the ridge lead directly to the summit. We left no permanent protection or anchors and called our route Chillin' the Most (600', III 5.10- PG13). While walking back to camp we stumbled across a meadow with hundreds of shooting stars blooming. We lay back and soaked in the High Sierra sun, the urgency of our planned afternoon climb fading away in a dreamy midday snooze.

— DAMIEN NICODEMI

MT. WILSON, DREAM OF WILD CHEESEBURGERS AND HEAD OF STATE

"YOU SHOULD TRY your hand at Mt. Wilson," touted a climbing partner. "I know a guy, he's always stoked." A quick phone call later, the plans were made. Before I knew it, Kyle Willis and I were on the summit of Mt. Wilson via the classic Inti Watana and upper Resolution

Arête linkup—our first route together.

Fast-forward to a year later, September 2016. After gaining some new-routing experience around Moab, I was back in Red Rock and looking for a bigger challenge. Kyle and I again turned our eyes to Mt. Wilson, this time to an unclimbed crack system to the right of Inti.

When we got up to the base we realized why such an obvious line had gone climbed: I'm not sure if I'd ever seen that much moss on a climb, and I'm from the Northwest! However, we were pleasantly surprised that the climbing wasn't as bad as it looked. We made it halfway up the fifth pitch before dark and fixed ropes back to the bivy ledge atop pitch two. The next morning we discovered pitch after pitch of fun climbing and increasingly good rock. Before we knew it we had reached the ledge system where Inti Watana links into the Resolution Arête and rappelled from there. Dream of Wild Cheeseburgers (IV 5.9+) climbs around 1,500' of new terrain.

Psyched on our success, we scanned photos of Wilson for another unclimbed line and spied a series of discontinuous ridges and cracks between Lady Wilson's Cleavage and Dogma. We approached from the old Oak Creek campground, and about halfway between the highway and the mountain we cut left onto an obvious ridge that led straight to the base of the route.

On day one we climbed a big, slabby feature to reach the top of Willie's Couloir. The hand crack above was one of the best pitches I've ever done in Red Rock. Some scrambling then led to our planned bivy site. The next day we proceeded slowly up a wide crack system and over a series of small towers to the base of the final headwall. We stashed gear here for our planned return and rappelled.

A few days later, we hiked to the summit of Mt. Wilson via Oak Creek Canyon and rappelled into our high point below the headwall. There appeared to be just enough thin gear on the headwall, but also some lichen. We left a fixed line as we rappelled, intending to top-rope and clean this crux pitch before a lead. After completing the easy pitch below, we went to work, but cleaning and rope-work shenanigans ate up precious time. We each top-roped the pitch successfully but ran out of time for a lead attempt. A continuous lead ascent of Head of State (3,000' V 5.11b R) awaits.

We climbed the route in 20 long pitches, with two 5.11 and several 5.10 leads, totaling about 2,800' of roped travel plus some scrambling. This is now, to my knowledge, the longest route in Red Rock. 🖻

— SAM BOYCE

[Below] The Aeolian Wall of Mt. Wilson, showing (1) Head of State (V 5.11b R) and (2) Dream of Wild Cheeseburgers (IV 5.9+), which lies just to the right of the classic Inti Watana. *Sam Boyce*

NOTCH PEAK, NOTCH YOUR BUSINESS

Late August in the western Utah desert is hot. Bird-size bugs terrorize the unsuspecting, scorpions dwell under tents, and tarantulas lurk in the shadows. High above the basin, however, cooler temps can be found on north-facing aspects. Seeking refuge from the Hadean heat, Jonathan Schaffer and I forged a new route up the north face of Notch Peak over the course of three days. Like other routes on Notch Peak (none of which either of us had climbed), Notch Your Business (450m, 5.11 R/X) features run-out climbing over often-loose terrain. Ten pitches (all of which deserve an R rating; some get an X) ascend the middle of the face between the classic Book of Saturday (5.11- R, Lyde-Price, 1999) and Nightmare (5.11+, Kofler-Steufer, 2011). The climb begins with an 80m pitch up a very prominent left-facing corner and continues up connecting features. Most belays have at least one bolt. Two protection bolts and one piton were placed. A rappel line exists, mostly following the route of ascent.

[Above] The 1,500' north face of Notch Peak. (1) Book of Saturday (Lyde-Price, 1999). (2) Notch Your Business (Fasoldt-Schaffer, 2016). (3) Nightmare (Kofler-Stuefer, 2011). The Swiss Route (Koch-Deinen, 1986) is farther right. Fin du Monde (Howe-Shewell, 2002) ascends the right arête. *Josh Oyler*

– PETE FASOLDT

Nightmare on Notch Peak: *Previously unreported in the AAJ, Nightmare was put up by Benjamin Kofler and Roman Stuefer in May 2011. The two Italian climbers completed 11 pitches over three days during their first attempt, using only nuts, cams, and pitons for protection, with hand-drilled bolts at some of the belay stances. They bivied once below the cliff and once at a sitting stance en route. Poor weather forced them to retreat and prevented another attempt until a week later. The night before their second attempt, 4cm (1.5") of snow fell and they decided the only way to complete the route was to hike up the south side of Notch Peak, rappel from the top, and climb the final three pitches to the summit. It is not known if an integral ascent has been completed.*

NOTCH PEAK, SOUTH FACE, AIRAVATA

From November 28 to December 9, Karl Kvashay and I established the first route up the prominent south face of Notch Peak (9,654'), a limestone mountain much better known for its huge north wall. This was our second go at the line after a strong but failed attempt in the spring of 2015.

We spent two days on either end of the climbing hauling our kit to and from the wall. We

[Above] **Notch Peak from the west. Airavata (VI 5.10 R A4) climbs the large south-facing wall marked with the arrow, with nine very long pitches on the headwall.** *Karl Kvashay*

accessed the route from the peak's south drainage until an obvious gully breached a maze of 3rd- and 4th- class steps. The headwall was climbed in nine pitches, totaling 1,755' of technical climbing, with a total of 18 belay or protection bolts drilled by hand.

Airavata (VI 5.10 R A4 PDW) was climbed ground-up, in full winter conditions, with temperatures regularly dropping into the negatives. [*Editor's note: PDW is a big-wall grading designation that originated in Zion National Park and stands for Pretty Damn Western. It denotes very serious climbing.*] One snowstorm pinned us down for 36 hours in our portaledge. The route required careful navigation through many teetering and fractured features; all belays were thoughtfully placed to protect against leader-induced rockfall. A full wall rack with ample beaks was key to protecting both the free and aid sections, and a 70m rope was utilized to its full extent. 📷

— **KRISTOFFER WICKSTROM**

UTAH / ZION NATIONAL PARK

KOLOB CANYONS, BLACK DIAMOND WALL, MELTING POINT

"GET OUT OF the way, quick!" I shouted, as calmly as possible considering the position I was in. It was summit day during the first ascent of the Black Diamond, an unclimbed wall in Zion National Park's Kolob Canyons region. I was 25' up the third pitch, stemmed out and surrounded by stacks of loose rocks, when I looked below to see Ana Pautler still jugging to the sheltered belay—she was right in the crosshairs. I turned 5.6 into 5.9 trying to avoid the trundle pile at all costs, and luckily it worked.

Brandon Gottung and I had planned this climb for half a year, each of us having stared at the wall for hours while exploring routes on nearby Tucupit Point (*AAJ 2016*). Brandon, Ana, and I spent our first day figuring out the approach, which involves multiple 3rd- to 5th-class sections. On day two we hiked up a second load and fixed the first pitch. The next day, in snow and cold, we fixed the second pitch. On day four we jugged to our high point, climbed the final three pitches to the top of the wall, and forged a heinous thrash through steep dirt and scrub oak to the top of Horse Ranch Mountain. The view was expansive and memorable.

Melting Point (600', IV 5.11 C1) has a beautiful, surreal character; in places the cliff was sculpted into giant huecos, gargoyles, and tunnels. We rappelled the route via bolted anchors. 📖📷

— **KARL KVASHAY**

RED SENTINEL, HUMAN CENTIPEDE V

I HAVE LONG dreamed of standing on top of obscure and puzzling big walls, and the Red Sentinel in Zion National Park has been on my list for nearly 15 years. The north-facing wall is on the left as you look into the Court of the Patriarchs. As far as I can determine, there are five routes on the wall, all of which are aid climbs. The oldest was established by Jeff Lowe and Cactus Bryan and is called the Toad (VI F8 A3, *AAJ 1972*). The other four aid climbs all were done in the late 1990s and 2000.

In late November 2015, I conned a few partners—Mike Brumbaugh, Curtis Chabot, Sean Lynn, and Darren Mabe—into trying to establish a ground-up free route with me over the winter months. After scouting the face numerous times over the years, I had a solid plan of attack. We would climb the middle of the wall, where the cracks seemed plentiful, wide, comfy, and continuous, until we reached the top. It would be just a matter of doing it.

Well, Old Man Winter had a different idea. It snowed every day on the 2,000'-plus, north-facing wall—so much so that we weren't just post-holing on the approach but also on the ledges up high. It was so cold that two out of the five team members (including myself) got frostbite on their feet during the 16 days (spread over five months) that it took to complete the first ascent. The cracks were not all wide and comfy—some were thin and filled with dirt. The rock was bomber, except for when it wasn't and we trundled massive teetering blocks into the peaceful canyon below. There were multiple days where we advanced only 200' up the wall.

All that being said, we were continuously impressed by the variety of styles the 21-pitch

[Below] North face of the Red Sentinel, showing the approximate route lines of (1) Brown Eyed Girl (VI 5.8 A3+, Nolte-Schock, 1999), (2) Red Dawn (VI 5.9 A3+, Dodds-Stratford, 1996), (3) Off to See the Lizard (VI 5.6 A3, Hill-Jones, 1998), (4) Human Centipede V (VI 5.13 or 5.11 C1, Brumbaugh-Chabot-Lynn-Mabe-Pizem, 2016), (5) The Toad (VI 5.8 A3, Bryant-Lowe, 1971), and (6) The Big Easy (VI 5.10 R A3, Denise-Hammond, 2000). *Brian Smoot*

climb presented. There are wonderful dihedrals that allow the climber to use every size of gear on the rack, from tips to sixes. There are traverses where the climber hangs out in dizzying exposure. There are Indian Creek–style splitters from tips to fingers to hands to offwidth. Finally, and most importantly, there was a good to very good ledge at every belay.

The two 5.13 cruxes (pitches 5 and 13) are both short-lived. The first is a tips layback dihedral, protected with a bolt, and a small roof. The entire hard section is only 15' or so. The upper crux is an arête that yields about 8' of desperate technical moves and an enjoyable stemming finish. Both cruxes can be aided using protection bolts.

We completed the route to the summit in February, and I finished freeing all the pitches in April, belayed by Mike Brumbaugh, Curtis Chabot, and Rob Warden. The effort that all the team members gave over five months was monumental. 📷 🔍

– ROB PIZEM

GREGORY BUTTE, FIRST KNOWN ASCENT

OVER SIX DAYS in July, during a cool spell of 90°F, I made the first known ascent of Gregory Butte (ca 7,700'), in the Kolob Canyons section of Zion National Park. I had previously attempted to climb the butte via a new aid line on the southwest spur, but there were no continuous crack systems. Eventually I found a gully described in by Fred D. Ayres and A.E. Creswell in *AAJ 1954*, leading to a hanging valley upon which the summit formation of Gregory Butte sits. Ayres and Creswell had climbed the gully to measure the span (ca 300') of nearby Kolob Arch. It was apparent this route sees very infrequent traffic. On the first pitch I used a knifeblade piton to scrape thick moss off footholds, and there were no cracks that would take pitons or cams. Higher up I found Star Dryvin bolts from the 1950s and rotten webbing at rap stations.

Once in the hanging valley, I explored the north and south sides of the upper section of Gregory Butte for a route to the summit. My route ascends the south face, starting where the west ridge meets the flatter summit formation. Overall, I rope-soloed ten pitches: five in the gully and five from the hanging valley to the summit (5.9 A2). 📷

– DAN STIH

MERIDIAN TOWER, FIRST COMPLETE ASCENT, AND CHAMELEON PEAK: *In 2008, David Everett and Dan Stih climbed Meridian Tower (7,332'), northeast of the Altar of Sacrifice at the head of Oak Creek (AAJ 2009). However, they did not attain a short summit block separated from the main tower by a deep chasm. In March 2016, Stih returned with Matt Mower, repeated the 2008 route up the north face (8 pitches, 5.8 A0), rappelled into the gap, and reached the true summit via a 5.6 pitch along a vein of basalt running through rotten red sandstone. En route to Meridian, they did the first ascent of Chameleon Peak from the north. Details are at the AAJ website.* 📷

PEAK 6,020' (THE LITTLE BISHOP)

IN MARCH, WALT Hutton, Courtney Purcell, and I did the first known ascent of Peak 6,020', a few miles due east of Checkerboard Mesa. We called it the Little Bishop due to its resemblance to the Bishopric, another Zion peak. It is best approached by a longish overland route through the pass between Checkerboard Mesa and Crazy Quilt Mesa. There were two short pitches of roped climbing near the top, between 5.4 and 5.6. The crux was marginally protectable with pins.

– DAN STIH

TEXAS TOWER, EAST FACE, FIRST FREE ASCENT

I HAVE BEEN frequenting the desert of southern Utah for over a decade, concentrating mostly on the obscure and wide cracks. Texas Tower had always been on my list, but it was a challenge for which I wanted to feel fully prepared. Located in a remote canyon outside Blanding, Texas Tower is 800' tall, and its only free passage involved difficult offwidth and chimney climbing for nearly the entire route. Last spring I finally felt ready.

In late May, I met Jackson Marvell and other friends and we headed into Texas Canyon. The classic south face route (5.11+, Toula-Zaiser, 1987) on the tower was cooking in the sun, so we decided to check out the east face, an aid route first climbed by Jeff Pheasant and Paul Ross in 2002. As it turns out, the east face route is the analog crack to the south face, has just as much offwidth climbing, and had never seen a free ascent.

Beginning with a sparsely protected crux traverse with ledge-fall potential, Jackson linked the first two original pitches (5.9 C2) and (5.9 C1) into a 55m free pitch, onsight at 5.11+ R. He fixed the rope, cleaned the pitch, and we raced toward the rim in the dying light.

[Above] **Texas Tower, located in Texas Canyon, near Blanding. The east face route follows the obvious offwidth crack. Climbers are barely visible on the summit.** *Parker Cross*

Next day, Jackson and I jugged our rope and climbed a 5.8+ chimney to access the offwidth splitter on the tower's headwall. The original fourth pitch (5.9 C2) started with two bolts that led to a crux traverse into a finger crack and crimping section above a very poor single piece (5.12a R). The pitch then eased into 5.10+ offwidth to the anchor.

The next pitch (5.10 C2) was the final question mark, but thankfully looked to be all offwidth and wider, making a free ascent feel more probable. Tunneling inward to avoid two large roofs, I found the feature to be even tighter than the infamous Liquid Sky chimney on North Six Shooter. After 140 feet of strenuous offwidth and squeeze chimney (5.11+), I made a belay in the middle of the tower—a spot we dubbed the Heart of Texas. The final marathon chimney pitch (5.9 X) was shared with the south face.

Every pitch was led onsight, and no fixed gear was added to the route. Jackson followed every pitch free, but I neglected to follow the first lead, opting to ascend the fixed line to save energy for the upper half. The east face (IV 5.12a R) is a spectacular route on an amazing tower in an absolutely beautiful setting. 🗎 📷 🔍

– PATRICK KINGSBURY

SEDONA AREA, LONG NEW ROUTES

FOR THE PAST 15 years I have climbed on the often weird towers and canyons around Sedona. While the town's New Age vibe is pretty lame, there are miles of cliffs to explore and occasionally a good climb. In the last three years I have become absorbed with new routing there, adjusting my work situation to allow maximum time off in the winter when the conditions are best. The year 2016 was notable with five new routes, all of which I feel would hold their own to established classics in the area.

In February I was looking at pictures of Marg's Draw in Sedona, and found a beautiful crack system that didn't quite reach the ground, ending at the featured limestone band that exists low in the stratigraphy. Recruiting Blake McCord to dispatch with the limestone via ground-up bolting, we were able to link between two great thin-hands cracks and romp to the previously unclimbed summit of a feature we dubbed the Self-Loathing National Monument. Rotor Rampage (5 pitches, 5.11+) has good rock (for the area!), three crux pitches, and fun, physical climbing.

In April, Blake and I climbed a new route in the west fork of Oak Creek Canyon. The subfork where the climb is located is known as Insomnia Canyon, and was previously unexplored by climbers, although it is locally known among canyoneers for a 300' overhanging rappel. Pictures from a search and rescue slideshow tipped Blake off that there might be overlooked potential. Valhalla (5.12-) ascends a beautiful varnished face for two pitches, leading into a single crack system for four more pitches.

During the six days that we worked on establishing Valhalla, we spied a slender 500' tower across the drainage. It was first climbed just the year before, but we saw a system of cracks that ran from the ground and would add four pitches before joining the existing route at the notch between the tower and the canyon rim. Eventually this line became Denied Bail (5 pitches, 5.11+), named because the first ascensionist of the tower had returned to climb this system just two weeks after we started up the route and bailed once he saw we'd been there already.

While establishing Denied Bail, we spied a pure splitter line on the south face of the same tower. We were unsure if it was possible to climb into the thin seam at the bottom of the widening, 250' crack, but once we made it to the base of the system, miraculous face holds appeared to link the 30' to the crack. The crux was one of the best pitches I have ever climbed, with improbable face climbing, arête slapping, and a slightly overhanging finger crack, all in the depths of a steep, beautiful riparian canyon. Life without Parole (6 pitches, 5.12) is incredibly varied and was a real blast to establish with help from local crack ace Jeff Snyder.

After finding new routes on such quality sandstone, a rarity in the Sedona area, where muddy blobs are the norm, I got to thinking about a line I had seen while climbing in Mormon Canyon two years prior. In October I teamed up again with Blake McCord, who appears to never have a job. We explored a varnished wall and found a line we named Hot Hookers (5 pitches, 5.11), after I sandbagged us by establishing the route in the sun in 85° heat. While the wall has few crack systems, patina edges and some creative gear allowed us to do less bolting from hooks then we'd anticipated to protect the 500' route. In fact, we were so surprised by the climbable nature of the wall that we returned to explore a seam that sits in the middle of the wall. It turned out to have great face holds and took fickle nuts for most of the pitch. Plural Pleasures (5.11+) has 250' of independent climbing after starting on Hot Hookers and rejoining that route at its fourth pitch. While not the straightest line, every pitch is good and the setting is top-notch. ▣

– ZACH HARRISON

[Photo] Zach Harrison on the crux third pitch of Life Without Parole (5.12-) in Insomnia Canyon, a sheer offshoot canyon in the west fork of Oak Creek Canyon. *Blake McCord*

GLACIER NATIONAL PARK, MT. EDWARDS, NORTHWEST FACE

GLACIER NATIONAL PARK is a wild and remote place where alpine climbing often involves dodgy or nonexistent beta, long approaches, bushwhacks, bear encounters, and creative anchor-building in sedimentary rock. Combine that with fickle weather and tricky avalanche conditions, and you have a place that, well, attracts only a few alpinists. It is, however, a perfect place for adventure climbing. On November 7, Stefan Beattie, Kevin Oberholser, and I set out

[Above] **Adam Clark climbing thin ice and mixed terrain during the first ascent of Jedi Gordon Edwards (2,500', IV WI3 M3).** *Kevin Oberholser*

in the dark for the northwest face of Mt. Edwards (9,072'), looking for just that kind of thing.

At 8:45 a.m. we stepped onto the northwest face at about 6,200'. Easy snow slopes gave way to steeper rock slabs and short vertical steps draped with a thin but climbable layer of ice and snow. The climbing was delicate and scratchy, with gentle spindrift falling from above. Screws were useless, but the knifeblades came in handy.

About a third of the way up the face, our progress was blocked by a formidable cliff band. During the approach, we'd seen what looked like a single white ice pillar bisecting this headwall—it appeared to be the key to the upper face. But our "pillar" turned out to be a thin veneer of rotten snow over steep rock. Unwilling to climb this—or to head down—we made a lengthy traverse to the right on a snowy ramp, finally reaching the base of a continuous weakness through the headwall. More steep snow with sections of rolling ice and mixed climbing led to a steep and excellent ice curtain at about 7,800'.

Above the ice our route crossed the upper west face, first climbed in winter by locals Nathan Sande, Don Scharfe, and the late Scott Sederstrom in the early '90s. I drafted off Kevin and Stefan as they kicked steps and led us up into a cloud layer. The terrain steepened once more near the top, and some deliberate moves over rime-plastered rock put us on the crest of the west ridge at 8,700'. With limited visibility and only an hour and a half of daylight remaining, we began our descent, feeling our way along snow ledges and over rock towers. Once off the mountain, this superb day concluded with post-holing and hiking seven miles back to the car.

Despite a tradition of unreported new routes in Glacier, after checking with several longtime locals we believe our route is a first ascent. We named it Jedi Gordon Edwards (2,500', IV WI3 M3), a reference to one of Glacier's pioneering climbers and to the mountain. 📄 📷

– ADAM CLARK

MISSION MOUNTAINS, SHEEPSHEAD, NORTH FACE

ON MAY 1, Damien Mast and I made the first ascent of the 2,200' north face of Sheepshead (9,417') in the Mission Mountains of northwest Montana. (*This peak is also known locally as Sheep's Head or West McDonald Peak.*) The face had been attempted many times, but due to poor conditions was never completed. We walked five hours from McDonald Lake to get to the base, bushwhacking through extremely dense forests for three miles.

Upon arrival at the bottom of the face, we found perfect climbing conditions, and we soloed about 1,000' of AI3 and 70° névé to a series of cliff bands. Here, we roped up and climbed two 60m pitches of M5. Then we put the ropes back in the packs and escaped climber's left, out from underneath the 30- to 40-foot cornices that loomed high above us. Another 850' of névé up to 80° brought us to the summit ridge. After about five hours of climbing we reached the summit of Sheepshead, where we ate food in T-shirts and then descended off the west ridge and then down the south face.

[Above] The north face of Sheepshead in Montana's Mission Mountains, showing the line climbed by Damien Mast and Justin Willis in May 2016. *Ken Turley*

– JUSTIN WILLIS

WYOMING / WIND RIVER RANGE

TITCOMB BASIN, VARIOUS NEW ROUTES

IN JULY 2015, Jake Frerk and a variety of partners (Kevin Chuba, Mark Evans, and Greg Troutman) climbed new routes on Red Tower, which sits jus below Fremont Peak's large west face, the north face of Elephant Head, and the east face of the Buttress, and also added a new finish to Indian Paintbrush (Deshler-Jenkins, 5.10, *AAJ 2012*), heading straight up from the "obligatory 5.10 traverse" and adding about four new pitches (5.11-). The full report and photos are at the AAJ website.

– *INFORMATION PROVIDED BY* JAKE FRERK

CLEAR CREEK, FORLORN PINNACLE, SOUTH FACE

IN MID-SEPTEMBER, OLIVER Deshler and I returned to the Clear Creek drainage in the northern Winds to attempt the south face of Forlorn Pinnacle (11,660'), which is actually a rooster comb of separate spires at the south end of Osborn Mountain. (*Deshler and Jenkins climbed several new routes in this area in 2009. See AAJ 2010.*) Staying in the gully directly west of the Fickle Finger—a stunning pillar—we climbed the central tower in eight pitches, 5.10 C1, topping out at 3 p.m. The summit was a true pinnacle, so we chopped off a chunk of the rope and slung the top to rappel. We had hoped for more ascents, but a snowstorm swept in that night. It was still snowing two days later, so we slip-slided our way out.

– MARK JENKINS, AAC

WASHAKIE LAKE, BIG CHIEF BUTTRESS, THE NON-OBVIOUS GARDEN TOUR

IN AUGUST 1993, Lorna Corson and Norm Larson climbed one pitch up Big Chief Buttress, an unclimbed 900-foot tower in the Washakie Lake cirque. They descended after that first pitch, as they felt the climbing was not within their ability.

[Above] **The Big Chief Buttress above Washakie Lake, showing the 12-pitch line of the Non-Obvious Garden Tour, climbed by Anne Gilbert Chase and Kate Rutherford.** *Jason Thompson*

Twenty-three years later, Big Chief was still unclimbed when Norm and Lorna showed Kate Rutherford and me a picture of the buttress, asking if we wanted to go in and climb it. We said yes without hesitation.

In late July, the four of us, along with Jason Thompson and Ken Etzel, made the 13-mile approach into Washakie Lake. Loaded with climbing gear, fly rods, whiskey, and good food, we made our camp for seven days on the beautiful lake below the buttress. Kate and I spent a total of three different days on the tower, trying to find the best line to the top.

During our first two attempts, we found very loose rock, thick black lichen, and dead-end crack systems. We wanted a line that followed a clean crack system and had the potential to go free, so we kept the bolts in the duffel back at camp and continued looking. Finally, on the third attempt, our perseverance paid off and we made it to the top of the buttress after climbing 12 pitches of varied rock, including run-out slab at the start and steep cracks and exposed face climbing higher up on the wall. Although our route was not the splitter, clean line we were hoping for, it was still a wild adventure in a beautiful alpine setting, filled with some intense gardening (deserving of a jungle grade) and rope shenanigans.

In retrospect, the experience was more about Norm and Lorna's story than that individual climb. Norm has done more than 160 trips into the Wind River Range, and together Norm and Lorna have put up over 30 first ascents there. While Kate and I were adventuring on the Big Chief Buttress, Norm and Lorna were attempting a new route in a nearby area. After Norm took a good-size fall, they decided to back off and instead re-climbed a route called the Obvious Crack, which they had put up many years before. This trip represents the essence of climbing for me—sharing passions across generations and passing the torch to enable progression. As a play on Norm and Lorna's nearby climb, we named our route the Non-Obvious Garden Tour (IV 5.11 C1 J1).

— **ANNE GILBERT CHASE**

SPEARPOINT LAKE, NEW ROUTES AND POTENTIAL

IN MID-AUGUST, SCOTT Kice and I spent a week exploring the extensive walls above Spearpoint Lake in the southern Wind River Range. The formation is identified as Chess Ridge in the Joe Kelsey guidebook. Untold hours of surfing the Web had convinced us the cirque was a treasure trove of untouched rock; to our knowledge, no routes had been climbed on the sheer cliffs directly above the lake.

After an outfitter deposited our gear at trail's end, we spent the better part of the next day scrambling up the final two steep miles to our destination. [*Spearpoint Lake, elevation ca 10,620', is located in a very isolated cirque about five miles, as the crow flies, north of the*

The east-facing walls above Spearpoint Lake, described in Joe Kelsey's guidebook as Chess Ridge, showing Josh Drexler and Scott Kice's routes and attempt from August 2016. (1) The Southeast Ridge (600', 5.10+). (2) Cheddar and Whiskey (1,200', IV 5.8). (3) Attempt on the central prow (hidden behind the short buttress in the center of the photo). *Josh Drexler* [Bottom] Josh Drexler at the base of the technical climbing before he and Scott Kice attempted the center prow above Spearpoint Lake. The two climbed about 350' before bailing below a large overhang. *Scott Kice*

Cirque of the Towers.] Viewed from the lake, the cirque has three fairly distinct formations, each approximately 1,200'–1,500' tall and a quarter mile wide. The leftmost (or southeastern) wall, directly above neighboring Lake 10,682', is dark and vertical to overhanging, chaotically streaked with dikes and fissures, reminding us of the Painted Wall in the Black Canyon. The center formation consists of fairly solid, light-gray granite, easily identified by the black streaks running down from the top of the cliff. The wall on the right is steep and has few obvious weaknesses.

Scott and I first set our sights on the middle formation. The center prow, a few hundred feet to the right of a deep chimney system, is one of the only direct lines in the cirque offering less than vertical rock. Nevertheless, the climbing was slow going, requiring substantial cleaning and a pendulum early on. Foreseeing the likelihood of an unplanned bivy, we bailed at a 10'–15' overhang about 350' up. For more patient climbers, this line should offer a good reward.

The next day we headed for more moderate terrain on the periphery of the cirque. The Southeast Ridge (600', III 5.10+) above Lake 10,682' presents spectacular positioning for six pitches, mostly 5.5 with occasional 5.7 and 5.8 moves. Near the top we were rewarded with perfect hands in a beautiful 60-foot dihedral, though this crux pitch could easily be avoided. Due to its position near the Washakie Lake Basin, I would guess this ridge has been climbed before.

We then turned our attention back to the middle of the walls. A deep gash/gully system separates the left and middle formations. Our route Cheddar and Whiskey (1,200', IV 5.8) heads up the vast, nondescript wall immediately to the right of the gully for 12 pitches.

Starting 50 feet up the gully, we followed good crack systems on a rounded prow for the first couple of pitches, then pushed left to avoid being sucked into steeper territory. Nonetheless, all the crack systems seemed to lead to a sizable bulge at three-quarter height. Just when it looked like we might be shut down, salvation presented itself in the form of a short chimney leading through the heart of the steepest section. While no destination route, Cheddar and Whiskey offers solid rock and ample protection in a spectacular setting.

In general, the walls above Spearpoint Lake are too big, blank, and steep for mere mortals like Scott and me. Our lines were sideshows to the main event in this beautiful cirque.

– JOSH DREXLER

CIRQUE OF THE TOWERS, WARBONNET PEAK, WHO'S ON FIRST?

IN LATE AUGUST, Andrew Andraski and Matt Zia climbed a likely new route up the east buttress of Warbonnet Peak, to the right of the well-known routes on the southeast face: Who's on First (8 pitches, III 5.11+). Zia's full report and photos may be found at the AAJ website.

– *INFORMATION PROVIDED BY* MATT ZIA

DOG TOOTH PEAK, WISDOM TOOTH, INFINITE JEST

OVER THE COURSE of two weeklong trips, one in September 2015 and one in August-September 2016, Trey Warren, Tyler Barker, and I established Infinite Jest on the Wisdom Tooth, a prominent formation on the east face of Dog Tooth Peak, a few miles east of the Cirque of the Towers. We completed two distinct starts that meet at approximately 350', and

the route shares perhaps five or six pitches of what remains of the formation's original route, climbed by Ken Nichols and Al Rubin (*AAJ 1981*). According to Joe Kelsey, the bottom 250' of the original climb exfoliated sometime between 1983 and 1992, and the "tantalizing crack" described by Nichols is now a striking dihedral capped by a large roof.

In September 2015, Trey Warren and I climbed Infinite Jest via our left start, using aid and free climbing (5.10+ A2). Our plan was to begin from the gully to the left of the main face and traverse into the crack system above the large rock scar. This start begins in the second obvious finger crack up the gully. Two 5.10 pitches lead to a ledge with a bolted anchor. Pitch three (5.10+ A0), which is mostly bolted and required an extreme amount of work to hand-drill, continues up a wide crack until you are level with a bolt on the right-hand face. A couple of A0 moves lead to good holds and then a long, wandering face. A short fourth pitch gains the main crack system on the wall.

After two pitches in solid cracks, pitch seven involves tricky aid climbing on small nuts through an overhanging dihedral and then free climbing to the base of a vertical chimney of

[Left] The Wisdom Tooth, first climbed in 1980 by Ken Nichols and Al Rubin, showing the line of Infinite Jest and its two starting options (IV 5.11 A2, right, or IV 5.10+ A2, left). *Mark Daverin*

stacked blocks. Although the climbing on this eighth pitch is moderate and fun for the second, it will likely have the leader's full attention.

From the top of pitch nine, which ends in a large chimney, we believe the original Wisdom Tooth route exited to the right. Infinite Jest escapes the chimney to the left (the belay may need to be moved up the chimney) and follows two pitches of discontinuous cracks and face climbing (5.9) to the base of some stepped roofs. Pitch 13 follows the line of least resistance through the roof, a wide crack on the right side with good stemming (5.10). One or two more pitches should find you at the end of fifth-class terrain.

In August 2016, Trey was busy with work, so I returned with Tyler Barker with hopes of freeing the striking dihedral at the bottom. After a couple of days of work aiding and cleaning some scary flakes, Tyler and I were able to free all but the roof pitch on the direct start to this climb, with two 5.11 pitches. After the roof (A2), one more long, challenging pitch (5.10+/11-) gets you to a good belay at the top of pitch four of the left variation.

After two dedicated trips, Infinite Jest goes at IV 5.11 A2 (dihedral start) or IV 5.10+ A2 (left start), and we feel we've only opened the door to this climb's potential. The A0 moves on the left variation will be easily free climbed by someone stronger than us, as will both of the overhanging aid pitches on the direct line. Future parties looking for a challenge will have a splendid climb to themselves, just two miles away from the crowds in the Cirque of the Towers.

– MARK DAVERIN

CIRQUE OF THE MOON, NEW ROUTES

LONGING FOR A true wilderness experience, in August I made two trips to the Cirque of the Moon, a desolate cirque approximately four miles east of the Cirque of the Towers. This compact horseshoe of walls and buttresses lies south of the North Fork of the Popo Agie River, between Long Lake and Papoose Lake. On August 2, Adam Ferro and I left from Big Sandy to embark on the 16-mile approach. Upon arrival, we found a series of north- and east-facing buttresses that hosted a variety of unclimbed natural lines.

First we climbed a 13-pitch nightmare on the beautiful, prominent east-facing buttress in the cirque. Unfortunately, Mare Frigoris (IV 5.11 R A1) ended up being an extreme exercise in choss tolerance. [*Editor's note: In 1978 and 1979, climbers attempted a route on this formation that they called Cowcatcher, retreating after seven pitches. See historical note below.*] Our route follows the obvious left-leaning system that begins at the bottom of the formation. From the middle of the wall, a leftward traversing pitch gains a striking system that is predominantly composed of fist cracks. The second to last pitch seemed to be the crux, and we placed one pin. The last pitch is 5.11 offwidth. This route was

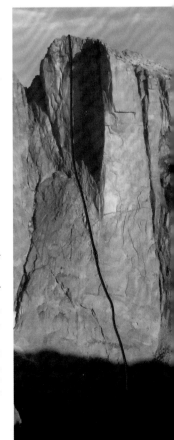

[Right] Cirque of the Moon's prominent east-facing buttress, showing the line of Mare Frigoris (IV 5.11 A1 R). A route dubbed Cowcatcher, attempted in 1978 and 1979, climbed seven pitches up this impressive buttress, to the right of Mare Frigoris, but the party retreated from below roofs at three-quarters height. *Andy Hughes*

hard to grade accurately because it is horrendously loose and lichen-covered. Mare Frigoris, the "Cold Sea," is a region on the Northern Hemisphere of the moon and refers to the open bivy that occurred atop the climb. While the route awaits a free ascent, I would strongly discourage it.

After a rest day, we then climbed an incredible 10-pitch line that was the exact opposite in quality. Space Ghost (IV 5.10+ C1) goes up a natural, leftward-curving line on the right side of the main northwest-facing wall of the cirque. [*Editor's note: Early climbing parties in the cirque named this the Tycho Wall, with three distinct buttresses.*] The route begins up an aesthetic, left-facing dihedral (hands), goes through a roof, and then quickly turns to offwidth. After one more short pitch, we reached the crux. One bolt was placed here, and this pitch will likely go free at 12a. Above, the route follows a moderate yet amazing leftward-trending system.

At the end of August, I recruited Garrett Reigan and returned to the cirque to climb the prow to the right of Space Ghost. On day one we climbed eight pitches, requiring much cleaning and trundling. On day two we climbed back to our high point in six pitches, involving flakes, chimneys, a 70-foot corner protected by number 6 cams, and two awesome 5.11- crack/seam pitches. The desperate crux pitch follows a laser-cut seam through a series of three roofs. We placed two pins, and just above the last roof the crack briefly terminated and one bolt was placed from a hook. I took two whippers trying to free the pitch with no success—it will likely go at solid 5.12. After the crux, a traversing pitch takes you to an amazing hands corner that leads to an immaculate slab. On this pitch, Garrett quested into a 40-foot runout over 5.10 terrain. He then traversed into a right-facing corner to access the summit, completing Moonquakes (V 5.12- R/X A1). 📷

– ANDY HUGHES

EARLY CLIMBS IN THE CIRQUE OF THE MOON: *New Mexico climbers David Baltz, Mark Dalen, and Mark Leonard put up the first known climbs in this cirque during a two-week trip in July 1978. The three climbed Pipeline (9 pitches, V 5.9 A3) and a six-pitch route (5.10) up a slabby wall they called Sunset Buttress, and Baltz rope-soloed the first two pitches of Cowcatcher, an attempted direct route up the right-hand (southernmost) buttress of what they named Tycho Wall.*

The following year, the three men returned with Bruce Bundy, Dave Dahrling, Mike Head, Paul Horak, and Tom Wells. Bundy, Head, and Wells freed Pipeline at 5.11d, and the same trio, along with Baltz and Horak, added five pitches to Cowcatcher but bailed at a band of chossy rock. The group added several shorter lines as well. Mark Dalen's full report about these trips is at the AAJ website. 📷 🔍

[Top] The right buttress of Tycho Wall, showing the two routes completed by Andy Hughes and partners in 2016. (1) Space Ghost (IV 5.10+ C1). (2) Moonquakes (V 5.12- R/X A1). The Pipeline buttress, first climbed in 1978, is just to the left of this formation. *Andy Hughes* [Bottom] Mark Dalen jumaring to the top of pitch four during the first ascent of Pipeline (5.9 A3) in 1978. The route went free at 5.11d the following summer. *Mark Leonard*

LOST TWIN LAKES
A LITTLE-KNOWN ALPINE WALL GETS SIX LONG NEW ROUTES

BY CHRIS HIRSCH

AT ROUGHLY 10,000', the Lost Twin Lakes of Wyoming's Bighorn Mountains sit right at timberline. Above the upper lake loom two 1,000' walls: The western Spider Web Wall is closer to the upper Lost Twin Lake, while the Thundercloud Wall sits back a little farther to the south. This area is home to many pika, marmots, martens, and the occasional visiting fisherman seeking large lake trout. Many climbers have hiked in the seven miles to investigate, but few have ascended the walls.

To the best of my knowledge, development of this tucked-away cirque began with Paul Piana in the early 1990s. He and the late Todd Skinner flew over the area and immediately were awestruck by the steep left side of the Spider Web Wall. While Skinner never climbed here, Piana returned several times throughout the decade, with Heidi Badaracco, Pete DeLannoy, and probably others. In 1996 he established Great Spirit (14 pitches, IV 5.12-) and later put up Coup Stick (7 pitches, III 5.10+).

Piana kept these climbs quiet for years, sharing them only with a few friends. In 2011, he revealed his best-kept secret to me while climbing near our homes in the Black Hills, and a friend and I ventured out the next summer to check it out. We managed what was likely the second ascent of Great Spirit and

[Above] **Tony Schwartz casts off on the crux fourth pitch of Mixed Signals (8 pitches, IV 5.12+ C1), the most difficult of the new routes on the Spider Web Wall, above Lost Twin Lakes.** *Chris Hirsch*

were blown away by the rock quality and potential. Since that trip, I've returned every summer to further develop the Spider Web Wall. In the last three summers, we've put in six new lines that average one bolt per pitch. With Paul's blessing, I'm sharing this information now.

Labor Day weekend of 2013 was our first attempt at ground-up new routing in this cirque. After scrutinizing many photos all winter, antsy to test these potential lines, I recruited Lee Terveen to help me. Our first choice of line failed when the free climbing came to an abrupt stop on the second pitch. We did not want an A or C attached to the grading of this route. So we eyed up another line on the shorter, western side of the wall. An obvious line of cracks and dikes split the center of this smoother section. Two days of route-finding, hand-drilling bolts, and trundling blocks led us to the summit and the FA of Strange Designs (7 pitches, III 5.11-).

With my fire stoked even more for the alpine season of 2014, I planned to spend two weeks in the Bighorns that year, the first with Tony Schwartz and the second with Dan Brazil.

In August, Tony and I set out with intentions of establishing a new route on the nose of the formation, just to the right of Great Spirit. With a portaledge, gear, food and water, and several printed pictures of the proposed line as our topo, we hoped to make a single-push, ground-up ascent in two days. The first day went very smoothly—each pitch was falling into place perfectly, with no storms, and we made it halfway up the wall.

The next morning we tackled the most questionable section. To our relief, it gave way to some thin 5.12- laybacking and required only two protection bolts. At the top of this seventh pitch, however, it began raining. We quickly deployed the portaledge rainfly and hung from the inside like we were in a giant cocoon, our legs going numb. (Naturally, this was the only hanging belay on the whole route.) Tony wanted to bail after the first clap of thunder, but with no rap stations, and being only 200' from the top of the 1,000' wall, I said "Hell no!" The rain still hadn't subsided after a couple of hours and it was getting too late to try for the summit. So, we decided to spend another night on the wall and struggled for a good hour to set up the ledge from inside the rain fly.

We woke the next day to a helicopter buzzing into the cirque. A rescue? No, they were just stocking the upper lake with cutthroats, a unique sight from our vantage. Blue sky and only two pitches remaining had us psyched to finish. But with an unplanned night on the wall, we were cramping from lack of water. Thankfully the climbing didn't get any harder than 5.10. We hiked back to camp, and the next morning went back up and freed the full route, Vision Quest (9 pitches, IV 5.12-), in five hours.

Dan's week in the Bighorns would be part of his "50x50" project (50 significant climbs before he turns 50). One of his goals was to achieve an alpine first ascent, and I had just the line picked out: a linear set of creases up the center, lower-angled part of the wall. With support Dan received from the AAC Live Your Dream Grant, we set out to tick this off his list.

Despite Dan's inexperience with drilling bolts and ground-up venturing, we established five pitches the first day, even after hitting a dead end and having to reroute. The fifth pitch was a phenomenal, varied corner system that checked in around mid-5.11. We rapped and fixed a couple of the pitches for easier access to our high point the next day. Only two pitches remained, but the last one had to break through the overhanging capstones that make up the summit rim. After a chimney/offwidth on pitch six, we reached the critical moment. A weakness revealed itself through some pumpy 5.11+ terrain, followed by the worst top-out of all the routes, with loose scree and moss. We dubbed our route Wild, Wild West (7 pitches, IV 5.11+).

With time remaining, I wanted to make a start on another route for the following summer. So, just to the left, we established two long pitches of what I've been calling the Greenway Project. I returned in July 2015 with Harrison Teuber to push the route higher, but immediately above the 2014 high point, some 5.11 face climbing required a couple bolts. Before we'd finished the third pitch, the sky let loose, so we rapped and then hiked out in the rain.

I called my friend Luke Ross to join me over Labor Day weekend. Back on the Greenway Project, I navigated through unknown ground, running it out more than I would have liked, because time and Luke's patience and body heat were limited (bolts still need to be added). On the last pitch, a wet transition between cracks forced our retreat just 30' from joining Wild, Wild West and 60' from the summit. The Greenway Project (6½ pitches, IV 5.11+?) remains unfinished.

Luke and I returned in June 2016, but mid-June, as it turned out, was a little early for Lost Twin Lakes—they were still partially frozen! However, comfortable temps could be found on the sunny southeast face of the Spider Web Wall. A ways to the left of Great Spirit, we climbed three pitches before rapping down and finishing our trip with some fly-fishing.

A couple of weeks later, on July 4, Harrison came back and we swapped leads to the summit on the new line. Pitch seven, which looked like 5.9, turned out to be the crux, at 5.11+. Surprise! Our nine-pitch route became Astro-Pika (IV 5.11+ PG-13). Every multi-pitch crag needs an Astro route, right?

[Above left] Harrison Teuber traversing to the belay on pitch eight of Astro-Pika (IV 5.11+ PG-13), high above Lost Twin Lakes. [Top right] The southeast face of the Spider Web Wall. (1) Mixed Signals (IV 5.12+ C1, Hirsch-Schwartz, 2016). (2) Astro-Pika (IV 5.11+ PG-13, Hirsch-Ross-Schwartz-Teuber, 2016). (3) Great Spirit (IV 5.12-, Badaracco-Piana, 1996). (4) Vision Quest (IV 5.12-, Hirsch-Schwartz, 2014). [Bottom right] The northeast face of the Spider Web Wall. (1) Vision Quest (IV 5.12-, Hirsch-Schwartz, 2014). (2) Greenway Project (IV 5.11+ unfinished, Brazil-Hirsch-Ross-Teuber, 2015). (3) Wild, Wild West (IV 5.11+, Brazil-Hirsch, 2014). (4) Wandering Spirit (III 5.6, Badaracco-Tolle, 1996?). (5) Coup Stick (III 5.10+, DeLannoy-Piana, early 1990s). (6) Strange Designs (III 5.11-, Hirsch-Terveen, 2013). *Chris Hirsch*

For my third trip of the summer, Tony and I spent a week at Lost Twin Lakes in August. Of the many potential lines remaining, we chose a set of very steep dihedrals on the far left side of the wall, not visible from the lake. The first three pitches varied from 5.7 to 5.9, but above that it was on. The crux fourth pitch was amazing, but we were unable to piece together the last 15 feet all free. After a couple of pitches of superb corner climbing, we encountered a large suspect flake, ready to calve from a roof with the slightest touch—there was no passing it safely. After much deliberation, we opted to descend and rap in from the top the next day to remove the flake. We made the 1,000'-plus trudge and rappelled to the flake, and to my amazement it wouldn't budge! We finished placing anchors and protection bolts, and rehearsed pitches on top-rope. After three days of work and a rest day, we came back to climb our brilliant new route Mixed Signals (8 pitches, IV 5.12+ C1).

EDITOR'S NOTE: *The Thundercloud Wall, at the head of the cirque, has seen some activity by others, but to the author's knowledge it remains unclimbed. Topos of all routes described here are at the AAJ website* 📷 🔍

CLOUD PEAK, EAST FACE, MEDICINE CROW

AFTER SEVERAL YEARS of aborted trips, Alex Marine and I climbed a new route on the east face of Cloud Peak (13,166') in early July. Our route begins about 100' left of the 1986 route, A Shimmering Abstraction (Ilgner-Petro), the only other climb known to have been completed on the main east face. [*An easier route was climbed left of the main wall in the 1970s, and another route is in progress on the main face and is expected to be completed in 2017.*] After a three-day approach from the east, including two days shuttling loads from Mead Lake to Glacier Lake, we climbed the stunning, taffy-swirled wall over four days, mostly following a ghostly white dike.

Given the wall's reputation for few continuous cracks and the melted-out snow couloir that was formerly the standard descent, we opted to fix lines and establish bolted rappel stations. We climbed ground-up for three days, retreating each day to our tent by Glacier Lake as afternoon storms arrived. We summited on the fourth day and rappelled the route, using our six new two-bolt rappel stations (two 60m ropes), the bottom four of which double as belay anchors.

Medicine Crow (1,100', 8 pitches, 5.11+ R) goes clean except the first pitch, which required several knifeblades to make it safe. (No fixed protection was left on the route.) The movement is exciting and athletic, with heady face climbing interspersed with chimneys and laybacking. On the crux fourth pitch, through a golden roof, Alex jumped off after nearly dislodging a large flake directly above the belay. We cleaned the flake, and on a second go some hidden crimps allowed passage. We did not bother to redpoint this pitch, so a ground-up clean ascent of the route still awaits. Above pitch six the route shares much ground with A Shimmering Abstraction. Our fun and improbable final pitch tops out through a series of nested roofs directly on the lip. We believe this finish is different from the 1986 route, but it's hard to say for sure.

With the addition of our rappel route, we believe that approaching from the west would now be the best option. If approaching from the east, it may be best to arrive early in the summer to avoid the dangerous rockfall on either side of the glacier that can occur in warmer conditions.

We named the route after the inspiring Dr. Joseph Medicine Crow, the last surviving Crow

war chief and a celebrated historian, who passed away shortly before our climb. The Bighorns have long been sacred ground to the Crow Nation and others. Nine days on ancient rock only recently emerged from the earth was strong medicine. [*This trip was funded in part by an AAC Live Your Dream grant.*]

— SPENCER GRAY

[Left] The 1,000-foot east face of Cloud Peak, showing the two full routes up the wall. (1) Medicine Crow (Gray-Marine, 2016). (2) A Shimmering Abstraction (Ilgner-Petro, 1986). The 1986 route line was placed farther left in AAJ 2015. Cloud Peak's 13,166-foot summit is out of picture to the left. *Spencer Gray*

[Top] Summer can be a relative term in the high mountains of Wyoming. [Right] The north face of the Merlon (ca 13,000'), first climbed in 2016. (1) Guillotine. (2) American Direct. (3) Jenga. Each route has seven or eight pitches. *Mark Jenkins*

THE MERLON, NORTH FACE

THE GLACIER WAS calving every half-hour all day and all night. A thundering boom would reverberate off the narrow cirque walls, then a wave of water would roll across Glacier Lake. During the day we could get used to it, but at night the detonations would blast us right out of our dreams.

This was my fifth climbing trip into the Cloud Peak Wilderness, but my first to the cirque below Cloud Peak's tremendous east face. It was mid-August and I'd come in with two fellow Wyoming climbers: towering, pencil-thin Julian Poush and Chris "Slim" Murray. Poush's father had actually attempted a route in this cirque over 40 years ago. We had help from horse packers getting our gear to the west end of Cloud Peak Reservoir, then humped heavy packs up past Diamond Lake, from which we scrambled northwest, gaining 700' to reach Glacier Lake (11,490'). Our goal was to climb the north face of the Merlon, a separate tower (ca 13,000') just south of Cloud Peak's east face. We accomplished this the first day: Jenga (8 pitches, 5.8 R). We rapped off the eastern prow of the Merlon, replacing old slings that Ken Duncan and I had put in eight years earlier when we climbed No Climb For Old Men on the south face. [*Editor's note: The Merlon was first climbed, by its eastern buttress, in 1961. The south face has three known routes, all 5.11. See "Recon" in AAJ 2015. The routes described in this report are the first known on the north side, above Glacier Lake.*]

The second day we ascended the left-hand side of the face up a left-facing dihedral. We got caught in a snowstorm at the second belay, waited it out, and continued climbing wet rock an hour later. The rock and climbing were superb, although sometimes scary—snow-covered face climbing, stemming through overhanging, guillotine-like slabs, and a final exit via a very reachy (if you're not 6-feet-4-inches tall) finger crack yielded Guillotine (7 pitches, 5.10+).

On the third day, Poush and I climbed a line up the middle of the north face through overlapping overhangs to a right-facing dihedral. The first pitch was run-out, the dihedral pitches spooky because of car-size blocks: American Direct (8 pitches, 5.10+ R).

It snowed the next day and we did a half carry back down to Sapphire Lake, finishing the hike out over the next two days. Seven gorgeous days in the Cloud Peak Wilderness. As per tradition, no pins, no bolts, no fixed gear, no aid.

– MARK JENKINS

[Above] **Cody Scarpella on the 40-meter 5.13+ crux pitch of Full Facial on Cynical Pinnacle.** *Rob Kepley*

SOUTH PLATTE, CYNICAL PINNACLE, FULL FACIAL

THE SOUTH PLATTE region of Colorado has a strong history of scrappy rock climbing and a staunch ethic of bolting new routes on lead. So when Dave Montgomery and I set out to climb the west face of the iconic Cynical Pinnacle, we knew there would be a good adventure.

Strappo Hughes first envisioned climbing this face ground-up in the late 1980s. After a short, four-bolt section of climbing Hughes retreated, leaving what he called the "Only the Lonely" project untouched for many years. For both Dave and me, the history and ethics of the South Platte are firmly embedded in our climbing experiences. So, early on, we were torn between stubbornly upholding those ethics versus the possibility of adding useless hardware to one of our favorite local spires. As a compromise, we rappelled the west face to preview the wall. We did not rehearse any moves, but only made sure there were enough features to be climbable.

Confident there was a line, we pulled our ropes and started up from Strappo's high point. Free climbing between hook placements and drilling when the hooks held, we were happy to make any small bits of progress. With each day's end, we fixed ropes at the new high point and retreated. In December 2014, after several weeks of effort, we made the summit. We had completed the line but were only halfway to our original goal.

Between seasonal falcon closures, temperature-dependent face climbing, and the overall difficulty of the route, it would be more than two years before we completed our vision. On January 27, Dave and I shared a day we would not soon forget, climbing the west face of Cynical Pinnacle all free. Though not the longest of routes, at 400', Full Facial (a.k.a. Only the Lonely) has a nearly 40m crux pitch and difficulties up to 5.13+. The bolts are in place for future challengers, but the piss-shivering memories of trying to place those bolts from thin, teetering hooks will remain exclusively Dave and mine. [*Editor's note: In January 2014, Cody Scarpella, with support from Joe Mills and Dave Vuono, free climbed Buffaloes in Space (5.13b), an old aid line up the west side of Cynical Pinnacle's summit block.*] 📷 🔍

—CODY SCARPELLA

ROCKY MOUNTAIN NATIONAL PARK, 2016 SUMMARY

IN A SUPERB effort, Josh Wharton completed the three hardest free routes in the Park in one year: Sarchasm (5.14a, a sport route below Longs Peak), the Honeymoon is Over (5.13c) and Dunn-Westbay Direct (5.14a), both on the Diamond. Wharton didn't redpoint the latter until October 10, well into usual ice climbing season on Longs. In what he called a "Triple 14" challenge, Carlo Traversi bouldered Jade (V14) in Chaos Canyon, then hiked to Chasm Lake and climbed Sarchasm (5.14a), then followed Pervertical (5.11a) to Longs' 14,259' summit, a 20-hour day that included about 23 miles of hiking. Also on the Diamond, Madaleine Sorkin ticked the first female ascent of Honeymoon is Over, breaking the final 5.13a pitch into two leads.

Just west of Longs, Ryan Gajewski and Dakota Walz toured all eight towers of the Keyboard of the Winds in a 27-hour round trip from the car, creating the Glissando Link-up, with about 3,800' of scrambling and roped climbing, likely including some new ground. The ever-active Ben Collett partnered with Ben Rosenberg to climb Brexit (6 pitches, 5.10 R) on the northeast spur of Taylor Peak. Ken Duncan and Dede Humphrey found Magic in the Middle (7 pitches, 5.9), a direct and reportedly excellent new line up the south face of Zowie spire. On the far right side of Hallett Peak, Mark Jenkins and Dougald MacDonald did a possible new line up the prominent fin leading to Point 12,308': the Fourth Buttress (750', 5.9 PG-13). At the foot of Hallett, during the winter season, various climbers found short lines near Bullet (M6+, Grohusky-Sievers, 2001), including the difficult Ms. Inferno (M7).

– DOUGALD MACDONALD

MICHIGAN

NORWICH LEDGE, PARMOTREMA ARNOLDII

NORWICH LEDGE IS a 100m rhyolite escarpment north of Bergland, in Michigan's Upper Peninsula. In February 2016, after a roughly 5-mile ski approach, Kim Hall and I did the first known winter ascent of Norwich via the summer rock route Book of Saturdays (solid M5). Additional potential was apparent.

Soon after this first climb, Dave Rone and I made the first ascent of Parmotrema Arnoldii (WI5/6 M7+ A0), which climbs four short but involved pitches through breaks in the many roofs that make up the tallest part of the escarpment. A bolt was used for aid turning the third roof, but the second followed free. The exit groove on pitch four, covered in the lichen that gives the route its name, holds the route's hard-to-protect crux.

[Below] Jon Jugenheimer below the first roof on pitch one of Paramotrema Arnoldii. *Dave Rone*

To our knowledge, as of last winter, this route was the hardest traditionally protected mixed climb on the U.S. side of the border in the Midwest. The best conditions are likely to be found in February.

– JON JUGENHEIMER

ALASKA

[Above] Nick Pappas pauses on the approach to the north buttress of the Albatross. Pappas and Katie Mills followed the prow facing the camera to the striking shaded dihedral splitting the upper tower, which gave the route its name: Eye of Sauron. *Katie Mills*

THE ALBATROSS AND THE SHIV: NEW ROUTES

POURING RAIN, NIGHTMARISH mosquitos, tussock bog–hopping with 90-pound packs—the struggle was real when Cigdem Milobinski, Nick Pappas, Todd Torres, and I began our approach into the Arrigetch Peaks on July 2. But the objectives we'd dreamed of climbing kept us going, and in the end we completed two new routes during our three-week trip.

Due to various unfortunate factors, including carrying too much gear and Cigdem spraining her ankle and subsequently self-evacuating, it took us nine days to approach and establish our base camp in the Arrigetch Valley. On July 12, Nick Pappas and I set out to climb the Albatross (5,565'), a twin-summited peak that had been climbed to its southern (true) summit twice before—first in 1969 via its southeast face and southwest ridge and then in 1993 via cracks up the south face. The north buttress commands the view upon entering the Arrigetch cirque. Its top is split in two by a giant dihedral that never sees sunlight, making it appear as if the watchful eye of some great god overlooks the valley. I couldn't believe that it remained unclimbed.

A beautiful 400' splitter crack system led us up to the shoulder of the north buttress, and some nerve-wracking climbing over giant loose blocks got us to the base of the dihedral. The corner was slammed shut at the bottom, and we spent four hours exploring various options and then retreating to a ledge to rest. Finally we followed a line of tiny crimps directly up to the dihedral, which eventually opened up to a decent crack. We climbed the wet, crumbly corner, full of flora and fauna, and exited to find a perfect safe nest for a well-deserved nap. After climbing a licheny slab to the north summit of the Albatross, we simul-climbed the ridge to a low point between the peak's two prominent high points. From here we made six 70m rappels off the west side to the glacier below. We returned to our tent 30 hours after leaving and named the route after the stunning dihedral that glowers over the valley: The Eye of Sauron (1,200', 5.10c).

[Above] Nick Pappas racking for the northwest ridge of the Shiv, with the crux lurking above, during the first ascent of Go Big or Go Home (5.10d R). *Todd Torres*

After scouting the area and finding nothing else we desired to climb, we moved base camp to the beautiful Aquarius Valley. On July 18, Nick and Todd climbed the northwest ridge of an unnamed peak attempted in 2002. [*Editor's note: This peak lies northwest of the Badile in the Aquarius Valley and is represented on the Survey Pass (B-3) Quad as a long ridge between two glaciers at the head of the valley. The 2002 party called it "Notchtop."*]

Classic 5.6–5.8 on the first few pitches led them to a knife-edge sidewalk and wild face, devoid of crack systems. It was clear that the 2002 attempt had ended here—Todd used the previous party's bail nut as part of the belay. Nick managed to free the next pitch onsight, calling it the culmination of 10 years of climbing and the best pitch of his life. Tricky ridge climbing took them to the summit, from which they continued down the ridgeline to a notch and then rappelled the west side of the peak. Since it was our last day to climb before hiking out, they named the route Go Big or Go Home (5.10d R, about 800' vertical but considerably longer climbing distance) and dubbed the formerly unclimbed mountain the Shiv. This trip was made possible by the Bob Wilson Grant from the Mazamas.

– KATIE MILLS

ARROWHEAD PEAK, WEST FACE AND NORTH RIDGE

IN LATE JULY, Tim Halder and Jason Schilling made the possible first ascent of a peak along the ridge between the Alatna and Kobuk rivers, north of Coolage Tower. Starting from a fork of Hot Springs Creek, they climbed over a pass to the Kobuk side of the Continental Divide, then climbed three long pitches up the west side of the Divide, followed by four pitches on the north ridge of the mountain they called Arrowhead Peak (ca 5,000', 5.8).

– *INFORMATION PROVIDED BY* JASON SCHILLING

[Above] Craig Muderlak leads a splitter hand crack on the second pitch of Red Dihedral (IV 5.10a) on the Dog Tooth. The team expected—and climbed—long snow and ice routes in the Neacola Mountains, but they also were pleasantly surpised by the quality of the rock climbing. *Drew Thayer*

THE LONG WAY HOME
FIRST ASCENTS AND EXPLORATION IN THE NEACOLA MOUNTAINS

BY DREW THAYER

A PHOTO OF unclimbed spires rising out of glacial ice sparked the inspiration for our expedition to the Neacola Mountains, a remote subrange of the Alaska and Aleutian ranges. The dream soon grew beyond climbing to include forging an overland route back out of the mountains. Craig Muderlak, David Fay, and I planned to fly into the Neacolas, attempt climbs on the granite spires, and then make our way back to civilization using skis and packrafts.

The obvious problem was the amount of gear we'd need. Climbing big, technical mountains and surviving on a glacier requires lots of equipment—the fact that we'd be returning by boat and on foot meant we'd have to cut corners. We crammed food into burnable containers and hand-sewed camera bags out of Dyneema fabric and foam. Seats came out of the packrafts—we'd use sleeping pads. David constructed the Settlers of Catan board game out of cardboard. We even hand-made wooden skis that we could use on the glacier and then burn to avoid having to bushwhack with them. When the plane dropped us off on the Pitchfork Glacier on May 12, we didn't really know if the skis would last for three weeks, but we were committed.

With much favorable weather, we were able to make attempts on several mountains above the Pitchfork and Neacola glaciers. We set our sights on the prominent northwest buttress of the Citadel, attempted by a British team the year before (*AAJ 2016*). Our first attempt ended early due to warm conditions, as the ice melted to slush and wet avalanches rumbled all around us. When we returned to the peak we aimed for a narrow slot on the northwest face that we called the Sliver. Climbing at night when the snow was firm, we ascended névé and ice through some mixed steps to a corniced ridge atop the northwest buttress. Facing deteriorating snow conditions and a prominent headwall above, we retreated after 3,000' (AI4 M3 90°). Our line provides an expedient and fun climb to the upper headwall and would be best completed in colder conditions.

The real prize on this expedition turned out to be what we least expected: splitter rock climbing. While ice melted and wet avalanches rumbled all day, we turned our attention to the east buttress of Dog Tooth (ca 7,150'), a 1,200' gem of clean granite first climbed in 2011 (Chriswell-Johnson-Thrasher, *AAJ 2012*). We first established Red Dihedral (1,200', IV 5.10a) on the main south-facing wall of the east buttress, left of the original route, and then a week later returned to attempt the picturesque south prow. After climbing four pitches up to 5.11c, we retreated when the cracks disappeared into shallow seams. The good weather continued, and the next day we tried another crack system, clad in the cut-off jean shorts we'd carried because you can't put a price on morale. Following continuous finger cracks linked by tricky face climbing, we put up Birthday Jorts (1,000', IV 5.11a) on David's birthday, all free and onsight. *[Editor's note: The group's two completed lines and their attempt all lie to the left of the 2011 route, which generally follows the eastern ridge of the Dog Tooth. Both of the 2016 routes end atop the east buttress, without continuing to the summit of the mountain.]*

Climbing at night when the snow was firm allowed us to make the first ascents of two peaks. On May 18 we ascended to the west-northwest col of a triangular peak at the head of the north fork of the Pitchfork Glacier, then followed snow couloirs around the northwest aspect to a mixed step near the summit, completing Shred Mode (2,000', 70° M4). We named the peak Spearhead (ca 7,200').

A week later we skied down to the Neacola Glacier and climbed an attractive spire along a shoulder east of Peak 6,310' that we called the Wing. *[Peak 6,310' was first climbed by Joe and Joan Firey and George and Frances Whitmore on June 25, 1965. See "Recon" in AAJ 2016.]* We climbed at night via snow slopes on the northeast and north sides to the west col, from which we climbed 100' of fun, steep 5.7 rock to the top (ca 5,700').

During our time spent on the Pitchfork Glacier, a larger unknown loomed in our minds: our return to the sea through some 60 miles of wild terrain. Our loads weighed 110 pounds each when we began skiing down the Pitchfork in the Arctic twilight. Sixteen miles later we reached the toe of the glacier,

[Top] David Fay leading the Sliver during the team's second attempt on the Citadel. [Bottom] Drew Thayer pulls onto the arête on the second pitch of Red Dihedral (1,200', IV 5.10a) on the Dog Tooth formation. *Craig Muderlak*

where we shuttled loads over moraine to the headwaters of the Glacier Fork of the Tlikakila River. The next morning we inflated our packrafts and pushed off into the rushing current.

Camped at the confluence of the Glacier Fork and the main Tlikakila the next day, we faced a major decision. We either had to schlep 330 pounds of gear over a mountain pass and then descend the Drift River, or we could try to bushwhack and raft our way to the Big River over terrain where no map would be of any use. This territory had been submerged beneath a glacially dammed lake when the map was drafted in the 1950s. That glacier has since receded, and now we had to hope that a descent through thick forest and along a rushing river would lead us to a new lake at the head of the Big River. Eager to be done with snow travel, we burned our wooden skis on a gravel bar and committed ourselves to making it to the Big River.

After hauling our boats over Lake Clark Pass, we encountered Class IV and V whitewater and were forced to portage. Shuttling loads through slide alder was slow—in two days we gained less than four miles—and we spent the night camped in the rain and mosquitoes, dreading our return trip for more gear. Stress, doubt, and scant rations wore us thin, and countless grizzly tracks meant we couldn't let our guard down. After two days of bushwhacking and running rapids, we finally reached the iceberg-studded lake at the headwaters of the Big River. The next day we floated 35 miles into the vast coastal plain. Shorebirds and seagulls appeared, and Craig spotted a harbor seal. On the sixth day of our voyage from base camp, we paddled to the river's mouth and awaited our pilot at the edge of the ocean.

[Top] The climbers started toward the distant ocean with 110-pound loads. Fortunately, their handmade wooden skis held together for 16 miles of glacier travel. *Craig Muderlak* [Middle] "It was hard to part with our homemade skis, but they would become a hefty burden in the thick alder forests that we knew were coming." *Drew Thayer* [Bottom] Treacherous rapids during the exit from the mountains sometimes demanded arduous portages. *Craig Muderlak*

SUMMARY: New routes on the Dog Tooth, first ascent of Spearhead (ca 7,200') and the Wing, and attempt on the northwest buttress of the Citadel, by David Fay, Craig Muderlak, and Drew Thayer, May 2016.

KICHATNA MOUNTAINS

THE CITADEL, WESTMAN'S WORLD

ON APRIL 21, after six weeks of watching from a distance as a gigantic storm system pummeled the Alaska Range, Jess Roskelley and I saw a forecast for a weather window long enough to fly into the Kichatnas. With our primary objective out of condition, we returned to the Citadel (8,520'), where we had climbed a new route up the east face, with Kristoffer Szilas, three years earlier (*AAJ 2014*). This time we set our sights on the peak's unclimbed west face, above the Cul-de-Sac Glacier. Zack Smith and Josh Wharton had attempted a line there in 2008 but retreated after Wharton took a lead fall, ripping gear and injuring Smith with his flying crampons. Jess and I planned a completely different line to the left of their attempt.

After fixing the first two pitches, we returned to camp and consumed a generous dinner, eating for the hunger to come. The next morning at 3 a.m., Jess and I committed to the wall. The steep rock yielded physical mixed pitches, switching between free and aid. Moving onto the rightward-traversing snow ramps in the middle of the face, we made our only bivy on the route when a horrendous windstorm pinned us down with driving snow. The following morning we climbed the remaining ice runnels, encountering thin, wandering ice in shallow granite grooves. Near the top we linked into familiar terrain from our ascent of the east face. From the summit, we descended via our ascent route, completing Westman's World (4,000', VI A3 AI4 X M7 70˚), named in honor of our dear friend and mentor, the Alaskan legend Mark Westman. Our trip was supported by the Mugs Stump Award.

– **BEN ERDMANN**

[Top] The west face of the Citadel, showing Ben Erdmann and Jess Roskelley's line Westman's World, the first route to be completed on the face. The X shows the approximate high point of the Smith-Wharton attempt in 2008. [Bottom] Jess Roskelley coming up the final snow slope leading to the summit of the Citadel, with Kichatna Spire behind. *Ben Erdmann*

[Above] **Rob Smith at the end of the technical difficulties on Mt. Foraker's Infinite Spur, with the Lacuna Glacier stretching out below. The first ascent of the Infinite Spur (Alaska Grade 6 5.9 M5 AI4) in 1977 took Michael Kennedy and George Lowe seven days from the bergschrund to the summit. Haley and Smith climbed the route on May 27 in 18 hours 20 minutes.** *Colin Haley*

SPORT + ADVENTURE
SPEED RECORDS AND A SOLO ASCENT OF MT. FORAKER'S INFINITE SPUR

BY COLIN HALEY

SOMETIMES ALPINE CLIMBING is all about the adventure, sometimes it is all about the sport, and usually it is partly about both. Adventure is not superior to sport, and sport is not superior to adventure, they're simply different. In 2016, a place like the Mont Blanc massif provides an alpine climbing experience that is 90 percent sport and 10 percent adventure. By contrast, a place like Alaska's Hayes Range provides an experience that is more like 70 percent adventure and 30 percent sport. I deeply appreciate and enjoy both these aspects of alpine climbing.

At the end of a long trip in the central Alaska Range in 2012, I skied from Kahiltna base camp toward the base of the Infinite Spur (ca 2,750m, Kennedy-Lowe, 1977) on the south face of Sultana (Mt. Foraker, 17,400'/5,304m) with a heavy backpack, hoping to make the route's first solo ascent. Having never been on the route before, I would've been in for a very big adventure had I not bailed near the end of the approach, convinced that conditions were too warm.

Before the 2016 season, my friend Rob Smith, who knew of my Infinite Spur solo intentions in 2012, suggested that we could climb the route together, and that afterward I'd be all primed to solo it. I was into the idea straight away. I knew that climbing the route beforehand would detract from the adventure of soloing it, but also would allow me to try the route in a super-lightweight, fast style that would be greater in the sport realm, and simply damn good fun. I also really liked the idea of descending the Sultana Ridge with a partner before doing it alone, as I knew this descent would be one of the most dangerous aspects of soloing the Infinite Spur.

After a period of acclimatization on Denali's West Buttress and the lower portion of the Sultana Ridge, Rob and I skied to the base of the Infinite Spur on May 26. On the 27th we crossed the bergschrund at 5:46 a.m., and after about 2,700m of simul-climbing and simul-soloing, we reached Sultana's summit just past midnight. Our schrund-to-summit time of 18 hours 20 minutes was a new speed record, aided by good conditions and by tracks left on the first half of the route by three British friends.

We moved at a more leisurely pace on the descent, stopping in crevasses twice to take naps while sheltered from the wind. At around 6 a.m. on May 29, Rob and I arrived back in Kahiltna base camp. After a few hours of sleep, I gave Rob a hug as he boarded a TAT plane bound for home, a great and successful trip already achieved.

[Above] **Looking back down while soloing through the first crux in the Black Band of the Infinite Spur on Mt. Foraker.** *Colin Haley*

Around 7 a.m. on May 31, after less than two full rest days, I departed Kahiltna base for a second lap on the Infinite Spur, this time by myself. When I crossed the bergschrund at 3:43 a.m. on June 1, I had gotten only a couple of hours of fitful sleep. I think conditions were still a bit better than average, but the earlier tracks were filled in with fresh snow and the snowpack had only partially refrozen during the night. I was nonetheless able to make good time, thanks mostly to my very lightweight kit. I had my crampons, ice axes, helmet, a swami belt, ice axe umbilicals, and two key-chain carabiners (for clipping the axes to my swami belt on the rock climbing portions). I did not carry a single real carabiner, nor a single piece of protection. My only rope was a 15m section of 5mm perlon, which I used to haul my pack twice on the hardest bits.

Considering that the forecast was supposed to be solid until the afternoon of June 3, I was a bit surprised to see it start lightly snowing around 8 a.m. on June 1. Nonetheless, the vast majority of the route felt very casual ropeless, although the sustained blue ice on the upper portion of the Knife Edge Ridge was certainly tedious. The only section where I felt I had to move very slowly to do it safely without a rope was in the Black Band. Despite being only two rope lengths long, this section took me over an hour to ascend.

At 11:20 a.m. I finished the Knife Edge Ridge and settled in for a rest and brew stop for about an hour and a quarter. I was off again at 12:36 p.m., my pack reloaded with about three liters of warm water. After a bit more 60° ice, I was soon slogging on Sultana's upper slopes. The snowfall from a couple of days earlier made for a bit of trail breaking, but still much better conditions than average. With the technical climbing behind me, I switched from bars to gels, busted out my iPod Shuffle, and dropped the hammer. I had an absolute blast pushing hard on the upper slopes and arrived on the summit at 4:18 p.m.—12 hours 29 minutes after crossing the bergschrund. Considering how big and serious a route the Infinite Spur is in general, it had been a shockingly casual and joyful ascent. [*Editor's note: The fastest previous times on the*

[Above left] The "Freezy Nuts Castle," where Rob Smith and Colin Haley sheltered during acclimatization for the Infinite Spur. The cache they left here was Haley's salvation during his solo descent. [Right] Haley near the end of the long descent. *Colin Haley*

Infinite Spur were about 25 hours, by Rolando Garibotti and Steve House in 2001, and by Samuel and Simon Anthamatten and Andreas Steindl in 2009.]

I made decent time on the first portion of my descent, which follows the upper 1,500m of the Japanese Route (northeast ridge, 1966). By 6:45 p.m. I was taking a break at the junction of the Japanese Route and Sultana Ridge, swapping socks, eating some snacks, and melting more water. I was moving again in less than an hour, and almost immediately the weather socked in badly. From here on, the descent was a long, harrowing blur, done entirely in storm, in which I became progressively more sleep-deprived. From the moment the bad weather came in on the evening of June 1, it took me nearly 48 hours to reach Kahiltna base. During this descent it snowed something like 50–60cm up high, with a lot of wind transport. Avalanche conditions were the sketchiest I have seen in 20 years of skiing and mountaineering.

My biggest problem by far was visibility. I did a decent amount of probing and backtracking, and in one particularly bad instance I did an extra 300m of elevation gain and descent (all with deep trail breaking), when I convinced myself I had accidentally veered off the main ridge. I finally concluded that wasting so many calories to route-finding was dangerous, and I switched to a program where I would only move if could see something, and then go as fast as I could (not easy with the deep snow). When the visibility was absolutely zero I would simply wait. In one instance I spent six hours in one spot, sitting on my backpack and alternating between bouts of light exercise to stay warm and extremely brief naps with my head resting on my knees. I had consciously packed my clothing fairly conservatively, since I didn't bring bivouac equipment, and was very glad I had.

It was a huge relief to finally arrive at the "Freezy Nuts Castle" (a crevasse where Rob and I had taken shelter while acclimatizing on the Sultana Ridge) around 1 a.m. on June 3. I hadn't had any water or food in about 20 hours, and I was very happy to find our small cache of food and fuel. I also knew that a lot of the route from there out was wanded. When I finally arrived at Kahiltna base around 7:30 p.m. on June 3, I had been awake nearly three full days.

I succeeded in soloing the Infinite Spur in a fun, sporty fashion, and by accident I ended up getting all the adventure I ever could've wanted—and way more. In the end it wasn't "worth it" in terms of all the risk I faced. It was simply way too dangerous, and I'm not proud of that. I am proud, however, that given the very serious situation I stayed levelheaded, made the safest decisions possible, and got back without incident. 📷

Summary: One-day (18 hours 20 minutes) ascent of the Infinite Spur (Kennedy-Lowe, 1977) on the south face of Mt. Foraker, by Colin Haley and Rob Smith, May 27, 2016. Solo ascent of the Infinite Spur (12 hours 29 minutes) by Haley, June 1, 2016.

CENTRAL ALASKA RANGE

DENALI, FATHERS AND SONS WALL, MOTHER'S DAY VARIATION

BETWEEN MAY 10 and 12, Mike Gardner and I climbed a variation to First Born (Helmuth-House, *AAJ 1996*) on Denali's Fathers and Sons Wall. To our knowledge, ours was the fourth ascent of the wall. [*Editor's note: The Fathers and Sons Wall, which rises above the Peters Glacier to Denali's northwest buttress, was named by the late Mugs Stump, who dreamed of climbing it. The ca 6,000' face has three full-length routes.*] Our climb took 73 hours, 30 of which were spent waiting on ledges or in a snow cave for weather to improve. Like all previous parties, we were too gassed to continue to the north summit of Denali.

Our line deviated to climber's right of First Born above the second rock band, in order to climb an attractive steep ice section that appeared to be in much better condition than the original line. We climbed 200' up a snow arête to the base of the third rock band, 150' up an overhanging pitch of waterfall ice, and then 200' up a 60° ice slope to a break. From there we did one short rappel and traversed approximately 500' left to rejoin the original line. Since we weren't there to hug our moms on Mother's Day, we named it the Mother's Day Variation. In the spirit of the past ascents of the wall, we graded it Alaska Grade 5, Scottish Grade VI. Our trip was supported by the American Alpine Club and Mountain Hardwear's McNeill-Nott Award. 📷

– JIMMY VOORHIS

PURPORTED 1948 ASCENT OF DENALI'S WEST BUTTRESS

IN THE SUMMER of 2015, I learned that a man claimed to have completed the West Buttress Route on Denali three years before the well-known 1951 first ascent by Bradford Washburn and team. Bob Jones, a maverick cement truck driver—apparently 95 years old and a World War II infantry hero—said that he had secretly parachuted from a military plane onto the Southeast Fork of the Kahiltna Glacier and climbed the route in 1948.

Jones seemed to embody the inverse of Washburn, who paved the way for thousands of climbers by generously sharing hundreds of his breathtaking aerial photographs, a laser-precise map of Denali, and specific information on what has become the most popular path to the top. Skeptical that Washburn would have knowingly ignored such an important predecessor in the mountain's history, I repeatedly interviewed Jones over the telephone, and, like others, was taken in by his story. Mention of his climb, along with his many escapades in WWII, had already appeared online and in newspapers. There were niggling holes in his tale, but it seemed ungracious to doubt him until sitting face to face.

When I visited Jones at his Bellevue, Washington, home, I discovered that he was a neophyte climber and that he claimed to summit Denali in five days, with two other men, without using crampons, ropes, or sleeping pads. He said one of the men had died during the descent, from altitude illness, and was buried in a crevasse. They did not carry a camera. When I expressed my doubts, he clung to his story. After further research, I discovered that Jones was five years younger than his stated age and had missed most of World War II, despite his claims to medals and behind-the-lines combat bravado. For the full story of what I believe to be Bob Jones's false claim on Denali, see *Adventure Journal* issue number 3. Jones died from cancer in January 2016.

– JONATHAN WATERMAN

MT. HUNTINGTON, MACHO MADNESS

ON APRIL 29, Nik Mirhashemi and Mark Pugliese established a 1,500' alternate start to the French (Northwest) Ridge of Huntington. Their line begins near the start of the 1984 route Polarchrome and climbs straight up to the ridge, reaching it below the First Step, the first significant difficulty of the French Ridge route. The pair did not continue to Huntington's summit but instead downclimbed snow slopes to climber's left of their route. They suggested their line is a good, lower-commitment objective during unsettled weather. They named the route Macho Madness (M6 75°).

— INFORMATION FROM DENALI NATIONAL PARK *AND* MARK PUGLIESE

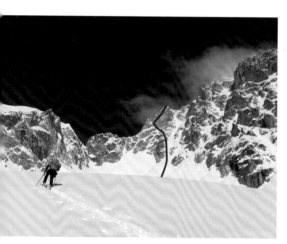

[Above] Kim Hall skiing below the south face of Mt. Providence. The line of Outside Providence (800m, IV M5 WI4, 2016) is shown. *Andy Anderson*

THUNDER MOUNTAIN, SOUTH FACE, THUNDERSTRUCK; MT. PROVIDENCE, SOUTH FACE, OUTSIDE PROVIDENCE

THE REPORTS BEGAN trickling in before we even got on the plane to Anchorage—shoulder-deep snow on the glacier, rivers of spindrift, and helicopter evacs due to avalanche danger. The snowiest spring in recent memory had left the Alaska Range buried, and the extended forecast didn't look promising.

Kim Hall and I quickly sidelined the large, funnel-shaped face that was our primary objective and scrambled for a backup plan. After much debating over beers in Talkeetna, we hopped in Paul Roderick's plane and flew to the southwest fork of the Tokositna Glacier on April 11. Much to our surprise, during our two weeks on the glacier we had stacks of bluebird days and primo conditions, and we climbed three routes on the south faces of Mt. Providence (11,200') and Thunder Mountain (10,920').

Upon landing we immediately spied a pyramidal rock buttress on the left side of Providence that looked to be split by an aesthetic mixed couloir. The next day we had a leisurely breakfast, clicked into our skis around 9:30 a.m., and skinned up to the central bowl that funnels Providence's expansive south face. We crossed the bergschrund around 11 a.m. and began climbing up the leftmost couloir toward the triangular rock formation.

After approximately 1,500' of simul-climbing up 50°–70° snow, we took an obvious left exit out of the main couloir, over a small fluting, and up a left-trending snow ramp toward the base of the buttress. The end of the ramp revealed the beautiful, narrow cleft we had seen from base camp. Three stellar, rope-stretching pitches of mixed climbing followed, including some rolling ice and névé, a bouldery step, and a slightly terrifying bout of unprotected vertical trenching through sugar snow. We arrived at the prominent notch at the top of the buttress, slightly detached from Providence's heavily corniced west ridge, around 6 p.m., and began our descent from there. Despite not going to Providence's summit, Outside Providence (800m, IV M5 WI4) is an aesthetic line with quality climbing.

After several days of rest and a quick ski up the glacier, we turned our attention to the south face of Thunder Mountain, where we saw a narrow, possibly unclimbed system that looked to be choked with ice. Crossing the bergschrund at 7 a.m. on April 15, we climbed 1,000' of steep snow before branching right on a steep, rising traverse. After some simul-climbing and an easy mixed choke, several 70m pitches of steep, wild, and difficult ice steps brought us to some blue-collar sugar trenching, with decent rock gear, which took us up and out of the gully. From a spectacular belay on top of a fluting, we headed right up a narrow, moderate mixed slot, after which a short, spicy step of vertical ice led to more unprotected trenching and the ridge. We traversed several hundred feet east to a corniced high point at 10,850', beyond which lay a massive blank gendarme and overhanging cornices. We descended from there. Thunderstruck (1,000m, V WI5 M4) shares its start with Maxim (Huisman-Isaac, 2004) in the major couloir system just left of Ring of Fire (Cordes-DeCapio, 2001).

After a week of base camp lounging, many sausage breakfast sandwiches, and a pair of nasty head colds, we recovered enough to load our packs for one more outing. On April 22 we repeated Deadbeat (Cordes-DeCapio, 2001) to the base of the 60-foot summit cornice, which looked ready to part ways with the mountain, in 20 hours round-trip from base camp. With pitch after pitch of challenging ice and mixed climbing and a direct, aesthetic line to the summit, this route alone was worth a trip into this rarely visited fork of the range. 📷

– ANDY ANDERSON

HISTORICAL NOTE ON THUNDER MOUNTAIN: Geoff Hornby, long believed to have made the first ascent of Thunder Mountain with David Barlow in 1993, via a snow couloir on the right side of the south face and the upper eastern ridge, now says it's unclear whether they climbed beyond a corniced high point to the true summit, as they were in a whiteout with no altimeter. If that is the case, then the first ascent of the peak may have been by Kelly Cordes and Scott DeCapio in 2001, via their route Deadbeat.

CENTRAL ALASKA RANGE / RUTH GORGE

MT. BARRILL, BIRTHDAY PARTY

FROM APRIL 29 to May 1, Teresa Au (my wife) and I climbed a new route on the northeast face of Mt. Barrill (7,650', a.k.a. Barille or Barrille). This was our first trip to Alaska, and we flew to the Mountain House airstrip in mid-April, planning to warm up on moderate routes in the Ruth before attempting classic climbs on the Mooses Tooth and Mt. Huntington. But while skiing below Barrill, we spotted a series of stunning, long vertical ribbons of ice flowing down the entire height of the face.

That must be a classic, but what is it? I wondered. We hadn't seen anything describing this striking line in our pretrip research. "I don't care if it's been climbed or not, or even if it will go," I declared. "It looks amazing—we've got to try it!"

[Right] Nicolas Preitner leading difficult mixed terrain low on Birthday Party on the northeast face of Mt. Barrill. *Teresa Au*

[Above] **The northeast face of Mt. Barrill.** (1) Birthday Party (Au-Preitner, 2016). (2) Alaska Primer (Gilmore-Johnstone, 2011). Arrow marks the start of the Cobra Pillar (Donini-Tackle, 1991). At least two other routes are in between. The top of Mt. Huntington is visible in upper right. *Nicolas Preitner*

On our first attempt we were moving too slowly. On our second, when we were partway up the route, the early afternoon sun triggered showers of ice from the rock faces above. A small block smashed into my helmet and broke off a large chunk. Fortunately, I wasn't hurt and was able to duct-tape my helmet back together on the spot before rappelling.

Teresa vowed not to return, but after gazing at that glimmering, tantalizing line while resting in base camp, she had a change of heart and was ready for more. Our strategy for our third and successful attempt, beginning April 29, was an anti-alpine start: We slept in and started climbing in the afternoon, so we would reach the slopes that were exposed to icefall once the sun had stopped shining on the faces above. We climbed light, carrying no bivy gear except for a stove.

The climbing started with 60m of high-quality, steep waterfall ice (WI5+), with an exciting, slightly overhanging finish of chandelier ice and some mixed moves. We continued on a steep rock chimney and corner system (M5), with traces of ice—an equally aesthetic pitch, with balancey moves and good protection. We then climbed steep snow for about 250m until we met another vertical ice flow with chandelier ice (WI5+). We switched on our headlamps and kept climbing into the clear, star-filled night. Higher up, I spotted a little cave just big enough for the two of us to crouch inside after some chopping. Fortunately, the night was short and not very cold. We melted a few icicles to cook a freeze-dried meal, brewed up, and dozed for a bit before starting again. We finished the steep ice at first light.

A few moderate mixed pitches then led to a long vertical strip of sn'ice (AI5). The soft, hollow ice was hard to protect, and my crampons and tools would sometimes shear through without warning. My mind raced, but after two pitches the slope eased a bit and the ice became denser. Night fell again, and this time we rested and refueled while standing awkwardly on a narrow ice ledge. We yearned for a brief snooze, but snow started to whirl softly around us, and the icy chill seeping into our limbs made sleep impossible. The climbing had been spectacular, but I now felt a growing sense of urgency to get off the mountain, before either our judgment or the weather seriously deteriorated.

We resumed climbing before sunrise, and after a few moderate ice and snow leads we reached the final pitch before the summit ridge. Delicate moves on verglassed rock (M5) slowed us again, but we finally reached the snowy summit ridge about 45 hours after leaving the ground. It was now snowing heavily, and we were in a complete whiteout as we climbed the few hundred meters of deep snow to the summit. The total absence of visual cues made it hard to orient or even keep balance, but we found our way over the top to the northwestern snow slopes, which offered an easy but avalanche-prone walk down to the Ruth.

Birthday Party (850m, V WI5+ AI5 R M5, steep snow) had been packed with quality technical climbing from the first pitch to the last. It was the perfect way to celebrate my birthday, which was just a few days before. [*Editor's note: The 2016 route begins and finishes to the left of Alaska Primer (Gilmore-Johnstone, 2011), crossing that route twice in the middle section but sharing little ground with it.*] 📷 🔍

– NICOLAS PREITNER

MT. CHURCH, LES DÉMONS DE MINUIT; LITTLE JOHN AND OTHER ROUTES

DURING LATE APRIL and early May, an expedition of the Groupe Excellence Alpinisme National, a mentorship program of the federation of French alpine clubs (FFCAM), led by Mathieu Détrie, Frédéric Gentet, and Christophe Moulin, completed several new routes and significant repeats in the Ruth Gorge.

On April 28, Moulin, Mathieu Rideau, Antoine Rolle, and Steve Thibout climbed a mixed route on a small tower attached to the southeast face of Mt. Johnson, immediately to the left of the Escalator. The route (500m, 5.10 WI4+ M3 90° R) begins on ice smears left of a large corner. Sustained WI4 ice leads to a ridge, where the route passes a gendarme on the south side. Difficult rock then leads to steep and unprotected snow climbing on the summit mushroom of the tower, which they called Little John. They descended to the pocket glacier to the right and continued down the lower portion of the Escalator to return to the glacier.

On May 5, Détrie, Camille Marot, Benjamin Ribeyre, and Vincent Rigaud completed direct new route on the north face of Mt. Church. Les Démons de Minuit (1,300m, ED+ M7 R 90°) starts about 100m to the right of Memorial Gate

[Above] The ca 1,000m north face of Mt. Church in the Ruth Gorge. (1) For Whom the Bell Tolls (Bracey-Helliker, 2009). (2) Amazing Grace (Clapham-Pike, 2009). (3) My Friends Forever (Amano-Masumoto-Nagato, 2010). (4) Memorial Gate (Ichimura-Sato-Yamada, 2007, first ascent of the face). (5) Les Démons de Minuit (Détrie-Marot-Ribeyre-Rigaud, 2016). *Frédéric Gentet Collection*

(Ichimura-Sato-Yamada, 2007) and climbs directly up the imposing wall, utilizing a prominent chimney system. The lower part of the route featured sustained difficulties, including vertical snow and hard mixed; the crux sixth pitch required caving between a snow plug in a chimney. Above a prominent rock band, the technical difficulties eased, but the remaining 700m of steep snow flutings offered very little protection. The round trip took 22 hours.

Other significant ascents by the group include the third ascent of the Warrior's Way (4,400', AI4+ M5 R, 2006) on the east face of Mt. Grosvenor, by Moulin, Rideau, and Rolle; The Trailer Park (1,000m, WI6 M6, 2000) on London Tower, by Léo Billon, Gentet, Mathilde Oeuvrard, and Benjamin Védrines; and the east buttress of Mt. Bradley (1,600m, 5.10b M7 snow, 1987) by the same group. The latter may have been only the second ascent of the full east buttress.

Billon, Oeuvrard, Gentet, and Védrines also climbed the north buttress of the Rooster Comb (1,200m, AI5 M6 A2+), a route that has seen many attempts but few successes since it was established in 1981 by Britons Nick Colton and Timothy Leach. Mathilde Oeuvrard is believed to be the first woman to reach the summit of the Rooster Comb by any route. 📷

– ANDY ANDERSON, *WITH INFORMATION FROM FRÉDÉRIC GENTET AND DENALI NATIONAL PARK*

ALASKA RANGE / DELTA RANGE

TRIANGLE PEAK, WEST FACE, POSSIBLE FIRST ASCENT

IN APRIL 2015, Bryan Sehmel and Jason Shorey climbed the west face of Triangle Peak (ca 7,200'), which is typically accessed from the Castner Glacier and climbed via the moderate north ridge. Sehmel and Shorey camped below the Broken Glacier and then followed this to a short icefall and an obvious couloir in the center of the west face. About 1,000' up, they passed a rock band by a moderate ice and mixed step, then continued on solid snow, which steepened to 70° near the top. A quick jaunt up the northern ridge brought them to the summit. They descended by an easier section of the face to the north of the direct line. In total they spent about eight hours on the route (2,600', 70°). 📄 📷

– *INFORMATION PROVIDED BY* JASON SHOREY

TALKEETNA MOUNTAINS

SHEEP RIVER GLACIER, NEW ROUTES

OVER SEVEN DAYS in mid-July, Chris Williams, Gus Barber, and I climbed three new routes above the Sheep River Glacier, in the Talkeetna Mountains, north of the Matanuska Valley. I had seen photos from a friend's ski trip in this area, and the mountains were reminiscent of Little Switzerland. As far as I could tell, little or no rock climbing had been done here (or at least reported).

After a helicopter flight from Sutton and a stormy night, we skied up the glacier to the base of Peak 8,733'. A 300' splitter crack went up the lower south-facing wall to gain a ridgeline. We climbed this in two long pitches on excellent rock (5.9 and 5.10), followed by easier climbing (5.2–5.8) up the ridge. We descended our line of ascent by rappelling and downclimbing, and returned to camp at 2:30 a.m., having established Funding Denied (1,300', IV 5.10). [*The route tops out the prominent main buttress of the peak, without continuing to the true summit of Peak 8,733'.*]

Our second route was on the east side of a short, unnamed buttress west of Peak 8,733'. Life Insurance Policy (650', III 5.10 X) climbs deceptively good-looking rock that deteriorated as we went higher. One excellent pitch in the middle of the route went at mid-5.10, but without any good protection. After six pitches (5.7–5.10), a thunderstorm developed and we decided

[Above] Gus Barber exits the chimney on the first pitch of Funding Denied (1,300', IV 5.10) on Peak 8,733'. The "Life Insurance Policy" buttress is visible at far left. *Lang Van Dommelen*

to descend from a pinnacle about 500' shy of the summit. We also made a brief attempt on the central southeast face of Peak 8,733', to the right of Funding Denied, and then climbed a 100' crack, Hypothermic Sending Temps (5.11-), on a small wall between the Life Insurance Policy buttress and Peak 8,733'. 📷 🗎

— LANG VAN DOMMELEN

CHUGACH MOUNTAINS

CRACKED ICE ARENA: NEW ROCK ROUTES

OVER MULTIPLE WEEKENDS throughout July and August, a group of friends and I completed nine long rock routes in the Cracked Ice Arena, a popular backcountry skiing zone near Thompson Pass. These peaks are better known for their remarkable steep powder skiing than for technical climbing; it is one of the few ranges where it is easier to obtain summits in the spring and winter months, due to the cohesive nature of the coastal snowpack. As such, it is entirely possible some of these routes, or parts of them, may have been ascended or descended in winter conditions by heli-skiers or ski mountaineers.

We climbed the northwest arête (1,500', III 5.7 AI3) of Cracked Ice (6,513'), as well as numerous routes on Cracked Ice Spire and Graywacke Tower, both of which we named after finding no record of technical climbing. All of the routes were approached from the Richardson Highway, and each offers a pleasurable day of alpine climbing that includes glacier travel, high-quality rock (for the Chugach), river crossings, and of course bushwhacking. Brief descriptions and and photos of all routes can be found at the AAJ website: publications.americanalpineclub.org. 🗎 📷

— TAYLOR BROWN

WEST FACE DIRECT

A MAJOR NEW ROUTE ON CELENO PEAK IN THE UNIVERSITY RANGE

BY GRAHAM ZIMMERMAN

As THE PLANE swooped toward the Canyon Creek Glacier, Chris Wright and I caught the first glimpse of our objective: the 6,000' west face of Celeno Peak (13,395'). With our eyes glued to the window, we watched as it simultaneously towered above and fell below us, our plane dwarfed by its fantastic mass. Our pilot, Jay Claus, had made the first ascent of this peak, with Kevin Ditzler, in 2012 (*AAJ 2013*), and as he circled in he pointed out the route they had climbed up the peak's northwest ridge, which we planned to descend.

Later, when the sound of the plane had long faded and base camp was partially situated, we stood staring at the face, still 4km away, scanning upward along our proposed route. On paper it had seemed so reasonable, but now, from the glacier, it looked dark and wild, hanging high above us. Storm clouds closed in that night, giving a reprieve from the looming presence of the mountain. Our forecast showed 24 hours of storms before the onset of a large high-pressure window that was sure to give us an opportunity to attempt the wall.

On May 12, after waiting two days for the mountain to clear, we launched at 1 a.m. The route began with 2,000' of snow and ice to 70°, which we climbed unroped. A small section of this climbing was exposed to objective hazard from above, and we climbed quickly to cross this gauntlet in less than 15 minutes. This placed us on the mixed spur that we planned to climb directly to the summit.

I led the day's first block of pitches through fantastic mixed terrain, sustained at M4 to M5, with a stout M6 chimney crux. Chris then led two moderate yet extremely loose pitches that placed us 3,000' above the start of the route. There, we stopped in late afternoon to bivy, digging a platform into a thin snow ridge on the crest of the spur.

A hundred feet above the bivy was a geological contact between the granitic lower half of the mountain and the metamorphic upper half. The bottom of the metamorphic rock presented a severely overhanging headwall. On the morning of May 13, Chris led two moderate pitches that brought us to what appeared to be a weakness in the barrier. He then spent more than three hours leading the route's crux: a wildly steep and loose pitch of 5.10 X A2+ that can only be described as totally fucked—a very compelling reason for this route never to be repeated. Making the final aid moves through a roof, he dislodged a large section of rocks, damaging one of the ropes and crushing a carabiner lower on the pitch.

Fortunately, the core shot was close to one end of the rope. After repairs, I took the lead through two more loose but moderate rock pitches to the top of the band, where we found a 3' by 4' platform on which to brew up water

[Below] **The 6,000-foot west face of Celeno,** showing the 2016 route and bivouacs. *Chris Wright*

and sit out the heat of the afternoon. We'd climbed only 500', but lower-angle climbing lay above.

Departing our small perch at 2 a.m., I led through two final pitches of easy mixed before the route changed to steep snow and ice. We simul-climbed to the top of the spur before cutting hard right to reach an ice gully that led toward the summit. The day's climbing consisted of approximately 2,500' of sustained 70˚ ice, with short sections of 90° to 95˚ ice and snow as we crossed over flutings. During this time the weather deteriorated, with visibility reduced to around 100'. It came as a huge relief when we reached a large, flat snow ledge just below the summit in the early afternoon.

On May 15, we once again started before sunrise, making our way up 200' of moderate snow to the summit, under clear skies. As the sun rose over the range, we marveled at the ocean of mountains surrounding us, including Mt. Logan, Mt. Saint Elias, University Peak, and the Atna Peaks.

For the rest of the day we reversed the first-ascent route, down the northwest ridge and along the edge of a massive hanging plateau, dubbed the Balcony by Claus. The three miles of elegant ridge climbing were reminiscent of sections of the west ridge of Mt. Hunter. At around 1 p.m., at the top of the Black Couloir, which Claus and Ditzler had climbed during the first ascent of Celeno, we waited until the evening before rappelling and downclimbing the 4,000' chute. We reached our skis on the Canyon Creek Glacier at 11:30 p.m. and made it to base camp an hour later, exhausted and hungry. Our trip was supported by the Mount Everest Foundation (U.K.) and the New Zealand Alpine Club's Expedition Fund.

SUMMARY: First ascent of the West Face Direct (6,000', 5.10 X A2+ M6 95°) of Celeno Peak (13,395') and second ascent of the peak, in the St. Elias Mountains, by Chris Wright and Graham Zimmerman, May 12–16, 2016. 📷

[Right] Chris Wright on the crux rock pitch of the west face of Celeno. This lead, on day two of the climb, took more than three hours and went at 5.10 X A2+. *Graham Zimmerman*

CENTRAL TOWER OF RAPA NUI, THE NORTHERN BELLE

On June 18, Chris Moore, Cooper Varney, Will Wacker, and I completed the first ascent of the Central Tower of Rapa Nui (7,015'). This formation is the centerpiece of a collection of granite towers two miles east of Klukwah Mountain (7,000'), to the north of Haines. The Central Tower caught my eye while scouting for rock around Haines by air and ground over the past three years, a search I began after reading Will's report exposing the area he called Rapa Nui (*AAJ 2013*).

All the rock towers in this region are truly remote, and ski-plane access is what makes this whole dream possible. In the same spirit that alpinists hear the calling toward unclimbed terrain, Drake Olson, the owner and operator of Fly Drake, enjoys the challenge of finding new landing zones in these unexplored areas.

After flying in on June 9 and establishing our base camp on an unnamed glacier below our objective, we got right to work, utilizing the endless light of the Alaskan summer. Over several days we worked through mostly marginal weather, pushing our high point up through immaculate steep, white granite. We'd work the pitches free during the warm hours of the day, establish a high point by evening, then rappel down to our skis and ride back to base camp at night.

A few nights before the full-moon solstice of 2016, we set up our portaledges high on the tower and enjoyed incredible views of the Fairweather Range. The following day we established two more pitches to the top, completing the Northern Belle (1,500' of climbing, V 5.11+ A2 50˚). The route features a 300' approach pitch of snow, followed by seven long pitches of rock. It was our intention to establish a pure free line to the

[Above] **The Central Tower of Rapa Nui, the most prominent formation in a cluster of spires outside of Haines, showing the Northern Belle (1,500', V 5.11+ A2 50˚).** *Will Wacker*

top, but we were forced to aid a steep headwall section at A2. I'm positive that under the right conditions a variation could be established that would turn this into one of the wildest, steepest, and cleanest free routes in Alaska. Right now, the free climbing crux is the 220' third pitch, with steep, sustained, sport-like climbing, protected by gear and bolts, through highly featured terrain (5.11+). All the belays are bolted and equipped for rappelling.

This was one of the best trips any of us had ever done, and each team member had to draw upon all of his past experiences to make our goal a reality. Seeing our strategies, teamwork, and climbing skills prove effective has left us even more inspired, and this is certainly just one of many more expeditions to come in this powerfully beautiful area of Alaska. 📖 📷

– TYLER BOTZON

[Top] Tyler Botzon scopes the next pitch on the Central Tower of Rapa Nui. [Bottom] Cooper Varney contemplates donning rock shoes in chilly temperatures as Chris Moore leads out. *Will Wacker*

CANADA

FIGHTING TILL DAWN
TWO ROUTES IN THE RAGGED RANGE

BY PAT GOODMAN

I MADE MY ninth expedition to the Ragged Range in Nahanni National Park in 2015; it was the second for both Jessa Goebel and James Q Martin. The year before, Jessa and I had attempted the first ascent of the south face of Dawn Mist Mountain (a.k.a. Moraine Hill), and Q was with Jeff Achey, Jeremy Collins, and me when we made the first free ascent of the Phoenix Wall, via Phreenix (VI 5.11, *AAJ 2013*).

Kluane Airways dropped us at Vampire Lake in mid-July with 18 days of provisions. The weather, for the most part, was quite wet; it would rain for a few hours then dry up for a few hours, like clockwork. We had one clear 27-hour window and a mostly clear 23-hour window, during which we sent our two new routes.

Moraine Hill was first climbed in 1968, via the fourth-class west rib, by Bill Buckingham and party. He named the peak Dawn Mist Mountain during an expedition in which they named most of the prominent spires in the Vamps and climbed them by the way of least resistance. Jessa and I faced several unexpected hurdles in 2014, from deep snow and slush on the North Moraine Hill Glacier, which must be crossed for several miles to reach the wall, to Jessa fighting the reality of this area's extreme solitude. She rallied, though, and fought with determination while climbing—it was inspirational watching her take control of her mind and try HARD! However, we had terrible weather that kept us tent-bound except for one attempt that ended after four cold pitches in a snowstorm.

When we got to Moraine this time, we found the wall running with water after a big snowstorm. We opted for a line to the right that looked less "splitter" but, in all honesty, was probably a better, more consistently steep rig than our 2014 attempt. The cruxes were more about staying calm while free climbing with wet shoes and numb fingers than any particular sequence. (A dab of fresh snow crowded many of the lesser-angled features on the wall.) That said, pitch four was pretty feisty—we had to do a big iron-cross, backhand move left from a fingery flake (wet, bad feet) into the base of a slightly overhanging, stem-box corner—one of those features in which you jam your shoulders and wiggle around until you can get your feet under you. My fingers were about as sensitive as chopsticks, but I reckon that section was solid 5.11. Most of the pitches had some sort of wide (5.10ish) funkiness to overcome.

[Below] The south side of Dawn Mist Mountain (Moraine Hill) showing (1) 2014 attempt and (2) Fighting Till Dawn (Goebel-Goodman-Martin, 2015). The buttresses to the right are unclimbed. *Pat Goodman*

[Photo] Pat Goodman, pitch four of Fighting Till Dawn. James Q Martin

I led the entire route, free and onsight, with no bolts. Jessa followed with only one fall, while Q ascended a rope I fixed as we went, in order to capture the action in photos. We reached the summit around 11:30 p.m. as the sun was beginning to set. The sky was on *fire—a* stunning display of colors. It was Jessa's first big, remote summit, and she was glowing with delight. These kinds of moments are fleeting and few people ever get to experience them. To be a part of that, and to witness her struggle and success, especially after getting skunked the previous year, was a high point of my life.

We rapped a series of lower-angled gullies left of our ascent route to our 2014 high point, then down the anchors from that attempt—nine raps in all—and returned to the tent 22 hours after leaving. The south face of Dawn Mist has more adventure value than high-quality free climbing, but three shorter (500–1,000'), neighboring buttresses that top out on a separate, unclimbed spire look to offer excellent splitters up golden granite.

After this climb, we wanted try something a little less committing, since the weather was fickle at best. Three distinct sub-walls flank the southern aspect of the massive granite formation known as the Sundial (a.k.a. Mt. Dracula), whose northeast aspect hosts the Phoenix. Hank dubbed the wall Bela Lugosi, in honor of the original Dracula actor.

Our route wandered from crack to crack, ledge to ledge, avoiding bottomed-out grooves and trying to find clean cracks. We eventually traversed from the right side of the wall to the left, but it was a very fun outing and a pretty good route. This wall offers excellent free climbing potential, especially if you have time to clean and work around the crackless features. We descended via a fourth-class scramble to the west, going 16 hours tent to tent.

Our trip was sponsored by Parks Canada in exchange for historical, logistical, and climbing information I'm providing. Parks Canada is working with the Alpine Club of Canada to build a website that will cover climbing throughout Nahanni National Park. Can you imagine our National Park Service sponsoring climbing trips? Me neither. No wonder I love climbing up here so much.

SUMMARY: Two new routes in the Vampire Peaks (Ragged Range), a subrange of the Logan Mountains in the Northwest Territories, by Jessa Goebel, Pat Goodman, and James Q Martin (all USA). Fighting Till Dawn (460m, V 5.11- R) was the first ascent of the south face of Dawn Mist Mountain (Moraine Hill) and second ascent of the peak, on July 19–20, 2015. Ramshackle Affair (330m, IV 5.11+ A0) was the first ascent of the Bela Lugosi Wall, on July 26, 2015. 📷 🔍

NORTHWEST TERRITORIES / RAGGED RANGE

THUNDER MOUNTAIN (MT. NIRVANA), UNSUPPORTED ASCENT, AND PEAK 46

ON JUNE 13, Len Vanderstar and I set out to make the first ascent of Thunder Mountain (9,097', a.k.a. Mt. Nirvana) without air support. Before 2016, this peak—the highest in the Northwest Territories—had seen five documented ascents, all relying on support from helicopters or floatplanes. I had also made an unsuccessful attempt on the summit in 2015, helicoptering in from Watson Lake to try a new route on the southwest face with Dave Custer and Susan Ruff (*AAJ 2016*).

From the mining town of Tungsten, Len and I paddled down the Flat River with Ron Vanderstar and Luke Weyman. After two days of difficult whitewater, involving many portages, we took out at an unnamed stream, stashed our boats in the trees, and headed into the Ragged Range. Three days of tough bushwhacking, a glacier crossing, and alpine meadows brought us to the foot of the east face of Thunder Mountain.

[Above] The east face of Thunder Mountain (9,097'), seen from a helicopter, in September 2015. The only known route on this aspect zigzags up the sunlit central face to the saddle, then follows the ridge rightward to the top. The roughly 500-meter wall in right foreground is on the Minotaur and was climbed in 2000. *Mike Fischesser*

After one false start when sunny, warm weather released multiple avalanches from the upper snowfield, Len and I returned to camp, slept for a few hours, then started another attempt at midnight on June 20. This time we reached the upper snowfield at 3 a.m., when it was still firm, and easily made it to the base of the upper face. I believe our line here roughly followed the route of the 1996 expedition that climbed the first and only known route up the east face (*AAJ 1997*). We reached the summit ridge around midnight, and after a nap continued up easy snow and fourth-class rock to the summit, where I lay on my stomach to tap the highest point, a cornice overhanging the north face. We took another long nap on the ridge, waiting for the evening chill to firm up the upper snowfield, then rappelled the route through the night, returning to camp 51 hours after leaving.

On June 25 Len and I started our journey back to the truck at Tungsten, Ron and Luke having headed to the boats a few days earlier. We scrambled partway up a gully just east of the Minotaur, then climbed four pitches of moderate snow and rock to a high col, and then rappelled into the north cirque. Three days of hiking brought us to the west edge of the Ragged Range, where we had enough extra time for a brief side trip to unclimbed Peak 46. We crossed the northern glacier, Len led a few steep snow pitches, and then I led a moderate rock pitch across a knife-edge ridge to the crumbling summit. The next day we dropped into the Flat River Valley, and three more days of difficult bushwhacking brought us back to Tungsten. 📷

– ERIC GILBERTSON, *USA*

[Above] Toshiyuki Yamada on the 5.10 corner crack of Happy Trio, belayed by Noboru Kikuchi. *Takeshi Tani*

WADDINGTON RANGE, ASPERITY MOUNTAIN, HAPPY TRIO

WHILE I WAS taking my ACMG apprentice alpine guide exam, Craig McGee, one of my instructors, told me about the Waddington Range. "It's like Chamonix, but ten times as big," he explained. "Also, there is still a lot of potential for first ascents." I immediately decided to go.

Noboru Kikuchi, Toshiyuki Yamada, and I flew in to Rainy Knob and set up base camp on April 30. While scouting around the Tiedemann group, we found ourselves staring up at Asperity's massive southwest face. It's so big it hurts your neck just to try to see the top!

At 4 a.m. on May 5 we left camp, following the Asperity Couloir (leading to the Asperity-Tiedemann col) until we moved up a snow gully to the right, with about 200m of WI3. From here, we picked our way up into good, mostly dry rock. Just before sunset, we stood below what appeared to be the crux, a 60m hand crack in a corner. We debated whether to continue or bivy—we did not have many number 2 cams, and there was ice throughout the crack. Eventually, Yamada took the rack and started up. In spite of some serious runouts, he made it through the pitch (about 5.10a). Above the corner, we joined him on an icy ledge and established a small bivy site around midnight. The next day, in perfect weather, amazing cracks and some snow sections led us to a knife-edge ridge at the headwall. We made it to the summit around 4 p.m. and then descended into the night via the Asperity Couloir. We established our route without bolts and called the line Happy Trio (950m, ED- 5.10a WI3). [*The Japanese route starts near the original route on the southwest face (Elson-McLane, 2010) but stays to the left in the first half and then to the right in the upper section.*]

— TAKESHI TANI, *CANADA*

MT. BUTE, SCHOOL OF ROCK, FIRST FREE ASCENT

IN 2009, BRUCE KAY, Jimmy Martinello, and Jay Sinnes put up School of Rock (1,900m, VI 5.11 A2), a 50-pitch route up the complete west buttress of Mt. Bute. In July 2015, after a three-day approach from Homathko Camp, near the north tip of Bute Inlet, Jason Ammerlaan, Nathan MacDonald, and Luke Neufield free climbed the route in two days at 5.12.

— DOUGALD MACDONALD, *WITH INFORMATION FROM THE CANADIAN ALPINE JOURNAL*

SQUAMISH, STAWAMUS CHIEF, LONG ROUTES AND FREE ASCENTS

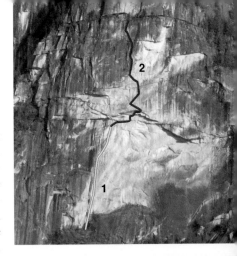

OVER THE PAST few seasons, the mighty Chief has continued to yield stellar new routes, with several big lines. In August 2015, Tony McLane and Jorge Ackermann finally punched through the top of the Sheriff's Badge on the North Walls with their brilliant extension to the Daily Planet (4 pitches, 5.12a) dubbed Daily Universe (5 pitches, 5.12b). The full nine-pitch route traverses through overhanging blocks, corners, and cracks to breach the very apex of the Badge formation—a long-anticipated feat.

At the start of May 2016, Sonnie Trotter made the coveted FFA of the steep, sweeping Prow Wall (8 pitches, 5.14a), directly across the South Gully from Squamish Buttress. Trotter spent five days prepping and cleaning the central line, which had thwarted numerous parties over two decades. The free Prow Wall is the Chief's first multi-pitch 5.14.

Another recent addition to the Prow (from 2014) is Colin Moorhead and Andre Ike's Written in Stone (8 pitches, 5.11d), which was the first route to breach the left side of Prow Wall. While belaying Trotter on his Prow Wall send, Tom Wright took note of the huge dike that runs between these two routes and returned a few days later to bolt and climb Written Into The Prow (5.12c), a high-quality link-up of some of the best pitches from both routes.

On the sunny west face of the Chief, the two most notable big lines from the past couple seasons are Sunset Strip and Labyrinth. Yet another Moorhead classic, Sunset Strip (12 pitches, 5.10d) is quite sustained and utilizes short sections of existing routes in the Western Dihedrals (The Gauntlet, Crap Crags, Millennium Falcon, Sticky Fingers), with about 70 percent new terrain. Meanwhile, on the Tantalus Wall, Labyrinth (5 pitches, 5.12c) was added by Marc-André Leclerc and Luke Neufeld. This incredibly technical route climbs elegant, thin dikes that are a unique hallmark of the Tantalus Wall.

[Top] **The Sheriff's Badge formation on Squamish's North Walls, with (1) Daily Planet and (2) Daily Universe, climbed in 2015.** [Bottom] Sonnie Trotter on the crux pitch of the Prow Wall (8 pitches, 5.14a), a "last great problem" in Squamish that went down in 2016. *Rich Wheater*

A cold snap in mid-January of 2017 brought another kind of climbing to the Chief: a full-length ice climb, mostly following the route Ultimate Everything, for 10 pitches of Chamonix-like runnels. Jia Condon, Jason Kruk, Paul McSorley, and Tony Richardson were first up the line, followed quickly by several other parties before the rare flow disappeared. [*The online version of this report, at publications.americanalpineclub.org, documents many other Squamish-area developments from recent years.*]

– RICH WHEATER, *CANADA*

[Above] Marc-André Leclerc follows pitch two of Hidden Dragon on the Chinese Puzzle Wall. *Brette Harrington*

HIDDEN DRAGON
CHINESE PUZZLE WALL CLIMBED AFTER YEARS OF ATTEMPTS

BY BRETTE HARRINGTON

MARC-ANDRÉ LECLERC FIRST pointed out the Chinese Puzzle Wall three years ago, as we climbed the Northeast Buttress of Mt. Slesse. Across the Nesakwatch Creek valley, on the south side of the west buttress of South Illusion Peak, was a diamond-shaped outcrop of steep, white granite. Why hadn't this beautiful 500m wall, just an hour's hike from the trailhead, seen an ascent? I would later learn that, within the small community of climbers who actually knew about the wall, it had a formidable reputation. It is almost entirely overhanging, with looming blocks the size of grand pianos suspended by unknown forces. The Chinese Puzzle Wall is aptly named.

The wall has had five known attempts. In 1986 and '87, Nick Jones, Bill Noble, and Kirt Sellers made two unsuccessful ground-up attempts on a line near the middle of the wall they called the Warlock. Then, in 1994, Fred Beckey, Mark Maffe, and Steve Must tried to climb the wall, but were stymied after the first two pitches. In 2000, Michael Crapo and Ben Demenech got a few pitches up and bailed due to loose blocks. Finally, Tone McLane and Dan Tetzlaff made an attempt in 2008 but took a scary gear-ripping fall on pitch one and bailed.

In August, Marc and I hiked our gear up the steep and forested slope to the base of the wall and spent a total of eight days establishing its first complete route. As we climbed the route, we had to establish nearly every pitch by aid, just to clean out the moss-filled cracks so typical of the Pacific Northwest. While one of us cleaned on a fixed line, the other aid-soloed new terrain above. In this manner, we divided and conquered, each of us ending up with dirt-plastered faces. After establishing a few pitches, we would rappel down, free climb back to our high point, then bump our camp higher up the wall.

By day three we made it to the "Mirage Corner," which appeared black from below and white from above due to a lichen that only grew on the underside of the textured granite. I spent all afternoon aiding and preparing this pitch. We were about halfway up the wall and had greatly underestimated the amount of cleaning that would be required to establish an all-free line, so we bailed to resupply and return in a few days.

I was now ready to try leading the Mirage. The crux was fiddling in gear, almost blindly, into the undulating flare while laybacking the slopey edge. Pumped out of my mind and just a few meters from the top, I ran it out in desperation. It was useless, as my hands peeled away from the crack and I took a mega-whipper. During the fall the rope jammed into the crack and suffered a severe core shot, leaving Marc and I with two options: Bail and return with a new rope or continue and be careful about the damaged line. We opted for the latter. Climbing the next pitch, we heard a deep rumble. Across the valley, the pocket glacier on Mt. Slesse was sliding. As thousands of tons of ice cascaded into the cirque below, we were reminded of the power of the mountains.

[Top] The south-facing Chinese Puzzle Wall, below North Illusion Peak (left) and South Illusion Peak, photographed from near Pocket Peak, south of Mt. Slesse. *Drew Brayshaw* [Bottom] Brette Harrington on the sharp end on the sixth pitch of Hidden Dragon, the first complete route on the Chinese Puzzle Wall. *Marc-André Leclerc*

Over the next five days we continued up more beautiful corners in the same relentless style. On the eighth day, we free climbed the final pitches. We then rappelled the entire face on our dangerously core-shot rope while carrying our haul bag and ledge. Using a hand drill, we equipped the route with bolted rappel stations at every other belay. We also equipped two variation pitches that go at 5.12c. Hidden Dragon follows continuous corners flowing gracefully around the giant roofs throughout the face. The rock quality was excellent, and the climbing was incredible. There is potential to establish more lines here in a similar, ground-up style, and we are confident this will become a popular wall in the future.

SUMMARY: First ascent of Hidden Dragon (11 pitches, 5.12b), the first route up the Chinese Puzzle Wall in the North Cascades. 📷

MT. SLESSE, INDIRECT EAST FACE

THE SECOND ASCENT of the East Face Route (ED2 VI 5.9 A3+) on Mt. Slesse—first climbed in 1997 by Sean Easton and Dave Edgar—has been on the minds of local rock climbers for almost 20 years. In spite of attempts by skilled climbers, the route remained unrepeated. Craig McGee and various partners freed the first seven pitches in the mid-2000s at 5.12c, but could not reach the easier upper wall. After studying photos, I came to believe a traverse could be made from the start of the East Pillar Route rightward into the East Face. It seemed like dodging the difficulty of the lower face could make for a nice moderate free climb.

On August 11, after scrambling up the lower ridge, Paul Cordy and I began some new pitches in the warm morning sun. Our long, traversing third pitch led to a particularly committing location above the steep lower east face. "This rock is super solid," Paul declared confidently during his first lead of the day. Encouraged, I looked up just in time to see Paul's only hand and foot holds break simultaneously. He fell a meter but somehow caught himself on a jug, preventing a much bigger fall. The impact broke two fingers, although not badly enough to stop Paul from following the remainder of the route. A more serious injury here would have proven very inconvenient.

We found the climbing to be well protected at times but also with big run-out sections. It wasn't clear how well we followed the original aid line. We may have done a variation on the last steep pitch, climbing left up a ramp. Belay bolts were not in good shape, nor did we find them at every anchor, as the East Face Route topo states. In the end, we climbed 16 pitches up to 5.10. Only a standard rack is necessary. 📷

— TONY MCLANE, *CANADA*

MT. MACDONALD, LITTLE FACE, POSITION OF COMFORT

HIGH ABOVE THE Trans-Canada Highway, in the Rogers Pass area, Mt. MacDonald (2,883m) holds a commanding view. The peak is comprised mostly of quartzite, and just like its neighbors, it boasts long, clean ridgelines of solid (enough) rock. What makes MacDonald unique is a particularly steep and sustained face of golden rock. This 500m to 600m wall is ironically known as the Little Face, first climbed by the visionary Waterman Route (600m, 5.8 A3, 1974).

[Left] Tony McLane on pitch six of Position of Comfort, at the start of the steep, golden quartzite on Mt. MacDonald's Little Face. *Jason Ammerlaan*

[Above] The North Pillar and Little Face of Mt. MacDonald (2,883m), showing approximate location of known routes. The North Pillar is ca 1,000m high, and the Little Face is 500m to 600m. (1) North Pillar (Kay-Walsh, 2005). (2) North Pillar Direct (Relph-Walsh, 2010). (3) Prime Rib (Moorhead-Walsh, 2003). (4) Waterman Route (Waterman-Waterman, 1974). (5) The Blind Watchmaker (Dorsey-Van Oort; incomplete line shown, as of 2016; dotted line shows 2016 connection to Position of Comfort). (6) Position of Comfort (Ammerlaan-McLane, 2016). (7) Dorsey-Mackaness, 2015 (the climbers found older pitons on this line). (8) Haley-Schaefer, 2014 (climbed during off-route attempt on Primal Rib; the climbers continued up the northwest ridge to MacDonald's summit). (9) Short Ribs (Cummings-Sproul, 2009). *Jon Walsh*

On August 4 and 5, 2016, Tony McLane and I established a new line on the Little Face, which we dubbed the Position of Comfort (510m, 5.11+ A2). Our route ascends an obvious line of weakness through the lower tier of the face to reach a large ledge with a perfect bivy cave. From the ledge it tackles the steepest section of rock all the way to the ridgeline that connects to the summit of Little MacDonald, and eventually to the northwest ridge of Mt. MacDonald.

Ryan Thorpe and I established the initial four pitches. A week later, after traveling back home to Squamish, I teamed up with Tony and returned to finish the new line in alpine style over three days. The first evening, following the approach, we slept at the base of the route. We began climbing early the next day, leaving our boots in a cave after the initial four pitches, having decided we probably wouldn't be going all the way to the top of the mountain. Tony had the bright idea of bringing our socks along, "just in case of an unplanned bivy." This proved to be a wise decision. Just a few pitches from the top, with daylight fading, we knew we were close. After so much hard climbing, it seemed our best chance to finish the route on this trip would be to shiver it out and finish the final pitches in the morning.

Overall, we freed the majority of the route's 13 pitches, with three pitches requiring short sections of aid (KBs, LAs, Peckers, and some thin cams). The real crux of the route came in finding the line of weakness and connecting features. The steep quartzite was difficult to read, and the corner systems were inconsistent.

We placed two bolts for an anchor on top of pitch 10 but did not place any protection bolts. We did not summit Mt. MacDonald after cresting the ridge, as climbing the wall was our goal and our appetite was sated after a cold night shivering together in the position of comfort on a small ledge.

After reaching the subsummit of Little Face, we made three 60m raps to join up with a line that Ben Dorsey and Harry van Oort are working on. We finished our raps down their anchor stations to the base, picking up our boots along the way. [*Editor's note: The incomplete line, which lies to the left of Position of Comfort and to the right of the 1974 Waterman route, is called the Blind Watchmaker and is 5.11d A0 to its high point, six pitches up. Shortly after the first ascent of Position of Comfort, Dorcey and van Oort returned to their own line and, seeking an easier finish, ended up joining Position of Comfort and following that route to the top, seeing the first ascensionsts' chalk along the way. They aided the same sections that Ammerlaan and McLane did.*] 📷

— JASON AMMERLAAN, *CANADA*

SNOWPATCH SPIRE, MINOTAUR DIRECT; EASTPOST SPIRE, SICK AND TWISTED

ON AUGUST 19, Colin Moorhead and I rolled out of Golden at 6 p.m. for the Bugaboos. Fifty-one hours later we returned, having completed two new multi-pitch routes.

Our first line, Minotaur Direct (16 pitches, 5.11+) on Snowpatch Spire's east face, was the culmination of a multi-year project dating back to 2011. That year, Colin and I started on Labyrinth (Simms-Walsh, 2009) and then ventured into new terrain on the Minotaur, beginning with what's now its sixth pitch. We rejoined Labyrinth for its last three pitches after completing seven new leads, including free variations of the aid route Les Bruixes Es Pentinen.

In 2014, Michelle Kadatz and I established a five-pitch direct start to Minotaur. Over several sessions in 2015 and 2016, we continued to work on Minotaur ground-up, cleaning the cracks, bolting the stations, and pushing the direct finish until we were only 60m below the summit ridge. When Michelle's schedule got too busy, she gave me permission to find another partner. On a whim, I reached out to Colin, who was living in Squamish and usually busy guiding. He cleared his schedule and made the nine-hour drive. We stumbled into Applebee Camp by moonlight on August 19. Next day, it took us about 14 hours round-trip to complete the route, including bolting the last two belays and brushing the final 60m on our way down.

The 500-meter east face of Snowpatch Spire has experienced a "golden age" of free climbing in the past decade, with many new free routes from 5.12 to 5.14. Jon Walsh, responsible for several of these climbs, has produced a high-resolution photo showing all known routes on the face. Find it with this report at publications.americanalpineclub.org. *Jon Walsh*

Despite feeling fully satisfied and quite sore, we decided we might as well attempt a shorter route before hiking out. Chris Brazeau and I had a project going on the south face of Eastpost Spire, just ten minutes' walk from camp. In late 2015 and early season 2016, we had put in the route ground-up, on sparse gear, and then added a few bolts. But neither of us had led the crux second pitch clean. Chris, who was at Applebee at the time, suggested that Colin and I go for it. We had low expectations, given our fatigue, but I ended up sending. After Colin arrived at the belay at the end of the fourth pitch, he said, "This is sick and twisted." I agreed, hence the route name: Sick and Twisted (5 pitches, 5.12a). It was surprising to discover something like this right beside the main climbers' campground. But it just goes to show, there's still plenty out there left to climb. 📖 📷

— JON WALSH, *CANADA*

MEN WITH OPTIONS: *Not previously reported in the AAJ, a new route on the east face of Snowpatch was completed in July 2014, between Labyrinth and Sweet Sylvia. Chris Geisler, Crosby Johnston, Joshua Lavigne, and Simon Meis worked on the 11-pitch line, Men With Options, which currently goes at 5.12 A1. A topo can be found with this year's Snowpatch Spire report at the AAJ website.*

THE MINARET, RETINAL CIRCUS, FIRST FREE ASCENT

THE MINARET IS a gorgeous prow shaped like a rocket ship that leans against the south side of South Howser Tower. Despite having made many trips to the Bugaboos, I'd never climbed on it. In August, Maury Birdwell, Leo Houlding, Jesse Huey, and I ponied up some loonies for a heli and set up a deluxe base camp a five-minute walk away from the Minaret.

Early in the trip we spied some impressive headwall splitters, and guidebook sleuthing revealed the line to be Retinal Circus, a 600m 5.11 A2 climbed by Aaron Martin and Zack Smith in 2001. On our first two attempts we made incremental progress, sussing out sequences and figuring out the best path for free climbing. Down low, slammed-shut corners necessitated some crafty, wandering face climbing. "Wish we had brought double ropes, mate," remarked Leo. The Brits love their double ropes. Note to future ascensionists: They definitely wouldn't hurt.

On our third attempt in two weeks (we took breaks from the project to climb other routes), we cracked the code and arrived at

[Above] **The Minaret, showing the line followed for the first free ascent of Retinal Circus (600m, 5.12+). The climbers likely deviated from the original 2001 route several times in search of free climbing terrain. Just left of this formation is the classic Beckey-Chouinard Route on South Howser Tower.** *Chris Weidner*

the centerpiece of the route: the much-ogled headwall splitters. One false start dead-ended me in the middle of nowhere. I rapped and tried a crack to the left, and this time the dots connected. I imagine those cracks had likely only been climbed once before, but they were absolutely immaculate.

By dusk we were on top of the Minaret and beginning a slightly tense descent along Doubting the Millennium, to climber's right of Retinal Circus, using Leo's 4mm tag line to pull down our main rope. It's hard to put much faith in a rope that skinny, but it worked out OK. Around midnight we scampered back to camp, cracked a Kokanee each, and toasted a stellar day.

— WILL STANHOPE, *CANADA*

NORTH HOWSER TOWER, WEST FACE, ARMAGEDDON, FREE ASCENT

IN AUGUST 1999, Jonny Copp and Mike Pennings climbed a new line on the 3,200' west face of North Howser Tower. They called their route Armageddon (VI 5.11+ A2) and free climbed most of it. "Arghh," Copp wrote in *AAJ 2000*, "a pecker and a blade; damn, we have to aid climb ten feet of the thousands that we've freed. No problem though. Our goal is to go up, so we do." [*Editor's note: Armageddon begins with All Along the Watchtower (Robinson-Walseth, 1981) and shares some pitches with Warrior (Burton-Sutton, 1973).*]

In spite of having only this brief stretch of aid climbing, the route did not see a free ascent until 2016, when Jesse Huey and Maury Birdwell climbed it at 5.12+. In a blog post for

[Above] Jesse Huey on 5.11+ ground, headed toward the crux (5.12+) corner of Armageddon on the west face of North Howser Tower. *Maury Birdwell*

Arc'teryx, Huey described arriving at what appeared to be the crux right-facing corner system: "The worst part was not knowing what [they] hadn't free climbed…. Was it that section? Or was it that one up there? It was all a question mark, so I paid attention to the only holds that mattered, the ones right in front of me."

After some sustained 5.12 to a no-hands rest, Huey fell on the technical crux pitch of the route. He aided the pitch, fixed the rope to the midway stance, and then he and Birdwell bivvied on a ledge below. In the morning, after both climbers rehearsed the moves on top-rope, Huey freed the pitch on his second lead attempt of the day and Birdwell followed it clean. "The questions then arose…." Huey wrote. "I have climbed enough hard corners to know that this pitch was for sure 5.12+, but [also] that Mike Pennings has a real tendency to sandbag me…. Oh god, we both thought, what if the 'A2' section is still above us?" No worries: Huey and Birdwell onsighted the final 1,000 feet of climbing, all under 5.12. 🔍

– CHRIS KALMAN, *WITH INFORMATION FROM JESSE HUEY, MAURY BIRDWELL, AND ARC'TERYX.COM*

HALL PEAK AND BLOCK TOWER, SEVERAL NEW ROUTES

IN AUGUST, JENNY Abegg, Alix Morris, Forest Woodward, and Graham Zimmerman visited the Leaning Towers of the Purcell Wilderness Conservancy. They made the arduous approach over two days, hiring a horse packer to carry gear for the first six miles before camping at the Dewar Creek hot springs. The next morning, with the help of a local friend, they humped loads over a pass to the base of Hall Peak and set up camp. Over the next ten days the four climbers split into two teams: Abegg and Morris, and Woodward and Zimmerman.

Abegg and Morris established Heart Like a Hippo (600', 5.10) on the right side of the east face of Hall Peak. Following this success, they attempted a variation to State of Wonder (1,000',

[Above] Known routes on the east side of Hall Peak. (1) East Buttress Direct (Morriss-Ramos, 2014). (2) East Buttress (McComb-Myers-Twomey, 1975). (3) East Face Ramp (Leary-Reimondo, 2013). (4) Affirmations in the Afternoon (Woodward-Zimmerman, 2016). (5) Heart Like a Hippo (Abegg-Morriss, 2016). (6) Post Credit Cookie (Morriss-Ramos, 2014). (7) Shoeless Solidarity (Woodward-Zimmerman, 2016). The formation to the left is the Pulpit. *Forest Woodward*

5.11- C1, 2015), established by Jasmin Caton and Kate Rutherford on the east side of Wall Tower (*AAJ 2016*). After six pitches on State of Wonder, including free climbing the formerly C1 first pitch and fourth pitch (followed at 5.11+), they started up a left-facing corner to the right of the 2015 route. However, after one new 5.10 pitch they were halted by a widening crack for which they lacked protection. They rappelled back to State of Wonder and continued up that route to the summit. Abegg is confident the full variation to the summit would go free, with steep crack climbing on high-quality rock.

Meanwhile, Woodward and Zimmerman put up two routes on the east face of Hall Peak: Shoeless Solidarity (400', 5.10a) and Affirmations in the Afternoon (800', 5.10b). Zimmerman said both offered excellent climbing on good, albeit dirty, stone and were well protected with a standard rack to a number 4 Camalot. Affirmations in the Afternoon finished with a 150' traverse to the right, joining Heart Like a Hippo for its final 60' of climbing.

Woodward and Zimmerman then climbed Pink Rabbits (1,400', 5.11 A2) on the east face of Block Tower. Their route began at the low point of "a very compelling buttress" between Trout Fishing in America (Edwards-Isaac, 1997) and Slim Princess (Caton-Rutherford, 2015), starting with a leaning finger crack to an obvious wide splitter. The resulting route involved 1,400' of finger cracks, sustained wide cracks (a number 5 is recommended), some serious gardening, a dash of run-out slab climbing, and a single aid pitch utilizing beaks, small cams, and tension traversing to reach a ledge where the pair bivied under an emergency blanket before finishing the route next morning. Zimmerman said the aid pitch could be freed at approximately 5.12 if the aid seam were cleaned out. 📷

— CHRIS KALMAN, *WITH INFORMATION FROM JENNY ABEGG AND GRAHAM ZIMMERMAN, USA*

WALL TOWER, WHITE TIGER

ON JUNE 25, Paul Bonnell, Vince Ryglis, Kale Semar, and I began the arduous approach to the Leaning Towers in the Purcell Wilderness Conservancy, with the goal of finishing a Fred Beckey and Carl Dietrich line first attempted in late 1986. We carried supplies for 12 days and adequate gear for a big-wall first ascent. After three days of hiking and exploration, Vince and I started up what we believed to be

The east side of Block Tower (left) and Wall Tower. (1) Approximate line of Trout Fishing in America (Edwards-Isaac, 1997). (2) Pink Rabbits (Woodward-Zimmerman, 2016). (3) Slim Princess (Caton-Rutherford, 2015). (4) State of Wonder (Caton-Rutherford, 2015). (5) White Tiger (Hanson-Ryglis, 2016). *Jasmin Caton*

the Beckey-Diedrich line on the east face of Wall Tower. We encountered rusty quarter-inch bolts and tattered webbing, but all signs of travel disappeared after three pitches. We continued climbing dirty, poorly protected cracks until, after another two pitches, the rock quality improved, allowing free climbing and better protection.

It took us two days to fix the first four pitches. On the third day, Vince and I made the summit in a push, finishing the 10-pitch route at night. After bivying near the summit ridge in an electrical storm, we rappelled the route. We named our route the White Tiger, due to the remarkable whiteness of the granite and the peculiar black stripes that cover the first third of the route. We drilled some bolts for anchors but did not place any protection bolts, and we propose a grade of VI 5.11 A3 (1,600'). *This team was supported by an AAC Live Your Dream Grant.* 📷

— AARON HANSON, *USA*

CANADIAN ROCKIES

VALLEY OF THE TEN PEAKS, MT. TUZO AND NEPTUAK MOUNTAIN, NEW ROUTES

BETWEEN APRIL 1 and 11, Canadian alpinist Marc-André Leclerc and I climbed three new routes in the Valley of the Ten Peaks. We had only recently tied in together for the first time, sharing a rope on March 27, when we climbed the Greenwood-Locke Route on the north face of Mt. Temple in a push, in quite wintery conditions. We worked well as a team, so I felt optimistic about doing more climbs together in the coming weeks.

We initially wanted to climb on the east face of Mt. Fay, near Moraine Lake, but warm temperatures and avalanches redirected us into the Valley of the Ten Peaks. We spotted a very nice and obvious line on the northeast face of Mt. Tuzo (3,248m). Our food and gas reserves were low after the disappearance of a food cache near Moraine Lake—apparently raided by an animal— but we were motivated by the promising line and started climbing around midday on April 1.

The first three pitches were very serious. Steep, loose rock and some thin ice brought us to a huge chimney, where we spent our first night on the wall. We started the next day by literally digging our way up through enormous snow mushrooms. A few moderate mixed pitches followed, bringing us to the base of the ice, about halfway up the face. The first pitch of ice (WI6+ R) proved to be the hardest and the most dangerous. A few more moderate ice pitches followed before we found ourselves below a steep rock step. We climbed this in three pitches of very steep dry-tooling (M7+). On the second, and hardest, dry-tooling pitch, we had to remove our gloves for a few moves to crimp on small side pulls and edges. We finally settled in to our second bivouac after a very long day, beneath a final ice chimney, where we spent another night with almost no food and liquid.

The next day, we climbed to the top of Mt. Tuzo, completing our new route, which we elected to call, simply, the Lindič-Leclerc (1,100m, WI6+ R M7+). [*The north face of Tuzo was first climbed in July 1985 by Jeff Marshall and Kevin Smyth, who started up the north buttress, traversed far left on ledges at mid-height, and finished directly on the upper northeast face, mostly to the left of the 2016 line (D+, 5.10c).*] We descended toward Mt. Deltaform, and from the col rappelled back to the north to return to our camp. During our descent we spotted a very good-looking ice line leading back up to this col.

On the 8th of April, after a couple days of rest, we climbed the ice line we had seen during our descent of Mt. Tuzo. The difficulties were never very high, but the climbing was always interesting: relatively steep and with some thin ice. We called our route Fantastic Mr. Fox (500m, WI5 M5) in honor of the food cache that had disappeared earlier in the trip, which we

suspected was stolen by a fox.

After a day of rest in our little base camp, we began our final route on the north face of Neptuak Mountain (3,241m). A steep, long line of ice on the upper part of the wall had motivated us to attempt this line, but the lower climbing turned out to be quite good as well. We climbed several superb mixed pitches of quality quartzite, with difficulties up to M7, before we started swinging our tools into perfect ice higher up. We didn't start our climb until noon, which is when the upper ice goes into the shade (making the line colder and safer). As a result, darkness fell when we were still on the steep ice, and we climbed the remainder of the route by headlamp. We reached the summit ridge around 1 a.m., and, an hour or so later, stood on top of Neptuak. We descended the west flank of the mountain and finally reached our base camp with the first morning light. We named our route the Psychological Effect (700m, WI5+ M7).

Of the routes that we climbed, the one on Mt. Tuzo is certainly the most serious, and the one on Neptuak Mountain offers the best climbing. To repeat the Lindič-Leclerc Route or Psychological Effect, one should bring a set of cams, a set of nuts, about 8 ice screws (including a few short ones), 3–5 different pitons, and 2–3 Peckers. To repeat the Fantastic Mr. Fox, one should be fine with 8–10 screws and a small set of cams and nuts.

[Top] Marc-André Leclerc on the second pitch of the Lindič-Leclerc Route on Mt. Tuzo in the Valley of the Ten Peaks. *Luka Lindič* [Bottom] The line of the Lindič-Leclerc Route (1,100m, WI6+ R M7+) on the northeast side of Mt. Tuzo. Deltaform Mountain is to the right. *Luka Lindič*

— LUKA LINDIČ, *SLOVENIA*

HUNGABEE MOUNTAIN, NORTHWEST FACE, MORDOR

IN MAY 2015, Steven Kovalenko and Maury Perrault climbed a 1,400m mixed line up the northwest face of Hungabee Mountain (3,490m) in a 30-hour round trip from Lake O'Hara (16 hours up, 14 hours down). Mordor (V 5.6 WI4 M4) topped out on the north ridge. Perrault and Maarten van Haeren had attempted the same line in 2014.

— DOUGALD MACDONALD, *WITH INFORMATION FROM THE CANADIAN ALPINE JOURNAL*

THE FINGER, NAPSIHU RIDGE

ON AUGUST 1, Mark Klassen, Tim Johnson, Margie Smith, and Larry Stanier did a new route up the northwest ridge (Napsihu Ridge) of the Finger in 12 pitches plus scrambling (AD 5.8). The route has some bolt protection and is now the preferred descent route from the Finger.

— DOUGALD MACDONALD, *WITH INFORMATION FROM DAVID JONES AND ROCKIES CENTRAL, VOL. 2*

[Above] **The incredible Mur du 51 at Rivière Nipissis in February 2016. An annotated photo showing all route lines, as of late 2016, will be found with this report at the AAJ website.** *Maarten van Haeren*

WARDLE TEETH, NORTH RIDGE OF NORTH TOOTH

JEFF DICKSON AND Tobias Link climbed the north ridge of the North Tooth, one of a pair of limestone towers just north of Mt. Wardle in the Vermilion Range. Their 600m route, climbed during a two-day outing in May, went at D 5.10a/b.

— DOUGALD MACDONALD, WITH INFORMATION FROM DAVID JONES AND ROCKIES CENTRAL, VOL. 2

QUÉBEC

NIPISSIS RIVER AREA, LE MUR DU 51, NEW ROUTES

THE NIPISSIS AREA is a premiere ice climbing venue in Québec that was discovered by Patrice Beaudet during a ski traverse in 1994. Over numerous trips, he gave the area his undivided attention, climbing many classics lines, including Le Filon (145m, III WI5) and Le Chercheur d'Or (160m, III WI5+). After creating a small PDF guidebook to the area, Patrice named some of the still-unclimbed flows, tempting other climbers to explore the cliffs.

From February 18–26, Jean-Philippe Belanger and Charles Roberge (both from Québec), Jasmin Fauteux (Alberta), Pete Takeda (Colorado), and I camped below the headwall of Le Mur du 51, named for the mile marker along the Tshiuetin Rail line, which we rode north from the city of Sept-Îles. We were excited to see plenty of ice, despite it being a substandard year for the area. Due to the dense boreal forest, the only easy camping and traveling we found was on the frozen Nipissis River. We established a base camp with modern luxuries, including a prospector tent with wood stove—crucial for drying ropes and equipment during the -35°C nights.

The best climbing at Le Mur du 51 is characterized by thin ice flows over granite slabs. The mineral-rich water produces beautiful golden ice climbs, almost dark brown in spots. These dissolved minerals also lower the freezing point of the water, which means the climbs keep rejuvenating even when the thermometer drops below -20°C.

Due to our timing, we were fortunate to climb several new lines, some of which were entirely unformed when we arrived. The most aesthetic of these lines was Âme du Nord ("Northern Soul," 125m, IV WI5 R M6). A well-protected M6 corner gains a thin flow out of a shallow chimney/crack through the granite slab. Stepping out from this belay, the crux second pitch climbs the thinly iced chimney, poorly protected by short screws and rock gear through a section of 1–2cm ice.

In addition to Âme du Nord, we climbed five other new lines and variations, from WI4 to WI5+. (*Details are at the AAJ website.*) None of the established climbing at Le Mur du 51 is cutting-edge, but the real value in climbing here doesn't lie in the next rad Instagram post. The remoteness, good people, and excellent climbing combined to offer something I haven't found anywhere else in my winter travels. 📷 🔍 📄

– **MAARTEN VAN HAEREN**, *CANADA*

GASPÉ PENINSULA, PIC DE L'AURORE, ALLER SIMPLE POUR MARS

THE PIC DE l'Aurore, in Percé, Québec, is a seaside wall at the tip of the Gaspé Peninsula, known for its long ice climbs. It's a five-hour drive from my home in Rimouski, but traveling here is always worth it for the awe and respect this wall commands.

In winter 2015, Carl Darveau and I tried to make the first repeat of Moby Dick (190m, WI5+ M7), a futuristic, high-standard line opened by Bernard Maillot and my late friend Benoit Marion in 2001. On the second pitch, I followed the first four bolts and then made a gigantic traverse into nothingness, unable to find the line—*had something changed?* We bailed and traded a

[Above] **Carl Darveau leading the 85-meter first pitch of Aller Simple Pour Mars (190m, WI7- M7+)..** *Dany Julien*

second attempt for Scotch. Comparing the 2001 photos with ours, it was obvious that a 10m by 50m part of the wall had collapsed into the deep blue sea, taking the climb with it.

In March 2016, we returned to Pic de l'Aurore, believing a new independent line was possible between Moby Dick and Double 7 (190m, WI7 M7). Armed with a drill, pitons, and cams, we rappelled down the wall and found an astonishing ice pitch and delicate mixed terrain. We placed eight bolts. The climbing was almost too nice. Unfortunately, the temperature climbed quickly and this alien-like red limestone is unsupportive—*Wham! Woof! Hoho, rockfall!* We couldn't climb the line that same day.

After a few days, the cold returned on March 17. Adding to our rack, we took courage like Vikings leaving home for a raid. Carl led the really long and thin first pitch, which finishes through overhanging ice mushrooms (85m, WI5). I took the second pitch, which starts with a technical traverse on loose rock, then thin tool placements on rock and ice, and, finally, 10m up overhanging pink ice petals and blobs (30m, WI6+ M7+). The third pitch, a mind-blowing ice pillar, started with an overhanging move onto the broken column and, then, after a puzzle of mushrooms, delicate climbing up thin and hollow ice with so-so screws (45m, WI7-). From here, a snow couloir (25m) led us to the top. The technical crux came later: It was really hard to get out from the Le Pub Pit Caribou in Percé.

This route is an ode to Benoit Marion, who died in a car crash in 2015. We called it *Aller Simple Pour Mars* (190m, WI7- M7+). 📷

– JEAN-FRANÇOIS GIRARD, *CANADA*

NEWFOUNDLAND

GROS MORNE NATIONAL PARK, THE CHOLESTEROL WALL, TWO NEW ROUTES

ON MARCH 7, 2015, Anna Pfaff and I completed Apocalypse Now, a traditionally protected mixed climb (220m, 7 pitches, WI7 M9) on the Cholesterol Wall, a large cliff above Ten Mile Pond on the west coast of Newfoundland. We climbed the route over five days, fixing ropes to our high point each day. All pitches were onsighted except the second, which we aided and then freed with the gear in place. The route awaits a single-push ascent, as of this writing.

A year later, on March 11, Ben Collett, Chelsea Rude, and I completed a harder variation of *Apocalypse Now* that we called *The Lion, the Witch, and the Wardrobe* (220 meters, 7 pitches, WI7+ M12). This line took 10 days, fixing ropes to our high point each day. Pitches two, three, and six were aided and then freed with the gear in place; the other pitches were freed first go. The climb has four pitches of M8 or harder and a wild ice roof, all protected without bolts. As of spring 2017, it has not had a single-push ascent. *Pitch-by-pitch descriptions of these climbs will be found at the AAJ website.* 📄

– WILL MAYO, *USA*

EDITOR'S NOTE: *In early 2017, Will Mayo returned to Gros Morne National Park and climbed several more new routes, with various partners, including Dreamline (1,250', WI6), a spray-ice route to the right of Pissing Mare Falls, climbed with Anna Pfaff and Newfoundland ice pioneer Joe Terravecchia. These routes will be documented in AAJ 2018.*

[Above] The Cholesterol Wall, above Ten Mile Pond in Gros Morne National Park. (Red) The Lion, the Witch, and the Wardrobe (220m, WI7+ M12, 2016). (Yellow) Apocalypse Now (220m, WI7 M9, 2015). *Will Mayo Collection*

GREAT SAIL PEAK, NEW ROUTES

In the summer of 2016, Joshua Lavigne, Marc-André Leclerc and I spent six weeks in the fjordlands of eastern Baffin Island, establishing two new routes on Great Sail Peak (ca 1,500m). Our journey began on June 21, when we set off from the community of Clyde River by snowmobile, guided by local outfitter Levi Palituq. Two days of travel over the frozen ocean landed us at the entrance to the Stewart Valley, an ancient fjord now blocked by a moraine to form a huge inland lake. We shuttled gear by sled for 10km across frozen Stewart Lake to the base of Great Sail Peak, and nine days after leaving Clyde River we were ready to begin climbing.

Josh, Marc, and I began our first route up the right side of the west-northwest face, where the rock is steepest. (Previous ascents of this face followed a line of ramps and ledge systems farther to the left. The wall was first climbed by an American team in the spring of 1998.) We spent a week establishing the first seven pitches, consisting of faint cracks and technical face climbing. Most

[Top] The ca 1,000m west-northwest face of Great Sail Peak, showing approximate lines of (1) Northwest Turret (2016). (2) Mascalzone Latino (2016). (3) Northwest Passage (2106). (4) Rum, Sodomy, and the Lash (1998). (5) Original start (1998). (6) Rubicon (2002). (7) Coconut Connection (2016, first free ascent of the wall, finishing on Rubicon). (8) Canadian-American start (2016). (9) West Buttress (2016). *Brette Harrington* [Bottom] Joshua Lavigne attempting a splitter granite crack on the northwest face of Great Sail Peak. *Marc-André Lelclerc*

pitches were cleaned on aid and then free climbed, with difficulties up to 5.12b.

These pitches led to a sloping talus ledge about the width of a football field where we collected water from melting snow. We traversed leftward under the headwall, past the high camp of a Belgian-Italian team that was working on their first route above us. [*This quintet climbed three new routes on Great Sail, including the first free ascent via Coconut Connection (5.12d); see feature article earlier in this edition.*]

Above the talus ledge, we first attempted one line, but it was obviously going to require far more aid climbing than we were after. We switched objectives to the leftmost buttress on the wall, a feature we named the Northwest Turret. The upper wall of the Northwest Turret showed apparent weaknesses and obvious free climbing terrain, but the lower wall had a blank slab, which posed the biggest question mark.

We prepared supplies for seven days, deciding to climb ground-up without the use of fixed lines. We set up our portaledge camp above the first crux, a thin and obtuse corner with a boulder problem crux, which we freed at 5.13a. While working on freeing this pitch a storm rolled into the valley. The Arctic cyclone lasted for six days, hammering our hanging camp with violent winds, rain, and snow. During breaks in the storm, Marc-André and I took turns working on the technical aid pitch above, hooking and copperheading our way across the slab in search of a free line. Our supplies were running low, and it soon became debatable whether we could finish the route. But the storm began to break on day six, giving us a very narrow window, given our resources, for a single-push attempt to the summit.

The evening of our push, Marc-André spilled boiling water on his foot and was unable to wear a rock shoe, so Josh and I took turns leading in blocks. The three of us climbed throughout the pale light of an Arctic night, using the fastest style possible to ascend each pitch. The leader would speed climb, using a mix of free, French free, and aid, depending on the terrain. The two seconds ascended the fixed lines, carrying the packs. It rained throughout the climb, and the upper wall was wet and partly iced up. Our bodies were tired from the incessant hanging belays, but we stuck it out and summited about nine hours after our middle-of-the-night start, around 10 a.m.

We spent the next ten hours or so rappelling. We had some difficulty reversing the traverse directly above our portaledge camp, but we made it work by reverse-jugging a line we had fixed over the traverse. We named our route the Northwest Turret (ca 900m, 22 pitches, 5.13a A2).

With a few sunny rest days, we took time to relax and boulder around base camp. The Belgians brought us fresh-caught Arctic char, quite a delicacy compared to our canned tuna.

Our next objective was the west buttress of Great Sail Peak, at the right edge of the main face, which we decided to climb in a single push. We led in blocks, with the seconds climbing with their packs. Intervals of steep climbing were split up by comfortable ledges and ramp systems. The climbing generally followed crack systems but had the occasional blank slab. We reached the summit around 3 a.m. as the golden glow of early morning cast upon the mountain peaks. Tired and worn, we rappelled the face via the Belgian/Italian anchors on Coconut Connection and were back at base camp in a full 24 hours. We named our route the West Buttress (1,100m, 5.12 C1).

It was now early August and the ice on Stewart Lake had broken up, so we resorted to paddling our gear back to the toe of the lake in two small blow-up rafts; each trip averaged four hours due to the strong headwinds. Taking a final look into the Stewart Valley, we hiked our gear over the moraine to Walker Arm, where Levi and a companion picked us up by motor boat two days later.

The 2016 expeditions were the first to the Stewart Valley during the summer season. Beyond Great Sail Peak, the entire valley has unimaginable potential for route development and exploration.

– BRETTE HARRINGTON, *USA*

[Above] The Mirror Wall in Stewart Valley, showing the first and only route up the ca 900m face: Sensaciones (2010). The formation to the left is the right side of the Citadel. The prow, dubbed Welshman's Peak, has two lines: Arctic Monkeys (2010) and Catacomb (2016). At right is the north end of Great Sail Peak. [Right] David Palmada on pitch 12 of Sensaciones. *Josep Maria Esquirol*

STEWART VALLEY, MIRROR WALL, SENSACIONES

THIS LITTLE-KNOWN FIRST ascent of one of the Stewart Valley's biggest walls was not previously documented in the AAJ. David "Pelut" Palmada and I flew to Baffin on April 27, 2010, and traveled by snowmobile to the Stewart Valley on May 10. From base camp, it was only a 30-minute approach to the unclimbed wall we planned to attempt. [*Editor's note: This ca 900m wall lies between Great Sail Peak on the right and Artic Monkeys (McAleese-Thomas-Turner, 2010) on the left.*]

We spent the first six days climbing and hauling the bags up the first 300m, in order to reach a ledge system at the base of the steepest climbing. This alpine section had some bad snow to 60°–65° and some vertical rock. After two rest days, we switched to the big-wall life.

We first tried to climb the wall directly, but we soon realized we wouldn't have enough time; it's extremely technical aid climbing, and there aren't ledges with snow for water. We moved farther left, toward the north buttress, and climbed about 800m up the main wall, with good rock and cracks, plus two snow and mixed pitches. Above this, another alpine section of about 300m led to the top. The wall finished with two spires that we baptized Genciana's Needle and Pelut's Needle.

The main wall took 19 days to climb, plus 24 hours for rappelling. During the climb, the weather was usually poor and cold. We enjoyed only two or three very good days on the wall. We used six portaledge camps. We called the whole face the Mirror Wall, because the main wall was nearly as blank as a mirror. We called our route Sensaciones; the total climbing distance was about 1,600m, and the difficulty was about 6c+ A4 M6 60°. 📷 🔍

– JOSEP MARIA ESQUIROL, *SPAIN*

[Top] Descending Peak 5 and **looking south at an unnamed, likely unclimbed peak.** [Bottom] View from the summit of Peak 9, looking south-southeast toward Peak 11. *Grant Dixon*

CUMBERLAND PENINSULA, GATEWAY GLACIER GROUP, ASCENTS AND EXPLORATION

SITUATED BETWEEN PANGNIRTUNG and Kingnait fjords on Baffin Island's Cumberland Peninsula, 35 kms northeast of the village of Pangnirtung, is a rugged, glaciated group of alpine peaks: the Gateway Glacier complex. Here, glaciers have carved an impressive selection of walls, narrow arêtes, and nunataks, and there are fine opportunities for ski touring circuits.

Grant Dixon (Australia) and four Canadians—Louise Jarry, Marshall Netherwood, Terry Winkler, and me—spent a month in the area, April 16 to May 17, skiing from Kingnait to Pangnirtung fjords. Including day trips, we traveled 225km and climbed 15 peaks, including 10 probable first ascents.

In mid-April, local outfitter Joavie Alivaktuk arranged for us to be snowmobiled in two stages to the mouth of an unnamed valley on the west shore of Kingnait Fiord, across from Qaiqsuki Point. We called the drainage "Tupeq Valley" after the peak at its head. After making the first ascent of an unnamed 1,554m peak, we slowly made our way up-valley, breaking trail in 25cm of new snow. With effort, we reached the mouth of our chosen side valley to "East Gateway Glacier."

At the crest of the eastern glacier, we camped two nights at "Gateway Pass." Peaks 3 (1,440m) and 4 (1,600m) on each side of the pass were ascended, both likely first ascents. On May 1, Grant and Greg skied, then cramponed, up the twin summits of Peak 5: west (1,617m) and east (1,620m). The remains of a note lay under a single rock at the west summit of Peak 5.

[Above] Panorama from Peak 4, looking south into the heart of the area explored by the 2016 team. In all they traveled 225 kilometers and climbed 15 peaks. *Greg Horne*

Only the words "1st August 19--, -- Carey, Jonas[?] --, Dave" were readable. A belayed traverse brought us to the eastern summit, which was small enough we took turns on our knees.

Moving across "West Gateway Glacier" and over 1,260m "Aanisittuq (South) Pass" put us at a high camp for several day trips to neighboring peaks. A peak 2 kms south of camp was the first objective. On top, Grant and Greg found a small cairn with another weathered note, this time some of it was readable: American David MacAdam and his son made the first ascent in 1974 from a lake, which we assume to be the 3km-long body of water that lies 4.5km to the southwest. From 1971 to the mid-1980s, MacAdam visited Baffin Island most summers, often solo, to explore many alpine areas.

The highest summit of our trip, Peak 7 (1,708m), was just west of "Aanisittuq Pass." We skied to its west col, then cramponed and short-roped to the top, where a cairn and no record was found. Peak 8 (1,650m), 1km to the west, permitted skiing to within 100 vertical meters of the top before switching to crampons.

We moved off the Gateway Glacier system by descending south from a high camp to a spot above "MacAdam's Lake," then east to the toe of a 6km-long glacier southeast of Gateway. Then we moved up to about the 1,000m level and established our best camp of the expedition, a hub for numerous day skis and climbs. Time was up for Terry and Marshall; they started their return to Pang ahead of the rest of us.

In fine weather on May 9, the rest of us skied east to a 1,170m pass and then up the south slopes of Peak 10 (1,530m) and its summit. On the way back to the pass, Grant and Greg broke off north, skinned to a high shoulder at 1,440m, and then climbed to the small, airy summit of Peak 11 (1,528m), probably the finest summit of the trip.

After attempting a narrow granite ridge about 1km north of Peak 9, Grant suggested an ambitious ski circuit around and over the mini-range south of camp on May 11. Leaving camp at 1,000m, we descended to nearly 800m then climbed up a lateral moraine and across a glacier to a nunatak with a spot elevation of 1,356m (Peak 12). We crossed over a glacial divide to 1,000m, where we left the glacier and ascended Peak 13 (1,422m), and then descended back to 1,000m. We soon intersected our earlier route to Peak 10 and returned home by the 1,170m pass, a 14.5km tour.

Degrading weather on May 12 helped soften the regret of beginning our journey back toward Pangnirtung. Soon we observed the sounds and sights of snow buntings, patches of grass, and open water. Our descent to Pangnirtung Fiord at Aulatsivikjuak Bay, with the full onset of spring, made for interesting snow, water, and grass skiing. [*The online version of this report has details of additional ascents.*] 📄 📷 🔍

— GREG HORNE, *CANADA*

GREENLAND

[Photo] Steep ground on the northeast ridge of Mt. Hannes (1,330m). *Barlow/Powell/Seabrook*

EAST GREENLAND

RENLAND: FOUR NEW ROUTES

FROM JULY 18 to August 19, an expedition to a little-explored glacier basin in the east-southeast corner of Renland climbed four new routes. After flying to Constable Pynt, David Barlow, Geoff Hornby, Robert Powell, and Paul Seabrook traveled 215km (12 hours) by rigid inflatable boat to Renland, where they established base camp at 71°8'52.25"N, 25°38'56.02"W, just above their drop-off point. A one-hour slog up the right-hand moraine, followed by a somewhat perilous descent to the glacier and another hour up the ice, led to advanced base at 526m. This was provisioned by multiple round trips from base. Unfortunately, during the first of these trips, Hornby sustained a knee injury and had to be evacuated.

On July 26 the remaining three climbers put up Arctic Monkeys (400m, 10 pitches, British E2 5b) on the east face of a formation at the entrance to a side glacier west of advanced base. They reached the crest of the south ridge at 1,114m, from where they made five rappels on the far side, then scrambled back down to the glacier.

On the 29th all three made the first

[Top] Starting the route Arctic Monkeys. The 800m-plus wall partially visible at left is unclimbed. [Bottom] Polar Daze generally follows the left skyline (northeast ridge) of Mt. Hannes (1,330m). The Double 00 Couloir begins immediately to the right. *Barlow/Powell/Seabrook*

ascent of Cerro Castillo (1,715m) via the southeast ridge (1,300m, AD+/D UIAA V). This was the first ascent of a peak attempted in 2012 by Michel Raab and Betsy Winston (*AAJ 2013*), who retreated after climbing a small summit partway along the ridge. Barlow, Powell, and Seabrook climbed a 600m snow gully to the start of the ridge, then followed it to a foresummit, where a 30m rappel led to a small col. A short traverse right, followed by a 50m pitch, led to the true summit. The three descended the route by rappel and downclimbing the snow gully, returning to advanced base after a 24-hour round trip.

On August 1 the three climbed the Double 00 Couloir (800m, AD 55°, rising to 75° at the top), which leads to a deep col on the ridge immediately west of what they named Mt. Hannes. They descended the route, largely from Abalakov anchors. On August 6–7, the team climbed the northeast ridge of Mt. Hannes, a fine alpine rock arête with 1,400m (20 roped pitches) of climbing at TD-/TD E2 5b. The 1,330m peak was named after Powell's climbing partner Hannes Esterhuyse, who was killed while climbing in the Alps. They bivouacked during the ascent—a cold night since they didn't take sleeping bags—and descended from the west end of the summit ridge in five rappels to the top of the Double 00 Couloir, which they again descended. The route was named Polar Daze.

This area has plenty of unclimbed summits, long snow and rock routes, and walls up to 1,000m. The east-facing rock wall behind Arctic Monkeys was thought to be between 800m and 1,000m high, and has two potential lines following dihedral systems. Various alpine summits seem accessible at a moderate grade via a heavily crevassed subsidiary glacier on the west, between base camp and advanced base. The expedition would like to thank the Montane Alpine Club Climbing Fund, ASP International Rope Access, British Mountaineering Council, Mount Everest Foundation, and Mountain Club of South Africa for financial support. A full report with GPS coordinates and topos is available at the *AAJ* website (publications. americanalpine club.org). 📷 🔍

— DAVID BARLOW, *U.K.*, AND ROB POWELL, *SOUTH AFRICA AND U.K.*

HISTORICAL NOTE: THE FIRST ASCENT OF HØNGBJERG (MT. MIGHTY)

In *AAJ 2016* we reported Jim Gregson's second known ascent of Mt. Mighty in North Liverpool Land and an addendum where he described finding the remnants of a cairn at the highest rocks, some 40m from the summit. Within these fallen stones he discovered a small bottle containing a faded, illegible message.

It turns out this message dates to July-August 1971, when Tony Higgins and Mike Townsend (U.K.), as part of the Greenland Geological Survey, were mapping North Liverpool Land. The two had a camp to the southeast of the mountain and climbed snow slopes to join the east ridge, which they followed to the summit. They christened the peak Høngbjerg after a particularly pungent Danish cheese. While Higgins does not remember leaving the bottle, he is sure they placed a message in a cairn on the summit.

The second ascent of this peak was in 2012 by Natasha Sebire and Gemma Woldendorp, via the northwest face and southwest ridge. (Unaware of a previous ascent, this pair named the peak Mt. Mighty.) The third ascent was completed in 2015 by Jim Gregson's party, via the northeast face. The 1971 party also made the probable first ascent of a 750m peak north of Høngbjerg. 📄 📷

— LINDSAY GRIFFIN, *WITH INFORMATION FROM MIKE TOWNSEND AND JIM GREGSON*

KANGERTITIVATSIAQ FJORD, MYTHICS CIRQUE, HIDDEN TOWER, CINDERELLA RIDGE; AURORA TOWER, SOUTHWEST RIDGE

MATTHEW IRVING (USA), Julian Kenchenten (Canada), Paolo Marazzi (Italy), Angela Percival (Canada), Vikki Weldon (Canada), and I left Isafjordur, Iceland, on August 18 aboard the sailboat Aurora. Captain Vidar Kristinsson and first mate Rasmus Jonsson piloted us to Greenland's East Coast over three days. We set anchor about 120km northeast of Tasiilaq in Kangertitivatsiaq Fjord, home of the Mythics Cirque, which had been visited only by an Australian-American-British team and an independent American team, who simultaneously sessioned the area in 2012.

Our first climb, on August 22, was from a high camp on an unnamed glacier south of the cirque. [*The two teams in 2012 made their base camp on the coast east of the cirque.*] Matt, Paolo, Vikki, and I climbed the southwest buttress of Hidden Peak (ca 1,400m; the southeast buttress

[Above] Aurora Tower (1,450m), highest peak of the Mythics Cirque, in center. The first-ascent route curved up the northwest ridge (center) and then the southwest ridge (right skyline). *Paul McSorley*

was climbed in 2012 for the first ascent of the peak; see *AAJ 2013*). We climbed approximately 17 pitches and scrambled several hundred meters for an estimated vertical gain of 800m. The climbing covered a variety of rock, from choss to immaculate, and offered difficulties to 5.11c. On the second rappel of 15, Vikki dropped a shoe, but with a bit of prosthetic taping she endured the rest of the descent like a champ. The route named itself Cinderella Ridge and was completed camp to camp in 18 hours.

After a few days of SUP'ing, cragging, and hiking, all of the climbers traveled on the 26th to the "backside" of the cirque, and after some very involved glacier travel we began climbing the southwest ridge of the highest peak in the Mythics (labeled 1,450m on the map; 66°18'23.71"N, 35°46'19.47"W Google Earth). To our knowledge, this peak was unnamed and unclimbed.

After a bit of rotten rock near the 'schrund, the ridge turned to mostly high-quality granitic rock. Difficulties on this 700m-long ridge never got harder than 5.9, with lots of exposed scrambling. The six of us topped out in late afternoon and descended partway down the ridge before making a bivouac 100m above the glacier. The next day we made it back to the boat in time for happy hour. The peak was christened Aurora Tower, as a tip of the hat to the vessel that provided such a commodious base camp. 📷 ▶️

— PAUL MCSORLEY, *CANADA*

QAQQAQ AOIFE, NORTHWEST RIDGE

WITH OUR TWO Icelandic mountain guides, Bjorgvin Hilmarsson and Leifur Orn Svavarsson, Mike Brinkworth, James Masters, Dave Minghay, and I made the first ascent of an unnamed peak of map height 1,194m, to the southeast of Niialigaq. This rises above the northeast side of Ikaasatsivaq Fjord, about 34km due north of Tasiilaq. We climbed a glacier on the west side to reach a ridge with a vertical rock barrier that formed the crux (British Severe). We named the summit Qaqqaq Aoife (Mt. Aoife), after my newly born granddaughter. 📄 📷

— CHARLES MASTERS, *U.K.*

[Above] The Daddy (left) and Daughter (a.k.a. Mt. Queen Lilliana) from the east. (1) Libecki Route (2016). (2) Libecki Route (2014). (3) Libecki Route (2016). (4) Way of the Banjo (Burcham-Libecki-Libecki, 2003). Both peaks are over 1,500m, with at least 1,000m of relief. *Mike Libecki*

DADDY AND DAUGHTER
SOLO FIRST ASCENTS IN EAST GREENLAND

BY MIKE LIBECKI

I HAVE BEEN on 10 expeditions to Greenland since first visiting in 1998. One particular area on the east coast, between Thor's Land and Tingmiarmiut, has been especially attractive to me, as almost no other climbers have been there.

I first traveled to this area in 2002 (solo), then again in 2003, 2008, 2014 (solo), and 2015, all trips resulting in first ascents. In 2002, I'd seen a huge rock peak at the end of Inugsuarmiut Fjord, which I referred to as Daddy Tower, and next to it another impressive formation that I climbed in 2003, the year my daughter was born. I called this Daughter Tower or Mt. Queen Lilliana in her honor. I returned and soloed another route on this tower in 2014, and then I finally felt the pull to solo Daddy Tower.

In mid-July 2016, Greenlandic friends took me by boat ca 500km south from Tasiilaq to Inugsuarmiut Fjord, where I set up base camp with a polar bear–protected perimeter system. After establishing a high camp about 9km up the fjord, I made a two-hour approach across a big, crevasse-riddled glacier to reach the foot of my chosen route. The climb meandered through wonderful cracks and features, and for the first 300m or so was 5.7 and 5.8. A few steeper sections bulged and pushed me out over the glacier below—oh, the flow of solo immaculate mayhem!

Above, it got steeper, with 5.9 and 5.10 sections. I felt solid and secure, often talking out loud to myself, double- and triple-checking verbally with my two partners (up there it was

me, myself, and I). With the rope still on my back, I wielded daisy chains with a few cams on each for protection and continued the sweet flow upward. I went through a couple of 5.11 sections, and sometimes would place a cam in a scary/crux moment, then remove or walk it. In all, I probably made 20 such cam placements on the climb.

Finally, I made it to a corner and ramp system (mostly 5.6 and 5.7) that led to the summit, where I looked over

[Above] Mike Libecki dons his Year of the Monkey mask on the summit of Daddy Tower. *Mike Libecki*

the ocean in one direction and the icecap in the other. I was exhausted and dehydrated, but was able to celebrate the success with my Year of the Monkey mask.

I was able to downclimb most of the route then started making single-rope rappels. With about 300m to go before I reached more downclimbable terrain, darkness and wind crept up on me. I was exhausted and had not yet found any water, so I decided to lay out my rope as a bed and shiver through the night. I put on everything I had, including the monkey mask, and waited for the sun. Next morning I made six more rappels, crossed the glacier, and descended to high camp, regaining it after a 32-hour round trip.

A FEW DAYS later I was back, as I'd spotted a cool new line on the Daughter Tower. It turned out to be classic. I spent most of the day in the sun on 5.6–5.7 terrain. High on the route, a few steeper sections of 5.9 or 5.10 made me place and walk a few cams. (I made about 15 placements in total.) I reached the summit for the third time, by my third different route, then walked off via a very dangerous gully (the second time I have descended by this route). I returned to high camp 13 hours after leaving. [*Editor's note: The 2016 line shares some ground with Way of the Banjo, Burcham-Libecki-Libecki, 2003, in its middle section. Both formations are over 1,500m high; the climbs described here each gained at least 1,000m.*]

SOUTH GREENLAND

TASERMIUT FJORD, HALF DOME, THE BAD MAN FROM BODIE

AFTER A FEW climbs in the popular Ulamertorssuaq region of Tasermiut Fjord, including perhaps the second ascent of Grmoland (Grmovsek-Grmovsek, 2008) on Ketil Pyramid, Duncan Barrack and Wil Treasure (U.K.) set off to repeat the Swiss route Les Temps Sont Dur (15 pitches, 6c, 1998) on the 600m, north-facing wall of the formation known as Half Dome. With only a hand-drawn topo, they couldn't identify the Swiss line or see the expected belay anchors. Instead, they decided to attempt a new line, working on the assumption that at least on this they couldn't get off-route.

The pair set off as the sun hit the face on July 29. Starting 50m left of the Swiss route and continuing up a blunt rib, the initial terrain had excellent granite, with positive yet run-out climbing. Toward the top was a frightening pitch on overlapping loose flakes, but it was short and the rock above improved. They joined the finishing pitches of the Swiss route and followed this to the summit. After a shiver bivy on a rope bed, seven hours of rappelling from the anchors of Les Temps Sont Dur took them back to the ground. They named the route the Bad Man from Bodie (E2 5b).

– LINDSAY GRIFFIN

[Photo] While climbing a new route on Igdlorssuit Havn Tower, Enzo Oddo and Siebe Vanhee kept staring at the 120-meter crack to the right. They returned for a second new line: The Splitter. *(Lionel Daudet)*

CAPE FAREWELL, NEW BIG-WALL ROUTES

Lionel Daudet invited me to take part in his Big Seas, Big Walls expedition, and I quickly accepted. At the end of June, Lionel and fellow Frenchman Enzo Oddo departed Scotland on Ada 2, skippered by the renowned French ocean sailor Isabelle Autissier. Because of my studies, I left Europe two weeks later by plane and jumped aboard the boat in Greenland.

Our main objective was clear: We wanted to climb a new route on the Thumbnail, one sector of the giant sea cliff Maujit Qoqarssuasia, above Torssukataq Fjord. However, first we aimed for something a little smaller. Ada 2 dropped us on Pamiagdluk Island, below the 650m northwest face of the Baroness. Here, we climbed a new line from July 5–8, using fixed ropes. The route is 13 pitches, has eight belay bolts and one protection bolt, and was climbed at 7c A2. Pitches six and 11 should go at approximately 8a+ and 7c, respectively.

We waited out some windy weather before committing to reach the Thumbnail using our inflatable kayaks. During this period, we made a one-day, all-free ascent of a new route on the west face of Mark (400m of climbing, seven pitches, 7a), higher up the Baroness valley. [*This ca 900m summit was probably first climbed, via the west face, by the line Called into Question (Mehigan-Sonnerdale, 2003).*]

The sun came out and the fjord now looked like a lake. We packed 15 days of provisions, as retreating from the Thumbnail in bad weather wouldn't be easy without any dry ground below the wall. Starting on July 13, it took us three days, moving camp every day, to reach the massive ledge that divides the wall in two. On our fourth day we fixed lines for a further 200m. The fifth day we were forced to lie in the sun after a night of constant rain that soaked the wall and Enzo's sleeping bag. On our last climbing day we ascended the fixed ropes and continued, light and fast, to the top of the Thumbnail, free climbing the whole way. Here we found the best pitches of the whole route, including two pitches of 7a cracks. From the top we could see the mighty Atlantic Ocean on one side and the thrilling Greenland icecap on the other. It was by far the most beautiful summit view I've ever had.

[Above] The 800m west face of Igdlorssuit Havn Tower showing the Mechanican (left) and the Splitter. There are at least seven other routes on the face, mostly put up in 2001. *Lionel Daudet*

In clear sky we descended to our camp at half-height on the wall, and the following day traversed the massive ledge to the left side of the wall and then followed a snow gully straight down to the fjord. It was scary but exciting sliding with 40kg haulbags to the base of the gully, where Ada 2 was able to pick us up. Our all-free route was 24 pitches and 1,355m of climbing. Pitch nine, the crux, was 7b (but felt like 7c+, as it was wet). The route lies entirely to the right of the 2000 British route (E6 6b, Bransby-Dickinson-Parnell-Parry).

We spent a few days on the boat before being dropped off in Prins Christian Sund, below the 800m seaward (west) face of Igdlorssuit Havn Tower. There are three existing climbs on the central section of this wall, and we opted for a possible new line straight up the middle, via a system of cracks left of the massive main dihedral. After one false start, it took three days of fixing rope, aid climbing, and then freeing some pitches in a slanting dihedral before we reached the roof system that guarded the upper cracks. The rock was not the best quality, and we did not climb pitches three, four, and five free. Pitch four might go at 7c/8a, and five at 8a+ or harder. Pitch six brought us above the roof system. After a rest day back on the ground, we continued the climb with a portaledge. Three days of sustained hand and fist cracks and stemming corners (between 6c and 7b) brought us to the summit. We called the route the Mechanican (850m of climbing, 19 pitches, 7b+/c A1).

On the last 300m of the Mechanican, our eyes had been drawn to a 120m splitter crack on the smooth face to the right of the main dihedral. Enzo and I decided to return, and on August 2 we ascended the static ropes we had left in place to the top of pitch six of our previous route. We then free-climbed nine more pitches to reach the base of the splitter. (We assume our pitches 11 to 14 share the same line as the 2003 Gibson-McClure route Twenty-one.) The next day we freed the finger-size splitter, which gave three pitches up to 7c+ and a fourth ending in poorly protected face climbing. The jamming was of very high quality and the exposure was incredible. We named the entire route the Splitter (950m of climbing, 23 pitches, 7c+ A1).

During our stay of more than a month, we nearly always had great weather—we didn't seem to waste a single day. 📷

— SIEBE VANHEE, *BELGIUM*

MEXICO

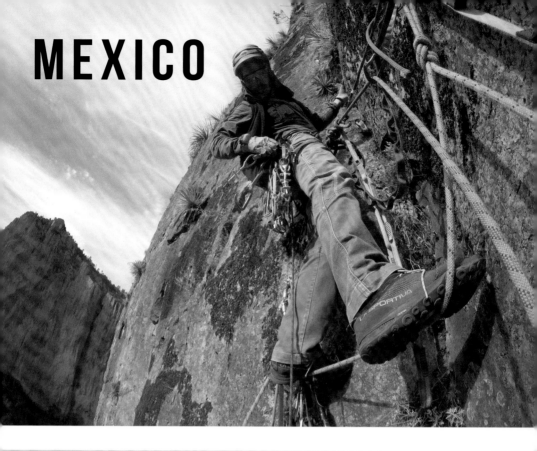

MIRADOR WALL, RARÁMURI SOUTHWEST

FOR SOME YEARS I have been captivated by the many big walls in Basaseachi Falls National Park. Candameña Canyon offers an infinite number of new lines, with vertical cliffs lining a canyon that runs more than five miles from Basaseachi Falls to El Gigante. At the end of February, the goal was a cliff we called Mirador Wall, right below a viewpoint (Mirador III) overlooking the waterfall. From our car it was less than two hours' walk to the base.

My partner for this climb was Larissa Arce from Chihuahua City. We carried about 140 pounds of equipment and food to the base of the Miraror Wall in two stages, collecting water at a natural spring, and established a camp in a small cave protected from rockfall. Over the next three days we fixed ropes to about 400', at the top of pitch four. We were happy to find cracks right from the start and move at a good pace. On the fourth day we decided to take everything up the wall and continue in capsule style.

[Top] Sergio "Tiny" Almada beginning the fifth pitch of Rarámuri Southwest in Parque Nacional Cascada de Basaseachi. *Larissa Arce* [Left] Rarámuri Southwest (1,000', VI 5.10c A2), the first route up the Mirador Wall. *Tiny Almada*

The following pitches were much less obvious, with blind cracks that couldn't be protected. We ended up aid climbing with hooks, micro-nuts, small cams in pockets—and runouts. We used only one knifeblade piton and three protection bolts on the entire route, along with bolted anchors.

By the top of the eighth pitch, 750' above the base, it had been four days since we began camping on the wall. Our only motivation was that we were still going up, little by little. On the last day of the climb, we started early, ascended our fixed ropes, and hauled everything to the top of the eighth pitch. It was past noon when Larissa began leading the last 130' to the end of the technical climbing. Right after this success, our tagline caught on some bushes, and it took us more than three hours to free the rope, bolt the anchors of pitch nine, and haul the gear to the top of the wall. We finally reached the overlook with all of our gear at 10 p.m.

After working on the route for 10 days, and living five of those days on the wall, we had completed Rarámuri Southwest (1,000', VI 5.10c/6a+ A2), naming it in honor of the Rarámuri people. With shade most of the day, the wall has a long climbing season. It could be repeated in two to three days by quick aid climbers, now that the loose rock has been cleaned.

—TINY ALMADA, *MEXICO*

RATTLESNAKE

A FRENCH "ROC Aventure Programme" team from the Fédération Française de la Montagne et de l'Escalade (FFME) completed a new route on the left side Candameña Canyon, about half an hour from Basaseachi Falls, in October. Six young climbers (Kevin Aglaé, Gaël Marty, Elsa Ponzo, Laurent Thevenot, Marion Thomas, and Sebastien Valran) and two FFME guides (Jonathan Crison and Antoine Pêcher) established the six-pitch route: Rattlesnake (200m, 7c, 6c obl). It is completely bolt-protected.

— JONATHAN CRISON, *FRANCE*

NUEVO LÉON

PARQUE LA HUASTECA, PICO PIRINEOS, EL LOBO DEL DESIERTO

ROLANDO LARCHER, ONE of my regular traveling companions, suggested the idea of climbing in Mexico. After some research on the Internet, Rolando was drawn to a stunningly beautiful wall in Huasteca Canyon and, without knowing anything about it whatsoever, explained to his sponsors that this would be the main goal of our expedition in January and February. Luca Giupponi joined us as the third member of our team.

Paolo Marazzi, who had climbed in Mexico a few months earlier (*see report on p.187*), put us in touch with Alex Catlin, an American who lives in Monterrey with his wife, Connie, and their two children; they devote much of their time to establishing climbs. We rendezvoused at a Starbucks in Monterrey. Despite heavy symptoms of espresso and croissant withdrawal, alleviated as much as possible with muffins, we immediately set to work examining the nearby rock faces. After two days we concluded that the wall Rolando had seen on the Internet, the east face of Pico Pirineos, was the most beautiful and interesting. But what had been climbed there? No problem: Alex called a local expert, and from what we gathered, picking up bits of their conversation in Spanish, it seemed the line we'd chosen was still virgin. [*Editor's note: The new route begins to the left of Primer Año on the lower east face of Pico Pirineos, then moves*

[Above] Luca Giopponi opening the eighth pitch (5.12b) of El Lobo del Desierto on the upper north face of Pico Pirineos. *Rolando Larcher* [Left] Rolando Larcher leading pitch four (5.12c). *Maurzio Oviglia*

to the north face in its upper half.]

We began our usual expedition routine: alarm clock in the middle of the night, a disgusting breakfast at a 7-Eleven, followed by climbing from first light to well past sunset. Then, exhausted, we'd dine in a restaurant in Monterrey to take in some protein. There was no time for alcohol or nightlife, not even for sightseeing or sport climbing. Completing the route was the main goal—we'd rest later. Is this perhaps why we've never returned from a trip empty-handed?

We climbed strictly ground-up, dividing the pitches evenly between us. We hung from hooks only to place a bolt, after free climbing the section below, meaning that we had to deal with some obligatory runouts! Many pitches used a few cams in addition to bolts.

After three days of hard work, we'd put up five long pitches to climb the spectacular lower east face of Pico Pirineos. Sometimes we were accompanied by a pleasant breeze, while other times it was hellishly hot. Cleaning the route cost a lot of time and energy, but we wanted to create a beautiful and safe line. So, while one of us established a pitch, belayed by another for up to three or four hours, the third jumared up and down to clean the previous pitch.

To climb the upper mountain, we didn't want to follow the easy arête directly above our start (already breached by an older route), so we abseiled 60m onto the north face, a nearly vertical 300m sheet of limestone. We decided to tackle this triangular face straight up through a brown section that resembled a howling wolf. A drastic drop in temperatures resulted in two days of freezing on this shaded face—it seemed as if we were in Patagonia! Luca grit his teeth and summoned his energy to finish the last hard pitch.

After two days of rest we redpointed the route on February 3, each climber leading the pitches he'd established. For my two friends, 7c climbing was probably a mere formality, but for me, having spent half the year recovering from a broken leg, redpointing my crux pitch was a significant undertaking, as was the first pitch of the route, which I also established: a 50m 7a+ with holds covered in dust from all the cleaning on the pitches above. We were pretty spent when we summited, and we abseiled by the beams of our headlamps, as usual. Mission accomplished, in less than 15 days. 📷

— MAURIZIO OVIGLIA, *ITALY*

[Above] **Pico Independencia (left) and Pico Pirineos,** with the new routes (1) Snail Trail (Fasoldt-Schaffer) and (2) El Lobo del Desierto (Giupponi-Larcher-Oviglia). Earlier routes not shown. *Rolando Larcher*

PARQUE LA HUASTECA, PICO INDEPENDENCIA, SNAIL TRAIL

IN EARLY 2017, Pete Fasoldt and Jonathan Schaffer established a nine-pitch sport route on the northeast face of Pico Independencia, between the older routes La Norte and Directisima. "The route was bolted ground-up, sussed top-down, and subsequently sent flawlessly," Fasoldt reported. Snail Trail (300m, 5.12) is protected mostly with bolts, supplemented by a light rack, and can be rappelled with a single 70m rope.

— *INFORMATION FROM* PETE FASOLDT

EL SALTO, EL CHAMÁN LOCO

IN NOVEMBER 2015, Italians Marco Maggioni, Paolo Marazzi, and Simone Pedeferri completed a 400m route up the El Chamán (Shaman) face at El Salto. The route was started about two decades earlier by Mexican climbers Paco Medina and Alex Patino. The Italian climbers spent six days aiding the line to the top of the wall (14 pitches). Marazzi and Pedeferri freed all but four of the pitches, with very sustained difficulty: The upper 11 pitches are mostly 7b to 8a+ (5.12b to 5.13c), with two pitches estimated at 8b or 8c but yet to be redpointed.

The new route, El Chamán Loco, is the second line up this huge face in El Salto, an area best known for difficult sport climbing. In 2006, Jimmy Carse (USA) and partners completed Samadhi after several years of effort. Alex Honnold and Chris Weidner free climbed the route (10 pitches, 5.13-) in 2009. 🔍

— DOUGALD MACDONALD, *WITH INFO FROM PLANETMOUNTAIN.COM, ULRIC ROUSSEAU, AND CHRIS WEIDNER*

BRAZIL

[Above] Sasha DiGiulian leads a steep pitch during the two-day free ascent of Planeta dos Macacos (650m, 5.13), the only known route on the main north face of Pedra Filhote. *Red Bull House Media*

MINAS GERAIS

PEDRA FILHOTE, PLANETA DOS MACACOS, CONTINUOUS FREE ASCENT

IN 2015, FELIPE Cazmargo (Brazil) told me about a climb in the "Yosemite of Brazil," near the town of São José do Divino. A decade earlier, a team of climbers, mostly from Chile, had equipped a route called Planeta dos Macacos up the north-facing wall of Pedra Filhote, just to the northwest of Pedra Riscada, but did not make a continuous free ascent. I met Felipe on July 19, 2016, in Belo Horizonte. From there we drove eight hours to the wall.

We spent two days climbing and two nights on the wall. Storms rolled through at night, and we had no cover from the rain on our portaledge, making for some wet, cold conditions. Planeta dos Macacos (650m) has several particularly challenging pitches, two of which are solid 5.13. We onsighted all the pitches, with Felipe leading the crux 10th pitch; I led the second-hardest pitch. I'd never done a first free ascent on a wall like this, so the achievement, especially with Felipe, whom I've known for 10 years now, feels extra special. 📷 ▶

— SASHA DIGIULIAN, *USA*

EDITOR'S NOTE: *Planeta dos Macacos was opened in 2005 by Bernardo Gimenez and partners. Gimenez said the route was established top-down, following one of the wall's only natural weaknesses. Every pitch was climbed free by at least one member of the team; however, they did not make a continuous ground-up ascent. The climbers proposed 7c+ (5.13a) for the hardest pitch, but Gimenez noted that the rock's sometime's fragile holds might make the climb feel harder.*

PEDRA BAIANA, EAST FACE, SANGRE LATINA

In August, Argentinean climber Horacio Gratton and Brazilian climbers Wagner Borges, William Lacerda, Valdesir Machado, and Ed Padilha opened a difficult 17-pitch route on Pedra Baiana. (Gabriel Tarso and Edson Vandeira were also present to document the ascent.) Pedra Baiana is about 20km southeast of Pedra Riscada, between the towns of Itabirinha and Nova Belem, on private coffee-growing land. The climbers asked permission for access and then established base camp 20 minutes from the east face. [*Editor's note: The big east face of Pedra Baiana is thought to have been previously unclimbed, with one prior attempt, in 2003, by 2016 team members Lacerda, Machado, and Padilha, ending 450m up the wall. Gratton and Ed Padilha had previously established new routes on Pedra Riscada; see AAJ 2010 and AAJ 2016.*]

The team began their ascent up a vertical panel (7c+/8a). The crux second pitch (believed to be 8b/8b+) ascends a dihedral with a finger crack that finishes through a roof that the climbers thought resembled the Great Roof on the Nose of El Capitan. For the next several days, the climbers made their way toward what looked like a ledge for a bivouac. The ledge didn't exist, but they were lucky and found a perfect cave with level ground 15m to the right, at the top of the sixth pitch. They called this bivouac El Buraco ("The Hole").

Above this, the rock became overhanging, with several pitches of 8 and only a few of moderate difficulty. Portaledges were essential. Several lower-angled pitches gained the top, which they finally reached on day ten.

They called their route Sangre Latina (800m, 8b/8b+, not yet redpointed), which means "Latin Blood," after the wounds they received during the ascent. Seven of the 17 pitches are believed to be grade 8, but not all have been led free. Although bolts were placed, many sections require traditional gear. The climbers recommend a rack of 20 quickdraws, two sets of cams from 0.3–6", and nuts. 📷 🔍

— MARCELO SCANU, *Argentina*

[Below left] **Scoping the options on Pedra Baiana prior to the ascent of Sangre Latina (800m, proposed 8b/b+). The completed route begins left of the obvious gash and climbs directly to the ridgeline.**
[Below right] **Exposed climbing midway up Sangre Latina.** *Gabriel Tarso / Edson Vandeira*

[Above] Looking out from Tabuleiro while working on the new route Para Temprano es Tarde. This sector of the wall overhangs at an average angle of 35°. [Left] Para Temprano es Tarde climbs through the huge roofs left of the waterfall on this 400-meter wall. *Horacio Gratton*

TABULEIRO, PARA TEMPRANO ES TARDE

In July, Horacio Gratton (Argentina) teamed up with Lucas "Jah" Marques and Gustavo Fontes (Brazil) to climb a new route up Tabuleiro, a 400m wall in the state of Minas Gerais. Tabuleiro is about an hour's drive from the town of Conceicao do Mato Dentro, followed by a one-hour hike to the base. The wall overhangs for 250m (at an average angle of 35°) and a waterfall runs down the center. Both Brazilian climbers knew the wall from a previous ascent of one the most difficult routes: Smoke on the Water (9 pitches, 8a+, Bean-Cuca, 2012).

The new route starts with the first two pitches of Smoke on the Water to reach a ledge, where the climbers camped, then breaks left through a big roof. It took two days to climb the first two pitches above their camp. The first is believed to be 8b/8b+, and the second ascends the 30m near-horizontal Pac Man Roof (8a).

Two more hard pitches—7c+/8a and 8b—lead to a 7a pitch connecting the new route into the final pitch of Smoke on the Water. The route, Para Temprano es Tarde (400m, proposed 8b+), has not yet been free climbed in its entirety. 📷

— MARCELO SCANU, *ARGENTINA*

ECUADOR

ALTAR MASSIF, CANÓNIGO, SOUTHWEST RIDGE (ELENA RIDGE)

DURING THE 1970S, when the Altar massif saw many of its first ascents, the well-known Ecuadorian climber Ramiro Navarrete attempted the southwest ridge of Canónigo (5,260m). Although he did not succeed, he dubbed the ridge Elena, after his daughter. [*Canónigo was first climbed in 1965 by an Italian expedition led by Marino Tremonti, who also led the first ascent of Obispo, the highest summit of the Altar group, in 1963.*] There had been several other attempts on this ridge since the late '70s, but the bad weather and loose rock in this region didn't allow passage until this year, when Pablo Falconí and I made the first ascent. As a way of honoring this area's first explorers, we suggest the name Arista Elena (Elena Ridge).

At the beginning of January we started from Hacienda Releche on the west side of the mountain and approached for two days to the base of Canónigo's southwest ridge. Knowledge gained from previous attempts helped us navigate through the area's tall grass páramo (tropical tundra). On the third day we started up the ridge, mostly simul-climbing but sometimes pitching it out. The hardest part was a rocky section we felt to be 6b; however, the majority of the climb was between 5a and 5c. The upper ridge presented mixed terrain up to M4, with snow ramps to 60°. It took us most of a day to complete the 800m climb and descend our line of ascent. ▣

– JOSHUA JARRIN, *ECUADOR*

ALTAR MASSIF, MONJA GRANDE, FIRST COMMUNION

IN DECEMBER, NICOLAS Dávalos (Ecuador) and I climbed a new line up the southwest side of Monja Grande (5,316m), one of the major peaks comprising the Altar massif. (*Editor's note: Monja Grande's elevation is frequently stated as 5,160m, but the author's GPS confirmed the 5,316m elevation, and the peak is not much lower than neighboring Obispo, generally given 5,319m.*) We approached Altar on December 2 and acclimatized the following day.

At 2 a.m. on December 4, we left the Italian Camp on El Altar's south aspect and traversed the glacier toward Monja Grande. Soft snow (55°–65°) led to the Obispo–Monja Grande col, from which we aimed straight for the summit, climbing three and a half new pitches up ice and snow (AI3), left of the 1968 south face route. We finished up a narrow ice gully to reach the summit. We descended our route by rappel from V-thread and piton anchors and reached the Italian Camp later that day. We named our route First Communion (700m, 250m of technical climbing, AI3). ▣

– FELIPE PROAÑO, *ECUADOR*

[Right] Felipe Proaño looking out on the east ridge of Obispo, highest summit of the Altar massif, from the summit ridge of Monja Grande. *Nicolas Dávalos*

PERU

[This page] Steve Fortune and Matthew Scholes high on the southeast ridge of Taulliraju. *Daniel Joll* [Facing Page] Taulliraju (5,830m) from the southwest. The west (northwest) ridge follows the left skyline, and the upper southeast ridge is on the right. (A) Third Buttress, showing the ANZAC variation to the GMHM Route (1988). (B) Taulliraju Sur (ca 5,400m), with the south ridge, climbed in 2016, on the right. *Ben Dare*

NEW ROUTES ON TAULLIRAJU AND OTHER ASCENTS

At the end of May, the Expedition Climbers Club set out from New Zealand for a five-week trip to the Cordillera Blanca. The team was comprised of Steven Fortune, Pete Harris, Daniel Joll, Alastair McDowell, Reg and Claire Measures, Jaz Morris, Rose Pearson, Lincoln Quilliam, Matthew Scholes, Stephen Skelton, and me.

Our group established a base camp at the head of Laguna Parón and divided into separate climbing teams. On June 3, McDowell, Quilliam, Skelton, and I set out to attempt the southeast face of a peak in the Caraz group. Splitting into teams of two, we tackled the 400m face via two independent lines. McDowell and Quilliam started up a gully just right of the center of the face, where they encountered moderate snow and ice to WI2 and mixed ground to M4. Skelton and I climbed directly toward the summit following a steep, névé-filled gully broken by a series of thinly iced rock slabs. Both teams climbed the face to the underside of the menacing cornices lining the ridge crest (approximately 30m below the summit), one of which collapsed on Skelton and I as we neared the top, fortunately without serious damage other than a smashed helmet. [*Editor's note: The 2016 team believed this face was unclimbed and called the peak Caraz IV in their reports. However, this peak is Caraz III and the face was climbed in 1997 by a U.S. trio who also stopped below the cornice (Erickson-Knoll-Wolf, AAJ 1998). Dare and Skelton repeated the 1997 route; the McDowell-Quilliam line to the cornice is new.*]

On June 6, I attempted a new route on the southwest face of Pirámide (5,885m), starting up a small avalanche cone to the left of the Wolf-Clarke Route. Mixed ground and thin ice led brought me to the west ridge about 500m above where I started. Confronted with unstable ice mushrooms, I rappelled the line without continuing to the top.

Following our time in the Parón Valley, we returned to Huaraz and then, on June 15, ventured into the Santa Cruz Valley, where we focused our attention on the primary objective of the expedition, the majestic Taulliraju (5,830m).

Without delay, Fortune, Joll, and Scholes set out to climb the south-southeast ridge on June 16. They intended to start on the GMHM Route (1988) up the third buttress, to the right of the main southwest face, but found the entire buttress devoid of ice. This forced them out left onto the crest of the buttress, where they climbed nine new pitches of sustained and often run-out mixed ground (M6) to reach the south-southeast

[Above] Traversing the knife-edged upper south-southeast ridge of Taulliraju Sur. *Steve Fortune*

ridge. Here, ice conditions improved and they were able to follow the upper section of the Guides' Route (1978) to the summit. They encountered overhanging ice steps to AI6 on the final pitches. They dubbed their new line on the third buttress the ANZAC variation.

Two other teams also launched climbs on June 16: Harris, Measures, Morris, and Pearson made it about one-third of the way along the unclimbed west ridge. (This is sometimes described as the northwest ridge, its orientation low on the ridge.) Meanwhile, Skelton and I set out for the far side of the peak to attempt a new route on the east aspect. Initially, we climbed the first five pitches of the Guides' Route to reach a campsite on the flat crest of the lower south-southeast ridge. From that point we fully committed ourselves by rappelling an overhanging serac down into the lower glacier basin on the eastern aspect. Here, we climbed a prominent rock rib— which we called the East Rib—for 12 pitches up mostly immaculate granite (5.10b), leading us directly to a junction with the upper northeast ridge. [*This route is 100m to 200m right of the 2006 Slovenian route El Centelleo (see AAJ 2007).*] We spent the night huddled on a small ledge below the ridge crest. The following morning we moved onto the upper north face, climbing another four ice and mixed pitches (AI5 M5) directly to the summit.

On June 21, Quilliam and I made an unsuccessful attempt at a new route on the south face of Pucajirca Sur (6,040m). At the same time, Fortune, McDowell, and Pearson made the first ascent of the 450m south ridge of Taulliraju Sur (ca 5,400m), the highest summit along the lower southern ridge crest. [*Taulliraju Sur was first climbed by Topher and Patience Donahue in 2001 via an ice/mixed route on its northwest flank they called Middle Earth (see AAJ 2002)*]. The trio encountered sustained mixed climbing on the lower ridge (M5). After a short diversion onto the northwest face, they regained the ridge, climbing moderate, blocky ground to the summit.

The last climb of the expedition was also one of the most noteworthy, as Pearson teamed up with McDowell and returned for a second attempt at the west ridge of Taulliraju. Setting out from base camp early on June 23, the pair soon reached the Taulliraju-Ririjirca col and made good progress up the lower ridge, surpassing their previous high point early on the second day. That day, June 24, Fortune and Measures also started an attempt on the ridge. Soon, both teams were weaving their way along the ridge crest, often in full view of the watching climbers at base camp. They were confronted with a multitude of difficulties, ranging from vertical unconsolidated snow and overhanging ice to thin mixed climbing and compact dry granite (5.8 AI5 M4). On the afternoon of the fourth day (day three for Fortune-Measures) all four climbers reached the summit. They briefly celebrated in the dwindling light before Fortune led the now-familiar descent down the south side. 📷 ▶

– BEN DARE, *NEW ZEALAND*

[Above] Max Bonniot starting up the east pillar of Siulá Grande on the first day of the climb: technical climbing on solid, sticky limestone. *Didier Jourdain*

THE EAST PILLAR OF SIULÁ GRANDE
A LIGHTWEIGHT PUSH UP A HUGE UNTOUCHED FACE

BY MAX BONNIOT

IN THE WINTER of 2016, Didier Jourdain presented a photo of Siulá Grande's east face to his teammates of the Groupe Militaire de Haute Montagne (GMHM) in France. Didier had visited the Cordillera Huayhuash 13 years earlier and climbed a wonderful new route on Jirishanca; he thought it would be possible to find good rock on Siulá Grande (6,344m). Our team did a lot of research but did not find any record of attempts on this wild 1,400m wall.

Didier and I became very motivated by the prospect climbing such a large and unknown rock face. The possibility of climbing in a party of two was exciting to us as well, since at the GMHM we usually climb in teams of four on high-altitude mountains. In a smaller party, there is more commitment; one has to bring more experience, physical and technical skills, and ability to handle doubts and fear. Didier is 10 years older than me and had taken part in 20 expeditions. I had only done a few expeditions, but I was efficient on alpine ground and fast at rock climbing. We would form a good team.

In late August, Didier and I, along with other members of the GMHM, traveled to the southern Cordillera Huayhuash. The other members of the team, Arnaud Bayol, Antoine Bletton, Cyril Duchêne, and Dimitry Munoz, climbed a new route on Puscanturpa Este (*see next report*). Didier and I began our first attempt on Siulá Grande on August 21. We climbed three pitches before snowfall covered the vertical limestone and the wall became impassable. We spent the night only 100m above the bergschrund, then abseiled down and escaped to base camp the following day.

Our true start took place on August 24. It seemed we would have five days of good weather—just enough time, we thought, for a round trip to the summit. The wall was immediately steep and provided technical climbing on sticky limestone, with good rock,

[Above] The east face of Siulá Grande (6,344m), seen from 4,500m during the approach. The line of Le Bruit des Glaçons is shown. The large rock peak to the right is Siula Antecima, first climbed by its northeast ridge (upper part seen in right skyline) in 2006. Between the two is part of Siulá Grande's northeast face, which has at least two routes. *Didier Jourdain*

plentiful holds, and easy-to-find protection. Higher up, we climbed two ice pitches to reach a big cornice, where we found a good ledge for our first bivy. It was the perfect place to study the next pitches, and a natural line appeared up the right side of the wall.

In the morning we ascended slabs on less solid rock. We found only superficial cracks, and belays were difficult to establish. We began to have doubts about our line, as we didn't carry bolts. Luckily, our intuition for the line proved correct, and we eventually reached a crack system leading toward the ridge atop the pillar. That night, August 25, we bivied at 5,600m, having climbed 10 varied pitches. Our bivy was just 100m below the top of the rock wall. The unclimbed southeast ridge of Siulá Grande hovered above us. This 700m ridge did not appear difficult, but in the Andes corniced ridges are never simple to climb, and it was also hard to see exactly how we would reach the ridge from the top of the rock pillar. A fine hail began as we dug out our two-square-meter bedroom.

On August 26 we woke at dawn to climb the final rock pitches. A short pendulum led us to the foot of a nearby crack system, which took us to the ridge with excellent 6b pitches. In all we climbed 24 pitches up the pillar.

At noon we finally saw the scene ahead: Connecting the pillar to the ridge would not be easy. We fixed our 60m haul rope, making one full length rappel down vertical slabs that would have been very hard to climb back up during our descent from the summit. After a second, shorter rappel, we reached icy ground approximately 100m below the pillar, at the col separating the pillar from the ridge. We cast off toward the ridge, which was lined with huge cornices. The forecast now promised a disturbance for the following day. We decided to climb as far as possible that afternoon. The snow conditions did not allow us to find good protection, and we often simul-climbed without anything to secure us. At 9 p.m. we reached a snow mushroom and dug a terrace just below it for a bivouac, at 6,200m, and plunged into a deep sleep by 11 p.m.

After an early start on August 27, we reached the summit without mishap at 8 a.m., far above a magical landscape. Despite the long descent ahead, we took time to enjoy the moment at this suspended place.

After retracing our steps down the icy ridge we found our way back to the col. We first had to climb a pitch of WI5 back out of the notch to reach the end of our fixed rope, which we then ascended to regain the east pillar. From there, the descent was committing: 700m of abseiling with our rack of about 30 pitons, nuts, and cams. We reached the glacier midday on August 28 and then base camp shortly after. During our five-day effort we felt both great pleasure and doubt on this untouched side of one of the most famous mountains of the Andes.

SUMMARY: First ascent of Le Bruit des Glaçons (1,400m, ED 6c WI5), the east pillar and southeast ridge of Siulá Grande in the Cordillera Huayhuash, by Max Bonniot and Didier Jourdain, August 24–28, 2016. This report was translated from French by Claude Gardien.

PUSCANTURPA ESTE, NORTH FACE, EL JUEGO SUMANDO

IT'S NEVER EASY to find a fine new line, especially when your requirements border close to arrogance: unclimbed, vertical, sunny, with good rock, and, of course, all free. However, we managed to find a jewel in Peru, realizing a new route up the north face of Puscanturpa Este. It was a complete success.

In late August our team from the Groupe Militaire de Haute Montagne (GMHM), which included Antoine Bletton, Cyril Duchêne, Dimitry Munoz, and myself (along with Max Bonniot and Didier Jourdain, who climbed a new route on Siula Grande (*see prior report*), traveled to the Cordillera Huayhuash. Puscanturpa Este (5,445m) is located at the southern end of the range. Unlike the famous limestone mountains here—Yerupaja, Siula Grande, Jirishanca—the Puscanturpa peaks are made of solid volcanic "organ pipes," where free climbing is quite enjoyable.

We initially aided the lower 200m of the wall, due to difficult protection. Our cams and ordinary pitons did not work well here—hard steel pitons would push aside the giant columns with a frightening noise, every hammer knock resonating and propagating through the column. We were forced to use classic soft steel pitons instead.

Operating in a team of four, two climbers would struggle to open the route above while the other two tried to free the pitches below. It took time to clean the cracks and add some bolts to belays or run-out sections. It took us seven days to reach the summit in this style, free climbing all of the pitches. We called our route El Juego Sumando (400m, ED 7b, mandatory 6b). We hoped to repeat the route in single-push, redpoint style over one to two days but ran out of time. Apart from the belays, the in-situ gear consists of 12 pitons, four

[Top] Dimitry Munoz leading a 7b pitch up a dihedral and wide crack on El Juego Sumando. [Middle] Aid climbing while establishing the initial 200m of the new route on Puscanturpa Este's north face. [Bottom] The north face of Puscanturpa Este (5,445m). (1) Poco Loco (Dutch, 2012). (2) El Juego Sumando (French, 2016). The north ridge, climbed by a British team in 1986 for the peak's first ascent, generally follows the left skyline, approached from the far side. *Arnaud Bayol*

nuts, and 10 protection bolts, plus anchor bolts. A full rack, including additional soft steel pitons, is required.

Although the abseil descent reduces the commitment, this climb remains demanding. The altitude at the start is 5,000m, and there are a lot of committing pitches, with long passages of 6b climbing lacking protection. Overall, this sunny and steep wall would fill lovers of crack climbing with great enthusiasm!

[*Editor's note: There are now five known routes on Puscanturpa Este: the north ridge (British, 1986), the east face (Kozjek-Kresal, 2007), the north face (Dutch, 2012), the southeast face (Noda-Yamanoi, 2013), and the new route up the north face (French, 2016).*]

— ARNAUD BAYOL, *FRANCE, TRANSLATED FROM FRENCH BY CLAUDE GARDIEN*

[Above] Duncan McDaniel climbing below a serac on Nevado Panta. *Waldemar Niclevicz*

CORDILLERA VILCABAMBA

NEVADO PANTA, SOUTH RIDGE; PUMASILLO, WEST RIDGE, NEARLY COMPLETE ASCENT

THE PUMASILLO GROUP has the most extensive collection of glaciated peaks in the Cordillera Vilcabamba, yet only a handful of ascents have occurred here. The west ridge of Pumasillo (5,991m) was climbed by five expeditions between 1957 and 1974, and Carlos Buhler and Paul Harris climbed its east face in 1988, making the most recent known ascent of the peak.

In 2014, Waldemar Niclevicz and I tried to repeat the west ridge but turned around at 5,700m. From trip reports, I could see that the west ridge had been snowier in the past, and therefore broader and easier to navigate. In late July, Waldemar and I returned to Pumasillo, this time accompanied by Florian Peter (Switzerland) and Duncan McDaniel (USA). On August 1, we climbed the west ridge to a point 50m below the summit cornice, where a large crevasse blocked our way. I felt the difficulties of this 1,000m climb were around TD+ WI4.

After a couple of days' rest in the jungle town of Santa Teresa, Duncan, Waldemar, and I set off for the remote, westernmost glaciated group of the Vilcabamba and our primary objective, Nevado Panta (ca 5,840m, a.k.a. Otaña). The mountain has had one known ascent, up the north face, by a Swiss team in 1959, one of their many first ascents in the Vilcabamba (*AAJ 1960*).

On August 15, from Huancacalle, we traveled on 4WD roads for two hours toward the south side of Panta. At a large curve in the road, southeast of the peak, there is a forest of Puya raimondii cactus where we started the hike to base camp. We followed a good trail up the

left-hand side of the valley and spent the night on ledges below the glacier at 4,800m.

On August 16, we began at 1 a.m., climbing the glacier below the broad south ridge. On the ridge proper, we picked our way through a maze of towering seracs and crevasses, with some sections of WI4. Once on the summit plateau, we post-holed to the top, reaching it by 10 a.m. The descent went smoothly down our route, with several fun rappels down ice blocks, and we were back at camp by 5 p.m. (850m, D+ WI4).

The 2016 route up the south ridge of Nevado Panta (ca 5,840m), the first ascent from this side of the mountain and the peak's second known ascent. *Nathan Heald*

The Vilcabamba remains one of the least climbed areas in Peru with great new-route potential, not just on glaciated peaks but also on large granite towers like those in Quelcamachay. Nowadays there are many roads offering easier access to these areas.

— NATHAN HEALD, *PERU*

NEVADO BONANTA, EAST RAMP

ON MARCH 9, Eduardo Baca, Yjeguel Camasa, and I climbed Nevado Bonanta (a.k.a. Bonomia, ca 5,300m), a rounded glacial summit on the ridge extending west from Nevado Veronica (5,893m). Our route up the east ramp had a short, easy, but very exposed 5th-class rock section to gain the glacier. Here, I found an old Charlet Moser ice axe; I believe it is from the 1958 Italian expedition that made the first ascents of Bonanta, Huakeihuilqui, Marconi, and the Chicon peaks farther east (*AAJ 1959*). The climb onto the summit plateau was straightforward on 120m of 50° ice, after which we post-holed up knee-deep snow until the summit (300m, PD+). Clouds blocked any views, but they would be spectacular on a clear day.

— NATHAN HEALD, *PERU*

[Above] Nevado Bonanta (lower peak on left) and Nevado Veronica, seen from the south. The 2016 route on Bonanta climbed a glacier toward the saddle right of the peak, then up the ridge to the summit. *Nathan Heald*

NEVADO HALANCOMA, WEST FACE (NOT TO SUMMIT)

ON JUNE 28, Andres Marin and I drove from Ollantaytambo up a paved highway (28B) that goes up a steep valley, with seemingly endless switchbacks, to a pass called Puerto Malaga and then down the other side to the large town of Quillabamba. Our goal was Nevado Halancoma (5,367m).

We started our approach at the largest left-turning switchback beyond the 117km marker, at about 3,900m. Our approach began up a steep, grassy valley, from which we climbed a steep hillside on the right for almost 700m to gain a ridge crest (4,570m), where we got our first view

[Above] The west side of Nevado Halancoma from Nevado Veronica, showing the 2016 ascent. The high peaks in the left background are (left to right) Chainopuerto (5,650m), Sahuasiray Norte (5,818m), and Sahuasiray Sur (5,770m). *Nathan Heald*

of the west face of Halancoma. Cliffs made it difficult to determine the best way down the far side and we traversed for some time. It took us five hours from the ridge to reach a lake camp below the west face at 4,650m.

The next morning we were up at 4:30 a.m. and began stumbling our way up the mass of boulders, steep scree, and rock slabs to reach the toe of the glacial ramp we planned to climb. The ramp was not any steeper than about 50°, so we did not rope up until the final 20m to the summit ridge, as this involved mixed climbing on ice and broken rock. We reached the ridge crest about four hours after leaving camp.

The main summit of Halancoma was a few hundred meters to the south and not much higher than where we were, but the loose rock ridge convinced us to descend from where we were. We found a large block to sling and began rappelling our ascent route, returning to camp around noon. Our climb was 700m, 50° AI2 5.5 and similar to climbing the north face of Mt. Sneffels in Colorado via its Snake Couloir. 📄 📷

– BRAD JOHNSON, *USA, WITH ADDITIONAL INFORMATION FROM NATHAN HEALD*

HALANCOMA HISTORY: *Nevado Halancoma has two tops: the south summit (5,367m) and the north summit (ca 5,300m). There has been some confusion between the peaks known as Halancoma and Huacratanca (ca 5,000m), which is just to the southeast. Additionally, Halancoma has also been called Helancoma or Alancoma. Local climber Nathan Heald believes that both the south and north summits of Halancoma were first reached by Piero Gighlione in 1953, when he also climbed Huacratanca. The route up the north face (F/PD) to the north top has become popular with local groups. The south summit has seen fewer ascents: The east face was climbed in 1981 by Tom Hendrickson and John Saunders; Peruvian climbers Cesar Cahuana and Alfedo Zuniga traversed from north to south along the ridge between the two peaks in 2015; and in 2016 Peruvian climber Coqui Galvez soloed a new route up the south face (PD 55–65°; see AAJ website for route line).*

NEVADO CHAINOPUERTO, EAST FACE

IN APRIL, EDUARDO Baca, Yjeguel Camasa, Coqui Galvez, and I climbed a probable new route up the east face of Nevado Chainopuerto (5,650m), an outlying peak of Nevado Sahuasiray (5,818m). I had seen this peak a few times from other summits in the area; its three-sided summit pyramid is 150m tall and comes to a sharp point.

On April 5, we started our approach from the northeast via Maucau. It took five hours to reach the eastern base of the peak, which was covered in dense clouds. Due to the low visibility, we unknowingly pitched our camp below an icefall, which led to a close call in the middle of the night. The following day we moved camp out of this shooting gallery to a more secure location and rested.

We left the tent at 2 a.m. on April 7 and navigated the eastern glacier through the clouds and dark until a beautiful sunrise. From the col between Nevado Can Can and Chainopuerto, we started up the summit pyramid of Chainopuerto, climbing 70° ice up the southern aspect. Clouds had rolled in from the jungle, reducing visibility to 40m. We could not stand together on top of the unstable summit cornice, so we went one at a time. We reversed our route, reaching the tent before dark.

Chainopuerto was first attempted by a Scottish team in 1964 by its southeast side; they came up 200 feet short of the summit (*AAJ 1965*). In 1968 an Irish team made the first ascent. It was attempted by Club de Andinismo Cusco a few times in the early 2000s without success. I believe our route up the east side of the peak to the col is new, but we likely climbed the summit cone via a similar route to the Scots and Irish—the 600m route was D AI3.

– NATHAN HEALD, *PERU*

CORDILLERA VILCANOTA

NEVADO JATUNHUMA, EAST FACE, NEW ROUTE

ON JUNE 1, Nathan Heald (Peru) and I climbed a new route up the east face (700m, D+) of Nevado Jatunhuma (6,141m, a.k.a. Tres Picos or Pico Tres). This is the only known ascent of the east face since a Yugoslavian team visited the Cordillera Vilcanota in 1980. [*Editor's note: Jatunhuma is a triple-summited*

[Top] Nathan Heald on the summit ridge of Nevado Jatunhuma (a.k.a. Tres Picos or Pico Tres, 6,141m). Callangate at left. *Derek Field* [Bottom] Nevado Jatunhuma and nearby peaks from the east: (A) Ausangate (6,384m). (B) Jatunhuma, showing the Field-Heald Route (2016, red line) and the approximate Yugoslavian Route (Kolar-Mihev-Radovič-Žagar, 1980, yellow line). (C) Callangate (a.k.a. Cayangate, 6,110m). *Nathan Heald*

peak first climbed by a German expedition in 1957. Search the AAJ website for reports of various routes.] Starting in the vicinity of Laguna Singrenacocha, northeast of Jatunhuma, this trip took us five days in total. On day four, we established a high camp in the moraine at about 5,300m and departed our tent just past midnight. Reaching the base of the main wall at sunrise, we cruised several hundred meters of 70° snow to the summit ridge, then carefully balanced our way northward along the outrageous knife-edge cornice to the top. Nathan's GPS recorded the height at 6,127m, close to the stated elevation. 🗎 📷

– DEREK FIELD, *CANADA*

NEVADO HUAYRURO PUNCO, WEST FACE; NEVADO PARCOCAYA, SOUTH FACE

ON JULY 16, I traveled into the Vilcanota Range with my client John Lewis (USA) and assistant guide Luis Crispin (Peru) to climb Ausangate's normal route. However, we abandoned this plan due to deep snow and instead turned our attention to smaller peaks in the area. Our first objective was Nevado Huayruro Punco (5,550m), a mountain that crowns the divide between the Pitumarca and Sibinacocha watersheds; it is also sometimes called Pacco. I could not find a record of anyone climbing the 350m west face (most ascents occur via the north aspect). The west face is the steepest, most heavily glaciated side of the mountain, with ice reaching down to about 5,200m.

At 3 a.m. on July 18, we left our base camp near the village of Jampa and hiked up Quebrada Chilcamayo. Luis left us after the 5–6km approach, at the base of the glacier, just after sunrise. John and I crossed the glacier to the main headwall, where the obvious crux presented itself: 30m of 70° blue ice with two bulges, all of it capped by a 5m serac. I spent over an hour leading this pitch, due to a full meter of fresh snow. Above the headwall, we marched up penitente slopes to the summit, where Luis awaited us. While John and I were busy climbing the west face, Luis had climbed the standard north ridge route with a random stray puppy as his partner. We decided to name the dog Pacco after the mountain. All four of us descended the standard north ridge. Our new route was 350m, AD+ WI3.

On July 22 we explored the vast moraine at the base of Ausangate's north face. We eventually reached a beautiful olive-green tarn at about 4,840m, at the base of Nevado Parcocaya (5,290m). Luis and John stayed to rest at the lake below while I made a solo ascent of the south face.

After weaving through dozens of crevasses, I arrived at the base of the major headwall. [*The author reports that Nathan Heald attempted this face alone*

[Below] Nevado Huayruro Punco (5,550m) from the west. The normal routes on this popular trekking peak ascend the left (north) side of the mountain. *Derek Field*

[Above] Derek Field stands on one summit of Papaccapac (ca 5,460m), with the impressive Screwdriver (ca 5,543m) behind. Screwdriver, first climbed in 1965, has three known routes. *Aaron Zimmerman*

two years ago but could not find a safe way through the vertical headwall of ice at ca 5,150m.] I chose a rock buttress on the far right side, which held a number of snow gullies. I ventured up the friendliest-looking gully (40–50° snow in a 3m-wide slot) and encountered a vertical rock step about 25m up. Awkward 5.7 chimney moves and a desperate belly flop landed me safely on the snow above. I continued up the gully to its junction with a 20m wall of blue ice (70°), then exited diagonally to the right on mixed terrain, manteling over a short ice step to gain the summit crest. On the west side of the 30m summit pinnacle, I found a way across the final bergschrund and continued up a steep dihedral (5.6) on quality metamorphic rock. On the summit I found a weathered sling, evidently used by a previous team climbing the normal route on the north side.

Cursing my foolishness for neglecting to bring a rope, I carefully downclimbed my route in its entirety. I was able to aid down most of the 5.7 rock step using the sling I'd found on top. My route on the south face of Nevado Parcocaya was 450m, AD 5.7 AI3. 📷 🔍

— DEREK FIELD, *CANADA*

CORDILLERA CARABAYA

"PICO CAROL," SOUTH FACE; PAPACCAPAC, SOUTH AND EAST FACES

On June 29, Vahi Beltrami (Chile), Yasu Beltrami (Chile), German Silva (Chile) Nathan Heald (Peru), Duncan McDaniel (USA), Aaron Zimmerman (USA), and I traveled to the Cordillera Carabaya. This seldom-visited range, with impressive snow and rock peaks rising to 5,780m, is located about 200km north of Juliaca in the Puno region of southeast Peru. The potential for new rock and ice routes remains significant.

[Above] The south side of ice-covered Allinccapac (5,780m map; 5,837m GPS), showing the new route up Peak 5,715m ("Pico Carol," at right). The west shoulder of Allinccapac, first climbed in 2008 and repeated in 2016, generally follows the left skyline. *Derek Field*

We drove north from the town of Macusani, capital of Carabaya province, and made our first base camp at around 4,600m in the Antajahua Valley. This moraine-bound basin is located below the unclimbed south face of Allinccapac (5,780m; 5,837m GPS), our main objective.

On June 30, after migrating to a high camp directly below the glacier at 5,000m, we climbed the gentle northeast face of Japuma (ca 5,550m), from which we identified a potential route on a runneled ice face below and slightly east of "Pico Carol" (5,715m), named and described as "a prominent gendarme on the east ridge of Allinccapac" by the 1960 Oxford Andean expedition.

At 3 a.m. on July 1, Nathan, Aaron, and I set off from high camp toward the runneled ice face, intending to reach the east ridge of Allinccapac from the ca 5,700m col just east of "Pico Carol." After crossing a penitente plain, slogging through deep snow, and overcoming a pitch of AI3 on the lower face, we crossed two significant crevasses and arrived at the base of the main headwall (ca 5,500m). This presented four pitches of steep, hard, and blue ice (80°). On the fourth lead, we traversed 20m left across a steep, unstable snow slope to gain the col. We proceeded along the east ridge of Allinccapac, bypassing "Pico Carol" on its north flank, but were unable to find a safe route, and so we retraced our steps to the 5,700m col. As a consolation prize, we climbed 15m of easy mixed ground up the northeast ridge of "Pico Carol" to the summit, protecting with cams.

We descended north down a snow slope, crossed a glacial plain at around 5,600m, and wrapped around the west shoulder of Allinccapac, making two rappels from its west ridge down to the base of the glacier. We made it back to base camp at 5 p.m., concluding a circumnavigation of the mountain. Our route up the south face of "Pico Carol" is 700m, D WI4.

On July 3, Aaron and I set out on a two-hour approach up a north-trending tributary of the Huayllatera Valley, aiming to enchain Papaccapac (ca 5,460m) and Mamaccapac (ca 5,450m) from the south. Mamaccapac was first climbed in 2007 by a British party via its north side, and Papaccapac was believed to be unclimbed.

We camped on the shore of a brilliant turquoise tarn (ca 4,700m) nestled at the foot of an awe-inspiring cirque of rock towers. Leaving the tent at 4 a.m. on July 4, we charged up a colossal mound of loose scree to a small rocky crest (ca 5,100m) dividing our base camp from the adjacent Chambine drainage to the east. From the crest, we dropped 100m (in a northeast direction) into the drainage to access the tongue of ice extending southward from the col between Papaccapac and Mamaccapac.

We navigated the lower crevasse field at dawn and then climbed the right side of the main south face, with about 200m of 70–80° ice. This brought us to the col between the two peaks (ca 5,350m), where we cached our ice gear and started up the complex east face of Papaccapac. After climbing a rock gully on the right side of the craggy summit, we switched to rock shoes and climbed three pitches of blocky but reliable rock (5.5–5.7) to the gendarmed summit.

With regard to the elevation of this previously unclimbed peak, Aaron and I made two observations: (1) Papaccapac is definitely taller than Mamaccapac, which was reported by the first ascensionists as 5,450m. We estimated the difference to be 10m, making Papaccapac roughly 5,460m; (2) It is difficult to tell which gendarme on top of Papaccapac is the true summit.

We returned to the col by rappelling twice from slung blocks. After a short rest, we began up the west side of Mamaccapac's summit tower. (This was called the "southwest ridge" by the 2007 British expedition. It's more of a blocky buttress than ridge, and it generally faces west.) The crux came early, with 50° ice transitioning directly into vertical rock. The upper part of this pitch featured an 8m horizontal traverse (5.7) on slippery but sturdy rock. Leaving our rope at the top of this pitch, we scrambled to the summit, where we found a cairn and rappel anchor left by the 2007 team. Two rappels brought us back to the col.

In the final hours of the afternoon, Aaron and I made four V-thread rappels down the first part of our route and then descended the lower glacier and moraine back to camp. We called our Papaccapac route Mom and Pop Shoppe (350m, D 5.7 AI3).

— DEREK FIELD, *CANADA*

NEVADO ALLINCCAPAC, WEST SHOULDER

IN EARLY JULY, I spent a week in the remote Cordillera Carabaya (*see previous report*). Our objective was the highest in the range, Nevado Allinccapac (5,780m, sometimes spelled Allincapac). However, after seeing the unclimbed south face up close, we climbed neighboring "Pico Carol" instead. Allinccapac remained in the back of my mind until October, when I returned with two friends from Cusco, Luis Crispin and Coqui Galvez.

On October 6, from the hostel in Macusani, we took a taxi to the lake below Allinccapac, and by the afternoon reached a high camp (5,200m) on the western shoulder. We left the tent around 2 a.m., heading for a line up the shoulder, where glacial ice is still prominent. After a pitch of WI3, we gained a lower-angle platform that led us to a prominent rock band. A couple of short pitches of easy climbing and traversing brought us to the summit ice cap. Two rope lengths of WI2/3 gave way to the broad summit plateau, on which we walked for 300m to the highest point. The GPS read 5,837m. We descended our route.

After this trip, local climber Renzo Leon reported that he and Angel Perez climbed Allinccapac on June 19, 2008. Their route appears to be similar to ours, if not the same, and is confirmed by a summit photo. [*Editor's note: The online version of this report contains two important corrections to a 2008 Alpine Journal article about climbs in the Carabaya.*] 📄 📷

— NATHAN HEALD, *PERU*

BOLIVIA

[Above] Pico del Norte (6,050m) from the north-northwest. The arrow marks the start of Ñeq'e Ñeq'e (Fava-Molina, 2013), which continued to the left of the prominent pillar above. In 2016, Rodrigo Lobo and Robert Rauch followed the same steep corner to start their new route Shit Happens, then moved right to climb the pillar directly, continuing up the upper face on more moderate terrain to reach the summit ice. The climbers descended the northwest ridge (right) before rappelling back to the north to return to the base of the peak. *Carlitos Molina*

PICO DEL NORTE: SHIT HAPPENS
A NEW ROUTE AND LONG DESCENT IN THE CORDILLERA REAL

BY ROBERT RAUCH

IN MY OPINION, Rodrigo Lobo is the strongest of the current young activists in Bolivia. Through extensive training together, we have built a mutual trust, and we are working to bring a new, more modern style to the harder Andean routes. Together we completed several significant first ascents in 2016 (*see below for more reports*). This one didn't go as smoothly as we'd hoped, but not for five minutes were we in a desperate situation. Thanks to our training, we always have some reserve in the tank.

Our goal was a new route on the northwest face of Pico del Norte (6,050m) in the Illampu group. In July, after waiting a day at our base camp because of snowy weather, we started up the left side of the face by climbing the initial corner pitches of Ñeq'e Ñeq'e (Fava-Molina, *AAJ 2014*) and then followed a parallel line to the right, more or less on the crest of the pillar that defines this side of the face. [*Editor's note: Some sources describe a prior route up this buttress at a grade of TD+ UIAA III AI4, but first ascent records are unclear—possibly German, possibly 1984.*] The first 300m were difficult but well protected; the remaining terrain was more moderate climbing, between 5a and 6a. The northwest aspect meant lots of sun, so the rock was warm and fun was guaranteed. We simul-climbed about half the route and unroped for easier sections to gain time. There were a few meters of ice climbing and loads of huge snow *penitentes* on the summit icecap.

We descended via the northwest ridge, which is mostly moderate ice with crevasses and penitentes. However, we made a mistake in route-finding and rappelled to the north too early.

Because of this, we were forced into an unexpected bivouac on a small ledge with no bivy gear. Next day, cloud covered the sky and we waited in vain for the morning sun to warm our bodies. We reached our camp in late morning and rested all afternoon, eating the rest of our food. Between 30cm and 40cm of snow fell during the ensuing night, and the granite slopes we had scrambled on the approach became impossible to descend. We sought and eventually found an alternative, with animal tracks showing the best way toward the end. We took many acrobatic tumbles on slippery, snow-covered rock.

When we finally reached the road, we didn't want to get chilled so we started walking immediately toward Sorata. We saw no cars for hours, but we had no worries; we were doing what we'd done many times before—we'd walk until we got back to civilization, no matter how long it took. It was a great surprise when suddenly three 4WDs stopped beside us in the pouring rain. It was a large group of Rodrigo's friends from Cochabamba and La Paz, who had driven 17 hours to look for us after Rodrigo was late for a hang-gliding competition. These are the kinds of friends I can only dream of!

Because of our experience on the mountain, we named the route Shit Happens (1,000m, 6c), a great climb on excellent granite.

L'HÉTACOMBE DES AVIONETTES: *Previously unreported is the route L'hétacombe des Avionnettes (900m, TD), climbed on the southeast ridge of Pico del Norte in July 2010 by Frenchmen Vincent Bailleu, Rémi Labourie, Benoit Montfort, and Josselin Perrugault. This is the prominent ridge or spur to the right of the Bettembourg Pillar. It seems likely this is a similar line to that first climbed over two days in the summer of 1972 by David Steel and Roger Skull, two U.K. alpinists who, later in the trip, died on Illampu after completing a difficult new route up the east face.*

CORDILLERA REAL

RUMI MALLKU, NORTH FACE, MINDFULNESS (NO SUMMIT); JAKOCERI, VARIATION TO SOUTH RIDGE

PIETRO SELLA, ANTONIO Zavattarelli (Padre Topio), and I made the second ascent of the south ridge of Jakoceri (ca. 5,800–5,900m) with our friend Davide Vitale, a great Andean climber and English teacher at the missionary in Peñas. Davide had climbed a new route on the west face earlier in the year, and a few days before our arrival, after consulting with Davide, two young Frenchmen climbed the south ridge and continued to the summit of Chachacomani. (*See reports below.*) On June 5, we climbed a steep snow slope to reach the ridge crest farther north than the French did. There was rock to 5c and ice to 60°. We descended from Jakoceri's south summit.

[Above] **Rumi Mallku seen from the north. (A) Ancohuma. (B) Pico Gotico (5,750m). (C) Rumi Mallku (5,982m).** This peak was probably first climbed in May 2006, via both the west and northeast ridges (reported to be scrambles) by guided parties led by G. Jaimes and J. Callisaya. As these two ridges look like the outstretched wings of a condor, they named the peak Condor of Stone. (1) Northeast ridge (Bolivian guides, 2006). (2) Northwest face (6a+, Flyvbjerg-Monasterio, 2006). (3) Mindfulness (6a, Italians, 2016, no summit). (4) West ridge (Bolivian guides, 2006). *Pietro Sella*

Antonio, Pietro, and I then moved to the northern end of the Cordillera Real and made camp by Laguna Glaciar, between Illampu and Ancohuma. Our plan was to try something in the Yacuma Group, but we were impressed by the huge bastion of Rumi Mallku (Stone Condor, 5,982m), which lies above the laguna, northwest of Ancohuma. The right side of its north face holds three pillars leading to a long west ridge, which rises directly to a shoulder beneath the summit.

On June 10 we made a reconnaissance of this face and stashed some gear. We decided on the left-hand pillar. We set off next morning at 4 a.m. and returned to camp at 9 p.m. The granite on the pillar was generally good, but on the more compact sections the cracks were blind and consequently difficult to protect. From the shoulder we descended, without continuing to the summit, by downclimbing ice slopes on the south face to reach the Ancohuma Glacier, which we followed back to our camp. We named the route Mindfulness (500m, with ca 700m of climbing, 6a). Various unclimbed objectives remain on the north face; perhaps most notable is the right-hand pillar.

– ENRICO ROSSO, *ITALY*

CHACHACOMANI GROUP, UNNAMED PEAK, LA TRAVESIA DE WINNIE APU

SHORTLY AFTER DAYLIGHT on September 22, Chris Knight (Canada) and I left our base camp at 4,800m in the valley that leads northeast to the Chearoco Glacier (between Chearoco and Chachacomani). We gained 500m and then scrambled along the west ridge of an unnamed peak at 15°59'44.13"S, 68°24'21.91"W (5,533m Google Earth). This dry mountain lies directly west, across the Chachacomani Glacier, from Jakoceri. We encountered cairns leading to the first top along the ridge but found no traces of prior climbing as we continued eastward along the crest toward the second and higher summit. We headed down to the east, witnessing a large rock collapse in the middle of the south face, and then turned north to descend to camp. Our route was named La Travesia de Winnie Apu, referring to the town of Winnipeg, from which both Chris and Winnie the Pooh originated.

– ALEXANDER VON UNGERN, *ANDEAN ASCENTS, BOLIVIA*

JAKOCERI, SOUTHWEST FACE, NEVER ENDING STORY

IN MID-MARCH, JOHNNY Ticona (Bolivia), Davide Vitale (Italy/Belgium, resident in Bolivia), and I made what we believe to be the first ascent of the southwest face of Jakoceri. (This peak is often quoted as ca 5,800m, but is possibly higher; it is shown as ca 5,900m on Google Earth.) The face, visible from Davide's kitchen window in Peñas, is beautiful, eye-catching, and among the most significant faces in this central part of the Cordillera Real. Davide had dreamed of climbing this ice and mixed wall for more than two years and had already visited a site for base camp below the mountain.

The approach, from Alto Cruzpampa, is long: about 25km up a valley. We had to cross rivers with high water from the rainy season, which gave us problems. Base camp was in a beautiful location, but given the demanding access it will probably never become overfrequented.

We left our tents at 4 a.m. and took a line on the left side of the face that was relatively direct, steep, and objectively safe. I led throughout. Several pitches were M5, with protection from cams and nuts. Continuing through a short-lived snowstorm, we found the upper part of the face to have rotten, rainy-season ice at 65–75°, with little or no meaningful protection.

After exiting onto the ridge we went up to the main (north) summit and then down the opposite (east) side of the mountain to the upper Chachacomani Glacier. From there we

[Above] High camp for Jakoceri (ca 5,800–5,900m) in early June 2016, in relatively dry conditions. (A) Chachacomani West (a.k.a. Sentinel). The main summit of Chachacomani (6,074m) is hidden behind. (B) Jakoceri main (north) summit. (C) Jakoceri south summit. The southwest face lies between the two summits, and the south ridge is the right skyline. (1) Never Ending Story. (2) Milanesa Patentada. (3) Italian start to south ridge. (4) French start to south ridge. All routes were climbed in 2016. *Pietro Sella*

headed back up west to the col between Chachacomani and Jakoceri, made one difficult rappel from an Abalakov anchor to the southwest, and then descended to our high camp at midnight. It was a complex and extremely long affair, and we named the route Never Ending Story (400m, TD).

Editor's note: It is not clear who made the first ascent of Jakoceri—possibly Japanese climbers as early as 1964. Until a flurry of activity in the first half of 2016, it had rarely been climbed. Full reports and photos of all the 2016 ascents can be found at publications.americanalpineclub. org. 📷

– ROBERT RAUCH, *BOLIVIAN TOURS, RAUCHROBERT@HOTMAIL.COM*

JAKOCERI, SOUTHWEST FACE, MILANESA PATENTADA

ON APRIL 3, Macelo Gomez (Bolivia), Nico Navarrete, and I (both from Ecuador) took a couple of buses and a taxi to Alto Cruzpampa and from there began a 25km walk up a valley to the foot of Jakoceri's southwest face. At 5 a.m. the next morning we started across a broken glacier, and after three hours we made it to the base of the wall. The temperature was low enough to keep the face in good condition, and we essentially climbed unroped, except for some pitches where we needed to assist Marcelo. Our line was well to the right of Never Ending Story, the first route up the face, and was mostly hard snow up to 80°, with some sections of mixed, and soft snow close to the ridge. We reached the south summit before noon, naming our route Milanesa Patentada (450–500m), and descended via the south ridge, downclimbing with one rappel at the end. 📄 📷

– ROBERTO MORALES, *ECUADOR*

JAKOCERI, SOUTH RIDGE AND TRAVERSE TO CHACHACOMANI

IT WAS 2 a.m. on May 25 at the 5,100m base camp for ascents of Chachacomani from the west. Jules Jenner and I woke up excited, but clouds obscured the peaks. We decided to sleep until 4 a.m. and then reassess the weather. Seven and a half hours later, we were gently woken by the sun. Damn! Neither of us had heard the alarm. But the weather was now nice and we wanted to climb, so at 10 a.m. we left camp and started up the Chachacomani Glacier.

At a large plateau around 5,450m on the normal route to Chachacomani, we headed east across the glacier to the south ridge of Jakoceri. Two poorly defined cracks led up to an obvious notch on the crest of the ridge; we chose the one on the left. After 40m of UIAA IV/V on good rock—once we had thrown off all the dirt—we reached the ridge. We turned the first gendarme on the right, then climbed exactly on the crest at UIAA IV. The ridge became easier and more mixed until it reached a small top, a point that could be gained more easily directly from the glacier, by a 65° snow slope. [*The Italian party that made the second ascent of this ridge, also in 2016, followed this "shortcut." See the Italians' Jakoceri and Rumi Mallku report above.*]

The ridge now became rocky again, with many short sections of climbing on beautiful

[Below] **Roberto Moralez and, below, Marcelo Gomez in the upper couloir of Milanesa Patentada on the southwest face of Jakoceri.** *Nicolas Navarrete*

[Above] On the north summit of Jakoceri with the south face of Sentinel (a.k.a. Chachacomani West) at left and Chachacomani to the right. Several routes ascend the shadowed south-southwest face of Chachacomani (6,074m). *Alexis Collette*

granite, reminiscent of Chamonix. We bypassed the third gendarme on the right via an amazing orange slab. We climbed the fourth gendarme on the left by a 3m crack (IV+) and then, after a short traverse, a second crack (V+) with a moving block. Above, we crossed the last notch and climbed easy mixed terrain, then snow, to the south summit of Jakoceri.

The traverse from here to the slightly higher north summit is largely an icy ridge with impressive cornices and amazing views toward Lake Titicaca and the Altiplano. We continued north, downclimbing to the 5,800m col between Jakoceri and Chachacomani, then continued up the south ridge of Chachacomani West, a.k.a. Sentinela or Sentinel [*AD+ and possibly first climbed in 1964*]. It was now 7 p.m. and the sun was beginning to set. We stayed close to the crest, enjoying fine mixed climbing (IV M3) to a final rocky section, which we overcame via a flake (V+). From the top of the Sentinel, it took only half an hour to traverse the ridge eastward to the summit of Chachacomani (6,074m).

In darkness we set off northwest down the normal route, trying to follow tracks that had been erased by the wind. We got lost and had to downclimb a 50m ice wall above a huge hole, leaving an ice screw for protection, but eventually made it back to our camp, arriving in the middle of the night—hence our route name: Back in Black (D+ V+). Although we made the ascent in May, this was a very dry year and we expect parties climbing the route during July and August of a normal year would find the same conditions as we did.

— ALEXIS COLLETTE, *FRANCE*

WILA LLOJE GROUP, PEAK 5,550M, NORTHWEST FACE

ON JUNE 26, 2012, I climbed a possible new route on Peak 5,550m, one of the subpeaks east of Wila Lloje. I climbed the northwest face at D-, a nice mixed route with a steep chimney near the top that provided the main difficulty. This peak was probably first climbed in June 1973 by Germans Georg Frey and Dieter Schoodt, via the east ridge. In July 1996, Brian Gebruers and Erik Monasterio climbed a couloir on the southeast face.

— GREGG BEISLY, *NEW ZEALAND*

NEGRUNI GROUP, CERRO MULLU APACHETA, TRAVERSE VIA SOUTHWEST RIDGE

ON SEPTEMBER 14, Chris Knight and Alexander von Ungern traversed Cerro Mullu Apacheta (5,368m), climbing the southwest ridge on solid granite and beautiful fields of penitentes. They descended via the upper northeast ridge and then to the northwest. The overall grade was AD+. The southwest ridge was followed in 1973 by Germans Heinz Goll and Alexander Schlee for what was most likely the first ascent of the mountain, although it is not certain at what point they accessed the ridge. 🖹 📷

— *INFORMATION FROM* **ALEXANDER VON UNGERN**, *ANDEAN ASCENTS, BOLIVIA*

[Above] **The Condoriri Group from the southwest. From left to right: Janchallani (Ventanani), Ala Izquierda, and Condoriri (Cabeza del Condor). The two lines are (1) Ave Maria and (2) Karakara, both climbed in April 2016.** *Alex von Ungern*

CONDORIRI GROUP, JANCHALLANI, SOUTHWEST FACE, KARAKARA AND AVE MARIA

ON APRIL 29, during a course for aspirant UIAGM guides, Carlos Vasquez and I, closely followed by a second team of Max Alvarez, Juvenal Condori, and Roberto Gomez, climbed a mixed line on Janchallani (IGM 5943 III map; other maps refer to it as Ventanani; ca 5,400m Google Earth). This peak is immediately southwest of Ala Izquierda. The "Ventanani" sometimes reported in earlier AAJs is well north of this (approximately 16°7'11.07"S, 68°14'46.22"W) and accessed from the Linco Valley.

We left base camp at 4,600m beside Lake Chiarkhota, crossed the pass to the northeast of Cerro Austria, down-scrambled, crossed the Ala Izquierda Glacier, and were roped up at the bottom of the southwest face of Janchallani after 2.5 hours. Above lay the crux: 10m of vertical mixed climbing to reach a snow/ice gully, which we then followed for five pitches at easy WI4. We reached the col between the two main summits and went right, climbing two pitches of easy but loose rock. This took us to the top we had estimated from below would be the higher, but in reality was 5–10m lower than the one to the northwest.

The following day, Pedro Sermini and Maximiliano Villar made the third ascent of the gully and reached the true summit. Meanwhile, Sebastian Rojas and Juan Señoret opened another new line, to the right of our route, starting with a 5.9 chimney and continuing with 40m of 70° mixed climbing to reach a snow/ice gully. They followed this, moving together, for 300m, until leaving it for easier terrain. They turned a lower summit and then carefully scrambled up to the main top.

Given that, from some angles, the summit looks like a mountain caracara (Phalcoboenus megalopterus), a common scavenger bird of this environment, Juan and Sebastian suggested the route name Karakara (450m of climbing, M3 70° 6a). We decided to name our line after this bird's local name: Ave Maria (225m, D). 📷

— **ALEXANDER VON UNGERN**, *ANDEAN ASCENTS, BOLIVIA*

HUAYNA POTOSI, NORTHEAST RIDGE VIA NORTH RIDGE OF PICO MESILI

ON MAY 19, members of the 2016 IFMGA aspirants guides' course, with instructors Roberto Gomez and Eduardo Unzueta, climbed a new line up the north ridge of Pico Mesili, a summit on the northeast ridge of Huayna Potosi. We approached the previous day, starting at the hydroelectric station (4,350m), joining the aqueduct, and eventually bivouacking at 4,850m on the northeast slopes of Huayna Potosi, just after passing the start of its northeast ridge. The steep, rocky lower section of the northeast ridge, which reaches the glaciated slopes above Pico Mesili at about 5,700m, is taken by the route Bicophobia (1,000m, TD+), climbed over three days in August 2010 by Vincent Bailleu, Rémi Labourie, and Benoit Montfort). We aimed to climb the north ridge.

We left around 4 a.m. and climbed the ridge in the dark, overcoming several short pitches in mountaineering boots. We believe some moves were 5a/b. We reached the snow line as the sun rose and slanted across the glacier to join the northeast ridge at the end of Bicophobia. Everyone then continued up the ridge to the main summit of Huayna Potosi, after which Roberto Gomez, Sebastian Rojas, and Juan Señoret climbed along the connecting ridge to the south summit and descended by the French

[Top] Huayna Potosi from the northeast, showing (1) Bicophobia (2010) on the northeast ridge of Pico Mesili and (2) Aspirante 2016 on the north ridge. (The 2016 group took two lines to minimize the consequences of rockfall.) Bicophobia and Aspirante 2016 join near Pico Mesili. The line drawn in the upper section is that taken in 2016; the French in 2010 continued up right to the ridge and then back left to the summit. [Bottom] Juvenal Condori climbing on the north ridge of Pico Mesili (Aspirante 2016) as the sun rises. *Alex von Ungern*

Route. The others descended more or less by the Normal Route. As far as we know, there is no report of our line being climbed in the past, and we have named it Aspirante 2016 (AD+).

– ALEXANDER VON UNGERN, *ANDEAN ASCENTS, BOLIVIA*

HUAYNA POTOSI, WEST SPUR AND SOUTH RIDGE

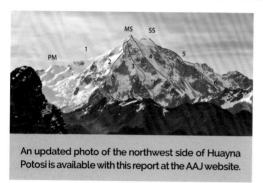

An updated photo of the northwest side of Huayna Potosi is available with this report at the AAJ website.

FROM JULY 21–23, 2015, Gabor Fuchs and Dominik Osswald (Switzerland) made a possible new line on Huayna Potosi (6,088m) when they climbed the obvious ridge to the right of the Argentinian-Spanish Route (Godö-Godö-Enriquez-Pagani, 1990, D+ 80°). The Swiss pair began on the right flank at ca 5,200m and climbed scree and mixed ground (M2), followed by a short, steep gully (M4 or F4a) to the crest. The crux lay just above: a badly protected steep slab of mostly good granite (5b). They continued up the ridge, turning obstacles generally on the left, until near the top it became steep and nasty. The pair made a slightly downward traverse to the right for about 20m before climbing direct (65° M3) to the south ridge. They followed the ridge easily to the top (south summit) and then went down the normal route.

The Swiss were in La Paz when protesting miners (*mineros*) from Potosi threw dynamite in the streets, hence the name of the route: Minero Dynamite (900m, D+ 5b M3/4 65°). 📷

— INFORMATION SUPPLIED BY GREGG BEISLY, *NEW ZEALAND*

PICO ITALIA, NEW ROUTE AND FAST LINK-UP

ON JUNE 8, Rodrigo Lobo and I made the first ascent of Al Fondo Hay Sitio on the east face of Pico Italia (ca 5,750m). We trained specifically for this 700m route, and as a result were able to climb most of it simultaneously, in only 2.5 hours. We roped up for the last 150m but climbed this section in one long pitch. Maximum difficulties were 6a+. We exited on the summit ridge a little left of the main top and then downclimbed part of the south ridge before descending a loose gully on the east face to return to the base. We took only rock shoes and one ice axe and one pair of crampons for both climbers, and we suffered with cold feet during the descent.

Later in the month, I returned to Pico Italia and made the first link-up of Arthritis (600m, TD+ 6a, Beisly-Monasterio, 2013) on the east face and the south ridge of Huayna Potosi. I climbed alone, making the first solo and possibly the second overall ascent of Arthritis.

I left the Elvira Hut at 5 a.m., started up the face at 9:30 a.m., and two hours later was at the top. I changed from rock shoes to mountain boots, spent three hours descending the north ridge of Pico Italia to the col, and started up the beautiful south ridge of Huayna Potosi immediately. I summited at 6 p.m. and arrived back at the hut at 9 p.m. the same day. The total ascent and descent amounted to around 3,500m. Although all the ground had been climbed previously, I feel this expedition deserves a name of its own: The Real Deal. I'd trained hard for this project, and on the ascent I pared my equipment to the minimum so I could travel fast.

In September, Rodrigo and I returned to Pico Italia and completed what's likely the second ascent and first alpine-style ascent of the Beisly-Monasterio Route (2012) on the east face. The first ascensionists fixed the first two pitches, then returned the next day, jumared the ropes, and reached the summit after a total climbing time of 16 hours. We spent two hours on the initial crux pitches (about 120m), including some time-consuming hauling of our 15kg packs.

Above this, we unroped and climbed the remaining 350m in 1.5 hours, for a total of 3.5 hours. The climb is steep and beautiful, with mostly good rock.

– ROBERT RAUCH, *BOLIVIAN TOURS*, *RAUCHROBERT@HOTMAIL.COM*

TIQUIMANI, NORTHEAST RIDGE ATTEMPT

SITUATED TO THE northeast of Huayna Potosi, Tiquimani appears as the guardian of the Zongo Valley and, indeed, in Aymara its name means "eternal guardian." The main summit barely rises above 5,500m, but the peak has a large, steep south face of great technical difficulty that has not been feasible in recent years due to dry conditions. After inspecting possible lines in mid-June, Anna Pfaff and I decided to attempt the unclimbed northeast ridge.

[Above] **East face of Pico Italia (ca 5,750m). (1) East face buttress (Beisly-Monasterio, 2012). (2) Descent followed by Rauch and Lobo in June 2016. (3) Al Fondo Hay Sitio (Lobo-Rauch, June 2016). (4) Arthritis (Beisly-Monasterio, 2013). The north ridge of Pico Italia and south ridge of Huayna Potosi are on the right.** *Robert Rauch*

From a bivouac by a small lagoon below the east face, at 4,800m, we reached the crest of the northeast ridge around 7 a.m. on June 21. The rock was loose, blocky, sharp alpine granite, though it improved a little the higher we climbed. Protection and belays were not great, and sometimes we had to run it out 15–20m. After nine or 10 pitches, when we reached an altitude of around 5,260m, one pitch below the east summit, we decided the way ahead was just too loose and dangerous to continue. We began rappelling, mostly from dubious anchors, leaving almost all our rack. The climb to our high point had been 5.10b R.

– JULIANA GARCIA, *ECUADOR*

TIQUIMANI HISTORY: *Tiquimani's highest (west) summit was first climbed in 1940, and the east summit in 1963. The steep south face was climbed by a Austro-German expedition in June 1973; this team likened the 1,000m ascent to the north face of the Matterhorn. Ten years later, Slovenians made an important variation in the upper part of the wall, and in 1997 a route up the left side of the face was soloed by Pere Vilarasau (Spain). These routes end on the west summit. Lines farther to the right on the face were claimed by Alain Mesili. The normal route climbs the rocky north face, while the long west ridge was climbed in 1976 by David Cheesmond and Phil Dawson, with reportedly good rock climbing to an icy, gendarmed summit ridge.*

ILLIMANI, SOUTH FACE, VARIATION TO ORIGINAL ROUTE

ON JUNE 22, 2015, French alpinist and Bolivian resident Anne Bialek, accompanied by Bolivian UIAGM guides Hugo Ayaviri Quispe and Rolando Tarqui Choque, made the second known female ascent of the south face, via Directa Boliviana, an important variant to the original route. Starting to the right of Directa Italiana (*AAJ 2016*), they followed a prominent gully of rock, snow, and ice back left to a point above the initial difficulties of the Italian route, and then climbed mixed ground and a shallow gully to reach 5,500m and the long snow slopes above. From thereafter their route followed very similar ground to the 1974 Laba-Thackray route and Directa Italiana. The new variation is relatively direct and might become the standard way on this face for parties not up to the more technical lines.

Anne Bialek is the first woman to have made the complete traverse of all five of Illimani's summits and to have summited all 13 of Bolivia's 6,000m peaks. 📷

— ANNE BIALEK *AND* AIMEE VERDISCO, *BOLIVIA*

NOTABLE ROCK AND ICE CLIMBS

Several new multi-pitch ice and rock climbs were completed in the central Cordillera Real. Brief summaries are provided here. Complete reports and photos of each climb may be found at publications.americanalpineclub.org.

• *Pacokeuta, south face, Wist'unasa Q'asadiente.* In October 2015, Mattia Buzzetti and Davide Vitale climbed a 120m icefall (WI4) on the south face of Pacokeuta (5,589m), calling it Wist'unasa Q'asadiente. They did not continue to the summit because of dangerous snow on the upper face. [*The online report includes a brief climbing history of Pacokeuta.*]

[Above] **The southeast face of the first buttress on the ridge leading eastward to the main summit of Khala Cruz (5,200m). (1)** Approximate line of La Muesca (1980). (2) Approximate line of Condores y Picaflores (2015). (The lower half of both 1 and 2 is drawn correctly, but the upper sections are approximate. See AAJ 2016). (3) El Techito de la Granja (2016). (4) 4 Estaciones (2016). *Alex von Ungern*

• *Pico Milluni, south face of unnamed buttress, Amuki.* On January 20, Sergio Condori and Alexander von Ungern climbed a five-pitch line, called Amuki (6a), up an unnamed buttress below the southwest face of Milluni, left of the main peak.

• *Pico Milluni, south summit, east face, GCP.* On September 21, 2015, Grover Rene Mamani, Sergio Dalenz Quispe, and Gregg Beisly added another route to the east face of Milluni's south summit. The four-pitch rock route, to the left of Black Condor, was named GCP (5c).

• *Khala Cruz Group: Patagonian Sunset, 4 Estaciones, and El Techito de la Granja.* Alexander von Ungern climbed three new routes with various partners. On June 3, he and Marcelo Gomez climbed a 150m, three-pitch route on the south face of a granite buttresses of the Khala Cruz group, to the east of the 5,200m highest summit. They called it Patagonian Sunset (6b). On October 23, the two climbed a 200m, five-pitch route on the southeast face of the most prominent granite buttress of the group, west of the 5,200m highest summit. They named it 4 Estaciones (6b) after the four seasons of weather they experienced on the climb. Later in the year, von Ungern and Damien Freemantle climbed El Techito de la Granja (6a A2) on the same buttress. The crux was a 5m overhang climbed with aid.

[Above] Sebastian Rojas on the first pitch (6c+) of Loro Paceño on Los Cuernos del Diablo. *Alex von Ungern*

LA CHANGA

On August 1, during the first stage of the Mujer Montaña and French Mountaineering Federation's High Mountain Women Group project, Susana Rodriguez (Venezuela) and Denys Sanjines (Bolivia) made the first ascent of a small, unnamed rock tower in the Araca region of the northern Quimsa Cruz. This summit (ca 5,000m) is known to climbers by its characteristic square top, and is situated to the northeast of Laguna Chillliwani. The climb went in three pitches (large cams useful) and was named La Changa (120m, 5.10b).

— *INFORMATION SUPPLIED BY* **DENYS SANJINES**, *BOLIVIA*

LOS CUERNOS DEL DIABLO, NORTHWEST FACE, LORO PACEÑO

On May 13, during a UIAGM aspirant course, Pacifico Machaca, Sebastian Rojas, and I climbed a sustained new rock route on the Cuernos del Diablo, right of the established route Inti Wiracocha. We believe our first four pitches were previously unclimbed. Sebastian led the first and most difficult 50m pitch (6c+), following a dihedral that was overhanging for short sections. All of the remaining pitches except the third were 6b or harder. The granite was excellent throughout, the only downside being that some cracks were filled with moss.

We called our route Loro Paceño (six pitches, 6c+), which means "Parrot from La Paz." Pacifico, who remained silent during the entire ascent (and generally is a rather silent person), earned this nickname while working in the lowlands of Bolivia, because he talks less than jungle parrots.

— **ALEXANDER VON UNGERN**, *ANDEAN ASCENTS, BOLIVIA*

ARGENTINA-CHILE

ANDES

MORRO VON ROSEN, QHAPAQ ÑAN

IN LATE APRIL, Argentine climbers Matías Cruz and Facundo Juárez Zapiola visited Morro Von Rosen (5,450m), a peak of compact granite in the Chañi Group, located in far northern Argentina. They made their base camp at a hut on the slopes of Nevado de Chañi (5,930m). The two climbers first attempted a new route on Chañi, climbing a dihedral with moves up to 6a+; however, they gave up after the first 100m.

On April 24, in windy conditions, they climbed a steep spur on the southeast aspect of Morro Von Rosen, with the majority of the route following a prominent dihedral. Not including the fourth-class approach, their route was five pitches. They called the route Qhapaq Ñan (300m, 6c+), which is the Quechan name for the Inca Road (phonetically, in Spanish, this may be written as Qhapac, Qhapaj, Capac, Capaj, or Capaq); one of the road's branches reached Chañi, which is reported to have had a child sacrificed on its summit. 🔲

MARCELO SCANU, *ARGENTINA*

CORDÓN LOS CLONQUIS, THREE FIRST ASCENTS

CORDÓN LOS CLONQUIS is the official name for a chain of sedimentary mountains south of Aconcagua and west of Mendoza. It contains five principal summits that separate Quebrada de Chorrillos to the south from Quebrada del Potrero Escondido to the north. One of the peaks, Cerro Tito, was climbed in January 2016 and reported in *AAJ 2016*. Three additional summits were claimed later in 2016. Only Clonqui Oriental (4,400m) remains unclimbed, primarily because of its vertical rotten rock.

Cerro Horqueta (4,565m), at the extreme south end of the chain, was climbed in March by Glauco Muratti and Adrián Petrocelli (Argentina). They climbed the northwest face from

Quebrada de Chorrillos. In the same month, the two climbers ascended the west face of Cerro Tropa (4,530m). Neither route has hard climbing, but there are some exposed steps to UIAA III. In October, Diego Molina and Pablo González (Argentina) climbed Clonqui Central (4,576m) from the Quebrada del Potrero Escondido. They reached the summit by a snow couloir with easy but exposed rock steps, ascending 1,300m from their base camp. 🄾

– MARCELO SCANU, *ARGENTINA*

VOLCÁN ANTOFALLA MASSIF, VARIOUS ASCENTS

A LARGE ARGENTINEAN expedition was active in the Antofalla massif, a mountainous high desert north of Catamarca, from January 9–20, 2017. They approached by a mining road and then off trail. The group made the first or second ascents of several peaks from 4,905m to 6,404m. Details can be found at the AAJ website. ▤ 🔍

– MARCELO SCANU, *ARGENTINA*

NORTHERN PATAGONIA / COCHAMÓ

CERRO CAPICÚA, WEST FACE, PICAFLOR

IN FEBRUARY 2016, Martin Håskjold Larsen, Clare Mains, Barry Smith, Fernando Virot, and I opened a new route on the west face of Cerro Capicúa, which we called Picaflor (meaning "Hummingbird"). The face has been estimated to be 1,200m; our route was fairly direct and covered ca 1050m of climbing.

Clare and I started the route together, starting with A Tirar a la Rarita (*AAJ 2014*)/Tigres del Norte (*AAJ 2009*) for nine pitches, then hauling our supplies to Plaza Cataluña (the large, tree-covered ledge around 400m up the wall). From there we began new-routing to the left of A Tirar a la Rarita. Clare and I were forced off the wall and back to camp after a few days, due to an injury, a couple of gear shortages, and weather. We retreated in dangerously wet conditions, and the river crossing was right on the edge of losing control.

When I went back up, it was with Martin and Barry. We also had some valuable logistical help from Fernando Virot, and a lot of friendly support and bits of old rope from Cooper Varney, Daniel and Silvina Seeliger, and various other climbers and campers at La Junta. The project took all of February. On the final push to the summit, we spent five nights sleeping on the wall using a portaledge and a hammock.

All of the 16 new pitches (except the final, 25th pitch) required some amount of aid. This was sometimes due to very hard climbing, but mostly due to near-impossible protection. Many of the cracks turned out to be closed-up seams, and a lot of them needed beaks, RURPs, or very shallow Lost Arrow placements.

We were keen from the start to make this a free line, and I talked a lot with the Cochamó regulars to get a feel for the local ethics. The accepted approach is that bolts should not be overused, but that it was better to place a bolt or two and provide a safe free climb than have it remain aid. Without bolts, very few of these pitches would have offered a reasonable level of traditional protection. For this reason, I chose to place bolts anyplace where only pitons would fit. I feel certain that every pitch can now be freed.

All this made the climb very hard to grade. I know the first ascent involved a few A2+/A3 pitches, but now that there are bolts on those sections, the grade is reduced to A1. My plan is to return and give Picaflor an all-free grade. I estimate at least three pitches will be around 7b. 📷 🔍

— TOM IRESON, *U.K.*

ANFITEATRO, WALL OF PATIENCE, IRON SKIRT

IN EARLY 2016, JB Haab and I opened a new route on the Wall of Patience ground-up, calling it Iron Skirt. This wall is located on the left side of the Anfiteatro, downstream of the route Al Centro y Adentro (*AAJ 2012*) on Atardecer; I don't think anyone had looked at it in years, but it was known to have at least one unfinished "open project," according to a topo left at the refugio. We chose our route based on a prominent line of vertical forest, which in Cochamó indicates there are cracks. On the first ascent, the grade was 5.11 R A2+ J2+ (J for jungle).

JB needed to return to the USA; however, I stayed to clean our route and work on a free ascent. Two and a half weeks after JB and I first climbed the route, I was able to free the first six pitches, with difficulties to 5.12-. The seventh and eighth pitches involved complicated mixed free and aid climbing (A2). Above this is a 200m blank slab leading to the very top of the formation, which I may try to climb in the future. 📷 🔍

— COOPER VARNEY, *USA*

CENTRAL PATAGONIA / AYSÉN REGION

TWO NEW ROUTES ON CERRO CASTILLO

CERRO CASTILLO (2,675M) is one of the iconic mountains of the Aysén Region in Northern Patagonia. Two new routes were climbed on the peak in the austral summer of 2016. On January 22–23, Sebastian Rojas, Diego Señoret, and Claudio Vicuña climbed Psyco Calma (850m, 5.10+ 85°), which ascends the steep, spiny southeast ridge. The route involved alpine terrain with bad rock quality. They bivied atop the seventh pitch of their 19-pitch route.

From February 28–March 3, Manuel Medina, Pablo Miranda, and Pere Vilarasu climbed the approximately 2km southwest ridge, calling their route Las 3 P (5.10+). Beginning at the toe of the ridge, they followed the entirety of the skyline, with much simul-climbing and scrambling, to reach the summit. 📷

[Above] Cerro Castillo (2,675m) from the south (1) Las 3 P (Medina-Miranda-Vilarasu, 2016). (2) Southwest face (Buscaini-Buscaini, 1987). (3) Psyco Calma (Rojas-Señoret-Vicuña, 2016). (4) Southeast face (Golnar-Hansel-Kyou Son-Waugh, 1982). (5) Si Mato Truco y Si Mata Quiero (Medina-Miranda, 2012). *Felipe Alarcon*

— PEDRO BINFA, *CHILE*

CERRO PENITENTES, SOUTHEAST FACE; CERRO COLORADO, WEST FACE

AFTER A WEEK in El Chaltén with bad weather, my brother Tomas Franchini and I decided in late January 2017 to move north toward Perito Moreno National Park. From Gobernador Gregores we drove to El Rincón, the end of the road on the Argentinean side. We were joined by Mariano Ignacio Spisso, who works as a park ranger, on January 24. Together, we warmed up on Cerro Colorado (2,301m), a rocky, volcanic peak in the lower grassland zone of the park, making an ascent of the unclimbed west face: La Ruta del Chinchillone (350m, VI-). This peak is easy to identify from El Rincón and has only a 30-minute approach and 20-minute descent.

In the following days, the three of us hoped to ascend Cerro Penitentes (2,801m) by its unclimbed southeast face. On January 25, we hiked in from the east, an unknown approach.

[Above] The route line of El Mariano (750m, 85° M4), leading to the northeast top of Cerro Penitentes. *Silvestro Franchini*

We first crossed the Rio Lacteo and then continued up a valley with many water crossings, eventually reaching moraine pouring out from the glacier. There were no signs of previous human passage, and Mariano said it was his first time in this zone.

Between us we carried one sleeping bag, one tent, food for three days, four ice screws, and a light set of cams, nuts, and pitons. We had not expected the wall to be so steep, and there was a lot of ice.

The following morning, Tomas and I started at 2:30 a.m. (Mariano stayed at camp.) The wall faces southeast and receives sun very early, but during the night the mountain was quiet, and we didn't see signs of stonefall or avalanches on the glacier below. We chose a line on the right side of the wall, climbing a goulette with waterfall ice. The climbing was fun and fast. Eventually we reached a large, white frozen waterfall, which we climbed on its right side. From here, snow slopes, mixed terrain, and a short ridgeline led us to the northeast summit (2,771m). We could see the east face of San Lorenzo in the distance—it was one of the best landscapes I've seen in my life. We called our route El Mariano (750m, 85° M4).

We tried to descend a ridge on the opposite side of the peak, but there was strong wind and the rock was incredibly rotten. We decided instead to rappel the face we had climbed. The sun was strong, and with the ice melting it was not possible to made V-thread anchors. We were forced to leave all our slings, pitons, and nuts to descend the 750m face. 📷

– SILVESTRO FRANCHINI, *ITALY*

[Above] **Marc-André Leclerc** celebrates at the kneebar rest on the crux lead (7b/5.12b) of Titanic. It would take him four tries to complete the next moves. *Austin Siadak*

TITANIC
A FIRST FREE ASCENT ON TORRE EGGER

BY AUSTIN SIADAK

In mid-September, I arrived in El Chaltén to meet up with my friend Marc-André Leclerc. Our goal was twofold: to climb Torre Egger and to film Marc-Andre as he re-enacted the mind-blowing solo of the peak that he'd accomplished just a week before. (*See feature article on page 34.*) We were more than three months earlier than most of the crowds that flock to this alpine-climbing paradise every austral summer. The town was quiet and beautiful.

On the east side of Torre Egger an enormous buttress of perfect granite juts out into the valley, taller than Yosemite's El Capitan. High on the route, a particularly striking pillar of stone stands out like a ship's prow, giving the route Titanic its name. In 1987 a group of three Italians—Giorgio Cominelli, Lorenzo Nadali, and Andrea Sarchi—climbed to the snow slope halfway up the route and fixed 500m of rope to their high point. Thwarted by storms, they left before finishing the route. A month later, two other Italians, Maurizio Giarolli and Elio Orlandi, jumared the fixed lines and then continued to the summit.

In the ensuing decades the upper half of the route has been climbed numerous times via different starts, but amazingly the original thousand feet had never been repeated. Intrigued by Rolando Garibotti's description of the original line—"the six-pitch hanging ice runnel in the lower half is the unrepeated hidden jewel of this climb"—and deterred by significant serac danger on the line Marc-André had just soloed, we decided to attempt the original start.

We first fixed two ropes to the base of an ice runnel 150m above the glacier. After a single rest day back in town, we returned to the route, ascended our fixed lines, and started up the ice runnel before dawn. Deep in the back of a chimney, a thin ribbon of ice and névé, often just a foot or two wide, shot up nearly a thousand feet above our heads. Marc-André cruised up the ice in the lead, shouting enthusiastically about the extremely high quality of the climbing.

Above the ice runnel we emerged into bright sun and climbed a few pitches of steep rock on which Marc-André soloed while I filmed. By 5 p.m. we had reached the mid-route snow slope and dug out a platform for our small tent. I have spent few nights in as picturesque a perch.

The next morning we had packed and set off before sunrise. Pitch after pitch, Marc-André would lead and fix a rope, I would jumar quickly, he would rappel back down as I got myself and my camera into position, and then he would free solo back up to me as I filmed. I was all too aware of the incredible risk Marc-André was taking, all for my camera (or so it felt to me), and at times I wondered if we were being incredibly stupid. But as Marc-André flowed over the rock it was clear that he was completely in control of the situation. Every step was precise, every move executed with confidence. After a couple of pitches my hesitations disappeared.

A couple of hundred meters above the snowfield we reached the crux: a long, leftward undercling traverse that had never been freed. Marc-André set off and moved carefully through the first 10m, underclinging the flake. The wall steepened, and I held my breath as Marc-André pulled around a small bulge. His foot flew off the wall and he screamed loudly, pulling himself back in at the last second and pawing through to a merciful no-hands kneebar rest. He shook out and looked back at me with a smile, collecting himself before the true crux: a blank downclimb traverse across a steep slab that still separated him from the belay. He stepped out of the crack and moved delicately onto the face, then his foot slipped and he flew off into space. He tried again from the kneebar but came off in the same spot. On his third attempt he kept his foot pasted to the wall with a yell, but slipped again just a couple of moves later.

We still had a long ways to go and I nearly shouted that we should keep moving, but I held my tongue. On his next go Marc-André moved quickly across the slab, pausing for just a moment before stabbing his left foot out and with a yell throwing his left hand to an unseen hold. As he hit the hold his body sagged and I thought he was off, but he pulled himself back in and scampered over to the belay as we both shouted in excitement.

Above the crux we continued quickly on easier terrain. By the time we reached the summit mushroom the sun was low in the sky and the weather had changed considerably. A constant wind blew from the west and thick clouds roiled all around us. Beautiful WI4 hero-sticks up a half-pipe of rime delivered us to an easier slope and finally the summit. I stood on top in disbelief. A small break appeared in the clouds and I looked west over the Southern Ice Cap, washed in the last light of the day. The imposing north face of Cerro Torre broke out of the mist, flying toward us above a sea of clouds like some mythical ice-encrusted battleship. Then it was gone as the clouds engulfed us once again. It was hard to leave such a magical moment and place, but it was clear we didn't belong. With night falling fast, we quickly began our descent.

Eight and half hours later we pulled our ropes for the last time and stumbled to our camp on the glacier. We crawled into our sleeping bags, brewed up a hot drink, and smoked a celebratory cigarette. The jagged silhouettes of the Chaltén massif materialized out of the starry, black sky and we watched our second sunrise of the day. I put down my camera, opened my eyes wide, snapped a mental image, and fell into a deep slumber. 📷

Summary: First integral ascent and first free ascent of Titanic (950m, VI 7b M6 90°) on the east buttress of Torre Egger, September 2016.

CHALTÉN MASSIF, SEASON SUMMARY

DURING 2016–'17, PATAGONIA witnessed one of the driest winters on record. By late November, the conditions were not unlike late February, with little snow in the mountains. It was so extreme there were fears of forest fires, an unusual occurrence in these parts. At the end of the first week of December, everything changed: It started precipitating and, except for a few short stints, it did not stop until mid-March. The low pressure that encircles Antarctica had moved north 3 to 5 degrees of latitude, and that dictated wetter and windier conditions for the entire season. In the Chaltén area, almost all climbs were limited to "consolation prizes." Cerro Torre was climbed only once, via the Ragni Route, and all but one ascent of Cerro Fitz Roy was done via the Supercwanaleta. Bad conditions did not allow for much more.

In early September, in winter, Markus Pucher attempted to solo the Ragni Route on Cerro Torre, reaching the base of the last pitch. He encountered difficult conditions throughout, with copious rime and very hard, cold ice. The last pitch had a layer of rime a meter deep. (Cerro Torre has yet to see a solo winter ascent.) A few days later he made an attempt on the Supercanaleta on Cerro Fitz Roy, climbing to within a couple of hundred meters of the summit. Soon after, Pucher made the first solo and first winter ascent of Cerro Pollone, via the south face.

In late December, Chris Mutzel, Austin Siadak, and Jimmy Voorhis (all USA) climbed El Tiburón, a new line from the north side of Cerro Solo, following a ridgeline that leads to the west ridge, then climbing several small towers to connect into El Dragón (Haley, January 2016). The rock quality is in the less-than-perfect category, but it is still a worthy outing. About a month later, Siadak returned to Cerro Solo with Andy Anderson and climbed a line on the virgin south face. They approached via Paso de las Agachonas and soloed all but one pitch.

In early February 2017, on one of the rare good weather days, Eneko and Iker Pou (Spain) opened a new route on the east face of Aguja Guillaumet: ¡Aupa 40! (400m, 5+ M7 85°). The name is in reference to Iker's 40th birthday, which was the day of the ascent.

Soon after, Jonathan Griffin and Tad McCrea (both USA) climbed a new route on the virgin east face of Cerro Huemul (2,550m). The upper headwall is 400m high and, except for the last pitch and a half, offers good rock. Their route El Tren Que No Puede Parar ("The Train That Cannot Stop," 400m, 5+ M5 80°) was named in memory of Iñaki Coussirat. This was a "blank on the map" that was begging to be filled. Barely a week later, the same pair climbed a new route on the east face and south ridge of Colmillo Sur. Califlores (350m, 5+ 85°) had eight pitches of mixed terrain.

As the practically nonexistent season came to a close, Takaaki Nagato and Yusuke Sato (Japan) climbed a new line on the north face of El Mocho. They started up Grey Yellow Arrow, but after two pitches went left into an amazing-looking corner, which they climbed in four pitches (160m, 6c+). At the big break, they joined Bizcochuelo, free climbing through it (6b+) to rejoin Grey Yellow Arrow to the top, free climbing its last pitch at 6c+. They named their new line Moribito, which means "guardian" in Japanese, a reference to their favorite novel.

The season, which had been surprisingly devoid of accidents, ended on a very sad note when two climbers fell to their deaths while climbing the Whillans-Cochrane on Aguja Poincenot. It's likely an anchor pulled or they were traversing a ledge without gear between them. This accident brought to the forefront, once again, the importance of seeking adequate insurance for trips to areas such as Patagonia. Your policy should include at least US $20,000 of rescue, search, and recovery coverage.

– ROLANDO GARIBOTTI

A PROPER FIGHT

A STORMY 19-DAY FREE ASCENT ON THE CENTRAL TOWER OF PAINE

BY SEAN VILLANUEVA O'DRISCOLL

It took a while for Nicolas Favresse, Siebe Vanhee, and I to get used to walking on horizontal ground again, after 19 days on the east face of the Central Tower of Paine. It was a powerful experience, with lots of bad weather and harsh climbing conditions. We just barely managed to pull it off!

El Regalo de Mwoma (VI 5.10 A4) was an aid line put up in 1992 by a British team comprised of Noel Craine, Paul Pritchard, Sean Smith, and Simon Yates (*AAJ 1993*). The line is obvious: a crack that cuts right up the steep east face. The route came to our attention when Nico and I free climbed the South African Route, to its right, in 2009. The crack looked very thin and reportedly there was a lot of knifeblade nailing, so it seemed unlikely this route would go free. However, the only way to be *really* sure was to put our noses right up against the wall.

We walked into the park on January 20 with our first load.

[Top] Siebe Vanhee on one of the lead attempts on pitch 13 (5.13b) of El Regalo de Mwoma. Nicolas Favresse eventually redpointed this pitch on the team's 19th consecutive day on the wall, after they had summited. *Nicolas Favresse* [Right] The line taken during the free ascent of El Regalo de Mwoma (26 pitches, 1,200m, 5.13b). The free ascent took a more direct line than the original aid route (VI 5.10 A4) through the lower slabs. About halfway up, they traversed into the left-hand crack system a pitch lower than the original route. *Sean Villanueva O'Driscoll*

On January 31 we committed to the wall capsule-style, utilizing two portaledges. Our first camp was above a nice comfortable ledge atop pitch seven. A few days later we moved to an impressive hanging camp atop pitch 13, right above the two crux pitches of the climb.

The first crux, pitch 12 (originally pitch 18, rated A4) is a stunning dihedral with hard friction stemming and a very hard move at the end (5.13b). The second crux, pitch 13, is a variation of the original route. For this pitch, we traversed left toward another crack system one pitch below where the British traversed—the section we avoided was A3 on the original topo. Our variation climbs a sustained and technical face that utilizes small crimps; it is mostly protected by small wires in a thin crack (5.13b).

The unstable weather, wind, cold temperatures, snow, and iced-up cracks made the free climbing very challenging. On the days that we managed to climb at all, we could only do one to three pitches before racing back to the portaledges for shelter and to get the blood recirculating in our fingers and toes. Six days were so bad that we didn't even come out of the portaledges. We spent a lot of time reading, playing music, meditating, and doing yoga. One memorable moment was my 36th birthday party, which we celebrated with popcorn and music: Nico played the guitar, I played the tin whistle, and Siebe was new to the mouth harp.

On February 14, our 15th day on the wall, we finally got a good weather day and raced to the summit under blue skies. Though it was Valentine's Day, there was not much time for romance on top because the wind was bitterly cold. We returned to the portaledges just as it began to snow again.

At this point, we still needed to redpoint pitch 13. We had more or less run out of food, having only brought enough for 15 days; however, we decided to ration and stick it out as long as we could. On February 18, our 19th day on the wall, after three days of bad weather and with no food remaining, we decided it was time to go down. Nico had already missed his flight back to Europe. We waited for the afternoon, though, hoping for a last chance at freeing pitch 13. And our miracle arrived: The wind and snow calmed down for a few hours, just barely enough time for Nico to redpoint the pitch! After this, we rappelled into the night through heavy snow.

We climbed El Regalo de Mwoma (1,200m) in 26 pitches (the original ascent was 36 pitches) at a grade of 5.13b. We completed the climb team-free, with the followers primarily climbing free without jumars, with a few exceptions when the weather was too stormy and cold. The hardest climbing is between pitches 10 and 16, with the two 5.13b pitches (I led the first of these and Nico the second), one of 5.12d, and two of 5.12b. The rest is mostly in the 5.10–5.11 range but often spiced up with icy cracks and snow-covered holds. No bolts were added, and a lot of the protection is on small wires. It was an incredible adventure, which took a fierce effort. It was a proper battle—a proper fight!

SUMMARY: Team-free ascent of El Regalo de Mwoma (1,200m, 26 pitches, 5.13b) on the east face of the Central Tower of Paine, with some new variations, January 31–February 18.

TORRES DEL PAINE, CERRO PAINE GRANDE, VARIATION

IN EARLY MAY, Nico Gutierrez, Cristobal Señoret, and Diego Señoret (all Chile) made the fourth ascent of Cerro Paine Grande. They climbed the 300m summit pyramid via a variation that involved three new pitches, left of the Garibotti-Sourzac Route on the southwest face.

— *INFORMATION FROM* ROLANDO GARIBOTTI

[Photo] Sean Villanueva O'Driscoll stemming hard up pitch 12 (5.13b) of El Regalo de Mwoma. *Siebe Vanhee*

[Above] **Ibai Rico beginning the climb of Torre Saia's east face.** *Evan Miles*

CLOUE ICEFIELD, TRAVERSE AND FIRST ASCENTS

In March and April, as part of the multi-objective expedition "Incognita Patagonia," Ibai Rico (Spain) and I (USA, based in U.K.) spent several weeks in southernmost Tierra del Fuego, based out of the sailboat Northanger. Among the expedition's goals were the first crossing of the Cloue Icefield (227 square kilometers), ascents of unclimbed peaks, and a survey of the glaciers and their behavior. Eñaut Izagirre accompanied us for the scientific objectives of our trip.

Cloue is located on a peninsula of Isla Hoste at 52.2°S, south of the Darwin Range, and is probably the area most exposed to Antarctic winds in all of Patagonia. Few have ventured into this region, with reports only from a Canadian-American team in 1989 (*AAJ 1992*) and a local Argentinean team in 2001. This second trip was completed by Luis Turi and Carolina Etchegoyen, who were prevented by poor weather from climbing any peaks. Cloue was also a favorite for the late, great Charlie Porter, who spent considerable time in the region establishing a network of weather stations (the maintenance of which was another expedition goal), but Charlie's exploits here were undocumented. Prior to our visit, many of the area's fjords were yet to be navigated and major peaks identifiable in satellite imagery were not even visible from sea—true *terra incognita* in the modern age.

Our team assembled in Puerto Williams on March 3. After paperwork and sailing challenges, we arrived at Coloane Fjord on March 14. Ibai and I had carefully planned a 30km route from here, crossing the peninsula and icefield from west to east. After a day of scouting, we left Northanger on March 16 with a promising forecast for several days. Carrying equipment and fuel for a week, we made good progress in warm, calm conditions, rapidly crossing the lower glacier, scrambling to the upper icefield plateau, and approaching the first major pass on skis. Here, the weather suddenly deteriorated and zero visibility forced us to camp among rocks exposed at the pass. As fog turned to snow and heavy wind, we were trapped in a storm that evening and the entire next day, unable to even see the skis on our feet during a short foray out.

Encouraged by a relative improvement in weather conditions—and hastened by a forecast suggesting a sustained, heavy storm after a short opening—we left camp at 2 a.m. on March 18. Soon we found ourselves in the worst storm either of us had experienced—and at night.

Snow fell heavily and we could barely see our skis or each other, making glacier navigation arduous and slow. Sequential *chubascos* (intense thunderstorms) tortured our calves with machine gun–like hail, and wind gusts of hurricane strength threw us several meters at a time.

In the darkness and guided solely by GPS relative to our own custom maps, we managed to avoid the worst crevasse zones. It was too windy to set up a camp and too cold to dig a cave. Instead, we were forced to continue carefully all night and the following day, when visibility improved slightly. Our traverse route passed near serac zones and over narrow passes, and involved scrambling along rocky ridges, rappelling down near-vertical forests, and finally traveling along a broken glacier tongue. We were on the move for 18 hours before *Northanger* collected us at Fouque Fjord.

Learning from our misery, we adopted a different strategy. Beginning March 23, Ibai and I set up a bombproof camp by Fouque Fjord, then provisioned a very secure advanced camp above a small icefall. Two peaks looked appealing: Monte Cloue (1,356m), the tallest of the island (but not the Monte Cloven/ Pafigliano mentioned in *AAJ 1992* and *CAJ 1990*, a fact we established via personal correspondence), and an unnamed tower jutting up a few kilometers to the south, showing a promising icy gully inside a big dihedral on its east face.

The weather suddenly warmed, and on March 26 we ascended the glacier aprons of Monte Cloue from the east in intermittent squalls of wind and rain. After crossing several large crevasses, we climbed steep glacier ice through the bergschrund and then made our way up several lengths of mixed climbing with rotten snow, hollow ice, and exfoliating rock to reach the top (300m, IV/M4 70°).

[Top] **Monte Cloue from the summit of Torre Saia.** [Bottom] **An icy Torre Saia before an intense melt-off.** *Ibai Rico*

The warm, wet weather continued the next day. We set off at sunrise on skis to the base of the unnamed tower. To access the ice gully, we passed a bergschrund and mounted a steep avalanche fan leading to a series of vertical rocky steps, intermixed with snow ramps. Despite a waterfall of icy meltwater flowing along our intended line, we climbed several pitches of tenuous mixed ground to the top of the great dihedral and on to the summit (350m, 75° V/M5). We have unofficially called this peak Torre Saia (1,320m, 52.2°S, 68.4°E), meaning "harpoon" or "hunting lance" in the language of the indigenous Yámana tribes. We made it back to Fouque Fjord and Northanger on March 28.

Before returning to Puerto Williams on April 8, we spent time mapping the glaciers of Cloue Icefield and Fiordo Pia Este of the Darwin Range. Documentation is limited, but we believe our traverse of the Cloue Icefield and the ascents of Monte Cloue and Torre Saia are all firsts. While logistical support and weather forecasting have greatly improved in some regions of Patagonia, enabling fast and light ascents, our experience strongly advocates for slower but more robust approaches in the erratic weather of the remote coastal zones. 📷

— EVAN MILES, *USA*

[Above] Crag Jones about to turn the corner during the first ascent of Starbuck Peak. The route spiraled around the west, south, and east faces of the spire. Behind, the Risting Glacier flows down to Drygalski Fjord. *Stephen Venables*

SOUTH GEORGIA
FOUR FIRST ASCENTS AND A TRAVERSE OF THE SALVESEN RANGE

BY SIMON RICHARDSON

ON SEPTEMBER 17, Henry Chaplin, Caradoc (Crag) Jones, David Lund, Skip Novak, Stephen Venables, and I left the yacht Pelagic Australis to attempt a ski traverse across the rarely visited Salvesen Range, in the southeastern part of South Georgia. Crag, Skip and Stephen hold a long-term fascination with the island and have more first ascents than anyone else. For Henry, David and me, it was our first visit to this mythical land of majestic icy peaks, rising straight out of the turbulent South Atlantic.

We were a classic case of a team being stronger than the sum of its individual parts. South Georgia demands a wide variety of boating, skiing, survival, mountaineering, and technical climbing skills, and although not all of us were experts, between us we covered the spectrum. Having never sailed before, and with only rudimentary skiing ability, I was very much a passenger until it came to putting on crampons. Throughout our five-day voyage from the Falkland Islands, it had been made clear that if we were lucky enough to attempt Starbuck Peak, our primary objective, then the team would look first to me to find a route.

We pitched two tents at the junction of the Harmer and Jenkins glaciers, just to the south of Starbuck Peak (1,434m), the dominant summit of the area. Disappointingly, the wind increased overnight and developed into a five-day storm, which battered our tents with 160km/h winds and buried them in 150cm drifts. On the fifth night the snow turned to rain, and next morning we woke to a spectacular sight of pristine white mountains shedding their storm clouds.

As a reconnaissance, Henry and I skinned up to the broad shoulder on the mountain's northwest flank, where we were irresistibly drawn toward a virgin snow peak to the north. Although it was late afternoon, the weather was calm, and for all we knew this might be our last climbing opportunity so we set off at pace toward the summit. An easy ridge of wind-blown rime took us to the top of Peak 1,318m, which lies 600m to the south of Black Crag South (1,245m), climbed by the 1955-'56 Carse survey expedition. During the descent we noted a spiral ramp up Starbuck's north and west faces, and on the east face a steep, tapering gully leading to the top. If these features connected, we might be in with a chance.

Next morning, September 23, all of us set off, in two ropes of three. The spiral ramp gave five pitches of exposed snow and ice climbing across the west face, interspersed with an awkward mixed section of Scottish 5, and led to a sharp notch on the southwest ridge. Fortunately, a narrow ledge led around the south face to within sight of the gully on the east face. Until this point the climbing had been relatively straightforward, which was just as well because the soft metamorphic rock was very friable, and the only reliable protection was ice hooks placed in narrow cracks, or better still, a Pecker hammered into a blank seam.

We downclimbed to a ramp of 70° poorly consolidated snow that led up and right to the mushroom-encrusted summit ridge. I tried

[Top] Starbuck Peak (1,434m) from the Novosilski Glacier to the northwest. The first-ascent route started on the ramp in lower left and moved rightward across the west face, spiraling around the south and east faces to the top. The main tower is about 150m high. [Bottom] Mt. Baume (1,912m) from the Spenceley Glacier to the east. *Simon Richardson*

four different lines until I found a streak of snow that had been hardened by drips from a rocky overhang. I wriggled up a hidden ramp below the overhang to emerge beneath the summit mushroom, which succumbed to massive excavation. The 40m pitch would not have been out of place on a Grade VI thin face route on Ben Nevis. One by one, the team climbed the remaining 20m of rime to the tiny summit.

We descended through the night and reached our camp at 1 a.m. Later that afternoon, Henry, Stephen, and I made the first ascent of the attractive twin-summited snow peak (ca 1,000m) that lies 2km southeast of the shapely Avalanche Peak (717m) marked on Carse's survey map. The following day we moved camp to the broad col at the head of the Spenceley Glacier, to the east of Mt. Baume.

Crag, Skip, Stephen, and I decided to attempt Mt. Baume (1,912m), the highest named unclimbed peak on South Georgia, by the northeast face, the line of a 2005 attempt by a British team. We started climbing at midnight on September 27 with a view to reaching the snowfield, which comprises the upper two-thirds of the face, at first light. Unfortunately, the lower rock spur, which neatly bypasses the hanging seracs on the right, was more difficult than expected.

Crag led several Scottish Grade 5 mixed pitches, and we emerged on the snowfield in the full heat of the day. After a careful ascent of the steep, convex face in bottomless, sugary snow, we gained the summit ridge in midafternoon. The 30m summit tower, resembling the nose cone of a rocket ship, loomed ahead. Fortunately, a huge flake of rime had created an icy tunnel up the back of the tower, and we took turns standing carefully on a tiny apex of snow. It was a spectacular climax.

The descent took all night, and we arrived back at the tents after a 27-hour push. Unlike Starbuck, which was very Scottish in nature, the climbing on Mt. Baume was more alpine, and we rated the 700m route TD. Meanwhile, Henry and David had made the second ascent of Mt. Pelagic (1,650m), following the 2005 line up the north ridge on skis. Henry skied off the summit.

On the 29th, after an unsuccessful attempt on the attractive 1,800m peak that lies 4km southeast of Smoky Wall, on the north side of the Spenceley Glacier, we skied down the Spenceley Glacier and over Ross Pass. Rather than continue down the detritus of the lower Ross Glacier, we spent three more days (including one day stormbound in tents) traversing the Webb and Cook glaciers to reach St. Andrews Bay, where the Pelagic Australis met us on October 2.

The expedition had been extraordinarily successful. We traveled 65km over 16 days, summited four unclimbed peaks, and repeated two others. Undoubtedly we were lucky with the weather, but Stephen's genius was to organize the trip for early spring, when glacier travel is easier and the weather gods are most likely to be benign.

SUMMARY: First ascents and a south-to-north traverse of the Salvesen Range, South Georgia, September 17–October 2, 2016. The online version of this report has many additional photos. 📷

ANTARCTIC PENINSULA

ANDVORD BAY, VARIOUS ASCENTS

FROM NOVEMBER 19–DECEMBER 19, Albert Argemi (Spain), Ken Ellison (Canada), Julie Jones (U.K.), Arnount Wittert (Netherlands), and I, as leader, summited and skied 12 peaks on the Peninsula. Six of these, located between Andvord Bay and Paradise Harbor, were previously unclimbed. From the yacht Iceberg, we accessed these summits from Andvord Bay via a narrow and initially very steep, unnamed glacial ramp, midway between Duthiers Point and Steinheil Point. We placed a camp in a high glacial bowl east of the Doktor Peaks and south of Mt. Hoegh; we believe this glacier had never been explored.

From this camp we ascended Peak 828m, Peak 1,030m, Peak 772m, Peak 652m, Peak 783m, and Peak 706m, along with various previously climbed mountains and the first climb of Mt. Hoegh from the south. All ascents were made on skis, although the summit slopes of several peaks required a few pitches using axes and crampons. 📄 📷 🔍

— PHIL WICKENS, U.K.

BRABANT ISLAND, PEAKS SOUTHEAST OF MT. PARRY

IN DECEMBER, a ski mountaineering party led by Bruce Goodlad (U.K.) was dropped off at Tarrada Point on Brabant Island. They skied up to a base camp in front of Mt. Parry (2,520m). The following day, with 50-knot winds over the summits, they skied a 1,983m peak to the south of Parry, at 64°16'59"S, 62°24'42.8"W. On the 3rd they skied an attractive mountain southeast of

Parry (ca 1,000m, 64°20'19.4"S, 62°21'11.9"W), which had a beautiful summit snow crest. It is not clear whether these two peaks had been ascended before—the only party that could have done so would have been the 1984-85 British Joint Services Expedition, which skied past this group. 📷

[Above] A ca 1,000-meter peak southeast of Mt. Parry, climbed on skis via the left skyline ridge, from the far side. *Bruce Goodlad*

– LINDSAY GRIFFIN, *WITH INFORMATION FROM DAMIEN GILDEA, AUSTRALIA*

HERITAGE RANGE

PIONEER HEIGHTS, ROGERS PEAK FROM NORTH AND EAST

AFTER SUMMITING Mt. Vinson on January 4, 2017, Larry Holmgren (USA), Nate Opp (USA), Liam Suckling (Australia), and I went old-school. Instead of flying back to the Union Glacier, we spent two weeks traveling with skis and sleds, descending the Branscomb Glacier from Vinson Base Camp to the Cairns and Tulaczyk glaciers, through the icefall onto the Zapol Glacier, and then traversing the Nimitz, Minnesota, Splettstoesser, Balish, Schanz, and Driscoll glaciers to reach the Union Glacier. During this journey, which covered nearly 200km of challenging glacier terrain, we made the first ascent of Rogers Peak (1,521m map, 1,500m GPS), at the junction of the Splettstoessen and Rennell glaciers.

We established base camp for Rogers at the entrance to a bowl shared by Rogers and Peak 1,400m. On January 17, we passed below most of the east face of Rogers Peak until the true summit at the end of a long north-south ridge was visible. We cut sharply right, climbing through a rock barrier to reach the ridge, where 300m of nicely exposed crest led south to the summit (79.3444°S, 84.2436°W). The round trip from base camp was 13.3km and was completed in a leisurely six hours. A couple of pitches were 45-50°. [*Although an obvious challenge, this is the first time a team has climbed any peak during a ski traverse to or from the Vinson Massif from either Patriot Hills or the Union Glacier.*] This remote section of the Heritage lends itself to first ascents, and the northwest ridge of Peak 1,400m is one of many beautiful lines we observed. The crux, as in most Antarctic endeavors, is getting there. 📷

– JEFF REYNOLDS, *AAC*

TRANSANTARCTIC RANGE / QUEEN MAUD MOUNTAINS

ROBERTS MASSIF

ON JANUARY 15, 2017, a British military group made the first ascent of Roberts Massif (ca 2,700m), while returning from the South Pole. While this is not so much a peak as a low, rocky feature at the head of the Shackleton Glacier, this is the first time a team traveling back from the pole has stopped to climb any summit in the Transantarctics since Roald Amundsen (with Johanssen and Wisting) reached the top of Mt. Betty (Herbert Range) in January 1912. 📖 📷

– DAMIEN GILDEA, *AUSTRALIA*

[Above] Eythan Sontag after the last hard (WI5) pitch through the final cliff band, one pitch before topping out the south face of Hrútsfjallstindar. The Svínafell Glacier below snakes out to the coastal plain and the Atlantic Ocean. *Spencer Gray*

LUCKY LEIF
A LONG ALPINE ROUTE IN SOUTHEAST ICELAND

BY SPENCER GRAY

IN LATE MARCH, Eythan Sontag and I (both from the U.S.) climbed a new route on the south face of the east summit of Hrútsfjallstindar ("Ram Mountain," 1,875m) in Vatnajökull National Park. The Hrútsfjalls peaks are situated on a volcanic crater rim at the edge of one of Europe's largest glaciers, squeezed between outlet glaciers flowing toward the coast.

After towing sleds over the five-mile approach up the Svínafell Glacier, with a heavily crevassed lower half, we dug out a camp under the face and away from an active icefall. The three-pound chocolate Easter chick we had recruited as our base camp sentry didn't survive the crossing. We glumly ate her, brooding that we'd just killed an albatross.

The south face has four steep snowfields separated by three overhanging basalt cliff bands. (The total vertical gain from the glacier to the summit is approximately 1,400m, of which the steep, technical headwall comprises about half.) Ice flows connect the snowfields and allow passage through the cliffs. There are now at least four technical routes up this aspect of Hrútsfjallstindar and several others on the western summit.

We began our new route on March 29, taking the leftmost ice line (three short pitches: WI5+, WI5, WI3) through the first cliff band. The lower 20 feet of ice had broken away, leaving the technical crux right off the deck: a mixed start up to an ice roof. We hauled packs through this initial section and bivied comfortably before dark at the second cliff band. Eight inches of new snow over the course of the day caused steady but shallow sloughing into the night. The rock took occasional solid knifeblades and angles, and we were glad to have pickets. The ice deteriorated steadily as we moved up the mountain, ending in degraded Styrofoam and janky rime that made the technically easier pitches the spicy ones.

On day two we continued up a variation (two pitches: WI4, WI3) to the right of the 1985 Doug Scott line (*the first technical route up the face*) through the second cliff band, followed by more steep snow and then a delicate winding traverse (two pitches: WI5, WI3) up the center of the final cliff band. This finish is between the final cockscomb buttress of the Scott line and a 2000 route ("Porcelain").

The summit glacier was easy walking, with crevasses mostly plugged. In the evening, the sun tracked just behind a thin cloud, an eye of Sauron beaming yellow and then pink down the western slopes. We downclimbed for several hours to climber's left of the seracs southwest of the west summit, keeping a wary eye out for glacial sinkholes and flowing waterfalls in the lower drainage.

We called our new route Lucky Leif (TD WI5+ M4). Leif "the Lucky" Erikson was an Icelandic Viking who established what was probably the first European settlement in the Americas, in the year 1000, in Newfoundland. Making the reverse trip, we felt lucky that conditions had allowed our ascent. We owe deep appreciation to Snævarr Guðmundsson and the Icelandic Alpine Club for their assistance.

After 10 days of trying to tap into our inner Old Norse, we still felt like rubes—but we certainly had held Iceland in our hands. Vatnajökull National Park was expanded and renamed in 2008, partially offsetting political fallout from the staunch government support for nearby hydroelectric dams and reservoirs that power a large smelter for aluminum exports. Clutching the aluminum that lets us do what we do—tool shafts, belay devices, carabiners—our adventure occurred squarely in the compromises we make on the land.

SUMMARY: New route Lucky Leif (1,400m, TD WI5+ M4) on the south face of the east peak of Hrútsfjallstindar in Vatnajökull National Park, Iceland, March 29–30, 2016. The online version of this report includes a climbing history and photo-topo of the routes on both summits of Hrútsfjallstindar, including two new routes climbed in April 2015 by Bjartur Ólafsson (Iceland) and Matteo Meucci, an Italian guide working in Iceland. 📷

[Below] Approaching Hrútsfjallstindar (1,875m) from the south. The 2016 route Lucky Leif is shown. See all routes on this face at publications.americanalpineclub.org. *Spencer Gray*

TRØLLKONUFINGUR, HUFFIN & PUFFIN

JACK GRINSTED, DAVE McKINNEY, and I, from New Zealand, established a new route, Huffin & Puffin (12 pitches, 7a A3), on the iconic Trøllkonufingur, a huge pillar along the coast of Vágar, one of the 18 Faroe Islands. The pillar previously had been climbed at least twice by Faroe islanders, via ramps on the left side leading to the notch behind the spire. We climbed directly up the 313m seaward face from the yacht Ljómer. After a first attempt during which we established two pitches before retreating in bad weather, the final ascent took five days, using a portaledge. We reached the top at 12:12 a.m. on July 31.

We aimed for as clean an ascent as possible, using trad gear where the rock allowed and placing all bolts on lead. Starting directly out of the ocean meant an exciting boat-to-rock transfer and made for a committing adventure. Another challenge was the resident population of fulmar seabirds, which roost on the ledges of the sea cliffs and defend their small territories with putrid vomit.

For our final ascent we hauled three days of food and water, but after three long and demanding days we were still two pitches from the summit. At this point we didn't have enough rope to return to our emergency food stash at the base of the spire without pulling down our fixed lines. We opted for a final push to the top the next day. This was a 26-hour camp-to-camp effort, as we were forced to bivouac just below the summit before descending to pack up our camp, removing all gear and waste.

[Top] Trøllkonufingur on Vágar, one of the largest Faroe Islands. The new route Huffin & Puffin (313m, 7a A3) climbs the right skyline, starting above the little bay on the left side of the prow (left of an arch), then moving to the arête about halfway up. Previous ascents had summited via the obvious ramp line on the left, leading to the notch behind the spire. [Bottom] Dave McKinney on Huffin & Puffin. *Jason Blair*

In addition to climbing Trøllkonufingur, we established a handful of new routes at Norðadalur, a new and exceptional crag on the west coast of Streymoy island, near Torshavn, the capital of the Faroes. Norðadalur is an impressive series of 15 to 50m columnar basalt cliffs with phenomenal scope for further development. With rock climbing really in its infancy on the Faroe Islands, there was great need for some beginner routes. We identified an area of rock that was slightly off vertical, which we named Kiwi Crag, and established ground-up ascents of eight new routes—six trad and two bolted. (*A photo-topo is at the AAJ website.*)

We got immense support from the local Faroese community, particularly Absalon Eysturoy and his family, who were instrumental in making this ascent possible. Eysturoy is a Faroese climber living in Copenhagen and was the instigator of the project; he also climbed with us on the first attempt on Trøllkonufingur. Our trip was largely funded by the Sport NZ Hillary Expedition Fund. 📷 🔍

– JASON BLAIR, *NEW ZEALAND*

LYNGEN, ULØYTINDEN, EAST FACE, STARLESS SPUR

I DISCOVERED ULØYA Island by accident. My longtime friend Peter encouraged me to invest in a fishing business with him, and after many months of persistent nagging, he finally achieved his goal. When I eventually went to Lyngen to see what I had bought, I saw mountain ranges all over the island.

Up to now there was not a single established alpine route on Uløya, only three icefalls that friends had climbed a year before. The faces rise to a maximum of 550m, and with two friends, I decided to go for the biggest prize, the central pillar of the east face of Uløytinden (1,115m), which rises above Isvannet Lake, just south of the highest peak on the island, Blatinden (1,142m). It looked to be the most striking feature, yet not particularly difficult.

I headed up to the wall with two of my most trusted friends: Marcin Chmielinski, a climbing veteran like myself, and Tomek Klimczak, a young lion. After a couple of hours we arrived at the foot of the pillar. It looked much steeper and harder than it had from a distance. "Well, folks, this is not going to be an afternoon stroll," I said, putting on my gear.

Our line climbed directly up the pillar in the first half, then moved left to a headwall. Tomek led the technical crux (M6+) on the lower wall, with a series of dry-tooling moves on small holds. At the top of the face, a huge, imposing cornice with solid, compressed snow loomed large over our heads. "Any ideas anyone?" I asked. "Scaffold?" Marcin replied.

It was getting dark and gray clouds filled the sky. With headlamps on, we made four rappels down to a snow ramp (climber's left of the route), where we unroped and slanted down to a large snow cirque. I have strong faith in the safety of Arctic snow, but as we plowed down the slope with snow up to my thighs, I had to keep repeating, "It's safe, it's safe." Two more rappels took us to the ground. We were tired, and skiing out was a bit of a struggle in the dark, starless night. On the last section I hit my head on a branch and the night was starless no more. A few minutes later we arrived at the welcoming door of our home. 🗎 📷

– ARTUR PASZCZAK, *POLAND*

[Below] Isvannet Cirque and east face of Uløytinden. (A) Icefalls. (B) Isvannet Lake (595m). (C) Uløytinden (1,115m), showing the line of Starless Spur (ca 550m, M6+) to the summit cornice. The climbers descended snow slopes to the left of the ascent route. (D) Blatinden (1,142m). (E) Skellettinden (930m). *Artur Paszczak*

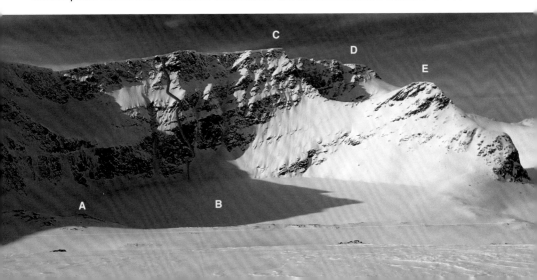

[Above] Abrahamstind from the north in evening light, with approximate lines of (1) *Wish You Were Here* (420m, WI4 M6 A0, Wright, 2016). (2) *All In* (400m, WI7 M8 R, Klarstrom-Olslund, 2012). (3) *Nothing Compares to You* (420m, WI5 M6, Rothl-Odermatt, 2009). (4) *Green and Grey* (WI4 M6, Eriksson-Frans-Melling, 2012). *Chris Wright*

LOFOTEN ISLANDS, ABRAHAMSTIND, WISH YOU WERE HERE

THROUGH MY WORK as a guide, I'm privileged to see corners of the Lofoten Islands that a short-term visitor might not. Abrahamstind (ca 900m) is not in one of those corners. The northwest face is front and center and staring at the road, though guarded from it by the not-inconsiderable finger of the Higravfjorden, as well as two problematic couloirs. My first attempt, in 2015, ended when an avalanche of spindrift in the second couloir made me question the wisdom of stomping up it alone. The second was over when my partner triggered a small slab in the same place.

The Nordland, more than anywhere else I've climbed, is a hard place to align everything for the ideal day out. Weather, conditions, free time, and the right partner rarely seem to come together. When I arrived in 2016, recent rain had left everything coated in ice, and the forecast showed no snow until the following night. However, as is often the case in these sparsely populated islands, the key thing missing was company. On February 26, I left the car at the end of a dirt road before dawn and set off alone.

As I exited the previously offending couloir and swung my tools into ice, I thought I would just go up and see how it looked, but the corner above pulled me in like a magnet, and next thing I knew I was on my way up, on lead by myself for the first time in nearly a decade. The corner was a beauty, with a crack running its length. It widened and closed from offwidth to seam, a mixture of gloved jams, torques, and swings into the "torf." The overhanging hummocks commanded wild positions, and I wished I had a witness for the drop knees as I reached for stick after stick, sometimes stemming on ripples, sometimes with a knee in the maw, or a foot on nothing at all. I wish I could know if it was really that steep or just tilted in memory. If I'd had a partner, I'd have had him watch me, keep me tight, and tell me how well I was doing. Instead I paid out a big loop of slack so that the rope wouldn't pull me at the crux, and lamented what an idiot I was for being out there alone.

Eventually the angle eased off, and after five or six roped pitches I stopped belaying and climbed to a notch. As the sun dropped into the sea, I made a short rap into a gully and continued up through the rocks to the summit, where I sat and ate the requisite Kvikk Lunsj, the Norwegian national chocolate. I downclimbed and rappeled the way I came up, and as I reached the wall's base the wind rose and snow started falling. I tramped back along the fjord, bashing through the woods and along the water's edge, crunching over sea ice, frozen kelp, and mussel shells as I strained to see into the gale. As I rallied the car up the road, it slid off into the snow. Sometime around 2 a.m. a friendly man from Viking Towing winched me 10m up onto the highway.

The photograph on the summit shows my icy glasses askew and my collar filled with dirt, but my eyes reflect the magic that gives the islands their name. It makes me happy every time I drive past Abrahamstind and remember: Wish You Were Here (420m, WI4 M6 A0). 🖼

– CHRIS WRIGHT, *AAC*

ROMSDAL, TROLLVEGGEN, SOLO WINTER ASCENT

FROM JANUARY 11–26, 2017, Marek Raganowicz (Poland) made the first solo winter ascent of any route on Trollveggen (the Troll Wall) when he reached the top of Suser Gjennom Harryland (18 pitches to east pillar, Norwegian 6 A3, Hagen-Ostbo, 1996). This was the third winter ascent of the route and its first solo. (The first "winter ascent" ended on March 25, 2007, just outside the calendar season.) Raganowicz climbed in a single push, hauling his portaledge up to his high point every day. The route lies on the left side of the face and ends at about half-height on the east pillar; he descended from there.

– LINDSAY GRIFFIN

ROGOLAND, PREIKESTOLEN, NORWEGIANSTYLE AND THOR

ON JUNE 13 the well-known tourist attraction of Preikestolen (Pulpit Rock), which rises above the Lysefjorden in Rogoland and is internationally famous with BASE jumpers, gained a five-pitch new route from local climbers Jon Egil Auestad and Øyvind Salvesen. The two rappelled 200m from the summit to the base of the rock and climbed back up a system of superb cracks, which they protected with traditional gear. They called the route Norwegianstyle (6a, 6b+, 6b, 6b+, and 7a+).

This ascent came a little over a week after Polish big-wall climber Marcin Tomaszewski climbed the single-pitch Thor (7c/7c+) up the top 20m of the formation, drilling bolt protection on rappel. The largest and most authoritative climbing club in Rogoland, Bratte Rogalands Venner, reacted quickly, declaring that bolting ethics in Rogoland are the same as in the rest of Norway: Bolts generally should not be placed in the mountains, and only on lines that are not possible to climb with natural protection; the local climbing community should be consulted before placing bolts, and bolting requires the consent of the landowner. Tomaszewski quickly returned and removed all the bolts, filling the holes so damage was minimal. The aim now is to try it with traditional protection.

Øyvind Salvesen stated, "Even though our project was conceived before Marcin placed his bolts on Preikestolen, his actions gave us extra motivation to finish it, and we would like to send a clear message to climbers visiting Norway: Please leave your drill at home and, if in any doubt, contact local climbing communities." 🖼

– LINDSAY GRIFFIN

TATRAS

TATRA RIDGE, TEAM SPEED RECORD

BETWEEN JULY 21 and 25, Polish alpinists Artur Paszczak and Adam Pieprzycki made what is likely the fastest crossing of the complete Tatra Ridge by a roped pair. The two took 106 hours 38 minutes to travel from Zdziarska to Hucianska Pass, across the main ridges of the Bielskie Tatra, the High Tatra, and the Western Tatra—about 100km with 22,000m of elevation gain.

The pair used as a benchmark the so-called Kurczab Variation, defined by Janusz Kurczab and Marek Woloszynski in their 1991 book *The Most Beautiful Peaks of the Tatra*. The Kurczab Variation is the most widely accepted crossing of the entire main ridge, at least by Polish climbers, and involves difficulties up to UIAA V-. The Bielskie is easy and grassy but with large ups and downs; the High Tatra has technical, exposed, and often loose ridges; and the Western Tatra is again easy but extending for over 50km.

The pair had made two previous attempts, the first in 2014 when Paszczak fell due to loose rock on the first day and suffered spinal injuries, and the second in 2015 when the pair gave up in very hot weather on the second day, due to slow pace and blisters. After these unsupported attempts, the two opted to have a team establish their bivouacs in advance, so they could carry lighter loads. But they had no caches of gear, food, or water between their bivies, other than two liters of water left during earlier attempts.

Paszczak and Pieprzycki were slow on the Bielskie, taking five and a half hours, due to muddy conditions after days of rain. The High Tatra took 76 hours and involved three bivouacs, while the Western Tatra took 25 hours 8 minutes and required another bivouac. After the first day, the sky then cleared, and for the next two days they pushed on for 17 or 18 hours per day to reach their rendezvous points with the support team. (These teams were led by Paszczak's wife, Alicja, also a notable mountaineer.) A storm moved in at noon on the fourth day, and after waiting it out at a cable car station they continued through miserable

[Top] Adam Pieprzycki climbing typical High Tatra terrain on the Rumanove Pinnacles (UIAA III) during the complete traverse. *Artur Paszczak* [Bottom] Artur Paszczak (left) and Adam Pieprzycki at the end of their odyssey, showing their elapsed time of 106 hours. *Artur Paszczak* [Right] Josef Kristoffy on the crux pitch of Corona, south face of Jastrabia veža. *Vlado Linek*

conditions to arrive at their fourth bivouac 30 minutes after midnight. On the last day the weather remained stormy, but they enjoyed a window of sunshine to move along the crest.

Both Paszczak and Pieprzycki consider this the hardest outing of their careers, and despite considerable trail ultra-running experience, they found it touched their limits. However, their time comes nowhere near the two outstanding solo records set in 1975. In that year Krzysztof Zurek completed the integral crossing in just 70 hours, with rappel ropes and food deposits in place on the ridge and a support team for the bivouacs. Wladyslaw Cywinski (who died, aged 74, in 2013 while climbing on the northwest face of Tepej in the Tatra) also soloed the traverse, in three and a half days, also with rappel ropes and food/water caches on the ridge. Zurek repeated the traverse in the winter of 1978 with two other climbers, taking 10 days.

The first team to achieve a complete traverse of the entire Tatra was Zbigniew Hegerle, Zbigniew Krysa, Jerzy Piotrowski, Ryszard Wiktor Schramm, and Jan Staszel over 11 days in 1955. The feat is rarely repeated—the last time before 2016 may have been as long ago as 1990. [*Editor's note: This report covers only Polish traverses of the range, from the Polish side of the frontier. Slovak climbers also have made significant Tatra traverses.*]

The main section of the High Tatra was first crossed in 1946 by Adam Gorka and Kazimierz Paszucha, the first winter crossing by Matras and Mlezák in 1953, and the fastest time to date by Vladimír Plulík, in 27 hours, during 1999. In 2015, Andrzej Marcisz, a great mountaineer from the golden era of Polish climbing, completed a super version of the High Tatra traverse, reaching all named topographical points, in four and a half days, with support teams for the bivouacs. He too said it was one of his hardest mountain experiences.

– **LINDSAY GRIFFIN**, *WITH INFORMATION FROM ARTUR PASZCZAK, POLAND*

JASTRABIA VEŽA, SOUTH FACE, CORONA

ON JUNE 17 and 18, Mišo Bado and I made the first ascent of Corona on the south face of Jastrabia veža in Slovakia. After a pitch of UIAA VIII, climbing through an overhang and a corner, with two bolts, the crux pitch overhangs 4m in its 38m length. I climbed it over two days using tiny cams, nuts, hooks, and a few copperheads (UIAA VIII and new-wave A3+).

Over the summer I visited Jastrabia veža several times, re-equipping the route for a possible free ascent. This is a mountain climb, so I protected the climb according to mountain ethics. On the crux pitch I placed only four bolts, leaving the rest to be protected naturally. I was successful in making a pinkpoint ascent on September 2. The grade of the crux pitch is UIAA XI- (solid 5.14), making Corona currently the hardest free climb in the Tatras. A person attempting the second ascent will need to know how to place their own gear and have the ability to make hard moves well above protection. 📷 🔍

– **JOZEF KRISTOFFY**, *SLOVAKIA*

MIDDLE EAST

JORDAN

JEBEL RUM, SULTAN UL-MUJAHIDIN

A VERY DIFFICULT new free route on the east face of Jebel Rum (1,754m) was redpointed in February 2017. In 2014, climbers Eliav Nissan (Israel-USA) and Elad Omer (Israel) began work on the 14-pitch, roughly 1,800' route. Over two winters and seemingly endless days of determining the line, cleaning soft, loose rock, and placing fixed protection, Nissan and Omer worked doggedly to establish a challenging yet relatively well-protected route, close to the village of Rum, which would attract strong climbers to Wadi Rum. In collaboration with their local Bedouin host and friend Muhammad Hussain, the route was named Sultan ul-Mujahidin, meaning "spiritual warrior," a name meant with good intent by these good men.

In January 2017, I joined Nissan and Omer with the aim of freeing the line. We decided to circumvent the difficulties of the original fifth pitch with a variation to the right, making the third and fourth pitch the hardest. I freed the third pitch at 5.13 and set to work with Omer on the fourth pitch. The rock is a delicate sandstone, and we added a little glue (as little as possible) on critical holds so they can bear future free climbing impacts. With the route prepared and all pitches freed aside from the fourth, I spent two more days attempting to redpoint the crux pitch. I came heartbreakingly close before it was time to leave. We proposed a grade of 5.13+.

The following month, two climbers from the Czech Republic, Jachym Srb and Matej Svotjka, obtained a blessing and topo from Omer and gave a very impressive effort to free the route. First, they worked on pitches three and four for several days, then made a continuous two-day free ascent. Srb and Svotjka praised the first ascensionists for their work on the line, saying it has some of the best climbing they'd ever done. 🔍

— **MADALEINE SORKIN,** *USA*

[Above] Matej Svojtka on Sultan ul-Mujahidin in Wadi Rum, Jordan. *Standa Mitáč/emontana.cz* [Next page] Marcello Sanguineti on pitch three of Ma che Guhl! (6a) in Wadi Nakhar, Oman. *Manrico Dell'Agnola*

WADI RUM, YALLA SHABAB

In November, British climbers Dan McManus and Calum Muskett bolted and climbed a difficult four-pitch line up a previously unclimbed face in Barra Canyon. The new route, Yalla Shabab (8a), went in four pitches: 7a+, 8a, 7c+, 7b+, the last three all 45m to 55m each.

– INFORMATION FROM CALUM MUSKETT, *U.K.*

OMAN

JEBEL MISHT, WER WIR WAREN AND MITTEN INS HERZ

In January and February of 2017, Philip Flämig and I climbed some big new lines on the beautiful and impressive limestone of the Western Hajar mountains. First we climbed Wer Wir Waren (460m climbing distance, 8 pitches, F6b) on one of the untouched Organ Pipes on the east side of Jebel Misht. [*This route climbs an obvious pillar between the Doc Bulle Pillar (Brachmeyer-Oelz-Precht, 2001) and Jilted (Barlow-Hornby, 1999)*]. Halfway up, we got caught in a huge thunderstorm and got washed off the wall. We might be the first climbing party that has ever experienced this at Jebel Misht—it had not rained for the previous eight months! Next day we recovered our gear and finished the climb, and we were treated to some spectacular mist and clouds in the steaming wadis. We left nothing on the wall.

Three days later, at 3 a.m., we started climbing up the fall line of the huge, heart-shaped depression in the middle of the massive south face of Jebel Misht. The steep and demanding, 60m crux pitch (UIAA 8-) gets a special place in my book of great climbing memories. Our line moved right and followed the left side of a pillar, 300' west of the route Paradies der Fakire. After a cold bivouac and a long descent, we were back at our tents by the afternoon of the next day. We left four pitons fixed. We called the new route Mitten ins Herz ("Straight to the Heart," 1,450m climbing distance, UIAA 8-/F6c+). [*Mitten ins Herz takes a line to the left of Paradies der Fakire (Jochler-Oberhauser, 2003) and right of Curry Power (Miskovis and friends, 2009)*]. 📷 🔍

– JENS RICHTER, *GERMANY*

WESTERN HAJAR, VARIOUS NEW ROUTES

Italian climbers Manrico Dell'Agnola, Daniele Canale, Tommaso Lamantia, Giovanni Pagnoncelli, and Marcello Sanguineti spent the first half of January 2017 in Oman, visiting the Western Hajar mountains and climbing several new routes. At Jebel Fokha (Al Hamra Towers), they climbed two 270m routes: Mia nei Giardini di Zaherd (9 pitches, 6b+) and Bahla coi Lupi (7 pitches, 6c+). On the Wall of Shadows in Wadi Bani Awf, they did No Wind, No Wine (210m, 5 pitches, 6b+). In Wadi Nakhar, they climbed Ma che Guhl! (100m, 3 pitches, 6a). And in Wadi Tanuf, they climbed Fantasia Trad (410m, 8 pitches, 6b). Some bolts were placed for protection and anchors, but all routes require a rack of traditional protection. 📷 🔍

– MARCELLO SANGUINETI, *CAAI, ITALY*

AFRICA

[Top] Gareth Leah attempting one of the crux pitches of Nubivagant.
[Left] Scoping 370-meter Pico Cão Grande from the end of the road.
Matthew Parent / Adidas Outdoor

SÃO TOMÉ, PICO CÃO GRANDE, NUBIVAGANT

I STUMBLED UPON Pico Cão Grande early in 2015 while searching for dream walls to attempt and Googling "super hero villain lairs." Cão Grande was listed as "the tower of Mordor" on one website. I was captivated by it. Formed millennia ago when high-pressure magma solidified inside an active volcano, Cão Grande ("Big Dog") is a 370m plug on the island nation of São Tomé, off the west coast of sub-Saharan Africa. Thanks to support from Adidas Outdoor's Claim Freedom project, Tiny Almada (Mexico) and I were able to complete this dream climb in June.

Arriving on the island in early May was a cultural eye-opener, with stray dogs running wild through the busy streets and a seven-person family riding a single 125cc motorbike. Navigating the narrow roads that wind south from the capital, Tiny and I, along with a small film crew, arrived at Agripalma plantation. A 3km hike through thick jungle brought us to the base of the wall, where we were surprised to find a 100m-high roof line that jutted out some 30m. We had not been able to find any information on the peak before arriving, and standing at the base we gained a very real sense of the task at hand.

After three weeks of 14-hour days, we stood on top of the peak on May 28, having established a new route up the east side. Tiny and I climbed 15 pitches up Nubivagant ("Wandering in the Clouds," 455m, 5.13d A0, with widely spaced bolt protection). Pitches two through four, passing the huge roof line, were the cruxes, with V8 moves off the belay to start the second pitch (5.13d A0), followed by two 5.13 A0 pitches. We made a redpoint attempt over two days, summiting again on June 3, but were unable to free the three crux pitches without rests. 📖 📷

— GARETH LEAH, *U.K.*

PICO CÃO GRANDE HISTORY: *The first known ascent of Pico Cão Grande was in 1975, when Jorge Marques Trabulo (Portugal) climbed the tower with São Toméans Constantino Bragança and Cosme Pires de Santos, after several earlier attempts. The team improvised various techniques and equipment, including the use of long aluminum ladders. In February 1991, a trio of young Japanese climbers from Waseda University (Naotoshi Agata, Kenichi Moriyama, and Yosuke*

Takahashi) spent two weeks establishing a route up the southeast buttress of Cão Grande (400m, 18 pitches, 5.10a A2). In 2014, Spanish climbers Hector Fernandez González and Victor Sánchez Martinez began a new aid route to the left of the 2016 route, but left without completing it.

KENYA, MT. POI, FAST FREE ASCENTS; OLOLOKWE, CAT AND MOUSE

AMERICAN ALEX HONNOLD, partnered first with Cedar Wright and then with Maury Birdwell, made one-day free ascents of True at First Light (21 pitches, 5.13b, Bechtel-Milton-Piana-Skinner, USA, 1999) and most of A Story About Dancing Dogs (5.13b, Fonda-Gruden-Jeran-Koren-Sisernik, Slovenia, 2002) on the east face of Mt. Poi. Bad bolts led Honnold and Birdwell to avoid the last crux of the Slovenian route and finish via the final crux of the American line.

Near Mt. Ololokwe, the team climbed two enticing towers: the Cat and the Mouse. Birdwell and Wright spent three days establishing the Samburu Direct (5 pitches, 5.12d R) up the Cat's 200m overhanging northwest face. Meanwhile, Honnold inspected and bolted a dramatic 15-bolt sport line—his first ever—up the southwest arête of the Mouse: The Mouse of the Rising Sun (5.12).

— INFORMATION FROM MAURY BIRDWELL

TANZANIA, MT. LONGIDO, ENDALATA ORPUKELY

KILIMANJARO IS A superb mountaineering destination, but for rock climbers there are only few interesting crags in the vicinity. Perhaps the best is Mt. Longido, easily accessible from Arusha via the well-paved "Nairobi Road." Its sharp western summit consists of solid granite faces up to 300m high. While some of the west face is covered in lichen, Gaby Lappe, Clemens Pischel, and I found a beautiful line on the east face in early January and established the first climbing route up this side of the mountain. (At least two long routes climb the west face.) Endalata Orpukely ("Savannah View," 215m, UIAA V, fully bolted) starts next to Longido's Northern Trail, a wild jungle path leading up from Kimokouwa village, and offers six pitches of pleasurable slab climbing with a few steeper sections.

— KAI MALUCK, GERMANY

NAMIBIA, SPITZKOPPE RANGE, PONTOK 3, BEYOND PLAISIR

IN EARLY MAY, Timmy ONeill and I climbed a new route on the South Face of Pontok 3 in the Spitzkoppe Range. This huge, clean granite slab is wonderfully featured, but with essentially no cracks for gear, bolts are the only option. Placing bolts on lead with a power drill (and only one battery) was new for Timmy, but he was a quick study. On the first day he brilliantly led three 60m pitches, placing three protection bolts on each before we all were drained of energy.

The next day, Timmy looked down from the middle of pitch five and proclaimed, "Let's take it to the top today." Two infinitely run-out pitches later, we were basking in the sun on top. Timmy named the route BEYOND (the Bachar Yerian of Namibia). Having made an early repeat of the notoriously bold Tuolumne route years before, it seemed fitting. Around the campfire, however, we lamented that, if better equipped, our new route could become a classic.

I returned with Franziska Garrett in August. Borrowing the Swiss term "plaisir" to identify well-protected long climbs, we offered Beyond Plaisir (12 pitches, III 5.10a/20).

— JAMES GARRETT, AAC, USA

GEORGIA

[Above] Climbing through the headwall on Ushba's west face, with Elbrus behind. *Archil Badriashvili*

USHBA SERENADE
A SPEEDY ASCENT OF A CAUCASUS TESTPIECE

BY ARCHIL BADRIASHVILI

USHBA IS SYMBOLIC of the Caucasus. It is no surprise that this double-summited peak was an emblem of Soviet mountaineering clubs—and of Soviet mountaineering itself. There are many legends, songs, and stories connected with this harsh mountain. There are also more than 60 routes on its flanks.

The Grigorenko-Prigoda Route (5B) on the west face was pointed out to me by my father, Zurab Badriashvili, who, despite the rules of the time, was a pioneer of solo climbing in the Caucasus. On the route's first ascent in 1972, a six-man team took 13 days to reach Ushba's south (main) summit (4,710m). Only two ascents have been recorded since, both in siege style. The route has long sections of mixed terrain and a slightly overhanging rock barrier below the summit. Giorgi Tepnadze and I intended to improve on the style, not only by making a continuous ascent, without fixing ropes, as just a pair, but also by traversing the mountain.

Try as we might, we couldn't get our sacks below 20kg for the climb, due to the uncertainty of the crux sections and not having the best lightweight equipment. On August 8, 2015, we started up the face, slanting left along the "Georgian Shelf." There was some loose stuff before reaching the middle rock barrier, which we climbed for 300m, with difficulties up to 5c. We climbed the last two pitches at night, and after 17 hours finally found a small ledge where we could pitch our tent.

Next day we climbed 200m of 45° ice, a few easy rock sections, and then two pitches on the headwall to a small ledge. Falling water obstructed the panoramic view, but did not touch us due to the overhanging, compact wall above. On day three we aided five pitches up the headwall, finding rusty bolts that gave no incentive to be bold. At the end of the wet fourth pitch we discovered both sheaths of our ropes had been cut badly. The pitch above had a retreat anchor and no in-situ protection above. I decided to go for it; Giorgi started to sing.

There is a fantastic legend about Mikheil Khergiani, the Tiger of the Rocks, one of the strongest Svanetians, climbing a new route on Ushba in 1964. (Svaneti is a mountainous province in northwest Georgia.) Five men are standing on a little ledge in the middle of the wall, with a very poor belay, while Khergiani is trying to free climb a wet, overhanging section with very bad protection and seemingly no holds. Retreat is impossible. Eventually he screams down to his friends to untie from the rope. In response, the Svanetians begin to sing. Khergiani makes it to the top with his inseparable friends.

Fortunately, so did we, receiving sudden applause from Polish climbers descending the Red Corner route to the right. At 8 a.m. the following day we reached the south summit, having climbed one new pitch to the right of the 1972 line. We rappelled four pitches and then downclimbed to the Ushba Saddle, traversed the northeast summit (4,694m), and went down the north ridge, which was in poor condition and had already repelled two parties. After another night out we reached the Ushba Plateau, regained our first bivouac at 2,000m, and made it to the main valley at 11:30 p.m. We graded our 2,300m ascent and traverse Russian 6A, 6b A2 AI2. The United Federation of Georgian Mountaineers named this the "ascent of the year 2015."

SUMMARY: First alpine-style ascent of the Grigorenko-Prigoda Route (5B, 1978) on the west face of Ushba, followed by a traverse of the mountain, August 8-11, 2015. 📷

CAUCASUS

DONGUZ ORUN, SOUTH FACE

IN JUNE MY six-man international party climbed the south face of Donguz Orun (4,454m) via the Dolra Glacier. We reached the glacier via a two-day trek up the Dolra Valley, followed by a final steep ascent over granite slabs below the hanging seracs forming the snout of the glacier. There was enough snow to facilitate passage—later in the season this would be much more difficult, or indeed impossible. We established a camp just above the snowline at 3,300m.

Documentation shows that Soviet climbers reached the summit of Donguz Orun from the south via the northwest ridge, the south-southwest ridge, and the southeast ridge. There is no record of climbs via the south face, though it is possible it may have been used in descent under good snow conditions. We climbed partway up a couloir to the east of the summit before crossing to the central couloir along a snow shelf. From here we reached the upper southeast ridge and followed it easily to the top. There were short sections of ice, but the angle never exceeded 50°. We descended the same way and rated the route Russian 2A. 📄 📷

– **MICHAL KLESLO**, *CZECH REPUBLIC*

DZHANGI-TAU, SOUTHWEST FACE, KARTVELISHVILI ROUTE WITH VARIATION

FROM AUGUST 19–22, 2015, Giorgi Tepnadze, Levan Tsibadze, and I climbed the Kartvelishvili Route on the southwest face of Dzhangi-tau (a.k.a. Jangi-tau or Janga, 5,058m, the second-highest peak in the Georgian Caucasus), creating a new variant of at least 150m, with sections of ice to 90°. First climbed in 1965, the Kartvelishvili Route had only been repeated once, in 1978.

Starting from the town of Mestia, we camped on the glacier at 2,750m, then twice on the face, at 4,340m and 4,630m. From the summit, we traversed the crest of the Bezingi Wall to the east (over

[Left] (A) The southwest face of Dzhangi-tau (5.058m). (B) Dzhangi-tau East. (C) Shota Rustaveli. (D) Foresummit of Shkhara West. Between C and D lies Sandro Pass, used in descent by the 2015 team. The Kartvelishvili Route with the 2015 Georgian variation is marked, following more ice than the first-ascent party on the upper wall. Of the handful of routes on the south side of Dzhangi-tau, this is the only one to climb directly to the main summit. *Archil Badriashvili*

Jangi East) to Sandro Pass (4,800m), from which we descended an icefall to the south. The weather was awful throughout, probably the harshest we've experienced on a mountain ascent. The 2,300m route was Russian 5B, 5c AI5.

– ARCHIL BADRIASHVILI, *GEORGIA*

SHKHARA SOUTH, FIRST WINTER ASCENT VIA SOUTH-SOUTHWEST RIDGE

FROM DECEMBER 16–19, 2015, Giorgi Tepnadze and I, with the help of Davit Mchedlishvili until the last camp, made the first winter ascent of Shkhara South (4,320m), a small top on the south-southwest ridge of Shkhara West (5,068m). The 2,100m ascent, with a total distance of more than 25km from the village of Ushguli and back, was rated 4A.

– ARCHIL BADRIASHVILI, *GEORGIA*

TETNULDI, NORTH FACE, NEW ROUTE

TETNULDI IS A beautiful, pyramidal mountain (4,853m) in the Central Caucasus. It is located in Upper Svaneti and was first climbed in 1887 by the British mountaineer and explorer Douglas Freshfield and party, via the southwest ridge. The steep, icy north face was first climbed in 1937 by Mike Taylor and John Jenkins during a productive Oxford University Mountaineering Club expedition. Tetnuldi's summit lies south of the border with Russia, meaning the north face is entirely within Georgia.

Maksym Kuraliesov and I visited Svaneti for the first time in July 2014, when we climbed the original route on Tetnuldi and two other mountains by challenging routes. Svaneti is a pleasant place, with friendly people and great cuisine. We enjoyed it so much we came back in July 2016 with plans for a few climbs. In the end we only completed one.

The north face of Tetnuldi had two existing lines: the British Route on the left and the 1982 Tulpanov Route in the center. Since the latter was first climbed, the face has developed huge, dangerous serac barriers. According to local climbers and border police, no one had visited the north face for many years.

From Mestia, Svaneti's capital, Maksym and I moved to the village of Jabeshi, from which the approach to the north face took two days via the canyon of the River Tsanner, the Tsanner Glacier, and the Oish Icefall. Worried that the hanging seracs on the north face might affect our planned line, we spent a day observing the face for falling ice or rocks, but nothing fell near our proposed route on the right side of the face.

At 3 a.m. on July 27, we left our camp at 3,570m on the glacier below the face. Luckily, we were able to find an easy passage through the bergschrund. The initial slope was névé at about 50°. The slope became steeper and icy, and as we had spent no time on acclimatization we moved slowly. We only reached the top of the couloir at 2 p.m. Climbing a little further, we came upon a big crevasse in which it was possible to camp comfortably. We decided to spend the night there.

The next morning we reached the upper northwest spur, which we followed to the summit. After half an hour's rest, we began our descent of the southwest ridge. Although it should have been possible to reach Mestia that day, a thunderstorm struck when we arrived at Nageb Pass and we decided to camp for the night. Our route up the north face of Tetnuldi was 1,100m, TD- WI3 55–60°.

[Above] The north face of Tetnuldi (4,853m). (1) Northeast ridge (4A, Shintlmeyster, 1931). (2) British Route (Jenkins-Taylor, 1937). A very similar line was climbed by Czechs in 1966 and graded 5B. (3) Tulpanov Route (5B, 1982). (4) Ukrainian Route (1,100m, TD-, Kuraliesov-Poddubnov, 2016). *Mykhailo Poddubnov*

— MYKHAILO PODDUBNOV, *UKRAINE*

KAZBEK, EAST FACE, NEW ROUTE IN WINTER

FROM FEBRUARY 9 to 13, Giorgi Tepnadze and I climbed a new route up the Dragon's Wall on Kazbek (5,047m, a.k.a. Kazbegi), which rises 3,200m above the village of Stepantsminda. Our route climbs the east face via a steep icefall through the left side of the crescent-shaped rock barrier at around 4,700m.

Kazbek (Georgians call it Mkinvartsveri, which means Icy Peak) is one of Georgia's sacred mountains, and associated with it are many legends and myths. The famous Dragon, visible from the valley as a crescent-shaped rock barrier, had been avoided for years due to its loose rock. One winter in the early 2000s, after several attempts, Georgian mountaineers Gezi Kakhabrishvili, Zura Kuchava, and Levan Tatarashvili made the first successful ascent of Dragon's Wall, grading their route 5B. Our ascent, to the left of this, was dedicated to the front man of the team, Tatarashvili, who was killed a few years later.

We took five days to reach the summit, camping first at 3,000m and 3,660m on the normal route (southeast side). Our third camp was on the east shoulder at 4,350m, and from there we began exploring unknown ground. Being winter, the slopes above comprised hard blue ice. We climbed about eight pitches on ice to reach the Dragon, where, at around 4,700m, after two hours of searching, we found a sloping shelf on which we could just pitch our inner tent. The lights of the village could be clearly seen far below.

Next day we followed a logical line over mixed terrain. The second pitch was thin ice over monolithic rock. Protection was psychological. The third pitch was a vertical icefall that Giorgi led, and the only pitch where the leader climbed without a pack. Above, we climbed 300m of

[Above] Stepantsminda village, Gergeti Trinity Church, and Kazbek (5,047m), with the Dragon's Wall and its curved rock barrier in upper right. The 2016 Georgian winter route is marked. The normal route, descended by the Georgian climbers, circles around the far side of the peak. *Peter Nasmyth* [Left] "Archil meets the Dragon." *Painting by Rusudan Badriashvili*

ice at 45°, closely chasing the sun's trajectory. Finally, at 8:40 p.m., by the light of our headlamps and the moon, we reached the summit.

We descended the long and tedious normal route, making two rappels, and finally reached the site of our Camp 2, by the Betlemi Hut and a disused weather station, at 4:30 a.m. We graded the route Russian 5B, AI5 (90°) M4 60°, with 800m of technical climbing. It is now acknowledged to be the hardest route on the mountain. The funniest memorabilia was presented to me by my younger sister: an exquisite painting of me meeting the dragon. 📷

— ARCHIL BADRIASHVILI, *GEORGIA*

CAUCASUS / CHAUKHI RANGE

ASATIANI, WEST-NORTHWEST BUTTRESS, BADRIASHVILI-TEPNADZE ROUTE

EAST OF THE higher and better-known peaks of the Caucasus, the Chaukhi massif is one of the most popular mountain regions of the range. It is only about 100km north of Tbilisi, Georgia's capital, followed by a short walk to base camp at around 2,600m. The existing routes climb rock and snow, from F to TD+/ED1, with vertical intervals of 800–1,250m between base camp and the summits. Most peaks are between 3,400m and 3,850m, and almost every summit is named after a beloved Georgian figure. Every year there are several official mountaineering events, which offer training for both beginners and the more experienced.

The hardest climbs in the region are found on the west-northwest buttress and east face of Asatiani (3,850m), and also on Mt. Agmashenebeli (3,854m). The Sindaura wall on Agmashenebeli is the hardest north face in the Chaukhi Range.

Over July 10-11, 2015, Giorgi Tepnadze and I climbed a direct new route on the right side of the west-northwest buttress of Asatiani. We climbed nonstop (though we carried bivouac equipment) in a round trip from base camp of 23.5 hours. The first pitch was quite close to the only other route on the buttress (5B, Khabazi-Kuchava-Ugulava, around 1996). The first dozen meters on the fourth pitch had no protection. The sixth pitch was wet and had a brittle overhang; we had to resort to aid for 15m, though we climbed the rest of the route completely free.

[Above] The west-northwest buttress of Asatiani. The approximate line of the new Badriashvili-Tepnadze Route is marked, with the summit ridge a considerable distance above (off picture). The original route up the buttress, climbed around 1996, starts in nearly the same place and lies mostly to the left until the top of the buttress, after which the two lines likely share ground to the summit. *Archil Badriashvili*

Above this, we were on ground known from our ascent of the face the previous year by the established route. The place where we had bivouacked in 2014 was now full of ice, so we kept going, traversed a foresummit, descended to the right, and within half an hour were on the summit. It was 20 minutes after midnight. We rested before starting the descent to our base camp. Our new route rose about 800m (1,200m above base camp), with difficulties of Russian 5B, 6b A2. 📖 📷

— **ARCHIL BADRIASHVILI,** *GEORGIA*

FIRST COMPLETE TRAVERSE OF CHAUKHI RANGE, SOLO

IN JULY 2015, after climbing a new route on Asatiani with Giorgi Tepnadze *(see report above)*, I was surprised by a fine morning on July 15 and hurriedly packed a rucksack for a long traverse. (I carried 7mm and 9mm ropes, some gear, a little bit of kitchen and bivouac equipment, and electronics, a total of 14kg).

Using a line I'd climbed a few years previously, I reached the summit of Javakhishvili in less than five hours. I self-belayed a narrow chimney of UIAA IV/IV+. I then traversed to Leonidze (IV+), belaying for a whole rope length, then continued along unknown ground (for me) to Cameron. Next I reached Asatiani, where it began to rain. I looked on the positive side and used it to replenish my water supply. Going down to a col, I built a stone shelter, got inside my bivouac sack, swallowed some awful scrambled egg, and went to sleep. It was a cold night, which got me going at 5 a.m. the following day.

Two-thirds of the remaining traverse of the main Chaukhi peaks was unknown to me, and I had no useful information—this part of the range is wild and remote. Several hours along the crest led to the two summits of Pirosmani (3,858m, high point of the range). Here

[Above] Badriashvili on the last day of the Chaukhi traverse, with bad weather developing. *Archil Badriashvili*

was a surprise: Between here and Mt. TSU were two summits of which I had not previously been aware. The first was difficult, with a section of 5c, which I back-roped. The way to the second "unknown mountain" proved to be longer, and on top of this I was attacked by a big bird. I rappelled the far side; the rope stuck and it took me some time to sort it out.

I crossed TSU and continued along a beautiful weathered ridge for 1.5km to a peak I had first climbed with my father when I was nine years old. Beyond this, the ridge, although only AD+, was quite dangerous and long. I crossed the summit of Takaishvili and in worsening weather slowly ascended Tikanadze, the last peak of the traverse. Lightning hit the top two minutes after I had left it, and I had an exciting time making a rapid descent of the classic route. After waiting for the lightning to ease, getting thoroughly wet and frozen, I descended to base camp, where I was able to calm friends who had witnessed the storm. Unfortunately, they told me the dinner they'd prepared had been eaten by cows, so, with nothing else to do, we packed up and descended to the valley by headlamp.

The full traverse, which took 31 hours, crossed 11 summits above 3,500m. I graded it 5B. According to my GPS I had made a vertical gain of 2,300m. Apart from 360m, on which I either self-belayed or rappelled, everything else was free solo. [*Editor's note: Peak elevations used in these Chaukhi reports are from the author's GPS readings during this traverse.*] 📷

– **ARCHIL BADRIASHVILI**, *GEORGIA*

AGMASHENEBELI, NORTH FACE

IN SEPTEMBER 2015, Giorgi Tepnadze and I climbed a new route on the north face of Agmashenebeli (3,854m, one of the highest peaks in the Chaukhi), which we dedicated to Alexander Ruchkin, who had recently been killed in Peru. Davit Agmashenebeli (David the Builder) was king of Georgia from 1089 to 1125, and Georgians consider him the most successful ruler in the history of our country. The first ascent of the north face of Agmashenebeli (Geldiashvili, Lukashvili, and friends, 1982) was awarded a silver medal in the Soviet Mountaineering Championships that year. The wall now has about six routes.

After scoping the wall for a day, we found a line toward the left side, beginning with the first 80m of the Tatsrashvili Route (2006). Levan Tatarashvili was an exceptional person and climber, who always liked trying something new; he tragically died soon after climbing this route.

We started up the face at 7 a.m. and continued directly up a crack system where the Tatarashvili Route went left. On the fourth pitch we had to resort to aid to clean mud out of a crack in an overhang. After that aiders were blissfully forgotten. Another six pitches of climbing up to 5c, and at least the same amount of simul-climbing above, brought us to the summit, where we set about preparing a bivouac.

The next day was a different story. We had to descend the south face into a totally different valley. On the last rappel a stone hit my knee and our party had to continue on three and a half legs. An inviting landscape lured us into a false exit: We were forced to cross four valleys and three ridges, and walk a total of 18km to reach Roshka village, where we were met by friends. The 850m new route was graded Russian 5B, 5c A2+. 📷

— ARCHIL BADRIASHVILI, *GEORGIA*

ASATIANI, EAST FACE

WHILE CLIMBING a new route on the north face of Agmashenebeli the year before (*see previous report*), it was hard not to notice the east face of Asatiani (3,850m) and wonder why it

[Above] **The north face of Agmashenebeli, left, showing the 2015 Badriashvili-Tepnadze Route, which shares the first 80m of the Tatarashvili Route (2006) and then continues straight up where the earlier route goes left. In all, about six routes climb this face. At right is the east face of Asatiani, climbed in 2016 by the same pair, finishing directly through the prominent headwall.** *Archil Badriashvili*

remained unclimbed. The wall seemed more monolithic and safer from objective danger than most others in the Chaukhi—it made our eyes sparkle with passion.

On September 7, from a camp on the glacier around 600m below the summit, Giorgi Tepnadze and I climbed a snow slope and then several hundred meters of rocky terrain to reach the headwall that forms the meat of the route. On the steep wall to the right of a huge open dihedral, a wide crack system slants up to the right. We followed these cracks, with several overhanging sections. After two pitches on the headwall, we carefully built a bivy site in the style of post-Soviet architecture. The next day we continued up the headwall, entering a narrow chimney that tested our caving skills. Another aid section, a wide crack, and finally, after six pitches on the headwall, we finished at a gendarme. From here, 20 minutes at rapid tempo took us to the summit of Asatiani.

After brief celebrations, we climbed down an objectively dangerous 300m couloir on the east face in the dark. With little left of our headlamp batteries, we packed our camp and descended to the village of Roshka, where we were taken hostage by Georgian hospitality for a few hours before driving back to Tbilisi.

It would be possible to free climb this route, but due to the compact nature of the rock, placing meaningful protection would require great skill. We aided much of it, with sections at A2+/A3, and gave an overall rating of 5B. 📷

— ARCHIL BADRIASHVILI, *GEORGIA*

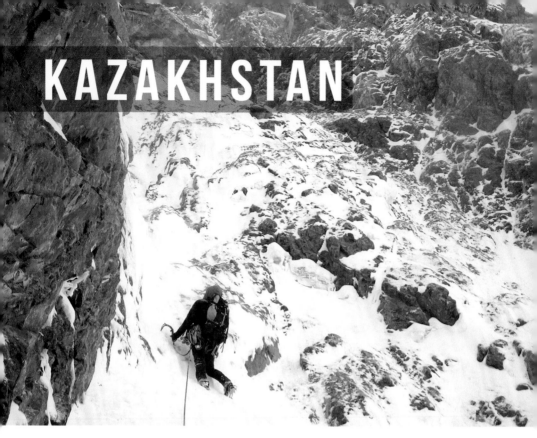

[Above] **Kirill Belotserkovskiy on moderate ground in the middle of the north face of Sairam.** *Max Ten*

SAIRAM, NORTH FACE, NEW VARIATION

SAIRAM (4,238m) is situated on the Ugam Ridge of the Western Tien Shan, approximately 150km northeast of Tashkent and 350km west-southwest of Bishkek (42°8'16.04"N, 70°28'50.44"E). The northern aspect is a fine alpine face, with room for new routes. I saw it for the first time in the spring of 2015, as I was driving around southern Kazakhstan and looking for walls to climb. With Polina Orendovskaya, I climbed a moderate five-pitch route on a limestone cliff at Boralday, then moved to the mountains south of Shymkent, where we put up a new route on Kyzyl-sau. That evening I went to look at the north face of Sairam, as I knew there were existing Russian routes of 5B—hard enough to be fun, but not so hard that they would involve lots of alpine suffering.

As soon as I saw the face, I was hooked. Back at home I did some research and found that the stunning direct line to the summit was unclimbed. But there was good reason. In summer the lower section is constantly bombarded with rockfall. In winter the access is very difficult, due to abundant snow in the approach valley. A friend suggested mid-spring would be the optimal time: The avalanche danger would not be too high, but there would be enough ice to bind loose rock.

Max Ten and I reached Shymkent on April 19, and the same day friends drove us toward the mountain. Next day we wandered up in thick mist, which later turned to rain. The following day was clear, so we continued. At noon we reached the moraine opposite the face and camped. For the rest of that day and all the following, we watched the gully that formed the initial section of our proposed line, trying to see or hear falling stones. The mountain was silent.

On April 23 we left the tent at 4 a.m., and one hour later were at the top of the avalanche cone, bombarded by steady spindrift. I started up the initial section of vertical, polished ice, looking at my feet the whole time to avoid a mask of snow building on my face. The ice led to a steep, snowy couloir, interrupted by sections of yellow ice. We climbed together for 150m to a rock section, where, from a nonexistent belay anchor, I headed up toward the huge dihedral that splits the central rock band. Without adequate protection, it proved too scary, so I downclimbed and Max led out left on a snow ramp.

[Above] The north face of Sairam (4,238m) in May 2015. (1) U. Svolik, 1988, 5A. (2) V. Sedelnikov, 1977, 5B. (3) A. Pavelyev, 2001, 5B. (4) A. Bobrov, 1986, 5B. (5) K. Belotserkovskiy and M. Ten, 2016, 5B. (6) V. Starlychanov, 1977, 5B. (7) V. Melnikov, 2001, 4B. *Kirill Belotserkovskiy*

This took us to a steep gully with 2cm of ice over monolithic rock. Much better!

I made another attempt to reach the dihedral but was stopped by a wide crack. Hoping to reach it from farther left, we climbed together for 150m on steep snow to a loose chimney, which, although steep, proved straightforward. I tried to move right again, as I still wanted to climb the central section of the face, but soon retreated when I found myself digging a trench for 30m through chest-deep snow over rock. I decided that if it collapsed it probably would not kill me, but it certainly would provide me with neither motivation nor pleasure.

Continuing up to the left, the next two pitches were the crux: 70° slabs covered with snow. It took me one and a half hours to lead the first of these pitches, hooking imaginary holds that miraculously worked. By this stage we were probably on the 1986 Bobrov summer route. With rock shoes, these limestone slabs would have been a breeze.

We finally reached the couloirs in the upper part of the face. The snow was deep, we were tired, and the sun was disappearing below the horizon. After a few hours I stood shivering on the northeast ridge as Max, exhausted and moving really slowly, approached. I was nearly hypothermic, and although the summit was only 50m above, we immediately set off down the northeast ridge, hoping that we were on the normal route (Timofeev, 3B). We weren't, and we had to make four rappels from one-piton anchors to reach the glacier, join the normal route, and rappel and downclimb a snow couloir to the moraine. Twenty-two hours after leaving, we reached our tent.

We didn't climb the direct line as planned, we didn't even summit, but we had fun. In that we succeeded. We graded our 700m route 5B, WI5 M7 A0.

– **KIRILL BELOTSERKOVSKIY**, *KAZAKHSTAN*

FIND MORE AT THE *AAJ* WEBSITE: *publications.americanalpineclub.org.*

FULL-LENGTH REPORT | ADDITIONAL PHOTOS | MAPS OR TOPOS | VIDEO OR MULTIMEDIA

The limestone escarpment of Hodja Gur Gur Ata rises 250m to 365m and extends for about 34km in an unbroken line. Entrances to the Dark Star caving system lie in the face below. *Robbie Shone*

DARK STAR
SANDBAGGED INTO THE FIRST ASCENT OF A 365-METER WALL

BY MARK SYNNOTT

"Misha, p-l-e-a-s-e, l-i-s-t-e-n, c-a-r-e-f-u-l-l-y," I said, holding up the frayed static line to which we were tied. "I don't want to climb any higher. If you won't go down with me, I will untie and solo to the bottom." Misha extended his lower lip and, with his brawny arms crossed over his chest, locked me in an icy stare and muttered something unintelligible. We had been arguing on a tiny ledge on the side of Hodja Gur Gur Ata, a 365m limestone wall in a remote corner of Uzbekistan, for nearly an hour. Considering we didn't share a common language, the situation was becoming ridiculous. One thing was clear: Misha adamantly refused to bail.

Earlier in the day, as we'd surveyed this vertical and overhanging cliff from the base, I realized immediately there was no way we could safely climb it with the motley assortment of old Russian caving gear we had scrounged in camp. I said as much to Misha and thought he agreed, but somehow he had cajoled me two-thirds of the way up the cliff on what I thought would be a few pitches of reconnaissance. Peering down the crumbling limestone we had already scaled, it dawned on me that my threat to downclimb was a bluff—and Misha knew it.

I found myself in this unsavory predicament because I had signed on with a 31-member expedition—led by and comprised mostly of non-English-speaking Russians like Misha—to explore a massive underground labyrinth called Dark Star that one day may become the Everest of caves. Our trip took place from August 3–26, 2014. Of the 22 different entrances that perforate the face of Hodja Gur Gur Ata, most can be reached only via technical climbing or rappelling. At breakfast our first morning in the area, Misha and I were tasked with getting to the top of the cliff and fixing a rope that would be used to establish a high camp on the rim. On the dozen previous expeditions, no one had ever actually climbed Hodja Gur Gur Ata; they had always hiked around the side. While that sounds easier, it's a good 40km trek, hence their plan to lure me into forging a shortcut. As the token rock climber on the team, I could see the logic in that decision, even if it seemed like Misha was trying to kill me.

The Baisun-tau Mountains are located in Uzbekistan's Surkhandarya province, near the border shared with Tajikistan and Afghanistan. The range consists of two main mountain chains, Ketmen' Chapty and Hodja Gur Gur Ata, the latter with a southeast-facing cliff stretching unbroken for 34km. A similar mountain range called the Surkhan-tau lies 15km to the southeast. The two ranges, which run in a southwest to northeast orientation, form the southwestern end of the larger Gissar Range. These mountains present as a series of wedge-shaped plateaus that rise to around 3,650m and end precipitously in 250–365m cliffs. In the deep valleys lie a hodgepodge of small villages where Tajiks and Uzbeks have lived for centuries. I was told the rugged track we traveled by Soviet transport to access these mountains was the same one used by Alexander

Mark Synnott rappelling the steep face of Hodja Gur Gur Ata, with entrances to the Dark Star caving system visible. *Robbie Shone*

the Great's army on its march to Afghanistan after sacking Samarkand in 329 BC.

When Misha called my bluff, I realized my only option was to go for the top. Though Mikhail "Misha" Rafikov is a world-class caver (and more stubborn than the donkeys that carried our gear into these mountains), he has little climbing experience. This left the dangerous job of leading the upper headwall to me, but I was in Uzbekistan for caving, not rock climbing, so I didn't even have sticky-soled rock shoes or a proper harness. What followed were three of the scariest leads of my life: rope stretchers on a static line, with a rack consisting of a handful of Russian bird beaks—none of which I was able to place in the compact rock. However, while I found not a single piece of protection on any of the pitches, I always managed to find an anchor just as I was running out of rope—a juniper bush with a trunk the width of my wrist, a chockstone, and finally a leg and elbow brace on a rubble-covered ledge just below the summit. When we topped out late in the day, Misha just shrugged and gave me a look as if to say, "See, I told you it was no problem."

Our route, which we named *Russian Roulette* (5.9 X), tackled the center of the wall, to the right of the entrance to a cave system called Festivalnaya. The rock was mainly choss, but later, while rappelling from the summit plateau in various locations, I discovered there is some solid rock on this wall. The Russians told me they know of no one else that has climbed Hodja Gur Gur Ata.

No trekking or climbing industry exists in this region. The Uzbek government requires foreigners to be registered in a hotel every night. This presents a thorny problem to anyone wanting to explore off the beaten path, but it has some merit, considering the area is the historic home of the Islamic Movement of Uzbekistan (IMU). To learn more about the icy caves we explored inside Dark Star, see my article on the expedition in the March 2017 issue of *National Geographic*.

Summary: First ascent of Russian Roulette (365m, 5.9 X), the only route up the southeast face of Hodja Gur Gur Ata in the Baisun-tau Mountains of Uzbekistan.

KYRGYZSTAN

KARAVSHIN, KARA-SU VALLEY, VARIOUS ASCENTS

GIAN LUCA CAVALLI, Pier Luigi Maschietto, Giovanni Pagnoncelli, Edoardo Polo, and I climbed in the Karavshin in August 2015. Unfortunately, floods the previous spring had destroyed many bridges, and landslides obliterated some paths along the approach from Uzgurush. Instead of the usual one and a half days, the approach took three. We established base camp in the Kara-su Valley at about 2,800m, finding the river quite wild; we had to install a Tyrolean to ease access to the true left side. We then had generally good weather, with only one or two days of rain.

On August 7 all four of us climbed the classic Diagonal Route (600m, 6c A1, 1987) on the east face of Yellow Wall (3,800m). Two days later, Cavalli, Maschietto, and I made the probable second ascent of Opposite to Asan (650m plus 150m of ridge, 6a+, 2006) on Silver Wall (4,000m), the next wall up-valley from Yellow Wall. We made a new variant in the middle section: Bye-bye, Globo de Gas! (200m, 6c A1, natural gear). We bivouacked on the ridge at 3,900m after completing the main difficulties, and the following day reached the summit.

On the 12th all four of us climbed a new line on Little

[Top] The northwest side of Asan (4,230m) from the Kara-su Valley. [Left] Little Asan showing (1) West ridge, (2) Waiting for Andrea, (3) Happy Birthday, Horses!, and (4) Italian Corner. Routes 2–4 were climbed in 2015. *Giovanni Pagnoncelli*

Asan (ca 3,900m), which we named Happy Birthday, Horses! (600m, 6b+). This followed dihedrals, slabs, hand cracks, and offwidths, generally using natural gear, with two pegs and one bolt. We rappelled the line, placing one bolt at each anchor. Later, Maschietto, Pagnoncelli, and Polo climbed a probable new variant to the west ridge of Little Asan, Waiting for Andrea (330m, 6a+), and then a new route on the west face, Italian Corner (150m of approach in a couloir and then 380m to 6b+, with two bolts). They also attempted a new line on a tower between the Yellow and Silver walls.

In the meantime Cavalli and I transferred to the Ak-su by horse and made an ascent of the classic Perestroika Crack (800m, 7a/b) on the Russian Tower (Pik Slesova, 4,240m). 📷

– MARCELLO SANGUINETI, *ACADEMIC ITALIAN ALPINE CLUB (CAAI)*

LOMO, NORTHWEST FACE; PIRAMIDALNY, NORTHEAST FACE

MAX TEN AND I established two new routes from the Kara-su Valley in July. First, in order to acclimatize, we climbed the northwest face of Lomo (4,750m). This shale mountain lies immediately south of Pik 4,810m and can be climbed from the pass between the two at 5B, as on the first ascent in 1988 by Buchinksy and team. However, it is rarely climbed, the last known ascent being in 1993.

We made the 2.5-hour approach from Kara-su base camp on July 19, our first day in the area. The next morning we left camp at 4 a.m. and reached the foot of the icefall at dawn. We were lucky to find an easy passage between ice and rock, and by 8:45 a.m. were on the plateau atop the hanging glacier.

[Above] **Lomo from the northwest. (1) The 1988 Buchinksy Route. (2) The 2016 Kazakh Route.** *Kirill Belotserkovskiy*

From there we chose the most obvious and easiest line up the northwest face, a steep couloir slanting left below steeper rock walls. We followed this to an exit high on the north ridge, where we joined the 1988 route. Apart from a 30m section of water ice, the couloir was no steeper than 65°. Once on the ridge, we climbed four pitches of black, sometimes loose, ice-plastered rock. We reached the summit at 5:30 p.m. and after half an hour's rest started descending one of the couloirs on the southwest face. In retrospect it would have been faster if we'd followed the south ridge to the col and then slid down the main west-facing snow couloir below. At 11 p.m., 19 hours after setting out, we regained our tent in the valley. Our route had difficulties of 5A (WI4 M4).

After a rest in base camp we headed toward our main objective, the northeast face of Pik Piramidalny (5,509m). Our idea was simple: reach the base of the face and decide where to climb. We knew the lines of the existing routes, and for us that ground would be taboo.

The approach to the 1,000m-plus northeast face is a complex affair. First we had to climb to a notch on the east ridge of Pik 5,000m and then rappel to the glacier on the far side. We started up toward this notch at 7 p.m. Brick-size rocks, released by snow and ice melt, were falling from the rock band above. Four pitches of 60–70° ice led to the notch, where we bivouacked.

[Above] Piramidalny (5,509m) from close to the summit of Lomo to the east. (A) Notch used to access the hanging glacier below the northeast face. (B) Pik 5,000m. (C) West Vadif Pass, used in descent in 2016. (The distant peak behind the pass is Snowy Ak-su.) (1) Southeast Ridge (French, 1993). (2) Russian Roulette (USA-Slovenia, 2002). (3) East-northeast ridge (Nazarov, et al, 1987). (4) French (2014). (5) Belotserkovskiy-Ten (2016). (6) Voronov Route (1989). (7) Paolo Tamagnini (1991, solo). (8) German Route (2016). (9) West and north ridges (British, 1991). *Kirill Belotserkovskiy*

Next day, at 5 a.m., we rappelled to the glacier. This place is a trap, as the steep, icy northeast face of Piramidalny, the east face of Pik 5,000m, and the steep-sided east ridge of Piramidalny rise on three sides, while to the east is a massive icefall. In a two-person party, if one of you gets hurt here, you're in trouble.

A snowy ridge rose from the glacier to the start of the difficult climbing on the northeast face. Two hellishly loose pitches, followed by six pitches of mixed climbing, brought us to a big ice slope. Two more pitches got us to the top of the slope, and a further pitch to a nice safe ledge for a bivouac.

Next morning, in order to bypass a huge cornice, we rappelled into an icy couloir and climbed it for 30m, where we were "woken up" not by morning coffee but by two pitches of vertical and extremely loose rock. No protection meant no falls. Three cool mixed pitches got us onto a snowy ridge, which in turn joined the east-northeast ridge of Piramidalny at around 5,100m. We arrived there at 10 p.m. and bivouacked in wet snow among crevasses.

Next day, July 29, we left at 7 a.m. and, following Piramidalny's original route (1987, 5B), we reached the summit by 11:30 a.m. In fine weather, we had great views of Lyalak Gorge to the west, Zarafshan Ridge to the south, and the Matcha Range to the east. Our ascent involved difficulties of 6A (WI5 M5).

We rested briefly then set off down the north ridge. (Often referred to as the "west ridge," this ridge descends north to Pik 5,000m, where it turns in a more westerly direction). Five rappels from Abalakov anchors got us to the col before Pik 5,000m. From there we climbed almost to the summit, then contoured the left side to reach West Vadif Pass. We made one rappel to the north, then downclimbed to the glacier, almost to the point where we had started climbing up to the notch four days before. Just before midnight we reached base camp. Two weeks later, three young Germans climbed another new route on the face, up the buttress right of center. [*Editor's note: No details of the new German route were available. See photo above for their route line.*] 📷

– KIRILL BELOTSERKOVSKIY, *KAZAKHSTAN*

JIPTIK VALLEY, MUZ TOK, NORTH FACE, ATTEMPT

ON JULY 5, after a two-day walk from Sary Zhaz, Phil Dawson, Ciaran Mullan, and I arrived at base camp near the snout of the Jiptik Glacier, a.k.a. the Schurovsky Glacier. (This was misspelled in past AAJs, the glacier being named after the Russian academic Grigori Efimovich Schurovsky.) Robert Taylor would arrive five days later due to a delayed flight.

The start of the trek to Jiptik base camp is shared with one approach to the rather more popular Karavshin, but in recent years access by this route sometimes has been impeded. The route used to pass through Vorukh, a Tajik enclave within Kyrgyzstan, and from time to time (e.g. 2014) outbreaks of violent conflict led to the border being closed. The tour operator Batken Travel Service has instigated a new route into the Jiptik and Karavshin areas that avoids the enclave and so makes these destinations less risky.

The Jiptik saw little climbing activity during the Soviet era—only a handful of easy routes were climbed. After the collapse of the USSR, this area remained untouched until 1996, when Paul Hersey's New Zealand expedition climbed Kyzyl Muz (5,127m on the Soviet Military Map), Muz Tash (5,040m), Kara-Eet (4,900m), and Pik 4,720m.

In 2009, Hersey returned to Jiptik with Graham Zimmerman and Yewjin Tan. This group climbed a new route on the north face of Kyzyl Muz and identified the north face of Muz Tok (a.k.a. Pik Schurovsky West, 5,066m) as an excellent unclimbed objective (*AAJ 2009*). Muz Tok was first climbed during the Soviet era via the southwest ridge and has probably been climbed more than once as a part of long traverses along the frontier ridge with Tajikistan. The north face would be our main goal.

Robert and I set off for Muz Tok at lunchtime on July 15. This was our third attempt, the first two (with Ciaran and Phil) having been abandoned very early because it was too warm or wet. As we waited on the moraine opposite the peak, the temperature fell in a satisfactory manner. It took much longer than anticipated to cross the complex glacier, and we began climbing, from 4,150m (GPS), at 1 a.m.

We continued through the night up névé and ice, past the first bottleneck, then up and right to a long couloir that we hoped would take us to the top. After daybreak we took to the solid rock rib for safety, as the sun was now hitting the snow. (Photos available to us before the trip had shown the Jiptik Valley to be limestone, so it was a pleasant surprise to find mostly granite from the snout of the glacier upward.) In the evening we arrived on the ridge marking the top of the couloir, where we could look down the far side onto what

[Above] Muz Tok (5,066m), showing the line attempted on the north face in 2016. The climbers descended to the right, just right of the prominent rock rib. The pyramid behind is Pik Schurovsky (5,490m). *John Proctor*

would eventually become our descent route. There was no space to pitch the bivouac tent, so we lay down in a line on a ledge at 4,928m. After food and drink, we "slept" from midnight to 1 a.m.

Our plan was to continue up the ridge to the summit and then descend relatively easily to the west. Unfortunately, we soon were wading through deep snow. When upward progress became impossible, we took to the east flank of the ridge, which had sections of 60° ice that took screws. However, after 50m we were stopped by a 20m rock barrier straddling the ridge, and due to technical difficulty, loose rock, and poor protection, neither of us could climb it. We started down, reached our bivouac site as it was getting light, and then descended the couloir on the west flank of the ridge with a combination of rappels and downclimbing.

We felt the 800m line we had followed to our high point to be around TD. We are grateful for the support given by the Austrian Alpine Club, BMC, MEF, and the Chris Walker Memorial Trust.

– JOHN PROCTOR, *ALPINE CLUB, U.K.*

MINDZHAR VALLEY, PIK 5,157M, PIK 5,390M, AND PIK 5,414M

BEFORE JOINING THE estimated 1,000 climbers at base camp for Pik Lenin in August, we went by jeep to the next main valley west, the Mindzhar, where there were no mountaineers. At the head of this valley, the Mindzhar Glacier rises west to Mindzhar Pass (ca 5,050m). This pass has been visited or crossed by "mountain trekkers," but there are strict rules that do not allow such "tourists" to climb to summits, so all the surrounding peaks have remained unclimbed. The highest unclimbed peak in this area, across the border in Tajikistan, is unnamed Pik 6,001m (39°18'46.52"N, 72°42'45.81"E). Immediately to the northeast of this peak lies Pik 6,130m, which was climbed in 2011.

Maksim Svoboda and I first camped on the Red Rocks ridge at 4,300m and then at 4,700m, and next day we arrived on Mindzhar Pass at around midday and pitched our tent on the border between Kyrgyzstan and Tajikistan. That afternoon we moved north along the frontier ridge and summited previously unclimbed Pik 5,157m (39°23'11.96"N, 72°36'38.22"E).

Next day we headed south along the ridge toward Pik 5,839m, which, first thing in the morning, when the weather was partially clear, looked like a Himalayan giant. We crossed Pik 5,390m, continued southwest over 5,414m (39°22'11.34N, 72°36'6.39"E), and descended the far side to MAI 50th Anniversary Pass. By now we could barely see each other at the end of 8m of rope, and after failing to find an onward route to 5,839m, we retreated to the tent. Next day we descended and subsequently drove back to Lenin base camp, where I summited the 7,134m peak, alone, for my sixth time.

OLEG SILIN, *LATVIA*

[Below] **The highest unclimbed peak in this area of the Pamirs, Pik 6,001m in Tajikistan, seen from Mindzhar Pass to the northwest.** *Oleg Silin*

BISHKEK SPORT CLIMBING

READERS MAY BE interested to know about Chunkurchak, a sport climbing area close to Bishkek, with both single- and multi-pitch routes, possibly useful for a couple of days at the beginning or end of a Kyrgyzstan expedition. Directions to these granitic cliffs and a partial topo guide can be found at the AAJ website: *publications.americanalpineclub.org.* 📷 🔍

– **KAI MALUCK**, *GERMANY*

TIEN SHAN / KYRGYZ ALA-TOO

SOKULUK VALLEY, CHON-TOR

IN JANUARY 2016, Egor Suzdaltsev and Ivan Temerev from Russian Siberia made what is thought to be the first ascent of Chon-tor (4,180m) in the Sokuluk Valley of the western Tien Shan. The valley is about 40km southwest of Bishkek, a little to the west of the well-known peaks of the Ala Archa.

[Above] **The northwest face of Chon-tor. (1) Spirit of Adventure. (2) Glazunov Route.** *Supplied by Anna Piunova*

Although they anticipated harsh conditions in winter, Suzdaltsev and Temerev were fortunate to have bright sunshine, little wind, and temperatures of only -5°C to -15°C. They approached via the Belogorka Gorge, and after two grueling days of ferrying their equipment, set their base camp tent below the central buttress of the northwest face. [*This area is easily accessible in the warmer months, but the climbers chose to climb in winter as part of the Russian Championships.*]

They began at 7 a.m. on January 22 and reached the top at 4:35 p.m. on the 24th. Two bivouacs were made on the wall, on small ledges, plus a third on the descent. After emerging from the wall, the two headed up the north ridge to what they thought would be a relatively straightforward summit tower. It was not. The tower was 200m high, and much aid and an unpleasant pendulum were needed before reaching the top (4,192m GPS; approximately 42°28'51"N, 74°20'46"E). The 900m route (1,200m of climbing) was graded 6A and named Spirit of Adventure. Rappelling only three times on the far side, they found an easy descent and returned toward their tent next day. [*Editor's note: A second route, also 6A, was added to Chon-tor a few weeks later by Evgeniy and Sergey Glazunov. See route line above.*] 📷

– **LINDSAY GRIFFIN**, *WITH INFO FROM ANNA PIUNOVA, MOUNTAIN.RU, AND ELENA DMITREKNO, RISK.RU*

ALA ARCHA NATIONAL PARK, VARIOUS NEW ROUTES

FROM AUGUST 4 to 28, Giovanni Pagnoncelli and I climbed three long new rock routes in Ala Archa National Park, all on trad gear. The weather was very bad throughout our stay, with only one fine day; the rest had at least two to three hours of rain or snow in the afternoon. We found plenty of good granite and potential for beautiful lines, particularly on north and west faces. We met only two (Russian) parties tackling semi-technical rock routes; the rest were climbing easy mixed ground, mostly the normal routes.

[Above left] **Homemade wooden "Big Bros"** in the third-pitch offwidth of the route called www.lookoutofthetent.com on Tower Gymnica 2000. [Above right] Giovanni Pagnoncelli climbing into the mist on one of the fine crack pitches of the route called www.lookoutofthetent.com on Tower Gymnica 2000. [Left] The west face of Baichechekey, above the Ratsek Hut in the Ala Archa. The left line on the crest of the pillar is the classic and fairly popular Shvab Route (1980,). The route on the right is Crêuza de Mä (2016, 6a+). It is thought the big corner in the lower section between the two lines has been climbed as a variant to the Shvab Route. *Marcello Sanguineti*

We made our base camp near the Ratsek Hut, at 3,400m, and on August 9 (the one continuously good weather day of the trip) climbed Crêuza de Mä (550m of climbing, 6a+) on the west face of Baichechekey (4,515m). This route climbs hand cracks and a corner entirely to the right of the classic Shvab Route (1980) for 10 pitches, four of which were 6a+, before joining the Shvab Route on the crest of the pillar for a final three pitches. This was an excellent climb on perfect Mont Blanc–style granite. We descended the normal route.

On the 11th we walked up the Uchitel Glacier and spotted an unnamed summit on the long west ridge of Korona (4,860m), between Korona and Ratsek Peak (3,980m). On that day we climbed three pitches up the east face. Bad weather kept us in the tents the next day, but on the 13th we went back to the face, climbed to the top of the third pitch by a different, easier line coming in from the right, and then continued to the summit in another three pitches plus some easy climbing. The route follows a splitter, then a corner, then slabs to reach a prominent "banana diedre" on pitches four and five, the crux of the route. The face is about 250m high, and we named the route Roulette Kyrghiza (330m of climbing, 6c A1). We descended the line by rappel in very bad weather. Although it is a beautiful line, the rock is loose in places and difficult to protect. We have dubbed the summit Chiavari Peak (4,145m).

Next we looked at a south-facing pillar leading to a tower on the walls between Baichechekey and Uchitel (4,527m). The pillar, about 220m high, is in two parts: first a narrow "candle," as one might find in the Mont Blanc massif, then a ridge to the summit. We have named the formation Tower Gymnica 2000 (4,020m) and the first section the Chandelle of Uchitel.

On the 18th we climbed the Chandelle in three pitches and left our ropes fixed. Third pitch was a flared and sometimes overhanging offwidth crux. Our cams weren't big enough, so at base camp we manufactured three wooden "Big Bros," which solved, at least psychologically, the protection problem.

Due to bad weather, we didn't get the opportunity to finish the route until the 21st, when we jumared the ropes, climbed a 10m pitch of A0 to the top of the candle, descended 15m on the far side, and continued up the ridge above for another six pitches (5a to 6b+) to the summit. The last two pitches were climbed through falling snow. From the top we rappelled into the couloir between Uchitel and Baichechekey. We gave the route the tongue-in-cheek name of www.lookoutofthetent.com (330m of climbing, 6c A0).

– MARCELLO SANGUINETI, CLUB ALPINO ACCADEMICO ITALIANO

ALA ARCHA, KORONA VI, SOUTH FACE, GEORGIAN DIRECT

AFTER STAYING A few days in the Ratsek Hut, Giorgi Tepnadze and I hiked up to the Korona Hut, a demotivating place due to its poor condition and interior design. We first went to the foot of Free Korea Peak to inspect a route we planned to try on the north face, and then set up camp below Korona's less frequently climbed Sixth Tower (one of the highest Korona towers at 4,860m), at the head of the Ak-Sai Glacier.

We began our climb on July 9, on a rightward slanting ramp to the right of known routes on the south face. After some moderate mixed climbing, we headed up a direct line for four difficult pitches: dry tooling with and without crampons; aid climbing up to A2+; free climbing with big (yet safe) fall potential, and then a final traverse left to cross a wide snow shelf and couloir. On the next pitch, starting up a steep rock wall, we spotted pitons and rappel slings; the rock pitches involved steep free climbing to 5c. The ninth pitch was wet, and above this we constructed a bivouac under a steep rock barrier, after several hours of dedicated effort.

Next day was Giorgi's turn to lead. The weather was horrible, and Giorgi had to dance the vertical in plastic boots. However, we tried our best to free as much as we could. Surprisingly, we found pitons on two pitches, before we made a leftward traverse, and more as we aided a wet chimney. A beautiful sunset accompanied us as we joined the last two pitches of

[Right] Traversing onto the steep upper pillar of the south face of Korona VI during the first ascent of Georgian Direct (900m, Russian 5B). *Archil Badriashvili*

the Glukhovtsev Route (5B). We climbed the last pitch under moonlight and bivouacked a few meters from the summit in clearing weather. Next day we traversed over Korona V, IV, and III before descending to the Ratsek Hut. The Georgian Direct is 900m, 17 pitches, 5B, 5c M3+ A2+, and is the first new route climbed by Georgians in the Ala Archa. After a few days of bad weather, we got halfway up the Bezzubkin Route (6A) on the north face of Free Korea, before having to bail in a big storm. 📷

ARCHIL BADRIASHVILI, *GEORGIA*

AT BASHI RANGE

SKI MOUNTAINEERING EXPLORATION

ISOLATED BY WIDE longitudinal valleys, the At Bashi Range extends 100km in a southwest to northeast direction, with an average width of 25km, and has a collection of mostly rocky peaks reaching about 4,790m. It is bordered on the northern side by the At Bashi River and the large town of At Bashi (2,200m), which is about 360km from Bishkek. Temperatures here can range from 40°C in summer to -40°C in winter.

In early April, our group of 12 arrived at At Bashi and stayed in the house of Eve Aka Turunkan, who offers half-board accommodation. On April 8 we drove to the Sary Tal (valley), which lies immediately west of the Karaili Bulak. There, we climbed Pik 4,159.2m, skiing from the summit on perfect névé until about halfway down, followed by more gentle slopes and a long valley, with a final surprise on reaching the last meadows, where afternoon melting plunged us up to our waists. Vladimir Komissarov (from the ITMC agency) later confirmed this peak had not been summited before, so we gave it the name Choku Chichi-bel.

On the following day the weather was poor and only a few of us decided to force an entry into the Acha Kayindy Valley, directly south of At Bashi town. This resulted in an ascent of Pik 3,671m, at the start of a ridge leading to several 4,000m summits.

On the 10th we headed back east as far as a village called Birinchi May, and then south into the beautiful wide valley of Tuyuk Bogoshti. Ascending this, we eventually branched right and reached the crest of the ridge at 3,954m. From there the ridge leading to the main summit is

[Below] Part of the At Bashi Range from the north. (A) Choku Kiara (4,016m GPS), climbed and skied in 2016. (B) Pik 3,808.6m. (C) Pik 3,560m. *Ruggero Vaia*

rocky, so we left our skis and continued on foot, finally reaching the top (4,016m GPS). We subsequently named it Choku Kiara.

On our last day, the 11th, we headed for a highly visible peak just southeast of At Bashi. Our vehicle reached the beginning of the forest, where we put on skis and continued through the trees. On emerging from the forest we saw immediately above us a beautiful snow-covered peak of 3,650m, which we reached easily and descended on good névé.

As a rule, I would not use the word "exploratory" to describe such trips, as I feel it is often used out of turn by those traveling for the first time in a place that has already been described and mapped. However, our experiences around At Bashi can only be described as true "ski mountaineering exploration." Who knows how many places like this still exist, hidden in the folds of the planet? [*Editor's note: The At Bashi Range has been visited extensively in August and September, and many of the highest peaks have been climbed. However, many lower summits remain unclimbed, and the ski mountaineering potential has barely been tapped. A comprehensive report from the Italian expedition, in English, is available at the AAJ website.*] 📷 🔍

PAOLO VITALI, *CLUB ALPINO ITALIANO*

KASHKARATASH VALLEY, VARIOUS ASCENTS

EMILY WARD MADE a solo trip into the At Bashi Range in mid-October, climbing or attempting several peaks, near or above the eastern Kashkaratash Glacier. Her full report is available at the AAJ website.

– INFORMATION FROM EMILY WARD, *ALPINE CLUB, U.K.*

DJENGHI-DJER

VARIOUS ASCENTS AND EXPLORATION

IN MID-JULY, MARK Chonofsky, Sandy Fowler, Sam Newmark, Calum Nicoll, Neil Smith, and I set out for unexplored and poorly documented valleys in the Djenghi-Djer, a subrange between the At Bashi and Borkoldoy. The Dejnghi-Djer, which in Krygyz means "new land," runs about 70km in an east-west direction, with the most prominent peaks clustered at the eastern end. We decided to travel on horseback for speed and flexibility, and to attempt unclimbed peaks at heights of 4,000–4,700m. We were confident the area would have potential for exciting first ascents, and we weren't disappointed.

After a ride of three days (which would have taken a week on foot with our gear) to the northern valleys, we explored widely, establishing four different base camps, using the horses to move camp every four or five days. Our second camp, at approximately 41°16'23"N, 77°4'36"E, proved to be the best for accessing a range of peaks.

We made five ascents of peaks up to 4,436m, four of which we believe to be first ascents. Two of the peaks gave nice mixed climbs, while three were on rock. Grades ranged from PD to D. The range still offers much potential for ambitious mixed-climbing first ascents in an extremely remote area. The nearest permanently inhabited settlement is 70km away, and we saw no evidence of other humans in most of the range.

On July 21 some of us climbed Pik 4,224m (PD), a little trip uphill from the first base camp to reconoiter access to other nearby peaks. A cairn was found on the lightly iced

[Above] View south from the summit of Stann Chonofsky. The 2016 expedition encountered a pack of wolves in the moraine below these peaks. [Left] The north face of unclimbed Pik 4,719m seen from the British expedition's horseback approach to their fourth base camp. *Djenghi-Djer Expedition 2016*

summit. On the 23rd, Mark, Sam, and I climbed Mt. Stann Chonofsky (4,412m, PD), a simple climb up steep scree and a small glacier directly to the summit. The team also climbed Pointsystem (4,157m), a prominent rocky pillar directly east of our base camp, offering challenging climbing to a point on the ridge north of Stann Chonofsky. We named our ascent route Kaleidoscope (D, F4 A0).

On the 26th, Mark, Sam, and I climbed Mt. Тризуб ("Trident," 4,436m GPS, 4,410m map, AD). The route we chose up the north ridge was long, steep, and punishing due to massive scree fields below the snow line. The mountain has a high glacier, but access to this was blocked from our side by vertical rock buttresses. After a very steep scree gully, there were long stretches of névé scattered all the way to the ridge. On reaching the rocky ridge, we climbed past several false summits, the last of which was reminiscent of Skye's Inaccessible Pinnacle, to reach the top.

On the 27th, Neil and I had a big day, making an 18km round trip to a valley west of our third base camp to explore and scramble two rock summits: An Trus (4,168m, PD-) and Clachan Niall (4,135m, PD-); the latter was the most westerly peak we reached during the expedition and had a good panoramic view, including peaks of diminishing size farther west.

We then moved base camp to this same valley and on the 30th attempted Pik 4,370m, which cut quite a nice jagged profile on the horizon. The scree route to reach the plateau, above which the peak rose sharply, was one of the most laborious we encountered, with abysmal granular rock. Once we reached the snow line it became more interesting, with mixed climbing and then continuous 55° névé leading to a rocky summit. The snow became softer and softer, and we eventually retreated around 50m below the top (PD+ to this point).

The weather was generally excellent and the terrain was great for riding, which was ideal, as none of us had much riding experience. By the end of the trip we'd certainly learned—although some of this had been the hard way with our highly strung Kyrgyz horses, including a kick to the thigh and a front somersault over the reins and into a river. There was also a lot of wildlife, including howling wolves, ibex, and many fish that we scooped out of rivers to supplement our rations. *A comprehensive expedition report may be downloaded at the AAJ website.*

– STRUAN CHISHOLM, *ALPINE CLUB, U.K.*

TERSKEY ALA-TOO

CHUNKER-KEL VALLEY, VARIOUS ASCENTS

From Tamga, south of Issyk-kul, Maria Dixon, Mike Ferguson, John McEvoy, Will McEvoy, Claire Stringer, and Guy Williams (all U.K.) drove over Tosor Pass (3,900m) and then used 4WD and horses to reach a base camp next to Chunker-kel lake (3,600m, 41°56'24.27"N, 77°27'7.8336"E). They then spent 11 days exploring the

[Above] **Looking southeast from the summit of Srnicova along the main ridge on the south side of the Chunker-kel Valley.** *Maria Dixon*

nearby mountains, climbing a variety of routes on six peaks above 4,000m. Only one peak next to camp had a name, Pik Srnicova (4,356m), and was known to have been climbed before, though others probably had been climbed as well. The team's routes ranged from scrambling to AD. Full details are at the AAJ website: *publications.americanalpineclub.org.*

– *INFORMATION FROM* MIKE FERGUSON, *ALPINE CLUB, U.K.*

PEAKS TO THE EAST OF SUEK PASS, VARIOUS ASCENTS

On September 19, Vladimir Komissarov, director of the ITMC agency, kindly met me in Bishkek to pass on some knowledge and homemade grappa. He pointed me toward the Suek Mountains, east of the pass of the same name—a range that, to his knowledge, had seen no previous mountaineering activity. Access was easy from the Kum Tor Gold Mine road, which made it perfect for a quick hit.

Callum Nelson had just climbed Pik Lenin, so he was much more acclimatized than me. We spent our first two days in the Suek Mountains slowly moving up to a glacier in the center of the range eventually placing a base camp at 41.828425°N, 77.849813°E.

[Above] Unclimbed Pik ca 4,500m in the mountains east of Suek Pass. *Emily Ward*

Over the next few days we climbed three peaks from this camp, including one on which we found a very large cairn and a decorative horse skull on top, suggesting that maybe we weren't the first people to be there.

On September 27, after some stormy weather and illness, we moved base camp farther east. Hiking through a thick blanket of snow, we camped at 41.844015°N, 77.884345°E. Here, we were lucky to witness Kyrgyz nomads taking their herds to Karakol for the winter.

With the weather remaining stormy, we spent a few days exploring, including a traverse of the rocky ridge east of camp, over pinnacles, to Pik 4,201m and an ascent of Pik 4,582m (41.797340°N, 77.876322°E), probably the high point of the range. *The online version of this report has coordinates and descriptions of all peaks climbed.* 📑 📷

– EMILY WARD, *ALPINE CLUB, U.K.*

TIEN SHAN / WESTERN KOKSHAAL-TOO

KOMAROVA VALLEY, PIK GRONKY, EAST BUTTRESS AND A BANG FOR THE BUCK; PIK ZUCKERMAN, PIZZERIA KOMAROVA

FROM AUGUST 21 to September 13, four members of the Austrian Young Alpinists Group—Maximilian Reiss, Manuel Steiger, Roman Weilguny (leader), and Michael Zwölfer—and two mentors, Alex Blümel and me, climbed in the Komarova Valley, east of Kyzyl Asker.

After a few days of enjoying great boulder problems around base camp at 3,800m, we climbed Pik Beggar (4,720m), Pik Lyev (4,710m), and Pik 4,963m for acclimatization. We then established an advanced base below Pik Gronky (5,080m).

On September 4, Blümel, Steiger, and I climbed the east buttress of Gronky (800m, UIAA IV+ M5 75°), while Reiss, Weilguny, and Zwölfer attempted an ice couloir on the mountain's east face. The ice quality was very bad, so they retreated after two pitches. However, while descending they noticed a fine-looking rock climb toward the right side of the face, and they explored 150m of this before returning to advanced base in

[Left] The last pitch on A Bang for the Buck, east face of Pik Gronky. *Lisi Steuer Collection*

the dark. The next day, Blümel and Reiss completed the rock line up the east face of Gronky. A Bang for the Buck ascends 350m of excellent granite, with difficulties of 6b+ WI5 and M6. In common with all other routes climbed during the expedition, no bolts were placed.

The same day, Weilguny and Zwölfer climbed the steep northeast face of Pik Zuckerman (5,045m) in a 14-hour push to create Pizzeria Komarova (600m, M4 90°).

This expedition was the culmination of a two-year project launched in 2014 by the Austrian Alpine Club for budding alpinists aged between 18 and 22. They were mentored by mountain guides and experienced alpinists such as Hansjörg Auer, Hannes Leitner, Much Mayr, and, in this case, Alex Blümel and me.

— LISI STEURER, *AUSTRIA*

PIK ROTOTAEV, NORTHWEST RIDGE

PREVIOUSLY UNREPORTED IN the AAJ: a long journey through the eastern end of the Western Kokshaal-too, in 1995, by Otto Chkhetiani, Vadimir Nikitin, Dmitry Oborotov, and Felix Weinstein, all from Moscow except for Weinstein, who is Swiss. From July 15 to August 9, in a round trip from the border outpost of Karakoz, the team traveled 231km, crossed seven passes, and made at least one first ascent.

The meat of this journey took them from the Chonturasu Glacier to the Palgov Glacier (an ascent of Pik Molodezhnyi, 5,330m, first climbed in 1969, was made en route). From the east branch of the upper Palgov Glacier, the team made an attempt on Pik Kosmos (5,940m), climbing the southwest flank of the northwest ridge to reach the crest southeast of Pik 5,681m. From here they continued as far as the western foresummit (5,820m), which they named Pik Rototaev. The ascent was graded 3A.

— LINDSAY GRIFFIN, *FROM INFORMATION SUPPLIED BY OTTO CHKHETIANI, RUSSIA*

[Top] Pik Gronky showing (1) Bang for the Buck (350m, 6b+ WI5 M6) and (2) the East Buttress (800m, UIAA IV+ M5 75°). Left of this peak lie Pik Carnovsky and the Ochre Walls (ca 4,800m). [Bottom] Pizzeria Komarova (600m, M4 90°) on Pik Zuckerman. The pointed summit on the left is Pik Unmarked Soldier (5,352m). *Lisi Steurer*

TAJIKISTAN

[Above] Seen from the southwest, Pik 5,722m (left) and double-summited Pik 5,623m, above the Darshaidara valley. Both mountains are likely unclimbed. *Jakub Gałka*

PAMIR / SHAKHDARA RANGE

DARSHAIDARA VALLEY: IMAST, NORTH-NORTHWEST RIDGE, AND VARIOUS OTHER CLIMBS

IN JULY, FIVE members of the Krakow Mountaineering Club visited the upper Darshaidara (Dara Darshai) valley, located in the far west of the Shakhdara Range in the southwest Pamir. After two days of trekking from Darshai village in the Wakhan Corridor, supported

[Above] Akademika Berga (left, climbed during the Soviet era) and Imast, seen from the east, are dominant peaks of the upper Darshaidara valley. The probable new route on Imast (Polish, 2016) is marked. *Jakub Gałka*

by donkeys and local guides, Mirosław Burzyński, Daria Mamica-Gałka, Radosław Stawiarski, Monika Wałaszek, and I set up base camp at the Tung pastures (ca 4,200m).

After establishing an advanced base on the glacier moraine southwest of Pik Mayakovsky (Quilla Mayakovskiy, 6,096m), Mirosław, Radosław, and I climbed the south face from a high camp at 5,300m, via the 1947 Burdenov Route (3A). We reached the southeast summit in very poor visibility and decided not to traverse to the main (northwest) summit. It was the only bad-weather day during our whole stay in the valley.

We then moved advanced base to the southern part of the upper Darshaidara valley, at 4,750m on moraine between the Ambarku and Ganzekh glaciers, just below the northwest slopes of Pik Imast (5,954m), the third-highest peak in the valley. We placed a high camp at 5,000m on the glacier between Imast and Pik Akademika Berga (a.k.a. Qullai Khirskhabol, 6,094m). Next day, after a six-hour ascent, Mirosław, Radosław, and I reached the summit via the north-northwest ridge, a probable new route (long sections of 50° snow/ice with a maximum angle of 70°). Just below the summit we found a cairn; we believe ours was the second ascent of the peak. We descended the same way after enjoying an excellent and extensive panorama of the Hindu Kush from the top.

We chose Pik Kolgaspornyi (5,604m) as our last objective, and Mirosław, Radosław, and I reached the top via the east ridge (snow/ice to 60°), which we approached from the Ambarku Glacier. We descended the same way. We think this was the second ascent of the peak. We spotted day-old spoor, belonging to either snow leopard or Pamir bear, above 5,000m during this climb.

Although most of the peaks in this valley have been climbed, a few are still likely untouched. One of the most interesting is Pik 5,722m, immediately southeast of Pik Mayakovsky. Its 500m icy north face might present a worthwhile climb. Farther south is Pik 5,623m, which has a rocky twin summit and has probably never been attempted. According to our research, Pik 5,395m, the first summit southwest of Mayakovsky, and Pik 5,622m (possibly named Bashiya), farther south, are likely unclimbed as well. On the other side of the valley, Pik 5,593m, northeast of Akademika Berga, also has no reported ascent. Some of the previously climbed peaks in the valley present interesting possibilities for new routes. 🗒 📷

– JAKUB GAŁKA, *POLAND*

PAMIR / RUSHAN RANGE

SHADZUD VALLEY, VARIOUS ASCENTS

AT THE END of August, Esther Baum, Stephanie Graßl (team doctor), Marie Hofmann, Veronika Krieger, Maria Pilarski, Susanne Süßmeier, Franziska Wiele, and I (team trainer) traveled to southeast Tajikistan as the last stage of the German Alpine Club's three-year young female alpinists' team program (DAV Expeditionskader).

The only known expedition to have visited the valley was in 2010, and Andrew Stokes-Rees and David Gladwin, who were on that expedition, provided us with information and photos. (*See report below.*) Sharaf Saidrakhmonov helped us with the logistics. He is well-organized and responsive. That being said, there is little experience with mountaineering expeditions in the area, so don't expect the level of service you can find in Nepal, Pakistan, or India.

[Above] **The east face of Farihta (5,437m GPS). A German team ascended the ice face more or less directly to the top.** *Veronika Krieger*

We flew to Dushanbe, then traveled by car to Khorog, a painful 16-hour drive. Here, we spent a day rock climbing with local young women at Tang, a small crag developed by Bo White and others. The contact was made through Christine Oriol, a Frenchwoman who has been doing great work teaching outdoor skills to local women.

[Above] The west face of Point Samba (ca 5,100m), climbed in 2016, with six pitches (6c A0) plus scrambling. *Doerte Pietron*

From Khorog we continued northeast by car to Shadzud (ca 3,200m), a small town in the Ghunt Valley. We hired local shepherds, who, with their donkeys, took our kit up to base camp (ca 4,050m, 37.81338°N, 72.34961°E). This took two days, mostly due to our loads falling off the donkeys every few hundred meters.

Once there, we realized that the glacier and mountains in this valley had changed dramatically since 2010. There was very little snow and ice, and the glaciers had receded significantly. We found much more loose rock and stonefall than expected. This made it difficult to choose objectives.

We divided into two groups and explored three different side valleys, acclimatizing slowly and working our way up to the highest peaks. In all we summited four peaks that we believe were previously unclimbed. Most of the climbing was on snow and ice, but we also established a very nice rock route on good granite.

During our five-week stay in Tajikistan we didn't have one day of bad weather. Temperatures were down to -20°C at 5,000m during the night.

In the following summary, the peaks' map altitudes and our own GPS measurements are given. (*Each peak's GPS coordinates and an annotated map can be found at the AAJ website.*)

• Peak 4,977m, which we named Point Samba and has a real altitude of about 5,100m. South ridge (250m, much scrambling and two pitches of French 4, Hofmann-Pietron-Wiele, September 12). West face (250m, six pitches, 6c A0 plus some scrambling, Hofmann-Pietron-Wiele, September 16).

• Peak 5,411m, which we named Farihta (Shugni for "the goddess," 5,437m GPS). East face (500m, 80°, Baum-Pilarski-Süßmeier, September 17; descent required ten 60m rappels).

• Peak 5,595m, which we named Safed Haikal (Shugni for "White Giant," 5,498m GPS. Southeast face, a long glacier with a short summit headwall (120m, 60°, Hofmann-Pietron-Pilarski-Süßmeier-Wiele, September 23). This is the highest peak in the valley.

• Peak 5,210m, which we named Azhdar (Shugni for "Dragon Peak," 5,264m GPS). North ridge (300m, French 3 60°, Süßmeier-Wiele, September 25).

There is more potential in the valley, but we recommend visiting in early summer, when there would still be a fair bit of snow. (This advice applies to the entire region, which seems to be suffering significantly from climate change.) Although there are many good-looking rock walls, up to 300m high, much of the rock is poor and there is considerable rockfall danger. 📷 🔍

– DOERTE PIETRON, *GERMAN ALPINE CLUB*

SHADZUD VALLEY, 2010 EXPLORATION AND ASCENTS

DURING THE SUMMER of 2010, a series of violent acts against foreigners in northern Afghanistan led our team to explore an area of the Rushan Range in Tajikistan instead of the Hindu Kush. We drove from Dushanbe to Khorog, from which I hoped we could reach the glaciers in a single day. We were successful, but it wasn't easy.

We made base camp at the highest green meadow in the Shadzud Valley, and during two weeks in September our team made a number of first ascents, enjoying the stable climate, moderate scale of the peaks, the variety of rock, snow, and ice features, and the sheer expanse of undocumented mountains. The most abundant climbing is on moderate ice faces (north aspects) that ramp from glacier valley to summit ridge. There also are "goulotte" routes that follow veins of ice through steeper rock faces. We made around 10 climbs, five of these being significant summits; we named the highest peak we climbed Asabek (5,354m map height, Michael Reid, Andrew Stokes-Rees, and Sam Williams, September 22).

Visible to the west of base camp was a peak we called Hourglass (5,022m map height) for its striking ice feature. This was climbed relatively easily by David Gladwin (solo). We also climbed a peak to the northwest, a striking feature we called the Sickle (TD, 65° and short mixed sections, Matthew Freear, Michael Reid, Andrew Stokes-Rees, and James Yip). *A full report from this expedition may be downloaded at publications.americanalpineclub.org.* 📷 🔍 ▶

– ANDREW STOKES-REES, *U.K.*

PAMIR / ALICHURSKY MOUNTAINS

BAZAR-DARA VALLEY, SKI MOUNTAINEERING FIRST ASCENTS

IN SEPTEMBER 2013, Jamie Bunchuk and Matt Traver traveled to the Alichursky Mountains to make a documentary about a Kyrgyz-Tajik hunter and herder called Orozbek, and while there ventured into both the north and south Alichursky ranges (*AAJ 2015*). After discussions with Traver, we concluded that the northern Alichursky Range would provide an ideal ski-mountaineering venue.

In April 2016, Anna Bushe, Stefan Jachmich, and I flew to Osh in Kyrgyzstan before driving over 4,280m Kyzylart Pass and into Tajikistan, then past Karakul Lake and the town of Murgab. Some 14km short of the town of Alichur, a track branches north up the Bazar-Dara valley. We planned to ski 20km north to Bazar-Dara Pass and the lake of the same name, from which we would explore major side valleys and attempt unclimbed peaks in the area.

Access to this region is relatively easy during the summer months, as a well-defined track follows the valley to a disused silver mine north of Bazar-Dara Pass (4,464m). In April, however, we found poorly consolidated snow, with travel impossible on foot. Donning skis and towing climbing and camping gear in haul bags, we spent several days reaching the pass, a journey that was made more arduous by our suboptimal acclimatization schedule.

On April 14, Stefan climbed the south ridge of the obvious peak to the north-northeast of our Camp 2. He used skis until he was able to scramble up the last few meters to the 4,952m summit, which we called Pik Perestroika.

After relocating our camp to 4,525m, north of Bazar-Dara Pass but still south of Bazar-Dara Lake, we explored the major valleys to the east and west. Under the prevailing conditions (high avalanche risk and unconsolidated snow), few peaks were safely accessible. Nevertheless,

[Above] Looking west from the north side of Bazar-Dara Pass. Pik Glasnost (4,918m), climbed on skis in April 2016, is the foreground summit left of center. The other peaks are above 5,000m, with the highest being Pik 5,617m (Russian map). *Derek Buckle*

Stefan and I climbed two other peaks we believe to be first ascents, both on skis until the last few meters: Pik 4,918m, which we called Pik Glasnost, via the south face; and Pik 5,021m, which we called Pik Druzhba, via its broad southwest gully and west ridge.

Following a return to Camp 2, we explored two of the easterly side valleys, and on the 21st made an attempt on the 4,879m peak at the head of the southern of these valleys. However, on reaching a well-defined col and a prominent pinnacle at 4,629m, it was clear there was no safe ski access to the summit. With obvious climbing opportunities now in short supply, we decided to return to the road. The team would like to thank the Austrian Alpine Club, BMC, Julie Tullis Memorial Fund, Mount Everest Foundation, and Mountaineering Council of Scotland for financial support.

– DEREK BUCKLE, *ALPINE CLUB, U.K.*

PAMIR / SARYKOL RANGE

BUZCHUBEK VALLEY, KARASAK FROM THE WEST

THE SARYKOL RANGE forms part of the frontier between Tajikistan and China, and virtually everything to the east of the Pamir Highway, between the border post at Kyzyl Art and the town of Murghab, is officially off-limits. However, the rules are rather vague and they appear not to be really upheld in the wild. The peaks of the Sarykol Range, most of which are probably unclimbed, are visible from the pastures that surround Karakul Lake, so Kyrgyz herders gave them names a long time ago.

In September, Stefan Matuska (Slovakia) and I made the long drive from Osh to the Buzchubek Valley in the Sarykol. From the highway, we walked southeast up this desolate and arid valley, and after 90 minutes came upon pastures and running water. We set up camp at 4,500m in the upper valley, by a stream flowing from the Buzchubek Glacier.

The highest peak of the surrounding mountain group is Karasak (5,747m, 38°49'52.86"N, 73°38'39.74"E Google Earth). After a one-hour walk from camp, we gained the Buzchubek Glacier via scree slopes on the left. The glacier turned to the left after 9km and rose more steeply to reach the southwest ridge of Karasak. We followed this on snow and a little ice to the summit, where we made a cairn. The ascent was similar to Elbrus—without the cable car. We rated it Russian 2A.

– MICHAL KLESLO, *CZECH REPUBLIC*

AFGHANISTAN

WAKHAN CORRIDOR, KOH-E-WAKHAN

SINCE 1964, at least four parties have ventured to the east end of the Wakhan Corridor in hopes of attempting the dominant summit of the Little Pamir, Peak 6,094m, sometimes called Qara Jilga I. In June, Matthias Müller and I made the first ascent.

[Above] The Qara Jilga valley. Greta Sar is the highest peak visible, second from the left. Koh-e-Wakhan is just beyond. *Steffen Graupner*

Since my first visit in 2008, the lower Wakhan has adopted more conservative Islam. The Taliban is at Warduj, only two hours away from Ishkashim, at the west entrance to the Wakhan. In addition, charges by local service providers have risen severely. However, the Wakhan itself still seems a safe and friendly place.

After numerous delays, Matthias and I, along with Christine Fischer and Kristina Kunze, made it over 4,257m Daliz Pass to Bozai Gumbaz in the Little Pamir. Christine and Kristina headed east to explore the source of the Oxus River (Amu Darya), while Matthias and I focused on the west and northwest aspects of Peak 6,094m. (Previous teams had tried from the northeast.) We reached a glacier, which we named Qara Jilga Glacier after the river valley, and then snowshoed to a high camp at 5,130m on June 23. Surrounding us were dozens of unclimbed peaks over 5,500m.

On June 25, at 5 a.m., we headed toward the roughly 900m west-southwest face of Peak 6,094m. Spring avalanches had wiped all loose rock and snow from the face, leaving good 40°–45° névé. A narrow 50°–55° ice gully brought us to the summit ridge at 5,852m, and we continued up on unconsolidated snow, at worst waist-deep. We reached the north summit (6,080m Russian map, 36°57.58'N, 74°05.42'E), which we called Greta Sar, at 1:30 p.m. Another summit loomed in the near distance, and we trudged over to this in an hour. Although our GPS had read higher on Greta Sar, Russian maps and our own eyes indicated this was the highest point (Peak 6,094m). There was no higher summit in a radius of 20km, and we thought it appropriate to call the peak Koh-e-Wakhan. Our route had been about AD+ and we descended the same way, reaching our camp at 10 p.m. Fifty-two years after the first attempt, the highest summit in the Little Pamir had been climbed. *For complete information on this expedition, including discussion of the Koh-e-Wakhan name, visit the AAJ website.* 🗎 📷

– STEFFEN GRAUPNER, *GERMANY*

WAKHAN ACCESS UPDATE: *A decade of open and relatively easy access to the Wakhan Corridor appears to be drawing to an end because of Taliban advances near the western end of the Corridor. However, one option that might keep the area accessible to mountaineers is a long-proposed border post at the Langar Bridge. This crosses the Oxus (Amu Darya) between Tajikistan and Afghanistan just upstream from Goz Khun, midway along the Corridor. When the German team (report above) was in this area, construction activity on the Tajik side of the bridge was clearly visible. A formal border post here would offer a much safer and cheaper way to enter the Wakhan. In addition, rumors abound of Tajikistan opening a border post at the eastern end of the Little Pamir, near the far eastern end of the Corridor. This could be accessed quickly, reliably, and cheaply by car from Khorog.*

– LINDSAY GRIFFIN, *WITH INFORMATION FROM STEFFEN GRAUPNER*

[Above] Ganalo Peak at sunset from high on the northwest face of Nanga Parbat, during a 2008 attempt on the northwest face. *Markus Gschwendt*

HIMALAYA

NANGA PARBAT, NORTHWEST FACE VIA DIAMA GLACIER, PREVIOUSLY UNREPORTED ATTEMPT AND OTHER HISTORY

IN 1895, HAVING attempted the so-called Mummery Rib of Nanga Parbat to 6,100m, the celebrated British alpinist Alfred Mummery, accompanied by two Gurkhas, Gorman Singh and Ragobir Thapa, headed up the Diama Glacier in an attempt to reach the northern (Rakhiot) side of the mountain via 6,300m Diama Pass on the east ridge of Ganalo Peak. They were never seen again.

In 1988, Karl Herrligkoffer began organizing a succession of expeditions to find a new route up the mountain, starting with attempts on the Mummery Rib in 1988 and '89. In 1990 he changed plans to an attempt on the northwest side of the peak via the Diama Glacier. Sepp Walter led the 1990 expedition, which did not get far due to serious objective danger. However, the following year, a ski expedition led by Peter Worgotter climbed the main northwest face toward the north summit, with Herbert Rainer reaching 7,400m.

In 2000 another team tried this line, ignoring past events and billing it as a first. Hanspeter Eisendle, Hubert and Reinhold Messner, and Wolfgang Tomaseth found the Diama Glacier truly treacherous but managed to progress up the northwest face to about 7,500m, where they intersected with the 1978 Slovak Route, which had reached Nanga Parbat's 7,816m north top (*AAJ 2001*).

A previously unreported attempt on this unfinished route came in 2008, when Markus Gschwendt and Clara Kulich (Austria) reached a new high point using skis. The approach up the Diama Glacier from the standard 4,250m Kinshofer Route base camp presented serious route-finding difficulties, due to impressive seracs and crevasses. (However, Gschwendt believes that in some years an easy passage could be found by keeping to the south flank.) Moving on skis over terrain rated F to PD+, the pair made camps at 5,100m, 5,800m, 6,400m, 7,000m, and 7,600m. Bad weather set in and prevented them from climbing to the north top; the pair retreated from a small col just below and south of it at 7,760m.

In January 2012, Simone Moro and Denis Urubko reached 6,800m on the same line, and during the winter of 2014-'15, Tomas Mackiewicz (Poland) and Elizabeth Revol (France) reported reaching 7,800m (likely the same point as the Austrians). Mackiewicz and Revol tried again in 2015-'16, making to 7,500m with Arsalan Ahmed Ansari (Pakistan)

From the small col at 7,760m, it would be possible to reach the 8,126m main summit either by following the original 1953 route or by traversing to the upper Kinshofer Route. 📷

— **LINDSAY GRIFFIN**, *FROM INFORMATION PROVIDED BY MARKUS GSCHWENDT, AUSTRIA*

HINDU KUSH

TIRICH MIR, NORTHWEST FACE, RARE ASCENT AND MINOR VARIATION

FRENCH CLIMBERS JÉRÔME Chazelas and Thomas Quillet reported reaching the summit of Tirich Mir (7,708m), the highest peak in the Hindu Kush, in July, via the normal route (1967 Czechoslovak Route) up the northwest face. The crux of this route is climbing a couloir above the normal site of Camp 3 (ca 6,700m). Here, rather than climb the couloir direct, the two moved out left onto snow slopes and climbed more mixed ground to the ridge above. They placed a high camp above the couloir at 7,200m and then took six hours to reach the summit.

More significant is that Tirich Mir, accessed through Chitral and lying very close to the Afghan border, has seen very little recent activity because of the perceived heightened terrorist threat in this area. This appears to be the first time the mountain has been summited since the summer of 2001. The pair reported no safety issues and added that a small Russian expedition was arriving at base camp just as they were leaving.

— **LINDSAY GRIFFIN**

KARAKORAM / BATURA MUZTAGH

BEKA BRAKAI CHHOK, NORTHWEST RIDGE ATTEMPT; PEAK 6,315M, NORTHEAST RIDGE

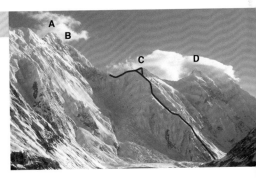

THIS EXPEDITION WAS not previously reported in the AAJ. In June 1998 my four porters left me alone at Lupdhor, a beautiful spot beside a lake on the north side of the Batura Glacier. My plan was to attempt the first ascent of Beka Brakai Chhok Central (6,882m, the highest of the three Beka Brakai Chhok summits), although I had never seen the peak nor a photograph of it. As I walked up the Batura Glacier, Beka Brakai Chhok (BBC) Central came into view and I was encouraged to see a feasible route up the snowy northeast spur of Peak 6,315m, from which it appeared possible to join the northwest ridge of BBC Central.

[Above] Seen from the upper Batura Glacier: (A) Beka Brakai Chhok Northeast (6,842m, unclimbed); (B) Beka Brakai Chhok Central (6,882m, unclimbed); (C) Peak 6,315m (Thompson, 1998); and (D) Sani Pakush (6,952m, climbed via the northwest ridge by Germans in 1991). Peter Thompson's 1998 solo attempt, the first on any of the Beka Brakai summits, is marked. *Peter Thompson*

On July 4, I reached the base (4,214m) of Peak 6,315m and began climbing up snow and ice, camping that night on a snowy shoulder of the northeast spur at 5,080m. Conditions were more difficult the next day, with deep snow, strong wind, and spindrift. I camped again at 6,160m. Next morning I bypassed the summit of Peak 6,315m on the east flank and descended steeply to a col at 6,150m. The northwest ridge of BBC Central is narrow and convoluted, and after climbing along it for 30 minutes I realized there was no way I could do it on my own. I returned to the col, climbed up to the top of Peak 6,315m, and then spent another night at my camp before descending. Beka Brakai Chhok Central is still unclimbed. 📄 📷

— PETER THOMPSON, *ALPINE CLUB, U.K.*

LUPGHAR GROUP, REVISION OF EARLIER AAJ REPORT: *In 2006, Lee Harrison (Norway) and Peter Thompson (U.K.) made the first ascent of a top they named Ghorhil Sar (ca 5,800m) on the southern rim of the Lupghar Valley (a.k.a. Lupgar, AAJ 2007). However, after returning to the Lupghar mountains in 2015, Harrison feels they were wrong to describe Ghorhil Sar as a "summit" and that it is no more than a point on the ridge. A photo of this top and neighboring unclimbed peaks is at the AAJ website: publications.americanalpineclub.org.*

[Above] Nicolas Preitner approaching Maiun Chhish by the Nasirabad aqueduct. The 2016 route climbed a hanging snow slope from bottom right, passing below the sunlit rock walls, then continued left along the skyline ridge to the highest point (marked). The ridgeline was reached from the opposite side in 1993 for the mountain's first known ascent. *Bruce Normand*

MAIUN CHHISH, EAST FACE AND EAST-NORTHEAST RIDGE

MAIUN (MAYUN) CHHISH (5,880m, 36°20'13"N, 74°27'58"E) rises directly above the western end of the main Hunza Valley and offers panoramic views of the Batura chain to its north and Rakaposhi to the south. The only known prior ascent was on August 9, 1993, when Peter Thompson (U.K.) soloed the north face and east-northeast ridge from the Muchuar and Mandosh glaciers.

In June, while Nicolas Preitner (Switzerland) and I were acclimatizing in the Hunza, we approached Maiun Chhish from the Hassanabad Nallah, starting at the bridge on the Karakoram Highway just below Aliabad. After a false start and then a long session of impromptu scrambling up gullies of caked mud and loose rocks, we finally gained the ridge crest at approximately 4,300m. Here we joined the line of a damaged aqueduct built by the village of Nasirabad; at least one local snow leopard had also been using it as a right of way. This led us very easily to the back of the drainage (*Hachindar Nala on the Japanese Miyamori map*), from which a scramble up scree allowed us to gain the small glacier below the eastern ramparts of Maiun Chhish. There we camped at 5,000m.

The east face is a steep snowfield (passages of 45°) by which we passed between cliff bands to reach the east-northeast ridge at 5,600m. We proceeded in softening low-angle snow and rising cumulus to the true summit. We camped at 5,600m for acclimatization, and a predawn start due to an approaching snowstorm had us back in Aliabad by midafternoon.

— BRUCE NORMAND, *SWITZERLAND*

[Above] Looking southwest from below Pregar at (A) Zartgarbin (ca 5,850m, likely unclimbed); (B) Tupopdan (climbed in 1987); and (C) Jurjur Khona Sar (likely unclimbed). *Peter Thompson*

PREGAR, SOUTH FACE TO JUST BELOW SUMMIT

AIDEN LAFFEY (IRELAND) and I hoped to make the first ascent of Gulmit Tower (5,810m), from the Bulkish Yaz Glacier, above Gulmit village in the Hunza Valley. [*This tower in the Batura Muztagh had witnessed five previous attempts. See AAJ 2012.*] On June 11, soon after our arrival, a large rockfall hit base camp. One rock came through my tent and hit me a glancing blow on the head. With no other suitable site for base camp, we decided to abandon the attempt.

Instead, we opted to attempt Pregar (ca 6,200m; 6,112m on the Soviet map)

[Above] Looking north from Karun Pir (Pass) at an unnamed and probably unclimbed peak of around 6,000m (left) and Pregar (ca 6,200m). The two routes attempted on Pregar's south face in 2016 are marked. *Peter Thompson*

from the Moorkhun Valley of the Karun Koh Group. The trail is fairly easy, and with three porters we walked from Moorkhun village to base camp at 4,420m in one day.

On June 23, after a period of acclimatization, we attempted the south face from an advanced base at 5,085m but were stopped at 5,500m by crevasses. On the 26th we made a second attempt by a different route farther right. Unfortunately, Aiden (who had the rope) took a different line and became separated from me by large crevasses. He waited in support at ca

5,700m while I continued solo on slopes up to 60° (AD). A final steep section of sugary snow on top of hard ice felt insecure, and I retreated just 20m from the summit.

We had thought we were attempting the first ascent of Pregar. However, the report of the Austrian expedition that did the first ascent of Karun Koh (6,977m) from the Moorkhun Valley in 1984 stated they also made "the first ascent of a 6,200m peak west of Karun Koh." I think this peak is probably Pregar, although our climb could be a new line.

Other reported climbs in this valley are the first ascent of Tupopdan in 1987, an attempt on the difficult Jurjur Khona Sar in 1988, the first ascent of Tapadan Sar in 1988 (all peaks a little above 6,000m), and two attempts on Zartgarbin (ca 5,850m), the last in 1997. All were made by British teams. In 2014, Phil De-Beger and Tim Oates attempted the south face of Pregar from a bivouac at 4,900m but met with bad snow conditions and retreated from 5,600m. 🗿

– PETER THOMPSON, *ALPINE CLUB, U.K.*

KARAKORAM / HISPAR MUZTAGH

YAZGHIL SAR, NORTHEAST RIDGE, HISTORICAL UPDATE

WHEN THEY CLIMBED Yazghil Sar (5,964m) in 2006 (*AAJ 2007*), Lee Harrison and Peter Thompson (U.K.) believed they were repeating the original route up the peak (*AAJ 1988*). Later, they learned that the first ascensionists had climbed the northwest flank and north ridge from the Yazghil Glacier. Harrison and Thompson followed the long northeast ridge, approaching directly from the north. Ironically, while making their ascent, the 2006 team had noticed the north ridge to their right and thought about cutting across to it, in the hope that it might be a new route, not realizing that they were in fact *already* climbing a new route. The team that first reached the main summit, in 1987, was Jack Brindle, Ernie McGlashan, and John O'Reilly, and their route is thought to have been repeated at least once. 🗿

– *INFORMATION PROVIDED BY* LEE HARRISON, *NORWAY*

MALUBITING GROUP, SHALTAR PEAK, NORTH SPUR AND NORTHWEST RIDGE

THIS CLIMB WAS previously unreported in the AAJ. In July 1989, I met a climber named Kees Dykwell (Holland) in Karimabad, and the two of us climbed a new route up Shaltar Peak, approaching via a side valley above the east side of the Bualtar Glacier, two days' walk from Hopar village. Shaltar Peak (map elevations ranging from 5,726m to 5,982m) is believed to have been climbed in 1987 by three British climbers, starting from the Barpu Glacier. [*The British called it Mongouo, but Shaltar is the name given by locals; the peak is visible from Karimabad and surroundings.*] From a bivouac in a cirque below the peak, Dykwell and I climbed a couloir to join the north spur, which we followed to the upper northwest ridge and then the summit. The difficulty was PD, and we bivouacked during the descent. 📄 🗿

– PETER THOMPSON, *ALPINE CLUB, U.K.*

FAROLING CHHISH SOUTH, SOUTH FACE; PEAK 5,594M, SOUTH FACE

THESE CLIMBS WERE not previously reported in the AAJ. In August 1988, Walter Phipps and I established base camp at Daltanas (3,922m), at the junction of the Hispar and Kunyang glaciers.

We had no particular objective and decided to walk up the hillside above base camp and see what we could find. This led us into a cirque to the northwest, where we set up an advanced base at 4,910m (36.193268°N, 75.092607°E) and attempted a number of climbs. This is the cirque above the last stream before reaching Daltanas.

First, we attempted Peak 5,643m on the west flank of the cirque. This is effectively a subpeak on the southwest ridge of Faroling Chhish. We climbed a couloir to the left of the peak, breaking right at two-thirds height to reach the difficult 10m rock pinnacle on the summit. This was badly iced and Walter was shivering uncontrollably, so we abseiled back down. The route was alpine PD to our high point.

From a bivouac at 5,230m, we next attempted the left side of the south face of Faroling Chhish South (ca 6,170m), the highest peak in the cirque. At about 5,950m, we began to traverse toward the summit. Moving slowly and with no bivouac gear, we decided to descend. The route was on snow and ice (D to the high point).

[Above] **The south face of Faroling Chhish South (ca 6,170m). (1) Attempt by Walter Phipps and Peter Thompson in 1988. (2) Solo ascent by Thompson in 1988. (3) Thompson's descent route.** *Peter Thompson*

Walter was still suffering from frostnip and split fingertips, so I decided to attempt Faroling Chhish South on my own, this time opting for the more direct central couloir on the south face. I set off at midnight on September 8. Conditions were good as I climbed the 800m or so of ice unroped to reach the southeast ridge. A long cornice guarded the summit, and I circumvented this to the left with some exposed moves over the south face, arriving at the top at 8 a.m. I descended the southeast ridge, with one short, tricky rock section, and eventually joined a couloir that led back to my bivouac at the base.

After resting at base camp, Walter and I returned to the cirque. On September 14 we climbed a rock peak (5,594m) on the right flank of the cirque, from a col to the south. The rock varied from loose to excellent granite, and the route was alpine D.

The online version of this report has coordinates for all peaks and also describes (with photos) a 14-pitch rock climb the two men climbed in the Ultar Nala, above the village of Karimibad. 📄 📷

— PETER THOMPSON, *ALPINE CLUB, U.K.*

MAEDAN GLACIER, POROK RI, WEST RIDGE; NERA PEAK, WEST FLANK

SUPPORTED BY THE German Alpine Club, Matthias Bohe, Harry Kirschenhofer, Philipp Moser, Chris Romeike, and I began our journey on July 14, aiming to explore side valleys of the Panmah Glacier. The approach from Askole took four days, following the Dumordo River and Panmah Glacier to reach the high meadow of Skinmang at the junction of the Chiring Glacier and Nobande Sobande branch of the Panmah. On the 23rd we established base camp at 4,175m on the lower part of the Maedan Glacier (called South Chiring Glacier on the Japanese Miyamori map). After some steep climbing we placed a high camp at 5,130m.

On July 30, Matthias, Philipp, and Chris left high camp and climbed 3km to the head of the

Maedan, then up a 100m névé slope (55°) to reach the west ridge of Peak 6,020m. They gained the crest by following avalanche-scoured terrain, then continued up the ridge over several steeper steps (65°), the biggest of which required downclimbing loose rock on the far side (UIAA II–III). Finally, they reached a big snow slope rising 200m (40°) to the final section of the north ridge. After negotiating the exposed summit crest, the team was surprised to find a black raven sitting on the highest point. The GPS recorded 35°51.074'N, 76°5.053'E, and the peak was dubbed Porok Ri (Raven Mountain in Balti).

On August 3, Matthias, Harry, Philipp, Chris, and I left high camp at 3 a.m. to attempt Nera Peak (6,143m). We climbed up the west flank, left of the steepest part of the glacier tongue, via a névé slope (420m, 55°). Shortly before reaching a high snow basin, huge crevasses blocked the way, so we roped up and bypassed them on the left. Deep snow and narrow crevasses hampered progress to the summit slopes, which involved snow and ice with steps up to

[Top] **Porok Ri (6,020m)** from the north. The 2016 first-ascent route generally followed the right skyline. [Middle] Granite towers on the west side of the Maedan Glacier. [Bottom] The west face of unclimbed Chiring I (Chiring West, ca 6,861m). *Christof Nettekoven*

80°. Five and a half hours after leaving camp, we reached the top (35°53.094'N, 76°05.171'E).

The Maedan Glacier still offers attractive unclimbed peaks above 6,000m. At the southeastern end of the basin lies S1 (ca 6,024m) and S2 (ca 6,000m). Opposite Nera Peak, on the west side of the glacier, are four unclimbed rock towers resembling sharks' teeth. The most spectacular targets can be found in the Chiring Range, on the east side of the Chiring Glacier. Here are unclimbed peaks up to 6,861m, as well as 1,000m granite walls and faces up to 1,400m. *The online version of this report includes a brief history of earlier attempts and climbs in the area.* 🗎 📷

— CHRISTOF NETTEKOVEN, *DAV, GERMANY*

MUZTAGH TOWER, SOUTHEAST RIDGE INTEGRAL, ATTEMPT

MATTHIAS KONIG AND I hoped to climb the southeast ridge of Muztagh Tower (7,284m) directly from the glacier at around 4,900m, a vertical interval of ca 2,500m and a climbing distance of 6km. Seen from the Baltoro, the ridge has three tops: a rocky tooth, then the Black Tooth at 6,702m, and finally the main summit. The unrepeated 1956 French Route on the upper southeast ridge followed glacial terrain and mixed ice and rock slopes on the southwest flank to join the ridge crest beyond the Black Tooth.

After eight days of exploring the beautiful Younghusband valley and acclimatizing, we began our attempt in early August, despite mediocre weather. We climbed a 500m snow and ice couloir on the northeast flank to reach a notch in the ridge at ca 5,500m. The rock improved as we followed the exposed crest, passing gendarmes mostly on their east side. Unable to find a tent site, we climbed into the night until we found an open bivouac, on a very small ledge, tied to the wall. We had been climbing for 19 hours.

[Above] **Muztagh Tower from the Baltoro Glacier to the south. The main summit (7,284m) and Black Tooth (6,702m) are prominent. The 2016 team climbed the lower southeast ridge (right skyline) to the top of the "rocky tooth" at 6,000m, and then descended to the southwest (left).** *Tom Richardson*

Next day, after more steep steps and gendarmes that slowed progress, we finally reached the rocky tooth at around 6,000m. To that point we had climbed a distance of 1,700m, belaying and simul-climbing around 24 pitches, up to 6a+ and 60° ice. Above, a beautiful snow arête rising to the Black Tooth promised faster progress. It was already 2 p.m. and now windy and snowing. As we were at the only flat spot seen so far, we decided to pitch the tent. During the night the wind increased, and when we woke next morning visibility was bad. We decided to descend.

Below us lay the only break in the steep walls of the southwest flank. After 700m of downclimbing and five rappels we reached the Dre Glacier. Descending the glacier and icefalls proved epic (the French had fixed ropes here) and led to an unwanted night out. Noisy cracks let us know the glacier was alive, and luckily, after a sleepless night, so were we. Two hours later we regained base camp. Above our high point the route to the summit is largely on snow, but linking it all would be a hell of a job. 📄 📷

– **FELIX BERG**, *GERMANY*

GASHERBRUM I, SOUTHWEST FACE, ATTEMPT ON NEW ROUTE

CZECH MOUNTAINEER MAREK Holecek was back for his fourth attempt at a new route on the southwest face of Gasherbrum I, this time with Ondra Mandula. The pair first acclimatized on the normal route, reaching 7,500m. They set off for a summit attempt on August 9, following a line previously attempted twice by Holecek and Zdenek Hruby, and a third time by Holecek and Tomas Petrecek. The proposed line follows the right side of the Afanasiev-Babanov couloir (*AAJ 2009*) before breaking right across mixed ground onto the main southwest face (above the 1983 Kukuczka-Kurtyka traverse) and then climbing more or less directly to the summit.

Holecek and Mandula bivouacked at 6,000m on day one, 6,800m on days two and three (after poor weather stopped play), and 7,000m on day four, and eventually reached 7,700m on August 15. Here, they were stuck for several days in very bad weather before making a difficult retreat, finally reaching base camp on August 22.

– LINDSAY GRIFFIN

[Above] Nancy Hansen in the couloir leading to the southwest ridge of Gasherbrum VI. *Ralf Dujmovits*

GASHERBRUM VI, SOUTHWEST RIDGE, ATTEMPT; PRAQPA RI, EAST-SOUTHEAST RIDGE, ATTEMPT

MY PARTNER, RALF Dujmovits, and I spent the months of June and July attempting two unclimbed 7,000m peaks, Gasherbrum VI and Praqpa Ri. After hiking more than 100km with our cook, liaison officer, several Balti porters, a few donkeys, eight chickens, and two goats, we established base camp at 4,800m on the spectacular Baltoro Glacier, southwest of Gasherbrum VI (a.k.a. Chochordin, 7,004m). Ralf and I found a way through the messy lower icefall into the valley southwest of the peak, and on our second trip we climbed the right side of a broad couloir to reach a spectacular high camp at 6,200m on the southwest ridge. The summit looked tantalizingly close.

We first tried a route directly above our camp, but the snow became shallow and faceted after we'd gained 250m. With just a few centimeters of sugar snow over steep, unprotectable marble, we decided to have a look at another possible route. We ran into the same predicament—it was impossible even to set a somewhat safe belay. We also could see that the mixed terrain above the rock band was going to present hundreds of meters of the same problem. German Walter Hölzler was stopped by the same issue on the southeast face of the mountain in the early '90s. The only other option for aspiring climbers of Gasherbrum VI is to risk the avalanches, seracs, and cornices on the northeast face, another unappetizing proposition. We believe ours was the fifth attempt on the mountain. [*A brief history of prior attempts, plus photos of each line, will be found in the online version of this report.*]

As soon as we returned to base camp, we sent for porters to help move our camp below our second objective: Praqpa Ri (7,156m), south of Skilbrum. Amazingly quickly, we were installed at the toe of the Savoia Glacier, an inspiring place less than a kilometer south of K2 base camp. We had found no record of any attempt on Praqpa Ri.

After a reconnaissance of the heavily crevassed Savoia Glacier and a short stretch of bad weather, we packed six days of food and fuel and headed back through the Russian roulette crevasse field. We climbed a steep 300m slope to access Khalkhal Pass (5,705m) at the base of the east-southeast ridge leading to the southeast summit. [*Praqpa Ri has three tops: southeast, 7,026m; middle, 7,156m; and northwest, 7,058m.*] It started to snow heavily and we quickly set up the tent to escape it.

Early next morning we started up east-facing slopes that quickly turned into a wet, sloppy mess in the blazing sun and started sloughing around us. After gaining only a few hundred meters, we were forced to make camp in a somewhat sketchy crevasse. We hoped to find better conditions on the more defined ridge above, but upon reaching the ridge at 6,300m the next day, we were immediately disappointed. A 2cm crust lay over deep facets, and before long we were in sugar snow to the tops of our legs. It was simply too dangerous to continue. For future aspirants, we suggest approaching the east-southeast ridge via the Khalkhal Glacier to the south. We could see from Khalkhal Pass that it would have been more straightforward and much safer.

It was a big gift to be able to spend almost two months in this wild place. We would like to thank the Gore-tex Shipton/Tilman Grant, Mountain Equipment Co-op Expedition Support, and the Alpine Club of Canada for partially funding this trip.

– NANCY HANSEN, *ALPINE CLUB OF CANADA*

KARAKORAM / HONBORO GROUP

JUDL PEAK, NORTHWEST RIDGE

THE HONBORO GROUP, with a high point at Honboro Peak (6,459m), lies northwest and west of the Hushe Valley, between the Hushe and Thalle (a.k.a. Yarkhor or Thalay) valleys. In 2011, Simón Elias, Ester Fresnada, and Berta Terres investigated the Apobrok River valley, northwest of Kande. From the upper Kande Glacier, they made the first ascent of Kande Peak (5,470m, *AAJ 2012*), which lies on the ridge between the Third and Fourth Kande cwms, as designated on Jerzy Wala's 2004 sketch map of the Honboro Group.

In May 2016, Elias returned with Gerald Boess to explore the possibility of ski ascents in the area. The pair reached the upper Kande Glacier and then headed southwest into the

[Above] Judl Peak from the northeast, showing the first ascent by Skiroute. *Simón Elias*

First Kande Cwm. From a camp at 5,060m, the pair climbed northeast-facing glacier slopes to reach the watershed ridge with the Thalle Valley, then followed the northwest ridge of Peak 5,871m to its summit. The mountain has been named Judl Peak (35.385584°N, 76.210153°E, Peak 146 on the Wala map), and the 800m ascent was called Skiroute.

– *INFORMATION SUPPLIED BY* SIMÓN ELIAS, SPAIN

[Above] Nya Kangri (6,480m) from the east-southeast. The 2016 Indian attempt was made on the face to the left. *Divyesh Muni*

EAST KARAKORAM

NYA KANGRI, SOUTHEAST FACE, ATTEMPT

AT THE START of May, Rajesh Gadgil, Ratnesh Javeri, Vineeta Muni, Roshmin Mehandru, and I arrived in Leh, hoping to make the first attempt on Shahi Kangri (6,934m). The approach was largely unknown, though Google Earth suggested traveling the Chip Chap Nala from Chongtash on the old Silk Road. However, the Chip Chap proved to be very narrow, with vertical walls, and we realized it would be impossible to carry loads around the bottlenecks.

We returned to the Nubra Valley, where the Army gave us permission for Nya Kangri (6,480m), which I had attempted in 2008. On the 21st we established base camp at Phonglas in the Arganglas Valley, and subsequently headed up the glacier on the south side of the mountain, establishing an advanced base at 5,430m. A spur appeared to offer a safe route up the southeast face. On June 2 we moved up to a summit camp on the spur at 5,965m. Steep blue ice slowed us the next day, and when it started to snow we turned back, about 250m from the top, confident we would finish the climb once the weather had settled.

We regained our top camp on the 8th but awoke next day to snowfall that lasted all day and then became heavy during the night. By morning it was more a question of how to get down safely than whether we would summit. We escaped during a break in the weather and made it down to base camp. Rajesh and other friends returned in August, but the weather proved even worse, with snow or rain every day for more than two weeks. 🗏 📷

— DIVYESH MUNI, *HIMALAYAN CLUB, INDIA*

NYA KANGRI, SOUTH-SOUTHWEST RIDGE, ATTEMPT

GIORGOS MARGARITIS, PETROS Tolias, and I aimed to make the first ascent of Nya Kangri (6,480m), above Sumur in the Nubra Valley. Starting August 24, we approached over several days by the glacier that flows initially west and then north from the mountain. Our high camp was at 5,810m on the upper glacier, beyond where it turns to the east-northeast and rises toward the rocky west face of Nya Kangri. To the east lay an ice slope of 50°–60° leading to the south-southwest ridge of Nya Kangri above 6,000m. The first part of the ridge is rocky, then it becomes snow and ice all the way to the summit. However, fresh snow made it too dangerous to continue above our high camp. 🗎 📷

– NIKOLAS KROUPIS, *HELLENIC ALPINE CLUB OF KOMOTINI, GREECE*

RASSA GLACIER, LAK KANGRI, SOUTHEAST FACE; THRUNG-MA KANGRI, SOUTH FACE

OBTAINING PERMITS FOR the remote valleys of the Indian East Karakoram can be a difficult and protracted process for non-Indian nationals; a positive outcome is far from guaranteed. Just days before leaving for India, our party of five Alpine Club members, Mike Cocker, Drew Cook, Gus Morton, and me (all U.K.) and Knut Tønsberg (Norway), who unfortunately returned home early due to altitude problems, received permission to attempt unclimbed peaks bordering the extensive Rassa Glacier.

From the village of Tirit, where the motorable road ends at a Buddhist shrine, we trekked for three days up the Tirit Valley to a base camp, at 4,756m, near the confluence of the Phunangma and Rassa outflows. Prior to our arrival, only two mountaineering parties were known to have visited the upper Tirit Valley. In 2001, an American-British-Indian team focused on the more southerly Phunangma Glacier, where they made a number of notable first ascents (*AAJ 2002*). In 2014, an Indian expedition led by Divyesh Muni broadly explored the Rassa Glacier, making the first ascents of Tusuhm

[Top] Looking southwest from Tusuhm Kangri at Lak Kangri (Peak 6,222m, foreground). This peak was climbed from the far side. Glacier 2 is to the right, and the fine distant pyramid is Nya Kangri, attempted by two teams in 2016. [Bottom] The south face of Thrung-ma Kangri (6,341m GPS) above Glacier 1, showing the route of ascent. *Divyesh Muni*

Kangri (6,219m) and the 6,250m Rassa Kangri (see *AAJ 2015 with map*). It was Muni's articles and photographs that inspired our 2016 expedition.

We had specifically identified Peak 6,315m, southeast of Tusuhm Kangri, as a major objective. We proposed to attempt this by way of the first side glacier, designated Glacier 1 by Muni's team, flowing from the northeast into the main Rassa Glacier.

After establishing base camp on September 5, we located advance base at 5,100m just below the glacial snout, and two higher camps on the side glacier. On September 10, from the higher camp at 5,675m, Cook and I climbed unroped up a prominent 35°–40° snow/ice gully on the southeast face of Peak 6,222m (GPS 6,266m). This is a summit on the ridge southwest of Tusuhm Kangri. The climb took five hours and was graded AD. Cocker and Morton made the second ascent by the same route the following day. We chose to call this peak Lak Kangri (Ladakhi for "Raptor Snow Peak"), after the unknown bird of prey that flew over the summit just as Gus and Mike were reaching the top.

Following a short spell of poor weather, we returned to Camp 2 to attempt Peak 6,315m. Setting out at daybreak on the 19th, Cocker, Cook, Morton, and I climbed alongside a narrow rock ridge forming the left arm of the second prominent 40° snow/ice couloir on the south face. We climbed unroped until crossing the thinning rock ridge into the main couloir, where the slope steepened to 45°–50° and became icier. The final 200m were climbed in roped pairs to gain the small, corniced summit. (D, GPS 6,341m). The ascent took seven hours and we descended the same way, making eight 60m rappels to easier ground. We chose to call this peak Thrung-ma Kangri (Ladakhi for "Protector Snow Peak") because of its prominent position when viewed from the lower subglacier.

We are indebted to the Mount Everest Foundation, the Alpine Club Climbing Fund, the Austrian Alpine Club, and the Norwegian Alpine Club for their generous support. We also thank Rimo Expeditions and the in-country support team, without whom our task would have been immeasurably harder. 📄 📷 🔍

– DEREK BUCKLE, ALPINE CLUB, U.K.

LADAKH

STOK RANGE, SUKHU KANGRI, NORTHEAST FACE AND SOUTHEAST RIDGE; KANG YATZE GROUP, DZO JONGO, NORTHWEST FACE AND EAST RIDGE

[Above] Unnamed peak of more than 6,300m (left) and Kang Yatze III (6,310m GPS) from the summit of Dzo Jongo to the northeast. Kang Yatze III was climbed in 2015 via the east face and northeast ridge, facing the camera (AAJ 2016). *Oskar Porras Aramendi*

SERGIO MARTÍN DE Santos and I arrived in Leh on June 30, and after acclimatizing near town we headed to Stok Kangri (6,150m), which we climbed on July 6 via the normal route. This completed our acclimatization and the following day we walked up toward Sukhu Kangri (6,005m), a summit on the watershed ridge that runs south-southeast from Stok Kangri.

In the dry conditions we found, we opted for a line on the northeast face, parallel to the one normally followed to climb the mountain; we saw there was no cornice at the exit. We climbed the first 100m (50°) unroped, then pitched a narrower stretch, with mixed ground and then snow and ice to 70°. At the southeast ridge, we joined the normal route and followed it to the summit. We have called our probable new line Animaren Oihua (250m, D), which means "Cry of the Soul" in Basque.

After a few days of rest in Leh, we set out on July 12 for the Kang Yatze Range (a.k.a. Kang Yissay) and reached Kang Yatze base camp (5,045m) on the 14th via a passage of the Konmaru La (5,200m). On July 15 we climbed Reponi Mallai Ri (6,050m) by the standard route. We saw the northwest face of Dzo Jongo was in good condition, chose a couple of possible lines, and decided to make a final decision at the foot of the face. [*Editor's note: Dzo Jongo (east peak, 6,214m, and west peak, 6,280m, 33°43.553'N, 77°34.491'E, both altitudes from GPS) is an accessible "trekking peak" immediately to the southeast of Kang Yatze. The normal ascent is via the easy east-northeast ridge. The north ridge of the higher western peak appears to have been climbed in the early 1990s.*]

On July 18 we camped on moraine in the middle of the glacier at 5,670m. In the morning, in cold, windy weather, we reached the foot of the broad northwest face, some distance right of the east summit. The bergschrund gave no real problem, after which a pitch of very hard snow and ice, followed by two poorly protected pitches of rotten snow, led to a sheet of hard ice. Above this we followed an attractive thin goulotte on the right, through the upper rocky part of the face, to a mixed section leading to the east-northeast ridge at 6,150m. From here we followed the unstable and bouldery ridge of the west peak to its summit, arriving at 3:30 p.m. Descending by the north ridge and then the northeast flank (45°), we reached our camp at 6 p.m. We named the route Elur (350m, MD 80° M4+) after my five-year-old son. ▤ ◙

– OSKAR PORRAS ARAMENDI, *SPAIN, TRANSLATED BY SERGIO MARTIN DE SANTOS*

SHAFAT VALLEY, VARIOUS ROUTES; Z2, EAST RIDGE

IN 2014, SIDARTA Gallego and I visited Zanskar and climbed a number of new routes (*AAJ 2015*). I realized the potential of the area, mainly for rock climbs, though there are possibilities for mixed, and returned in July with José Castanera, Alvaro "Tasio" Ortiz, and Lluc Pellissa. The result was seven new routes, on peaks up to 6,175m, with maximum difficulties of 7a and M5.

We based ourselves at 3,900m in the Shafat Valley, a side valley of the Suru and home to the Shafat Fortress (*see AAJ 2008*), where we first climbed established routes on Golden Sentinel (ca 5,200m) and Punta Georgio (ca 5,135m), put up by Italians (*AAJ 2006 and 2009*). The view from these tops gave us many ideas. Lluc and I first climbed Aguja Tunlup via the route Sangui (500m, 6c), then all four of us climbed Aguja Pomo Yan Le (ca 5,000m) by the route Tasio i es Desgraciats (500m, 6c).

Our next target was a bold pillar leading to the east summit of Shafat Fortress. We climbed this via Incertidumbre (700m, 6b A0 55° snow). The hand cracks were excellent, and just where

[Top right] **Estética Goulotte on the northwest face of the west summit of Shafat Fortress.** [Bottom right] **Z2 from the upper Rumdum (Rangdum) Glacier to the east. This photo shows both summits. Marked is the line of the Spanish route up the east ridge of the northern top.** *Oriol Baró*

we needed it, a tunnel led through rock, snow, and ice to the top. Luca and I next turned to the 5,700m west summit of Shafat Fortress and climbed the Estética Goulotte (900m, V/5+ M5). We also climbed shorter routes on the slabby rock buttress below the Golden Sentinel–Shafat Fortress north ridge.

After 20 days at this base camp we used horses to transfer all our equipment to the other side of the river, installing a tyrolean to make things easier. Next day we climbed two new routes: the Superestético Espolon (Lluc and José) and Mas Arrogante, Desplomada y Ordesina (Tasio and me) on the Pilares de la Tierra (600m, 7a A0; 500m, 6b). We also climbed a rock route at the entrance to the valley leading up to Nun Kun: 700m, mainly 6a but with a section of 6c. [*The Spanish provided few details of their routes, but photos at the AAJ website clarify some of the climb locations.*]

After our visit to the Shafat, José and Tasio went to climb one of Sergio Ricart's routes near Padam, and Lluc and I traveled up the road as far as the Pensi La, walked up the Rumdum (Rangdum) or Z2 valley, and climbed the east ridge of Z2 (6,175m, map height but possibly higher, 33°49'7.42"N, 76° 9'56.65"E Google Earth) via a 900m route of ED 6b M4+ 80°. From a camp at the base of the route, at ca 5,400m, we climbed the ridge on July 29 in a 23-hour round trip. On the 30th we descended to the Pensi La, and on the following day all four of us were reunited and relaxing over beers.

Editor's note: Z2 was claimed in 1977 by Italians Gino and Silvia Buscaini, who climbed the south ridge in a five-day round trip from the Pensi La. However, Z2 has north and south summits, and it is not certain which peak was climbed or attempted in past accounts. In 1982, Italians attempted the south ridge of the "lower summit (6,080m)," retreated, and climbed the southeast face, a difficult mixed climb. One member of this expedition, the accomplished skier Stefano De Benedetti, soloed the south face of the "main summit" and made a ski descent. In 2014, Baro and Gallego also attempted the south ridge of the "lower summit." 📷

— ORIOL BARÓ, *SPAIN*

MULUNG TOKPO, EXPLORATION

SINCE 2009 I have been exploring southern Zanskar and photographing many unclimbed peaks. I am pleased to see that many expeditions have been inspired by this information to visit the area.

From August 3–27, Toshio Itoh, Akira Taniguchi, and I visited the Mulung Tokpo (Mulong Valley), northwest of Padam. This is the next valley north of the Haptal. The Indian Mountaineering Federation does not hold any records of climbing on these peaks. Although there are few 6,000m summits here, there are a number of attractive lower peaks, in particular three I have designated M13 (5,902m), M15 (5,871m), and M16 (5,882m). Photographs and a map appear with the online version of this report. 📷 🔍

— KIMIKAZU SAKAMOTO, *JAPAN*

[Above] **M15 (5,871m)**, to the left, and to the right and further back **M16 (5,892m)** in the Mulung Tokpo. *Kimikazu Sakamoto*

RANGTIK, SHIMLING, AND DENYAI VALLEYS, EXPLORATION; REMALAYE WEST, SOUTH FACE

FROM MID-JULY TO the start of September, Anastasija Davidova and I explored the Rangtik, Shimling, and Denyai tokpos. The first two valleys are northwest of the Haptal, the last northwest of the Mulung.

We first spent 20 days in the Rangtik, where we acclimatized with an ascent of the south face of Remalaye (H5, 6,278m) as far as a prominent point on the west ridge, which we named Remalaye West (6,266 m). We then had a period of poor weather, during which we made attempts on Phobrang (5,800m) and H8 (6,193m), and repeated the 2008 Spanish route Rolling Stones (Pellissa-Ricart, 500m, D+ UIAA V+ 65° ice) on a peak they named Shawa Kangri. We measured the summit coordinates as 5,728m, 33°27'46N, 76°44'07"E.

With no improvement in the weather, we trekked up the Shimling Tokpo, crossed a 5,638m col to the Mulung Tokpo, descended to Zunkul Gompa, and then went up the Denyai Tokpo. We took no climbing gear but found many attractive peaks in this valley—it is possible that all of these remain unclimbed and unnamed.

In September the weather improved and we went back to the Rangtik, where we almost climbed H8. We climbed to a small col between the mountain and Peak 6,110m from the east, then moved onto the north flank and headed toward the summit. It got late and we had no bivouac gear, so we decided to retreat from 6,100m. There are many great opportunities for alpine-style ascents at all grades in this area. *Extensive reports from this expedition, including maps and many informative photos, are at the AAJ website.* 📷 🔍

— MATIC JOST, *SLOVENIA*

[Top] Base camp in Rangtik Tokpo (4,926m) and mountains on the south side of the Rangtik Glacier. (A) Phobrang (5,800m). (B) Shawa Kangri (5,728m). Rolling Stones (2008) more or less follows the left skyline rock ridge, approaching via the broad snow couloir. (C) H2 (6,085m). (D) Peak 5,680m. (E) Peak 6,095m. (F) Peak 6,005m. *Anastasija Davidova* [Middle] The southeast face (profile left) and east face of H8 (6,193m), seen from the summit of Ramalaye West, above the north side of the Rangtik Glacier. *Matic Jost* [Bottom] Peaks of the Denyai Valley. The snow-capped summit is M14 (6,135m), seen from the east. *Matic Jost*

HATTAL, HISTORICAL AND GEOGRAPHICAL CLARIFICATION

ON JULY 25, 1986, Japanese mountaineers made the first ascent of Hattal (ca 5,650m; H18 on the Sakamoto sketch map of the area) as well as unnamed Peak 5,550m in the Zanskar region. There has always been some confusion as to the location of Hattal, which has previously been listed in the Kishtwar Himalaya and quoted as 6,220m. It is essentially on the Kishtwar-Zanskar watershed (33°22'39.58"N, 76°39'5.02"E Google Earth) and lies more or less due east of Cerro Kishtwar (6,220m), its western flanks rising from the Chomochior Glacier. Confusingly, there are Haptal glaciers on both Kishtwar and Zanskar sides of the watershed.

On July 25, Naoki Sato, Yasuyoshi Tanaka, Akira Terada, and Kasumasa Yoshida climbed the southeast ridge over a foresummit and then for a further two hours to the highest point, which they named Hattal. On the 30th they established another camp on the ridge northeast of Hattal, and the following day Tanaka and Terada climbed northeast along this ridge to another summit, measured at 5,550m. On August 1, Sato and Yoshida repeated this ascent. 📷

– LINDSAY GRIFFIN, WITH INFORMATION FROM KASUMASA YOSHIDA AND KIMIKAZU SAKAMOTO, JAPAN

CHHOGO VALLEY, T16, SOUTH SUMMIT, SOUTHWEST FACE; T13, NORTHWEST RIDGE, ATTEMPT

BASED ON A report in the *Japanese Alpine News* by Kimikazu Sakamoto and some Google Earth imagery, but with limited information on the peaks we hoped to climb, my wife, Cristina Pogacean, and I planned a low-budget summer expedition to the Zanskar Range. Our targets were T13 and T16 on the Sakamoto sketch map (see *AAJ 2013*).

We traveled by public transport to Padam. Along with two Indian friends, Prerna Dangi of Delhi and Karn Kowshik of Pune, we trekked two days up the Chhogo Tokpo and established

base camp on moraine at 4,900m, at the entrance to a small side valley rising southeast between the T16 and T13 massifs. Three days later we all set off for the northwest ridge of T13 (6,436m), our planned acclimatization climb. Satellite imagery had led us to believe T13 would offer easy lines, but reality showed this was not the case, and we turned around from the long, complex ridge at around 5,900m. However, the climb presented a good view of the southwest face of T16 (6,431m) and an obvious route: a beautiful, natural couloir running from bottom to top.

On the 14th, after two days of rest and a gluttony competition, Christina and I camped 2.5km up-valley to the east at around 5,200m. Early next morning, we found decent névé and a couple of short 75° sections, and simul-climbed nearly all the lower couloir, with a short breakfast stop on a ledge halfway up. The snow section of the couloir ended with a constriction and a foretelling of what

[Left] **Cristina Pogacean climbing solid rock near the exit of the T16 Supercouloir on the final day of the ascent.** *Cosmin Andron*

was to come, with 5m to 7m of rotten ice and polished rock. By the time we were done, the sun was more or less upon us and we scurried to find a bivouac sheltered from rockfall. We were both queasy and sun-struck. As we went to sleep I said, "At least it's not snowing!" It wasn't longer than half an hour before the first snowflakes danced onto our bivouac bags. My wife told me, quite justifiably, to shut up.

Next day the cruxes were long: a 60m pitch of poor ice and a poorly protected mixed pitch of the same length. Fortunately, everything else that day was moderate. The site we excavated that night would have been good for one person, if he or she were small.

[Above] **The line of the Supercouloir to the south summit of T16 (6,431m).** *Cosmin Andron*

On the 17th we left most of our gear at the bivouac site, and after a few wet, snowy pitches on decent rock, we ended up on a beautiful face. The sun was out, the rock was dry, protection about right, and we were able to climb in rock shoes. We soon passed the false summit, a white triangle visible from base camp, on the right, by its east face. Close to the exit onto the final ridge, we experienced some of the best rock climbing either of us had done in the high mountains.

At the base of the final arête we left behind the rucksack and big boots. This arête was the meeting point of several ridges, including the two sides that bordered our couloir. We could see south summit of T16 directly above and the flat, tabletop northern summit at least a kilometer away, with a number of pinnacles along the connecting ridge. We had no idea which summit was the higher—IMF records only give one height for T16—so we stopped at the south top (33°22'45.57"N, 76°48'17.15"E, Google Earth).

Well after 5 p.m., we headed down, collecting our gear at the top bivouac and continuing into the night. By 3 a.m. we were in base camp with a hot mug of chocolate. Sleep was never sweeter, nor the sleeping bag softer. We have named the 1,200m route Supercouloir (ED, 6b C1 WI4+ M5/6 75°).

– COSMIN ANDRON, *ROMANIA*

KISHTWAR HIMALAYA

BRAMMAH II, SOUTH FACE AND SOUTHWEST RIDGE

IN 2011–12, KISHTWAR National Park reopened after a nearly 20-year hiatus. Jeff Shapiro and I were excited to explore this dramatic part of the Himalaya, and in our research we discovered an area for which we could get very little information: the Kijai Nala drainage, leading to a cirque between Brammah II (6,425m) and Arjuna (6,230m). Eventually we were able to find a few Polish reports, mainly describing the horror of the approach. Google Earth revealed two amazing-looking peaks. We had to go.

Access was prolonged and difficult, but we eventually established base camp 7km short

[Above] **The south face of Brammah II (6,425m) and American route. On the first ascent of the mountain, in 1975, the Japanese climbed the complete left skyline ridge, approaching from the far side.** *Chris Gibisch*

of where we had planned, thrilled, by that time, to get our gear even that far. We then explored the area, each day hiking more than 15km to acclimatize and search for peaks. It was incredibly warm and the lower portions of the mountains were dry. We focused our attention on the south face of Brammah II, since its base was at a higher elevation.

Bad weather intervened, and it was late September before we began our attempt. With heavy packs and difficult terrain, it took us two days to reach the base of the face. There were two obvious lines, but the warm temperatures eliminated the path we initially had chosen, and we shifted our attention leftward to a less objectively hazardous route.

Jeff and I were on the go at 3 a.m. on September 27. Conditions were favorable, and we made quick work of the lower face while a dramatic lightning storm illuminated the sky. After 13 hours I climbed onto the southwest ridge and found a great bivouac site. With pounding headaches from the altitude and dehydration, Jeff and I watched the sun set over one of the most magnificent landscapes either of us had ever witnessed.

The next morning, September 28, we were up early. We still had the crux rock band to come. [*Editor's note: At this point they were on the right flank of the southwest ridge. This ridge was used in its entirety in 1975 by a Japanese team to make the first ascent of the mountain. A similar route was repeated in 1981 by a Dutch team. The slightly lower Brammah I (6,416m), situated further northwest, was first climbed in 1973 by Chris Bonington and Nick Estcourt, and has been repeated several times since.*] The shallow mixed corner above turned out to be relatively straightforward—far more enjoyable than difficult. Some barehanded rock climbing and dry tooling kept us smiling as we climbed through the rock.

We were now near the top of the true south face in worsening snow. We continued to simul-climb through mixed terrain, inching our way to the summit. At 6:30 p.m. we enjoyed a spectacular view from the top as the sun dipped to the horizon.

We made around five rappels to get off the upper south face and onto the lower ice slope, where we chopped seats in the ice and settled in for the night. Lightning storms over the flats of India kept us mesmerized as we drifted in and out of sleep. The next morning we threaded the lower face, reaching the glacial basin before the dangers brought on by high temperatures reached us.

It was another day and a half before we were back at base camp and soaking up what we had experienced. We named our route Pneuma (1,300m, VI AI4 M5), and we sincerely thank the Mugs Stump Award and Copp-Dash Inspire Award for helping make this amazing experience a reality. 📄 📷

– **CHRIS GIBISCH,** *AAC*

[Above] Tomas Franchini on the lower east pillar of Kishtwar Shivling. *Silvestro Franchini*

KISHTWAR SHIVLING, EAST PILLAR, VIA DEI TRENTINI (TO TOP OF PILLAR)

For years my brother Silvestro and I had the east pillar of Kishtwar Shivling in mind, and finally we found two friends—Nicola Binelli and Luca Cornella—to join us. We arrived at base camp (3,360m) in May, and over the next 10 days we ferried all our gear to the foot of the east pillar. When we began climbing, we were surprised to find old rope and bolts from the 1992 Italian attempt still in place. After 50m these vanished and it was just us and the pillar.

The east pillar is surprisingly vertical, even overhanging in places, and our line was the only feasible option for climbing predominately alpine-style, connecting weaknesses on the face. We first climbed about 200m and then fixed lines straight to the ground. On June 1 we jumared the ropes at night, and as soon as it was light I started leading. I was cautious, as the rock alternated between sound and friable. Even so, I snapped a handhold and flew. It was only a few meters, but I was bruised, cut, and there was a worrying pain in my ankle—it had been injured before I left Italy.

Silvestro took the lead and climbed a few pitches before also falling because of rotten rock. Sharp pieces of granite hit him on the head, and Luca was struck hard on the shoulder. Two of our ropes were damaged. We were forced to retreat to our high camp (Vedetta Camp) at 4,960m. Next morning we decided to leave the tents and equipment and descend to base camp. Luca opted to head down to the valley—he was in pain and too shaken by events to continue.

On June 5, Nicola, Silvestro, and I returned to Vedetta Camp, took a day's rest, and then refixed our ropes and hauled gear to the top of them. On the 8th, even though it was snowing, we started climbing. By 12:30 p.m. we reached our previous high point. It was cold and misty, and I decided to lead in mountain boots. It took a long time to climb the overhanging chimneys above, and at the top I saw no good ledge, only snow hanging off the wall. There did not appear to be anywhere to stop, but when the other two joined me and checked out the snow, they found it was firm. We bivouacked there, at 5,600m, on the magical snow structure we named the Floating Meringue. Without sleeping bags and with only one dehydrated meal between the three of us, the night was long and cold, but at least we got the sun first thing in the morning.

The terrain above was difficult but the rock quite sound. At 12:30 p.m. we reached the top

[Above left] Monte Iñaki (left) and Kishtwar Shivling from the east-northeast. (1) Namaste Dost / Arista de los Sueños (2016). (2) Challo (Swiss, 2014). (3) Dawa (2016). (4) Chai-Chillum-Chapati (2016). (5) Via dei Trentini (Italian, 2016). [Right] On the second day of the first ascent of the southeast ridge of Monte Iñaki. *Caro North*

of the pillar, at 5,780m, a snow dome too small for a selfie. We were tired and started rappelling carefully into the mist, trying to make no mistakes. Before dark we had returned to Vedetta Camp, bringing down our ropes and the old ropes, so the wall was left clean. (We placed no bolts.) We named our 22-pitch route on the 800m pillar Via dei Trentini (VIII A1 M4+).

Editor's note: In 1992 the Italian team of Sonja Brambati, Adriano Carnati, PierAngelo Tentori, and Paolo Vitalli planned to attempt this pillar, but almost constant bad weather meant they hardly got started. Instead they made the first ascent of Bugjan (ca 5,600m). In 2014, Andreas Abegglen, Thomas Senf, and Stephan Siegrist from Switzerland climbed a hidden couloir on the left edge of the pillar and continued to the east summit at 5,895m (the first ascent of this top, AAJ 2015). The steep main wall between the Swiss and Italian routes will provide a future party with a taxing big-wall ascent.

— TOMAS FRANCHINI, *ITALY*

MONTE IÑAKI, SOUTHEAST RIDGE

FROM JUNE 5–7, Max Didier, Cristobal Señoret (both Chile), and I made the first ascent of the unnamed rock peak immediately south-southeast of Kishtwar Shivling. We climbed alpine style via the southeast ridge from an advanced base camp on the glacier below at 4,000m, making one bivouac on the ascent and another on the descent. There was only one ledge on the route that was big enough for our tent, in the col behind the very obvious spire on the ridge, where there was also enough snow to melt for water.

Just two pitches above our bivouac we were slowed by a massive slab that had no options for natural protection. Here, we placed two hand-drilled bolts. Above this lay the most technically difficult section of the route, a fine overhanging crack system (6c+/7a). The route had clean, solid granite throughout, except for three pitches in the middle where we had to climb a rocky gully hidden from the sun and thus quite icy. We measured the summit altitude at 5,370m and named it Monte Iñaki after Iñaki Coussirat, a good friend who died on Fitz Roy the previous January. We named the route Namaste Dost / Arista de los Sueños (700m, 17 pitches, 6c+/7a).

Later, we put up two rock routes on a little spire below and to the northeast of Monte Iñaki. Both had five pitches and difficulties up to 6b+ on good granite. The left route we named Dawa and the right Chai-Chillum-Chapati.

— CARO NORTH, *GERMANY*

GUPTA, NORTHEAST FACE AND EAST RIDGE

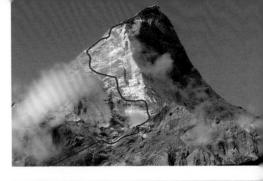

IN THE LAST few years eastern Kishtwar has been on the radar of an increasing number of climbers, drawn to a paradise of unclimbed granite walls and peaks. I already knew about the 5,618m unclimbed peak called Gupta, so I was determined to get there before anyone else. I sent a picture to my good American friends Mark Richey and Mark Wilford, with whom I had last been on a trip in 2009 (Saser Kangri II), and they signed on for a trip in the fall.

Military sensitivities required us to approach Kishtwar via Manali and the Rhotang Pass, and then make a scary, two-day jeep journey along the Chandra Bhaga Gorge. After completing formalities with the police at Gulabgarh, we started trekking up the Dharlang Nala on September 12, using horses to carry our gear. On the 14th we found a decent base camp opposite Gupta, but unfortunately on the wrong side of the river. [*Gupta lies on the south side of the Dharlang River, directly opposite the entrance to the Chomochior Valley.*] Richey came up with the bright idea that one of us—which was me— should swim across the river with a safety line, which then could be tensioned across a shorter

[Top] Gupta from the northeast showing the 2016 route. *Mick Fowler* [Bottom] The infamous road through Chandra Bhaga Gorge, the only permitted route to this area of Kishtwar. *Jim Lowther*

span of river between the framing of a collapsed shepherd's bridge. Amazingly, this worked.

On September 26 we ascended scree and a small snowfield to the base of a rope we'd fixed during acclimatization. We jumared this to the top of a pinnacle ridge that connected to the main northeast face of Gupta. Over the next six hours Richey led about six pitches up snow-covered rock to a decent bivouac site tucked well into the northeast face. Richey and I had the bivouac tent to ourselves; Wilford slept outside on an enormous, blow-up mattress.

Next morning Richey led across a snow ramp and then scratched his way up a strenuous overhanging chimney, followed by a snow-filled rake. The third pitch that day was the best of the climb: an upward-slanting, leftward traverse across snow-covered slabs, with frozen turf placements for tools and tiny incuts for mono points, all about M5. This led to the sunlit east ridge, where Wilford and I were greeted by an ebullient Richey. I led a couple of pitches, Wilford led a couple, and then Richey took us up to a snow patch that cut through the ridge onto the broad south face. Scrambling up for 100m, we reached a superb bivouac site perched hard on the east ridge, with the summit beckoning above. So far, no nasty surprises, so spirits were high.

On the 28th, Wilford set off with rock shoes, climbing three straightforward pitches. Richey led on for two harder pitches (5.9), climbed in big boots on truly immaculate, grippy granite, with lots of gear placements and chicken heads. I continued up snow to the summit ridge. The top was an arrangement of tottering blocks with unrestricted views into Zanskar, Pangi, and toward Kashmir. We spent the remainder of that day rappelling to our top bivouac, and the whole of the following day making 10 rappels to our launch pad and then descending to base camp. 📷

— JIM LOWTHER, *ALPINE CLUB, U.K.*

SERSANK REDEMPTION

A SEXAGENARIAN REUNIION ON AN UNCLIMBED 6,000-METER PEAK

BY VICTOR SAUNDERS

SOMETIME IN THE final decades of the last century, I used to have a battered climbing guidebook to someplace in Scotland. I cannot remember exactly which book it was, but I do recall the frontispiece, which displayed a quote from Colin Kirkus: "Going to the right place, at the right time, with the right people is all that really matters. What one does is purely incidental."

This is the incidental story of rediscovering an old partnership. It had been 29 years since Mick Fowler and I last climbed together. In 1987 we managed to find a route up the Golden Pillar of Spantik, and although we shared one more expedition in Pakistan, we had not climbed anything else major together. Mick built a successful twin career in the tax office and remote Himalayan mountains, while I became a mountain guide, working across the globe. We had barely spoken to each other in the intervening years.

Then, in 2015, came Frenchman Eric Vola with the idea of combining chapters from our books, a sort of literary version of a mash-up, translated into French. The book did well, winning the main prize at the Passy book fair that year. Working on this volume, *Himalaya: Les Tribulations de Mick et Vic*, and probably aided by some of Eric's excellent Sauvignon Blanc, we agreed to try one more mountain together. We were now much older, of course: In 2016, Mick was 60 and I was 66 years old.

Mick had built an extensive intelligence network, and a report from Martin Moran of a "tremendous north face of linked White Spiders" led us to Shib Shankar or Sersank or the "unnamed mountain," depending on which expedition reports we read. Two Italian and one British expedition had failed to make much impression on the 6,050m peak, while a Japanese team was told by the authorities that they could climb the mountain if they could find it, because it did not exist. This team turned back at the base of the steep summit block because, according to their timorous porters, Sersank was sacred. Fortunately for us, the nearest villagers held no such beliefs.

Much has changed in the world since the 1980s. Cell phones replaced telephone boxes, and in turn were displaced by smartphones. Back then, expeditions were booked by post, and we often beat our letters home. Climbers spent days in customhouses releasing freighted supplies, and most of us had no idea about local agents. Now, with an email or two, all is fixed. Our excellent local agent, Kaushal Desai from Manali, had us collected in Delhi, briefed by the IMF, and on the bus to Manali with our liaison officer, Sanju, within the space of a few hours. Only 48 hours later we were trekking up the Sural Valley.

Much of the logistical slickness was due to Mick's predilection for organization. And so it continued at base camp. Day One: unpack and setting up. Day Two: begin acclimatizing and reconnaissance. Day Three: reach the Sersank La (where we would get our first wondrous glimpse of the "north face of linked White Spiders." Days Four and Five: acclimatize on a minor summit in front of Sersank. Then back to base for exactly two days of R&R.

The reconnaissance showed that our proposed route was threatened by a line of seracs, whereas a longer but safer line from the toe of a buttress on the left side of the face looked good to both of us. It seemed our ideas of what is safe in the mountains were still in harmony. Armed with six days of food and gas, we headed back across the Sersank La and on to the face.

On Sersank most things were highly reminiscent of our former climbs. We recognized each other's climbing style. We re-enjoyed the discomfort of tiny bivouac ledges and spindrift

showers, the miserably small portions of food (not being strong enough to carry more), and we chatted aimlessly to pass the cold nights away. I think the one big change was the conversation: Where before it was the usual boys' blather, food and sex, now it was pensioners' talk: arthritic limbs, rheumatic joints, what to do about the children, the failing eyesight, and other interesting topics that filled the resting hours.

Bit by bit we linked the ice fields, the White Spiders. But in spite of the steady progress, the outcome was never quite certain. Every pitch we climbed made retreat less inviting and increased our commitment to traversing the mountain. In steep face climbing the best line is far from evident, and again it was modern technology that helped. In 1987, on Spantik, I had drawn a detailed route diagram while studying the face to help us find the way. Three decades later, we could examine the photographs on our digital cameras. But we couldn't quite work out from the reconnaissance what the finish would be like. The headwall loomed over our heads and in our imagination. On day five we found a way and flopped over the cornice to the southwest side of the mountain.

The next day brought a straightforward summit, a descent to a comfortable tent platform, and a cold night, followed in the morning by a complex descent through the steep and excessively crevassed and seraced South Sersank Glacier. We finally reached the comforts of base camp, where we wallowed in a pleasant recovery haze as we ate our first real cooked food for eight days, dozed on flat ground without being tied into the mountain, and generally enjoyed the warmth and oxygen of the lower altitude.

Mick was content to lie in his tent in a bubble of happiness, having ticked the adventure climbing boxes: new route, substantial length, sufficiently challenging, previously unclimbed summit, and descent by a different route. Meanwhile, I was in my own bubble, happy to have discovered that the old friendship had been redeemed. I lay in the dining tent, trying to force my old brain to remember exactly which guidebook it was that quoted Colin Kirkus: "Going to the right place, at the right time, with the right people is all that really matters...."

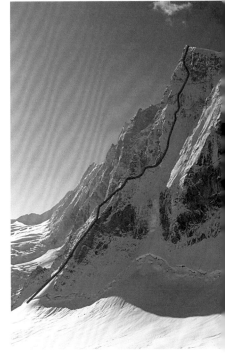

[Top] Mick Fowler on pitch three of day five on the first ascent of the north buttress of Sersank. [Bottom] The 1,100m north buttress of Sersank (6,050m), climbed with five bivouacs during the ascent and one more on the way down. The pair descended the opposite side of the mountain. *Victor Saunders*

SUMMARY: First ascent of the 1,100m north buttress of Sersank (6,050m, ED2) in the Pangi Region of Lahaul, September 28–October 4, 2016. A detailed report is at the AAJ website. 🗎 ⊙

[Above] Raja Peak (6,294m) from the Tidu Glacier with the British route on the north face. *Dave Sharpe*

RAJA PEAK, NORTH FACE, PEAK 6,036M, JAMES PEAK, NORTH FACE

JOHN CROOK AND I arrived in the Miyar on September 19. Our primary objective was the north face of an unclimbed 6,294m peak, hidden from view in the remote Temasa Valley. This was to be our first trip to the Himalaya, and with only an old photo of the face and Google Earth to send us on our way, trepidation was high.

We shared a permit with Ian Dring, Charlie French, Anette Kinde, and Martin Moran, who each had their own aspirations in the area. We had been invited on the trip by Martin, who had snared us easily by email: "*I have attached pictures of the north face of Peak 6,294m. The face height is 1,200m. The mountain is unclimbed, as far as I know.... To get to the face from here would be a real mission—totally committing.... In 2011 we saw no one for 10 days—no shepherds or trekkers in these valleys at all*". After receiving an email like this he had us hook, line, and sinker!

On arrival in the area conditions were good, and we wasted no time in establishing an advanced base camp high on the Miyar Glacier. Over the next two days we acclimatized on a nearby 6,036m peak (measured at 6,001m GPS), which is situated on the ridge running south from Peak 6,294m. Keen to capitalize on the continuing good weather, we began the approach to our objective the following day: over the Kang La (5,400m), down to 4,500m in the Temasa Valley, then up the Tidu Glacier. This took us three days.

We camped on the Tidu Glacier under our peak, and after a day of resting and observing the face, we began climbing on September 30, crossing the bergschrund at 4:30 a.m. The climbing on the lower half was varied, of good quality, and contained the route's crux in steep corners. By the end of the first day we had been moving for 16 hours and had reached a bivouac site roughly two-thirds of the way up the wall. With no good ledges in sight and unable to erect the tent, we had a sitting bivouac at ca 5,800m in an incredible location. Next morning we awoke to perfect weather and climbed as direct a line as we could, summiting at 8 p.m. after another 16-hour day. We named the route Transcendence (1,200m, ED2 Scottish 6) and the summit Raja Peak, which we measured at 6,267m with GPS. We descended the far side of the mountain, following the south ridge toward Peak 6,036m, for about 300m to a col, where we spent the night. We returned to advanced base the following day.

With time and weather still on our side, and after a couple of days' rest at base camp, we decided to return to the mountains to attempt another unclimbed peak lower down the valley, on the Jangpar Glacier, east of Marikula Killa (*climbed by Dring and Moran; see report below*). We ascended to a bivouac site under the face on October 6 and established Last Chance Saloon (1,300m, TD- Scottish 4) the next day. We followed a wandering line on the north face, christening the summit James Peak (5,870m GPS) after my nephew (not to be confused with the popular Point JAMES further south in the lower Chhudong Valley). We descended the same day. 🗏 📷

– DAVE SHARPE, *U.K.*

MARIKULA KILLA, NORTH SPUR

BETWEEN SEPTEMBER 26 and October 2, Ian Dring and I (both U.K.) made the first ascent of Peak 5,755m in the upper Miyar Valley. We climbed the 1,300m north spur via a route we named Crocodile Rock (ED, 21 pitches between III and 6a+ A0).

Peak 5,755m (33°4'10"N, 76° 47'39"E) is the rock bastion lying immediately north of Dali Got base camp, at the junction between the Miyar and Jangpar glaciers. A prominent pinnacle of ca 5,350m on the southwest ridge was climbed in 2004 by a British party and named Lammergeier Spire. However, despite its accessibility, the full mountain had not been climbed.

The north spur is an eye-catching line rising in a series of sweeping steps to a cluster of pinnacles. Our ascent was made in alpine style over six days. We were fortunate there had been a light snowfall two days before we started. Without the fresh snow patches, we would have had no water during the first three days of the climb.

The lower half of the route gave sustained, mid-grade slab climbing (UIAA IV and V), reminiscent of the Piz Badile north ridge or the Cassin on the north face. The pinnacles formed the crux, with strenuous cracks and corners to V+. A smooth slab was encountered under the largest pinnacle, named the Flaming Tower. The team carried five bolts and a hand drill, and with no alternative, all five bolts were placed to protect the slab, with 6a+ climbing complicated by patches of snow. Beyond the Flaming Tower, a beautiful section of granite pinnacles led to awkward climbing (V) on snowed-up rock.

On October 1, we reached the junction of

[Above] The north spur of Marikula Killa (5,755m) and the line of Crocodile Rock. *Martin Moran*

the spur and the northwest ridge at 5,600m, dumped most of our gear, and traveled light to the top with a deviation onto the west face. After a cold bivouac near the summit, we rappelled to our gear and descended the west face, using a combination of 14 rappels and downclimbing.

We propose the name Marikula Killa for the mountain, the citadel of the goddess Marikula. Marikula is an ancient local devi (goddess) for the people of Lahaul. The 1,000-year-old temple at Udaipur, at the bottom of the Miyar Valley, is dedicated to her.

The route was beautifully positioned, of high quality and consistent grade, and with good rock bivouac sites, comparable to an extended Frendo Spur or Gervasutti Pillar in the Mont Blanc massif. A younger and faster party, utilizing our bivouac sites and in situ gear, could repeat the climb in three to four days, given dry conditions.

– MARTIN MORAN, ALPINE CLUB, *U.K.*

SHAILAPUTRI, SOUTHWEST FACE

WE ARRIVED IN the Miyar Valley on September 20 and set up base camp close to Padang at 3,700m. Our objective was the peak referred to as Tharang II (32°50'15.22"N, 76°56'42.00"E Google Earth) by the 2012 British expedition that climbed Tharang I to the northeast.

We walked south up the Uldhampu Valley, making two camps, the higher at 5,030m, at a large in-filled lake west of the peak. On the 28th we attempted the southwest face of our peak, retreating from 5,900m due to weather conditions and lack of time. At 6 a.m. on October 1 we started out again from our top camp. We roped up at 5,400m and moved together up ramps and steeper sections to a shoulder on the pronounced spur left of center on the southwest face. We climbed the loose spur unroped (to minimize rockfall) until we reached its top at 5,800m. Here, we roped up again and, slanting right, moved together up 250m of 50°–60° snow to the summit. Our GPS recorded 6,025m. The overall grade was AD.

We descended the west face to the top of the spur and reversed unroped to the shoulder, from which we made three long rappels to the scree, reaching it at 8 p.m. We decided to call the peak Shailaputri, which means "daughter of the mountain;" her Navratri festival day coincided with our summit day. 🗎 📷

– CHARLIE FRENCH AND ANETTE KINDE, *SWEDEN*

PREVIOUS CLIMBS NEAR THE ULDHAMPU VALLEY: *In September 2012 a British expedition, led by the guide Mark Thomas, explored the valley immediately north of the Uldhampu. On the 25th, Steve Birch, Richie Mockler, and Thomas made the first ascent of Tharang I (6,066m, 32°50'39.77"N, 76°57'25.50"E Google Earth) via the west ridge (AD+). On the 28th, Thomas made the first ascent of Tharang Fang (5,490m), via the east ridge, with three different members of the expedition, and on October 2 Thomas soloed the southwest ridge of a peak to the northeast of Tharang Fang, which he named Jasminka (5,401m). The ascent was 1,700m from base camp and PD+ (mainly UIAA III, but a long pitch of IV on the summit block).*

GANGSTANG, NORTHWEST RIDGE

THE ATTRACTIVE PYRAMID of Gangstang (6,162m) is most often climbed by its southwest ridge, the route of the first ascent, approached from the Gangstang Glacier to the east. The east ridge was climbed in 2001 by a Japanese team supported by Sherpa professionals, after an approach from the northeast. In 2007 Martin Moran (U.K.) led a commercial expedition up the Thirot Valley, to the west of the peak, explored Gangstang's northern and western aspects, and climbed the west face onto the upper section of the southwest ridge. Moran's enthusiastic descriptions of the north face and northwest ridge lured Guy Buckingham and me to the Thirot Valley in late May.

We didn't like the look of the active seracs on the north face of Gangstang, so we set our sights on the sharp, mixed northwest ridge. From base camp we could see three distinct steps on the ridge, all of which looked worryingly compact. We dubbed them the First Tower, the Citadel, and the Grey Tower.

In the early hours of June 7 we climbed a 400m snow couloir to gain the ridge just under the First Tower. We knew it had been a very dry winter, so we were delighted to find good rock

[Above] Gangstang (6,162m), with the northwest ridge faicing the camera. The unclimbed north face lies to the left, and the southwest ridge (the line of the first ascent) is the right skyline. *Malcolm Bass*

on the ridge crest. We spent the rest of the day climbing rock (up to British 5a) and mixed terrain up and over the tower to a poor tent site partially overhanging the north face.

The next morning found us up against the Citadel. A couple of hard rock moves got us into a system of ramps and corners on the west flank. The climbing here was more mixed and rather scrappy, but it took us to where we needed to be, back on the ridge above the Citadel, at a luxurious tent platform below the Grey Tower.

We woke to a beautiful dawn with the valleys full of cloud. The snowed-up rock of the Grey Tower was steep and blocky, making for enjoyable mixed climbing, and the situation on the crest was superb. The mixed crux (about Scottish 6) involved torqueing up a crack, then rocking over onto a slab, then discovering that the slab was pierced by a body-sized hole that gave a view straight down the west face.

At the top of the Grey Tower the ridge merged with the north face, bulletproof ice became the norm, and it began to snow. Weary of calf and spirit, we considered bivouacking, but when no ledge appeared we kept on. We reached the summit in thick cloud, more concerned with finding our way off than celebrating. We camped 100m below the summit. It snowed most of the night and we ignored the first alarm. Later that morning we dropped about 400m down the southwest ridge in deep snow, then descended the Moran couloir on the lower west face in four rappels, lots of downclimbing, and some rash bum sliding. We would like to acknowledge the Montane Alpine Club Climbing Fund, Austrian Alpine Club, BMC, and MEF for their support. 📷

— **MALCOLM BASS**, *ALPINE CLUB, U.K.*

SHIGRILA
HARD GOING IN THE KULLU

BY CHRIS WRIGHT

WHILE PROBABLY BETTER known these days to vacationers and trekkers than to climbers, the Kullu region once was popular with mountaineers seeking easy access to its abundant, unclimbed, moderately technical peaks. By the end of the 1970s, predominantly British expeditions had climbed most of the region's major summits, including the highest, Dharamsura (White Sail, 6,420m) and Papsura (Black Sail, 6,451m), the so-called peaks of Good and Evil. The Shigrilas were two notable exceptions, and the reason we went to Kullu.

As far as we know, only the higher Shigrila (6,247m, 32°10'31.6"N, 77°35'03.2"E) had ever been attempted, and then only twice. The first time was in 1961, when a duo of fantastically tough-sounding British women, Jo Scarr and Barbara Spark, approached from the Bara Shigri Glacier to the northeast but were turned back quite close to the summit. Their effort and their entire expedition were remarkable for the era (*see historical note below*). The second attempt, in 1990 and again by a British expedition, climbed to almost 5,800m on the south-southwest ridge.

On September 18, after a three-day trek, Tico Gangulee and I reached a base camp at the junction of the Tos and East Tos glaciers, southwest of the Shigrilas. We spent the next week acclimatizing, establishing an advanced base camp in the upper East Tos at around 4,600m and a high camp at about 5,200m on the edge of the small glacier (which we referred to as the Shigrila Glacier) below the peaks. The travel between base and advanced base camps was continuously unpleasant and one of the major cruxes of the expedition. Luckily, travel higher on the glaciers was better, making for easier going and considerably less swearing.

By late September we were ready to go climbing and decided to start with the lower of the two Shigrilas, which we dubbed Lalsura ("Red Sail;" the 1961 expedition referred to this as Snow Dome) after its composition of handsome red rock. Opting for the relatively easy-looking northwest ridge, we left camp at 5:30 a.m. on the 28th and climbed unroped for the entire ascent. A few short mixed sections were negotiated as we bypassed gendarmes, but steep snow made up the bulk of the climbing, and we reached the top at 9:15 a.m. The peak had been reported as 6,187m, but we measured 6,004m. We returned the same way and were back at advanced base by midafternoon, naming the route Love and Biscuits (700m, M3 85°) in tribute to Tico's recently deceased cat.

We felt due for a rest, but fearing the weather was about to change, we trudged back to high camp the following day, got to bed early, and left at 2:30 a.m. on September 30. Half an hour later, we were crossing the bergschrund on Shigrila's southeast face and feeling our way through the dark up the snow and ice leading to the first rock band. We roped up, climbed a traversing rock pitch to a ledge, and then headed straight up via another fun rope length in a corner. We then simul-climbed for at least a dozen pitches, weaving through short sections of ice, mixed, and a considerable amount of steep névé as we made our way up to and then across a broad stripe of snow that cuts across the face. At its terminus, a few pitches of excellent climbing (WI4 M5) led to the eastern shoulder of the mountain. One more enjoyable pitch brought us to a ledge where we pulled out the bivouac gear and stove, ate, drank, and lazed in the sun for an hour.

When we left, it was, as I can now recognize, at comical speed, as we stopped frequently to rest our heads in our hands. Another few pitches of mixed led to the summit ridge, where my heart suddenly dropped. Above lay a smooth tower and, as Steve House once described it,

[Top] Tico Gangulee on the difficult ridge close to the top of Shigrila. The high, distant, pointed summit to the right is Central Peak (6,285m), climbed from the far side by the 1961 British expedition. The valley visible at far left is the Chandra. *Chris Wright* [Right] Chris Wright climbing the northwest ridge of Lalsura (6,004m GPS) with Shigrila (6,247m) behind. (1) Southeast face (2016). (2) East face and 1961 high point on the north-northeast ridge. The left skyline ridge was attempted to around 5,800m in 1990. *Tico Gangulee*

that classic alpinists' folly of dry snow over steep rock. Having left our one pair of rock shoes in the tent, we tried to bypass the tower by rappelling onto the snowfield below, but we found more powder on slab, and as darkness fell we retreated to our ledge.

After a fitful night we awoke late and coaxed ourselves out of the tent somewhere near noon, reaching the summit ridge under clear blue skies in half the previous time. I led out toward the tower and tried not to drop anything as I straddled the ridge, pried off my boots and crampons, pulled on the rock shoes, and removed my gloves. I climbed far away from my gear onto the smooth whaleback, until my hands were on top and I could mantel the crest. At a notch I reversed the procedure and headed back into the snow, and after another short pitch we were on top, laughing and hugging in the sun. The rock crux had been mercifully short, but Tico confirmed that following in boots was as hateful as I'd guessed. We descended almost directly from the summit in a series of rappels and traverses to regain the bivouac site, where we crawled into our sleeping bags and dozed for a few hours. We rappelled through the night, reaching high camp close to sunrise. Our nearly 1,000m route was 5.9 A0 AI4 M5.

We owe the AAC our thanks for a Lyman Spitzer Award, the Mazamas for an Alpine Adventure Grant, and our agents, Ibex Expeditions, for their excellent service and for helping us secure an effective permit workaround with the Indian Mountaineering Foundation, as our peaks were not on the permitted list. Despite our fine outing, I would not strongly encourage future parties to explore the area unless they're after heinous approaches and either very moderate or extremely difficult and/or dangerous climbing. This is not the India of 20-pitch splitters above grassy fields, but what the area does have going for it is solitude, and I'm very glad that we went. 📷

– CHRIS WRIGHT, AAC

NOTES ON THE SCARR-SPARK EXPEDITION: *In 1961 two women in their early 20s bought a Land Rover and drove it from the U.K. to India to make their first expedition to the Himalaya. With the help of two locals, Jigmet and Wangyal, Jo Scarr and Barbara Spark defied bureaucratic difficulties to reach the Bara Shigri Glacier, from which they ascended two previously unclimbed 6,000m peaks above a subsidiary glacier to the north: Central and Lion peaks.*

All four then attempted Shigrila. From a camp on the glacier below the steep rock and mixed ground of the east face, the party followed an intricate line to gain the upper north-northeast ridge, which they followed until, at 3:30 p.m., and after Wangyal had led an awkward section of soft snow over ice-covered rock, they decided that, with only three hours of daylight left and no equipment for a night out, they should retreat. "Fifty yards away and fifty feet above us I could see the summit, with ridges dropping away on the other side," wrote Scarr. They felt the mountain was as good as climbed, "after all, what's fifty feet in 20,000." However, it would appear they were looking at the intersection of the southeast and north-northeast ridges, and the start of what the Americans refer to as the summit ridge. Feeling their way down through the blackness, they reached their tents at 10:30 p.m., 16 hours after leaving.

Scarr and Spark were among the best British female climbers of their era, Scarr notably making the first female lead of the famous North Wales route Cenotaph Corner (E1 5c today).

UTTARAKHAND / GANGOTRI

THALAY SAGAR, NORTH FACE, MOVABLE FEAST

IN SEPTEMBER, DMITRY Grigoriev, Sergey Nilov, and I climbed a new route on one of the most famous and beautiful mountains in the Indian Himalaya, Thalay Sagar (6,904m). As far as I know, nobody has ever climbed the north face of Thalay Sagar without using a portaledge. We stopped using a portaledge for our climbs after No Fear on Trango Tower (*AAJ 2012*). It was an extra challenge for us, to try to achieve our routes with only a two-person tent.

When I first started looking at Thalay Sagar, I was pretty sure the buttress left of the central couloir had been climbed. But then Lindsay Griffin sent me a picture showing all the lines, and, to my surprise, it turned out that it had been climbed only in part. Our decision to go didn't take long.

We took a flight from Moscow to Delhi, a taxi from Dehli to Rishikesh, a jeep from Rishikesh to Gangotri, and, 40 hours after leaving Russia, we were discussing prices to Kedar Tal base camp with porters. At first we had no success, and we spent a day carrying part of the stuff ourselves. (The route to Kedar Tal takes one and a half days.) Next day we managed to hire some porters but immediately faced another obstacle: They had no food or tents, since they expected we would provide them. We were not prepared for this and had to open our high-altitude supplies to feed them.

Once we were finally in place, we started up our route on September 9. The first 500–600m were on a steep snow and ice slope. We then hit the first vertical rock buttress. Due to the wind and weather, even the steepest sections were covered in snow and ice. If we could see the rock, it meant it was probably very steep and smooth. It took us two days to climb 200m.

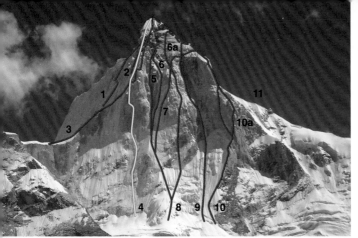

[Top left] The north face of Thalay Sagar. (1) Northeast face and southeast ridge—Dutch Route (2003). (2) Top section of northeast ridge (1983). This route climbs the left flank of the ridge and is mostly hidden on this photograph. (3) Italian attempt on the northeast ridge and right flank (1994, stopped at the shale band below the corner system later taken by Lindblade and Whimp, 1997). (4) Movable Feast (2016). (5) One Way Ticket (2003). (6) Central Couloir Direct (1997). (6a) Variation finish—Period for Friends (2006). (7) North Face—Original Route (1991). (8) Russian Direct—High Tension (1999). (9) Bulgarian Route—Between Light and Shadow (2003). (10) Northwest pillar—Harvest Moon (2004). (10a) Battiti di Liberta, to junction with west ridge (2015). (11) Top section of west ridge—original route up peak (1979). The online version of this caption contains all climbers' names and route grades. *Sergey Nilov* [Bottom Left] Dmitry Golovchenko on the first day (September 11) of the ascent of the lower rock buttress of Movable Feast on the north face of Thalay Sagar. The Russians were lucky to find a good crack system from bottom almost to top, but it was completely filled with ice. Sometimes Golovchenko had to clean the cracks to place cams, other times he could use ice screws. *Dmitry Grigoriev* [Right] Sergey Nilov wondering where to go on the headwall of Thalay Sagar's north face. It is early in the morning of September 16 and Nilov failed to find a climbable crack system at this point. *Dmitry Golovchenko*

Above, there was 300–400m of mixed climbing at 70°–80°. On one night we had to cut away ice from under overhanging rock in order to excavate a ledge, and there we discovered ropes and aid equipment, which we assumed had been abandoned by the 1994 Italian expedition.

Eventually we reached the summit barrier, which is loose black shale and overhanging at 110°. We tried to climb around it but were unsuccessful, and in the end had to climb it directly. Above, we were on the final slopes, and eventually snow led us directly to the summit. We reached the top on September 17, nine days after starting

We descended the original route on the west ridge, assisted by Indian fixed ropes, and got back to base camp at midnight on the 18th. We named our new route Movable Feast (1,200m, 1,400m of climbing, 6B/ED2, 5c A3 WI5 M7). There were five pitches on which we used aid (from A1 to A3).

— DMITRY GOLOVCHENKO, *RUSSIA*

CHAUKHAMBA III, SOUTH RIDGE TO JUST BELOW SUMMIT

[Above] **Chaukhamba III (6,974m) is the summit on the right. The south ridge faces the camera. The 2016 route began on the right side of the ridge and finished left of the summit.** *Paul Hamilton*

IN OCTOBER, THE American-Canadian team of Joel Kauffman, Jason Kruk, and Tad McCrea climbed the 1,600m south ridge of Chaukhamba III (6,974m), stopping on the summit ridge about 15m below and some distance from the top. The team spent 12 days away from base camp on the Panpatia Bank during their final, alpine-style push, with six days on the actual route. The only previously known attempt on this mountain, the highest unclimbed peak in the Gangotri, took place in 2004 when an Indian expedition reached ca 6,300m from the west. The 2016 route on the south ridge was named Sab Kuch Milega (5.10 A0 AI4+ 90°).

— LINDSAY GRIFFIN

VISHNU KILLA (5,968M), EAST GLACIER AND SOUTH FACE

ON MAY 21 an Indo-British party led by Francis Blunt, Adele Pennington, and I (U.K.), and Heera Singh and Mangal Singh (India), made the likely first ascent of the highest peak of the Vishnu Ghar Dhar Range. This range forms the southern fringe of the high Himalaya to the south of the Badrinath-Gangotri Massif. It is bounded by the Alaknanda Valley to the east, the Kedarnath Valley to the west, and the Panpatia Glacier to the north. The range contains over a dozen 5,000m peaks and several significant south-flowing glaciers, and only one major peak had definitely been climbed and recorded prior to 2016: Peak 5,919m, named Lakshmi's Peak by the first-ascent party, which approached from the Panpatia side (*AAJ 2001*).

Approaching from the Joshimath side, to the south, we followed the western flanks of

the Kalpa Ganga valley (also known locally as the Hir-na-wati) above Kalpeshwar. From the road head at Urgam, our route ascended 1,500m to Bansi Narayan Temple, then traversed a ridge called Acchari Dhar on a trail used by local people. Base camp was made at 3,830m below the Gimme Glacier (locally called Rund Glacier).

[Above] **The final ascent up the south face of Vishnu Killa, with unclimbed Peak 5,880m behind.** *Martin Moran*

Peak 5,968m was reached by climbing an icefall and crossing the 5,360m Gimme Khal (col). The final climb was a classic glacier ascent with slopes to 55°. Progress was facilitated by a full cover of spring snow; the icefall could be considerably more difficult and dangerous later in the year. We named the summit Vishnu Killa (30°39'25"N, 79°22'10"E), and the overall grade of the climb was AD or III on the IMF's Himalayan scale. The other summit members were Stephen Fletcher, Phil Griffiths, Martin Hulme, David Lohmann, Raymond McCourt, Simon Ridout, and Nigel Williams (all U.K.). Other peaks in the area appear to offer good rock and alpine-length climbs. 📷

– MARTIN MORAN, ALPINE CLUB, *U.K.*

DECCAN PLATEAU

SAVANDURGA, SOUTH FACE, DEEPAVALI WITH VARIATION FINISH

SAVANDURGA IS SITUATED 60km west of Bangalore and is among the largest monoliths in Asia, reaching an altitude of 1,226m. The first ascent of the main south face was made over two days in October 1984 by Kanhai Datta, Charu Sharma, and Mandip Singh Soin. They reached the top on the day of the Deepavali (or Diwali) Hindu festival, and named the route Deepavali. Since then, a number of new routes and variants have been established on this large granite face, including by well-known visiting climbers such as Lionel Daudet and Doug Scott.

[Above] **The south face of Savandurga, showing Deepavali with the 2016 direct finish (425m climb length, 6b/6b+).** *Samiran Kolhe*

On December 30, TT Niranjan and I climbed Deepavali with a new variant. Most of the climbing up to pitch seven is thin to offwidth cracks, slabs, and open-book features. About 75m below the top we struggled to find the previously climbed line, and so decided to finish directly on a steep and exposed slab. Protection was scant, but TT led this pitch confidently. I then led an easy slab to the top. The 425m route had difficulties from 5a to 6b/6b+. 📷

– SAMIRAN KOLHE, *INDIA*

[Above] Lasarmula (6,246m) seen from the Lor Khola. The east ridge faces the camera; the unclimbed north ridge is the right skyline. *Rebecca Coles*

FAR WEST NEPAL

HUMLA REGION, LASARMULA, EAST RIDGE

STANDING ON THE edge of the moraine and surveying the detritus of other climbers, Simon Verspeak and I saw our first ascent potentially unraveling. It was not surprising that another expedition had attempted the peak—its snowy pyramid of over 6,200m stood in grand isolation in the Lor Khola.

Until then our expedition had gone smoothly. The notoriously unreliable flights to Simikot had bumped us onto the airstrip on time, with all our bags. A local agent helped us find a man with two mules to transport our supplies and equipment, and after four pleasant days of trekking on a well-maintained trail up the Chuwa/Dojam Khola we arrived at the base of the peak we planned to climb: Lasarmula (6,246m).

After we got over the disappointing evidence of a previous climbing expedition (abandoned ropes and hardware, food packaging, and two tent platforms), we first assessed the north ridge, which is both steeper and longer than the east ridge. But a rock buttress looked impassable, and prolonged, post-monsoon cold temperatures meant the snow was unconsolidated.

Retreating to base camp in high winds, we resolved to attempt the east ridge. After just one rest day, we returned to our higher camp and the following day slogged through deep snow on the glacier. Circumnavigating crevasses, we spotted some abandoned fixed lines, but at around 5,200m these ceased. We bivouacked lower than hoped, setting us up for a long summit day.

On November 11, it took three hours in terrible snow to gain the crest of the east ridge, where snow conditions improved. The ridge was about AD/AD+. We pitched a couple of steeper sections but mostly moved together; it took us seven more hours to reach the top. We found no fixed ropes on the ridge, leading us to believe we may well have made the first ascent.

The peak is not named on any map we found. The name Lasarmula (also Lasarmu La) was given to us by our Simikot agent, Rinjin Lama, after he made some inquiries. I have also been informed that it may be called Chhamsark Daha or Chhamsacka. The expedition wishes to thank the Mount Everest Foundation, BMC (with the Julie Tullis Award), the Montane Alpine Club Climbing Fund, and the Austrian Alpine Club for funding. 📄 📷

REBECCA COLES, *ALPINE CLUB, U.K.*

BHANDAR LEK
THE SOLO FIRST ASCENT OF A 6,000-METER PEAK

BY JACK BYNUM

HAVING ONLY SOARED around the unclimbed mountain on Google Earth, it felt wild to cross a river into the winter-shadowed valley beneath its north face. The mountain was what I called Bhandar Lek (6,024m), what some locals call Dhaule, after the name of the river flowing from it, and what most people in Far West Nepal have given no name. The north face is split up the middle by one long ridge, rising about 2,000m from base to summit: the north-northeast spur. On maps it is the highest of a small cluster of mountains named the Bhandar Lek.

Carrying a 30kg pack, in mid-December I walked for 10 days along the Great Himalayan Trail, from Simikot over Margor Lek Bhanjyang Pass (4,037m) to Mathillo Pali, and then along a local trail to Nepka, through villages that rarely, if ever, have seen foreigners. Each village offered full welcome, everyone running to meet me and tick-tick-ticking in disapproval at my shredded trail runners. They were astonished that I was alone and spoke semi-fluent Nepali. (I had been living in the eastern part of the country for four months, researching environmental peace-building.)

Each day on the trail I would meet a new friend, who would often laugh at me, foolish *bideshi*, for not hiring a porter. Each evening I would set camp on a new friend's roof in the village and eat with them by their fire, explain each piece of ice climbing gear, and growl-laugh with the children circling my tent after dark, sing-songing the only English they knew: *"What is your name?"*

From Nepka I walked up the Take Khola. This valley is believed to have been accessed only once before by foreigners, the 2015 British Gorakh Himal expedition, which turned back in heavy spring snow. I turned southeast into the Dhuale Khola, leading to Bhandar Lek, and set up camp at 3,500m.

After two days of rest, I started up the spur with a 14kg pack, scrambling up 700m of rock to the snow line. I watched the first winter storms tumble by without ever obscuring the blue above. That night I perched the tent on a large, freestanding boulder. I so wished for wings to take me back to base camp. Through the whole climb I was chanting *connection, connection, connection* and picture-wheeling through the people I call home.

Day two brought technical rock and a

[Below] Bhandar Lek (6,024m) from the Dhaule Khola, showing the north-northeast spur (ca 2,000m, 5.7 M3 65° snow). [Bottom] Night visitors. *Jack Bynum*

300m traverse on steep snow to switch ridges. I rope-soloed two rock and mixed pitches at the end of the traverse. Seracs avalanched on either side of the knife-edge, but the ridge itself was safe. I pitched my tent on a body-width section of crest, overhanging free air for 30cm on each side. In the morning, wrecked, I repeatedly counted 15 steps and five-minute rests through the last of the technical ridge, in and out of a bergschrund, and up to a dug-in camp at ca 5,950m, dead-tired.

That night I watched the mountain's shadow stretch across the valley. I could see north into Tibet and southwest toward Saipal. The $50 sleeping bag from Thamel was holding up after all. After two more troublesome bergschrunds, on December 20, I sat on top saying my mountain prayer for the thousandth time that trip: *mother mountain, father mountain, brother mountain, sister mountain, genderless mountain, I come to you in loving kindness, humility, and respect, and ask for your safe passage.*

I guessed and headed down the west-southwest face into an unknown valley. Downclimbing and rappelling 2,000m of often objectively dangerous rock and ice with a 40m rope, through a wall of chaos, brought me safely and gratefully to the bottom. After six days on the mountain, and two days with almost no water due to lack of fuel, I slurped in a snowmelt stream for a long time, preparing for a six-day walk out to Gamgadhi and a five-day bus ride back to Kathmandu.

Far West Nepal is still full of opportunity for first ascents of 5,000m to 6,000m peaks. Hopefully, future parties will opt for light, self-sufficient, and culturally aware adventures that support the local communities they visit, on their way into the wild and epic mountains of their dreams. I am grateful to the AAC Mountaineering Fellowship Grant for support.

SUMMARY: Solo first ascent of Bhandar Lek (6,024m, 29°49'26.95"N 82°17'50.16"E) in the Humla region of Far West Nepal, by the north-northeast spur (ca 2,000m, 5.7 M3 65° snow), with descent by the west-southwest face.

PERI HIMAL

NAGORU EAST, WEST, AND CENTRAL PEAKS

IF SOMEBODY SAID you could still find 6,000m peaks in Nepal that were easy to approach, not technically challenging, and still unclimbed, would you believe them? In 2013, the German geographer Hannes Künkel published a short report about a recent trip to Phu, his exploration around an old village named Nagoru, and the three, still unclimbed "Nagoru peaks." I set out to climb Nagoru West (6,076m, 28°51'7.21"N, 84°17'45.38"E), the easiest of the three.

My party established base camp among Nagoru's old field terraces in late October,

[Left] The summit of Nagoru Central (6,165m) from Nagoru West. The distant snow pyramid just to the left is Himlung Himal (7,126m). *Wolfgang Drexler*

and the next day discovered a perfect place for an advanced base, 600m higher, at Nagoru Yak Kharka (4,900m). Setting out from this camp on the 30th, I climbed Nagoru West via its south slopes and upper southwest ridge in six hours, the summit turning out to be a bit of a disappointment as it had entirely lost its glaciation.

In contrast Nagoru East (6,116m) is still covered by a rather substantial glacier. Approaching via the southwest ridge, we found a small rock gully behind the glacier that led nearly all the way up the south ridge to a short stretch of glacier just below the summit. On November 1, only 4.5 hours after leaving camp, I reached the top accompanied by two Sherpa climbers and fellow Austrian Birgit Walk.

In 2016, I returned to Nepal to climb the third and highest of the peaks: Nagoru Central (6,165m). On October 21, my sirdar and I set out at 4 a.m., one hour before sunrise, and arrived on the summit at 10:15 a.m. For both myself and my sirdar, who had been with me on the other Nagoru ascents as well, this represented a "hand in hand" effort—neither would have been there without the other. 📄 📷

– **WOLFGANG DREXLER**, *AUSTRIA*

HIMLUNG HIMAL, SOUTHWEST RIDGE

HIMLUNG HIMAL, a classic 7,126m mountain above the Phu Valley, is usually crowded with big groups in the autumn, but in spring 2016 there was no one else there. We were able to climb as we wished, without fixed rope, even on a commercially guided expedition. From Camp 3 on the "new normal route" (*pioneered by Kari Kobler in 2013 after the 1992 route up the northwest ridge became increasingly exposed to avalanche danger*), we branched right, climbed to Lung La on the southwest ridge, and followed this ridge to the summit (V/PD). Benoit Clerc, Simon Garcia, Olivier von der Weid, and Cyrille Vuidel reached the top on May 12 and called their route Dedicated to the Braves.

On the same day, Frank Bonhomme and Rajan Bothe tried to climb the prominent western spur that reaches the southwest ridge between Himlung Himal and Himjung (7,092m). Due to soft snow and lack of time, they were only able to climb the technical part of the spur, then traverse left to the tracks on Dedicated to the Braves and descend. Their high point was 6,700m, and they named the line to this point Just for Him (V/D).

Even on the most classic and popular mountains, there are always other angles to explore. The climbing game in the Himalaya is endless. 📄 📷

– **PAULO GROBEL**, *FRANCE*

[Above] **Himlung Himal (7,126m) from Gyaji Kang.** The old normal route (the northwest ridge, Japanese, 1992) traversed the left skyline to reach the upper mountain. (1) The new normal route (Kobler expedition, 2013). (2) Dedicated to the Braves (2016), reaching the Lung La and finishing along the upper section of the southwest ridge. (3) Just for Him (2016), which joined Dedicated to the Braves below the ridgeline and then descended. Just off picture to the right is Himjung (7,092m), first climbed in 2012. *Paulo Grobel*

[Above] **Kim Chang-ho climbing steep ice at 7,100m, near the top of the rock barrier on the south face of Gangapurna.** *Korean Way Project*

THE KOREAN WAY
THE DIRECT SOUTH FACE OF GANGAPURNA IN ALPINE STYLE

BY KIM CHANG-HO

WHAT TO DO next? This question lingered in my mind after I completed all the 8,000ers without supplementary oxygen. Like everyone else, I don't have a compass that keeps me directed on the right line to follow. So I thought about my lifelong passion for authenticity in the spirit of mountaineering. This spirit has taught me principles: to overcome one's own limit, to pursue uncertainty, and to explore beyond the end of the road. Keeping these in mind, I devised the "Korean Way Project," which aims to create natural lines on unclimbed peaks and walls, climbing under our own steam, our own responsibility, with no extra equipment.

There is a specific set of criteria that determines the peaks to be climbed. Will the exploration required to reach the base of the mountain make a valuable contribution to the climbing community? While climbing, will we be able to respect local people's sentiments for the mountain? Is the proposed route a natural and "smart" line? Taking all these into account, I decided to try a direct route on the south face of Gangapurna (7,455m) and attempt the first known ascent of Gangapurna West (7,140m, sometimes called Asapurna), which the Nepalese government has recently renamed Lachenal Peak.

I invited two friends, Choi Seok-mun and Park Joung-yong. Seok-mun has climbed with me several times outside Korea, including an expedition in 2001 to five peaks in Pakistan, one to the Central Tower of Paine in 2007, and the first ascent of Batura II (7,762m) in the Karakoram in 2008. Joung-yong was with me in 2004 on the south face of Lhotse, and in 2008 on an ascent of Makalu.

Reaching base camp was not easy due to the swollen Modi Khola: At one point we had to make a makeshift 10m bridge, and another time a Tyrolean crossing to assist our porters. We eventually established base at 4,034m, by the stream flowing from the Annapurna East Glacier.

Gangapurna West came onto the permitted list in 2014 and has received no reported attempt. On October 5 we left base camp with plans to be out for five days. We went up onto the glacier and climbed a south-southwest-facing spur to a bivouac at 5,806m. Next day we climbed steep snow and some seracs to a second bivouac at 6,200m, below the upper south face. We spent two nights here as we explored a route through the complicated glacier terrain above. At 1:30 a.m. on the 8th we started for the summit, climbing fast, roped together, but only belaying occasionally on the steep face. Seok-mun and Joung-yong were rather slow due to insufficient acclimatization. Not far below the summit ridge, Joung-yong decided to stop and wait for our return. Seok-mun and I climbed three pitches to the ridge. The top was only 100m away. We halted and discussed the values of "an unsuccessful attempt" and "a colleague's safe return." An ascent without all colleagues was meaningless to us; we shared everything, and the expedition must be "from home to home." We decided to leave the top untrodden.

I first saw the south face of Gangapurna in the 1964 *Alpine Journal*, a rare aerial photograph taken in 1952 by Swiss cartographer Toni Hagen. Since a German expedition made the first ascent of the mountain,

[Top] **Choi Seok-mun and Park Joung-yong approaching the summit of Gangapurna after three days on the south face. In the background is Machapuchare (6,993m).** [Bottom] **The south face of Gangapurna, showing (red) the Canadian Route (1981), and (yellow) the Korean Way (2016). The camp shown on the left, at 5,806m, was used in 2016 to access the bottom of the face and also the south face of Gangapurna West, out of picture to the left.** *Korean Way Project*

via the south face and east ridge in 1965, seven parties had reached the summit. There were five different routes, mostly from the north, and in 1981 Canadians climbed the south face. We aimed to climb a direct route to the right of the Canadian line.

We planned to use the same approach as we had for Gangapurna West, climbing to our first bivouac then traversing east onto the upper glacier. The unstable weather concerned us. We had drizzle at base camp until the 12th, the date of the 2016 Dashain festival, which normally announces the start of dry weather after the monsoon. After a good rest at Machapuchare base camp, we returned to our own base camp and left for the mountain on the 16th with 8–10kg sacks, two 7.5mm 60m ropes, six screws, three pickets, one two-person tent, a short pad, a stove, and food.

After moving onto the upper glacier, we made our second bivouac at 6,000m, just below the south face. On the third day we simul-climbed the lower part of the south face, belaying occasional ice patches. That night, at 6,800m, was miserable, sitting on a chopped-out ice platform under a rock overhang. The next day we climbed the rock barrier directly: nine pitches of mixed terrain with thin ice over steep rock. Eventually, a narrow icefall led to a low-angle slope. We placed our tent in the middle of this slope, at 7,100m, and despite a very strong wind that kept pulling us away from the wall, we enjoyed being able to lie flat. The food was gone, but we had hot water.

We reached the top the next day, October 20, thankful that all three of us were there together. For the next two days we descended the 1,500m wall via the same route, using natural gear, snow bollards, and Abalakov anchors. Otherwise, all we left on the mountain were two snow pickets and 6 to 10kg of body weight apiece. The new route on the south face of Gangapurna (Korean Way, ED+) was a way of burning our bodies.

SUMMARY: Direct new route up the south face of Gangapurna (7,455m) in the Annapurna Himal, by Choi Seok-mun, Kim Chang-ho, and and Park Joung-yong, October 16–22, 2016. The same team also attempted the south face of unclimbed Gangapurna West, climbing the south face to the summit ridge. This report was translated from Korean by Oh Young-hoon. 📷

THE CANADIAN ROUTE: *The 1981 route on Gangapurna, climbed more or less in alpine style by James Blench and John Lauchlan, was a remarkable achievement for the era. After a four-day storm pinned them in a snow cave at around 5,480m, the pair set out on April 20 with Dwayne Congdon and Dave McNab, bivouacking that night in the bergschrund at the foot of the face. From there two climbers led the way, leaving ropes for the second pair to follow with heavy loads. Bad weather again pinned them down, and by the time they were in a position to attempt the rock band, on April 26, Congdon and McNab were too ill to continue. While they descended, Blench and Lauchlan went for the top, and after three more bivouacs and much technical climbing on 80° ice and mixed, they gained the upper snowfield and headed for the summit, which they reached at 3 p.m. on the 30th, amid a lightning storm. Blench was very sick the following day, and Lauchlan spent two days lowering him down the route to the bergschrund, where the two were met by Congdon and McNab, who helped them to base camp. Due to all the bad weather, the face was in far snowier condition than at the time of the Korean ascent.*

ANNAPURNA HIMAL

ANNAPURNA III, SOUTHEAST RIDGE, ATTEMPT

AUSTRIAN CLIMBERS HANSJÖRG Auer, Alex Blümel, and David Lama attempted one of the great unclimbed prizes of the Nepal Himalaya, the southeast pillar of Annapurna III (7,555m), in early May. They approached base camp by helicopter, and after three acclimatization trips on the east ridge, reaching a high point of 6,000m, they made an alpine-style attempt on the pillar. The weather was poor and the temperatures low, and under the circumstances they found the climbing quite demanding, sometimes having to resort to aid. They made their third bivouac at around 6,550m and received a bad forecast that night. Next day they retreated, and heavy snowfall prevented any further attempts. They feel they may have reached the same point, or perhaps slightly higher, than Nick Colton and Tim Leach did during the first attempt on this line in 1981.

– LINDSAY GRIFFIN

[Above] François Cazzanelli and Emrik Favre near the high point, about 200m below the summit, on their attempt to climb the southwest face of Kimshung (6,781m). Langtang Lirung (7,234m), visible behind, was first climbed by the east/northeast ridge (the right skyline) in 1978. *Giampaolo Corona*

LANGTANG HIMAL

KIMSHUNG, SOUTHWEST FACE ATTEMPT

STANDING TO THE east of Langtang Lirung, Kimshung (6,781m, sometimes called Tsangbu Ri)) has no recorded ascent. On October 6, François Cazzanelli, Giampaolo Corona, and Emrik Favre arrived at Langtang Lirung base camp (4,300m), on the glacier of the same name. On the 11th they placed a camp high on the right side of the glacier, at 5,300m, below the southwest face of Kimshung, and returned to base. On the 15th they made a reconnaissance of their proposed line up the large couloir right of the summit fall line, climbing 600m before descending.

The three men made their first serious attempt on October 21. Leaving camp early, they climbed for 15 hours to reach an altitude of 6,580m, a little short of the south-southeast ridge, where they were stopped by winds in excess of 70 km/hour. To that point they had belayed 12 hard ice pitches at an overall grade of TD+ (AI4/5).

Favre, a guide, left to accompany a trekking group, but the remaining two returned to their high camp on October 30 and prepared for a second attempt. At 5:30 a.m. on the 31st, at a height of 6,000m, a stone hit Cazzanelli on the right arm, producing a large, deep cut. Corona helped his partner descend by rappel. At 9 a.m. a helicopter rescued Cazzanelli and took him to hospital, where he stayed for the next seven days. 📷

— **GIAMPAOLO CORONA**, *ITALY, AND RODOLPHE POPIER, THE HIMALAYAN DATABASE, FRANCE*

URKINMANG, NORTH-NORTHEAST FACE AND NORTHEAST RIDGE; KIMSHUNG ATTEMPT

[Above] Urkinmang from the northwest, showing the Swiss line up the north-northeast face in 2016. In 1999, a French-Swiss pair started up the same line, then moved right to the north rib to reach the summit. The north rib (Japanese, 1994) is the direct route up the prominent rock rib just to the right of the marked line. The west ridge (Austrian, 1971) follows the right skyline. *Philipp Bührer*

ALEX GAMMETER AND I spent April in the Langtang Valley. After traversing Tsergo Ri (5,749m) via an ascent of the southwest face and descent of the north ridge, we made an attempt on Kimshung (6,781m, sometimes called Tsangbu Ri). It took us three days to get to the foot of the climb from Kyanjin village. On the fourth day, from a camp at the head of the Kimshung Glacier, we climbed the east flank of the south ridge of Kimshung to a brèche below the summit pinnacle, but above this the route was extremely dry—no ice, just plenty of loose rock. We rappelled and made it back to Kyanjin the same day. [*Editor's note: While it is believed that Kimshung has been climbed, there is no record of an ascent.*]

On April 15 we left Kyanjin again and set up camp at the little lake between Urkinmang and Ganchempo, north of Tilman's Pass. After a day inspecting a possible line on the north-northeast face of Urkinmang (generally quoted as 6,151m, but shown as 6,143m on the HGM-Finn map), we left our camp at 1 a.m. on the 17th and began climbing the north-northeast face at about 4,850m. The first 500–600m were moderate snow slopes (up to 50°) in a broad couloir, with two short, steep rock sections. At 5,600m the face steepened to 75°. Fortunately, the rocky sections above were plastered in good ice. We reached the northeast ridge at 5,900m and followed it to the summit.

We descended the west ridge and face. Down to 5,450m, this involved gentle snow slopes, but the next 250m descended a band of loose rock that was much trickier. However, with a lot of zigzagging and one rappel we reached the lower part of the glacier running down to the north from Tilman's Col. 📷

– PHILIPP BÜHRER, *SWITZERLAND*

EDITOR'S NOTE: *Japanese climbers made the first known ascent of Urkinmang in 1964 via the south ridge. The west ridge was pioneered in 1971 by Austrians. The most prominent feature on the north face is the north rib, which was climbed in the spring of 1994 by a large Japanese expedition led by Tamotsu Ohnishi. The team fixed 2,000m of rope from 5,000m all the way to the summit. On May 18, 1999, François Damilano (France) and Vincent Sprungli (Switzerland) climbed the north-northeast face via a 1,450m route that began in the same long snow couloir followed in 2016 by the Swiss, but then headed right through a difficult mixed section, comparable with the north face of Les Droites in the Mont Blanc Range. This gained the upper section of the north rib, which they followed to the summit. They descended the west ridge.*

[Above] Hari Mix climbing to the high point on Langdung's summit ridge. Behind, the dominant peak left of center is Chobutse (6,686m). To its left and farther back lies Takargo (a.k.a. Thakar Go, 6,771m). The big peak in distant right is Chugimago (6,259m). *Furtemba Sherpa*

LANGDUNG, SOUTH FACE TO SOUTHEAST RIDGE, ALMOST TO SUMMIT

IN THE AUTUMN, Furtemba Sherpa and I embarked on an expedition with permits for unclimbed Langdung (6,357m) and Omi Tso Go (6,381m), both situated above the remote and stunning Rolwaling (a.k.a. Ripimo Shar) Glacier. A four-day trek brought us from Furtemba's home village of Simigaon to Na, the Rolwaling's highest village. Accompanied by three porters and a cook, we established a base camp at 5,000m on the Rolwaling Glacier.

Next day we explored the upper glacier for access to Langdung's upper south face, bypassing an icefall with a series of loose but relatively easy couloirs (prone to rockfall) leading to clean, low 5th-class granite. We continued to 5,500m before descending.

Two days later we returned to our high point and established a comfortable camp with incredible views of the cirque. On November 1, we ascended talus and an easy snow couloir to reach a spectacular hanging valley. We then simul-climbed through the bergschrund and ascended ever-steepening snow and moderate alpine ice on the south face of Langdung, stopping only occasionally to chop a stance and rest our burning calves.

As Furtemba approached the last few meters to the corniced and incredibly loose southeast ridge, snow conditions plummeted. A short, corniced snow arête guarded Langdung's summit block, just 25m above, but the unprotectable sugar snow posed too great a risk to continue. We descended the face by rappels and, as night fell, packed our camp and headed back to base camp, leaving two short sections of fixed line to aid our descent.

While we were disappointed that the true summit of Langdung eluded us, we were thrilled to have climbed the entire south face (600m, 5.3 AI3 75°). The people of Rolwaling are among the most generous I've encountered, and the side valleys offer tremendous potential for alpine exploration. 📄 📷

— HARI MIX, *AAC*

KARBU RI, SOUTH FACE AND SOUTHWEST RIDGE, FIRST OFFICIALLY RECORDED ASCENT

IN NOVEMBER, I led a 13-member team to attempt Karbu Ri ("White Peak," 6,010m GPS), which I named after a reconnaissance to the area in April. This peak lies on the Nepal-Tibet border at the head of the Rolwaling (a.k.a. Ripimo Shar) Glacier, between the towering peaks of Langdung (6,326m) and Khang Kharpo (a.k.a. Ripimo Shar, 6,646m).

We placed base camp at 5,115m on the Rolwaling Glacier and a high camp at 5,345m. On the 16th, 14 climbers, including four Nepali support staff, set off at 2 a.m. for the summit.

Our route led through a 150m dry icefall onto a heavily crevassed, snow-covered glacier on the south face. This led to a col (5,700m GPS) on the frontier ridge, west of the peak, via 30–70° snow ramps. We used 600m of fixed line to protect the route through the glacier to the col. From there we walked along the southwest ridge. There are two summits, one on the border, which is higher by about 50m, and one to the south. We chose to summit the north peak, which was split into two small snow domes by a large crevasse running east to west. We all reached the top at 9 a.m. (PD, 27.954571°N, 86.494203°E). 📄 📷

– **BRIAN JACKSON**, *EXPEDITION WISE LTD., U.K.*

EDITOR'S NOTE: *Although the expedition believed this to be the first ascent, both summits of the peak were climbed in 1955 by Alf Gregory and Ted Courtenay. It was also known to have been climbed in 2005 by Paul Hartmann, Monika Hronsky, Bruce Normand, Marco Scarsi, Beatriz Vidondo, and Oliver von Rotz. Neither of these parties gave the peak a name. It has no spot height on the HGM-Finn map, but the north summit is recorded as 5,965m on the Schneider map. The summit is not yet on the list of opened peaks.*

YALUNG RI NORTH, POSSIBLE NEW LINE; CHUGIMAGO NORTH, NORTHWEST FACE TO NORTH TOP; CHUGIMAGO, WEST FACE, MIXED EMOTIONS

WITH THE HELP of a friend who had visited the Rolwaling two years earlier, Nik Mirhashemi and I contacted Mingma Gyalje of Dreamers Destination. Mingma grew up in the Rolwaling and has become one of the most accomplished and bold Nepali mountaineers of his generation. The level of service he provided was remarkable, to say the least.

We established base camp in the village of Na (4,150m), pitching our tents outside the house belonging to Mingma's mother. We acclimatized by trekking around the valley, bouldering, and doing a little sport climbing just outside the village. It's quite easy to get to 5,000m in 2.5 hours by taking the trail to Yalung base camp, where there is really good bouldering.

On October 23 we climbed possible new ground on Yalung Ri North (5,634m, a rocky summit first climbed by a 1952 Scottish expedition). Our route mostly ascended the north side of the peak to its very small summit: Wrong Way Bud (500m, 5.6 M4). We descended to base camp the same day, leaving a cache of gear at Yalung base camp.

Our next climb was Chugimago North (5,945m). This was significantly more difficult to access. Long talus fields and steep vegetated slopes put us at the rocky base of the glacier below the northwest face, where there was a flat, sandy spot to camp.

Early on the morning of October 28, we climbed a perfect 120m couloir onto the glacier and went up to the left-hand side of the face. Our 500m route initially consisted of moderately angled ice and snow couloirs, then large flutings and sugar snow over rock. The technical difficulties were M4 AI4 75°.

[Above] **Chugimago North and Chugimago (far right—top of west face visible) seen from the bouldering area near Yalung Ri base camp. (1) Mirhashemi-Pugliese route to the north top of Chugimago North. The Spanish route, Bums Dalbhat, climbed earlier the same month, appears to cover very similar ground except for the lower section, where it climbs right of an initial rock rib. It also does not finish on the north top. (2) Bajde-Kramer-Mucic-Strazar route (2015) on northwest face, finishing on the south top. (3) Infleti (Alegre-Baro, 2014).** *Mark Pugliese*

Our route ended at the north top; the ridge leading to the higher south top was spectacular but blocked by a massive, overhanging cornice. This true summit of Chugimago North is probably 100m higher than the top of our route. We followed old tracks down the north-northeast ridge to a notch at the base and then rappelled a 250m wall in the dark to reach the glacier. [*Editor's note: A little prior to this ascent, Spanish climbers Miguel Anta, Javier Palorames, Alberto Urtusun, and Lluis Vernich climbed a very similar line on the northwest face to the summit ridge, which they named Bums Dalbhat (500m, M4+ 90°). They didn't go to the north top but immediately descended the north-northeast ridge, regaining their camp after a round trip of 26 hours. The last four pitches to the summit ridge had very bad snow and were almost impossible to protect. Later, two of the team climbed new ground (V+ 80°) to 5,800m on the southeast face of 6,257m Chekigo before retreating.*]

Our last objective was the west face of Chugimago (6,259m). The peak had been climbed twice, both times via the impressive west face. We spied a line starting to the right of the 2015 Mucic-Strazar Route. We camped on the Yalung Glacier, and at 3:30 a.m. on November 1 we began walking toward the face.

Our route turned out to have the best climbing of the trip, with fun mixed pitches down low, snow flutings in the middle, and a final headwall. The latter had really fun mixed pitches, up to M6, with great névé in between. The snow became more rotten the closer we got to the ridge, but after six pitches on the headwall we reached the crest as the sun set. We bivouacked below a prominent pyramid-shaped rock on the ridge. Having chosen to go light and bring only a small tent, pads, and puffy pants and jackets, but no sleeping bags, this bivy sucked. I guess you live and learn. However, we made it through the night and next morning climbed the four remaining pitches along the crest to the summit. We called our route Mixed Emotions (900m, M6 AI5 80°). [*Editors' note: This route climbs more or less along the crest of the buttress right of the Mucic-Strazar Route, joins it in the middle section, and then climbs to the left of it through the headwall.*] In descent we took one of the prominent snow couloirs to the looker's right of our route and were able to rappel and downclimb to the glacier, reaching Na at 8 p.m. the same day.

The Rowaling is an incredible place and still a bit off the beaten track for Nepal. It holds lots of potential for new alpine mixed climbs on 6,500–7,000m peaks. Highly recommended! 📷

– **MARK PUGLIESE**, *AAC*

[Above] **Oriol Baró on the southwest pillar of Karyolung.** *Santi Padros*

KARYOLUNG, SOUTHWEST PILLAR AND SOUTHEAST RIDGE; NUMBUR, SOUTHEAST FACE, ATTEMPT

IN A FRUITFUL trip of less than three weeks, our Catalan team of Oriol Baró, Roger Cararach, and I did two climbs above the Dudh Kund Glacier. After flying to Lukla in mid-October, we approached up the Sor Khola and established base camp at Dudh Kund Lake (4,630m). The head of the valley was surrounded by the big peaks of Numbur (6,958m), Khatang (6,790m), and Karyolung (6,530m), and the southerly orientation of this cirque was favorable for new ice and mixed lines. The weather was stable but cold, with the morning temperature averaging around -14°C.

Less than a week after our arrival, we were already on our first route, the previously unclimbed southwest pillar of Karyolung, which rose close to base camp. We spent three days climbing what we christened Dudh Khunda Pillar (1,400m, ED 6a AI4 M4), reaching the summit on October 31. Our bivouacs were at 5,600m and 6,100m. From the top we descended the north ridge, loosing 700m in three hours before rappelling to the Dudh Kund Glacier and regaining base camp the same day. [*Editor's note: Rarely climbed Karyolung was first ascended in 1982 by Japanese, via the northeast face, also starting from Dudh Kund Lake.*]

After one rest day we set off for the southeast face of Numbur. We made this approach in two days, partly to make sure we arrived at the base relatively fresh. At 4 a.m. on November 4, Oriol and I started up the 1,100m face from a camp at 5,800m, aiming to reach the summit in one day. By 2:30 p.m. we had reached a height of about 6,900m. At this point, about 80m below the summit, we had climbed past the main technical difficulties on fantastic ice, but now were faced with totally unconsolidated snow slopes up to 70° that were impossible to protect. We decided the risk was too great and descended from this point. To our high point, the route was 1,000m, ED AI5 M4. [*Numbur was first climbed in 1963 by Japanese, via the southwest ridge, a route that has been repeated at least half a dozen times.*]

While in the area, Roger and I also climbed to the 5,850m col between Karyolung and Khatang via a diagonal line of around 600m and UIAA IV+, descending directly in six very long rappels (November 2). On the 6th, Roger and Oriol climbed what we dubbed the Aiguille d'Amitges del Karyolung (ca 5,200m), a rock pillar one hour from the lake. They named the route Ranxera Nepali (7a, 4 pitches plus 100m of easier climbing). Khatang, the other big peak in the area, has only been climbed once and has serious potential for new lines from the south. But cold, fatigue, and a certain satisfaction in what we had achieved drove us to the comforts of civilization.

[Above] The southwest pillar of Karyolung, with the 2016 line and bivouac sites marked. *Santi Padros*

— SANTI PADROS, *SPAIN, WITH ADDITIONAL INFORMATION FROM RODOLPHE POPIER, HIMALAYAN DATABASE*

LUNAG RI, WEST RIDGE, ATTEMPTS

In November, Conrad Anker and I traveled to the Khumbu. Just like the year before, our goal was Lunag Ri, an unclimbed 6,895m peak. In November 2015, we had failed to reach the summit during a three-day weather window, reaching a high point about 300m below the top,

[Below] The west ridge of Lunag Ri forms the left skyline, rising from a 6,026m col. On the left are the flanks of Lunag West. (1) The 2016 attempt by Conrad Anker and David Lama. In 2015 the same pair had continued up this line to the west ridge and then climbed about 600m up the ridge. (2) David Lama's 2016 solo attempt and bivouacs. *Archiv Lama*

because we had underestimated the complexity of the west ridge. [*The west ridge rises from a 6,026m col between 6,492m Lunag West and Lunag Ri, high point of the group. In 2010 a French team reached the 6,812m southeast top of Lunag Ri but did not continue to the main summit*].

During the first good weather period, we made an attempt on our previous line. On our first day, at about 5,800m, Conrad suddenly felt extreme pain in his chest. We immediately rappelled and called a helicopter, which picked him up at our advanced base and evacuated him to a hospital in Kathmandu. He had suffered a heart attack, but after emergency surgery he was doing better, and he soon left for home in Montana.

Knowing that Conrad was safe and wouldn't return to the mountain, I carefully weighed the pros and cons of a solo attempt. I felt well prepared from many solos in the Alps the summer before, but I had not planned for a solo ascent, and our rack was decimated after our first attempt. Ultimately, I came to the conclusion that I stood a fair chance.

Three days later, I left camp at night. I climbed ropeless up steep snow and ice slopes farther right than our previous attempts and reached a good bivouac spot about 700m below the summit. At around 2 a.m., I continued upward, and I was on the ridge by the time the sun started to rise. The terrain became more and more technical, and because I had to start belaying myself, things became slower and more toilsome. I felt great fatigue when I reached my second bivouac, approximately 250m below the top, and I knew that going further would deplete too much of my reserves to descend safely. In the morning I rappelled as far as I could before the sun set loose falling rocks and ice. I rested and then continued the descent at nightfall.

I look back at this as one of my most intense mountain experiences yet, not only because of the climb but also because of everything else that happened. Fortunately, Conrad has recovered well. He told me that he thinks Lunag Ri was his last expedition of that type, but he is climbing again and doing what we both love, being in the mountains.

– DAVID LAMA, *AUSTRIA*

MAHALANGUR HIMAL / KHUMBU SECTION

KANGCHUNG SHAR, NORTH FACE, ATTEMPT

ON OCTOBER 17, Simon Yates and I established base camp in a high and pleasant ablation valley on the north side of the junction of the Ngozumba and Gaunara glaciers. Our objective was the unclimbed 1,000m north face of Kangchung Shar (6,063m). Simon had taken striking photos of unbroken ice lines draping this face a few years back, but the 2016 post-monsoon season had been very dry, and the north face looked exceedingly lean. We changed our target to an indirect couloir line on the right side of the face, aiming to gain the col between Kangchung Shar and Kangchung Nup. From here we would proceed up the northwest ridge.

On October 25 we ascended a zigzagging line to the base of the couloir. A house-size chockstone blocked progress midway, requiring some Scottish 5 mixed to negotiate. As we got higher, what we'd thought would be enjoyable névé turned out to be thin, brittle crust over deep, sugar snow. We reached the col in the afternoon and camped on the northwest ridge of Kangchung Shar. On the morning of the 26th, progress was again frustratingly sluggish due to poor snow conditions. By late afternoon we reached a notch in the ridge at about 5,820m. Since we had no bivouac gear we decided to start down toward our high camp, which we reached just as daylight was fading. 🗎 📷

– PAUL SCHWEIZER, *ALPINE CLUB, U.K.*

KANGCHUNG SHAR, NORTHWEST RIDGE FROM THE SOUTH, FIRST OFFICIAL ASCENT

ON NOVEMBER 6, Ben O'Connor Croft and I (U.K.), Joshua Jarrin (Ecuador), Pasang Bhote Sherpa, and Ang Phurba Sherpa (Nepal) made the first official ascent of Kangchung Shar (6,063m), a peak on the list of 104 summits approved by the Nepal government in 2014.

We first climbed to the Kangchung La, the col between Kangchung Nup and Shar, via a large, broken icefall on the south face. From there it was about 500m (TD) up the northwest ridge to the summit. We left base camp (5,200m) at 1 a.m. and reached the top at 11:30 a.m., having fixed 400m of rope. The climb was not very technical but had passages of sugar snow and loose rock that required care. We descended the same way.

– MASHA GORDON, *U.K.*

EDITOR'S NOTE: *Although neighboring Kangchung Nup (6,043m) was first climbed by Edmund Hillary and other members of the 1953 Everest expedition, Kangchung Shar does not appear to have been climbed before November 1984, when it was soloed by Franci Knez (Slovenia) and later in the same month by Trevor Pilling (U.K.). Both climbers reached the Kangchung La from the south and followed the northwest ridge to the top, as did the 2016 team.*

PEAK 6,071M (KANG TARI), NORTHWEST FACE, TO HELL WITH OUR BODY

SPANISH CLIMBERS JORGE Cuadrado, Angel Salamanca, and Javi San Miguel arrived in Nepal in late April. They already had acclimatized in the Alps, and they added to this by trekking and climbing to nearly 5,800m in the Khumbu. The weather was bad during their time in the area, with lots of snow and poor visibility

The objective was Peak 6,071m (sometimes called Kang Tari), which Salamanca had seen on his trip to Nepal in 2015, when he climbed Peak 6,420m from the Mingbo Valley (*AAJ*

[Top] Climbing the northwest ridge of Kangchung Shar (6,063m). Behind is Kangchung Nup, first climbed by the 1953 Everest expedition. In the background are the peaks of the Rolwaling. *Masha Gordon* [Bottom] The Schweizer-Yates attempt on the north side of the Kangchung La. They continued up the northwest ridge of Kangchung Shar, facing the camera, to about 240 meters below the top. This ridge was followed to the summit soon afterward by the Masha Gordon team, which approached from the opposite side. *Martin Klestinec*

2016). Peak 6,071m, for which Salamanca could find no information, lies at the head of the Milingo Valley (Minmo on the HGM Finn map; sometimes designated Omaka on older maps). This valley rises more or less southeast from the village of the same name, immediately northeast of Tengboche. It is the first of the lower peaks on the ridge running northeast from Kangtega (6,783m).

The team established base camp in the valley at 4,600m and then a high camp at 5,000m, all without the help of porters. The initial plan was that Cuardardo and Salamanca would climb the route while San Miguel manned base camp. However, Cuardardo was ill and it was San Miguel who accompanied Salamanca on the northwest face.

Conditions for the ascent were poor, with continuous mist, wet snow, and cold temperatures. Nevertheless, the pair reached the top of the face and then descended via rappels and downclimbing, in a total of 14 hours. They have named their route to the ridge To Hell With Our Body (1,000m, MD+ M6 80° ice). This peak has no recorded ascent but would be much easier from the Hinku Nup Glacier to the south.

[Top] To Hell With Our Body (2016) reached the top of the northwest face of Peak 6,071m (a.k.a. Kang Tari). The summit is on the right. Kangtega Northwest (6,685m) is just off-picture to the right. [Bottom] Turning a rock barrier on the face. *Angel Salamanca*

– LINDSAY GRIFFIN, *WITH INFORMATION FROM ANGEL SALAMANCA, SPAIN*

OMBIGAICHEN, SOUTHWEST RIDGE

ON NOVEMBER 1 the Ukrainian team of Vitaly Golev, Yuri Kilichenko, Maxim Perevalov, Peter Poberezhnyi, and Yuri Vasenkov climbed a new route on Ombigaichen (6,340m), the beautiful, fluted peak that lies between Ama Dablam (6,814m) and the Mingbo La (5,845m).

Ombigaichen was first climbed in November 1960 by Jim Milledge (U.K.) and Ang Tsering from Ed Hillary's Silver Hut expedition. This pair climbed the northwest ridge and gave the peak the name Puma Dablam ("daughter Dablam"). An ascent was made via the south ridge, above Mingbo La, in December 2002, the year it was opened as a trekking peak, but the mountain is still rarely climbed.

The Ukrainian team left their camp in the Mingbo Valley at 4 a.m. on October 29 and headed up toward Mingbo La, before working left and setting foot on the southwest ridge a little before 10 a.m. The first part of this elegant ridge featured many mushrooms and was regularly cut by difficult crevasses. On the second day they climbed through the loose rock band that forms the middle section of the ridge. Protection was often difficult to arrange, on difficulties between 5b and 6a. Above, they spent the next three or four hours solving more "snow puzzles," before finding a place to stop for the night. On the third day it was more snow, ice, and mushrooms, and at dusk, with the altimeter registering 6,200m, they constructed a sitting bivouac and waited out the night. To their surprise, next morning it was only half a rope length to the summit, instead of the three hours they had anticipated—due to the extreme dryness of the air, the altimeter had underestimated their height.

The new route, Wild West, is 780m high with 1,100m of climbing, and has an average steepness of 55° and an overall Russian grade of 5B. The arête had average steepness of 50° below the rock barrier and 65° above. The route was considered objectively very safe, and the most taxing aspect of the climb was trying to construct bivouac sites on the crest of the ridge, where much ingenuity was needed. The climbers enjoyed more than a month of continuous fine weather during their stay in the Khumbu.

[Above] **Ombigaichen (6,340m)** from the southwest. The Ukrainian route Wild West (2016) follows the obvious central ridge. The south ridge (right skyline) was climbed by a small British team in December 2002. *Yury Kilichenko*

– **LINDSAY GRIFFIN**, *WITH INFORMATION FROM ELENA DMITRENKO, RISK.RU*

PEAK 5, SOUTHWEST PILLAR

ZSOLT TOROK AND I flew to Lukla and acclimatized on the southeast ridge of Kyajo Ri (6,189m, Holby-Kear, 2005). On October 26 we flew to the Makalu-Barun region, where our objective was unclimbed Peak 5 (a.k.a. Saldim or Saldim Ri) on the border with Tibet. On arrival, we quickly realized that every map we had was wrong, and our summit was located in another valley. [*Ascents of Peak 5 reported in the past, such as that of the 1989 British Makalu expedition, were actually on another peak farther east, with an altitude of 6,374m on HGM-Finn map, its southeast flanks overlooking the Lukuche or Saldim Valley.*] With considerable effort, we relocated to a base camp in the Barun Valley, and on October 28, thanks to accurate maps from the 1980s received directly from Doug Scott, we finally reached the foot of the mountain.

The weather was not the best, so we waited a day. Then, with no expectation of any change in conditions, we started climbing, alpine-style, on October 30, starting from an advanced base camp at the foot of the southwest pillar. We climbed the first wall directly, with passages of 6a/6a+ on solid granite. The climbing was really pleasant, but once we reached the small hanging glacier the weather changed and strong winds started to blow. This forced us to stop and camp, inside

[Left] The southwest pillar of Peak 5 (a.k.a. Saldim or Saldim Ri, 6,421m), climbed in a three-day round trip. *Vlad Capusan*

a crevasse at 5,800m. That night the temperature was very cold (-27°C). The following morning we left early with the intention of reaching the summit. We started the upper wall, dubbed the Caltun Wall, after a peak at home, and met difficulties of M5/M6 and WI4. After six pitches we got to the top of the headwall and found a somewhat easier ridge. This took us to the final ridge, which was a knife-edge and proved to be the most demanding part of the route, as we were unable to find any protection. Already exhausted by the wind and low temperatures, we took two or three hours to traverse the summit ridge, reaching the top a little after 2 p.m. According to our GPS, the altitude was 6,421m (6,432m on HGM-Finn map). On the upper route we found no trace of any previous passage. We spent only five minutes on top, due to high winds and poor visibility, and quickly started down the way we had come. After a 15-hour day we stopped at 5,900m for our second bivouac, and the following day made more than 20 rappels down our route to get off the mountain. We have named our route Romanian Flame (6a+ M5/6 AI4 90°). 📷

— VLAD CAPUSAN, ROMANIA

JANAK HIMAL

PANDRA, EAST FACE, ATTEMPT

KEI TANIGUCHI AND I attempted the east face of Pandra in November. In the fall of 2002, three Danes had made the first ascent of Pandra via the south face (TD-), recording a GPS summit elevation of 6,673m (*AAJ 2003*). This was the only known attempt on the mountain until 2016.

On November 11 we left advanced base camp (5,550m), crossed the Chabuk Glacier, and began climbing the east face at 1 p.m. After two bivouacs on the face, we reached a ridge and stopped again for the night, fixing one rope length above. The next morning we continued up the ridge, which soon became extremely difficult: A large cornice overhung a very steep drop to the right, while the left flank was formed of loose sugar snow. There was no protection, and when I'd finished my pitch and brought up Kei, I said to her there was no way we could reach the summit, even with our best efforts. Despite my doubts, Kei immediately continued, traversing onto the steep north flank. My body got colder and colder at the belay, and by the time I had reached Kei at the next stance, my mind had gone and she agreed to go down. We rappelled to the Chabuk Glacier and made it back to base camp the night of the 15th.

I soon regretted having abandoned the attempt and mentioned this to Kei. At first she seemed angry, but soon proposed that we return to the unclimbed mountains of eastern Nepal in the future. I was delighted to hear her generous and encouraging statement. Sadly, it was not to be: Within a month of our returning from Nepal, Kei died in a fall from Mt. Kurodake in Japan. ▤ ◙

– JUNJI WADA, *JAPAN, SUPPLIED BY TAMOTSU NAKAMURA, ASIAN ALPINE NEWS*

KANGCHENJUNGA HIMAL

GIMMIGELA CHULI EAST, NORTHWEST FACE

IN OCTOBER, ALEX Blümel and I trekked to the north side of Kangchenjunga and established base camp at 5,200m, a little higher than the classic Pangpema site. We acclimatized on Drohmo's southeast ridge, spending three nights at 5,900m. There are still great lines to do in the Kangchenjunga area, especially along the border with Sikkim extending northward from Gimmigela Chuli. *(The online version of this report includes informative photos of this area.)* Our goal was the northwest face of Gimmigela Chuli East (7,007m). I was unable to understand why this face had not been attempted: It's a king line.

Due to a wet monsoon, with high precipitation, the face was in perfect condition. Our main concerns were wind and the lack of obvious bivouac sites. Our tactic of going as light and quickly as possible proved to be the right decision. We left base camp on November 8 and bivouacked at 6,000m, at the upper bergschrund, above a large serac barrier. The next day we climbed the face to an exit leftward onto the final section of the north ridge, where we bivouacked at 6,850m. The difficulties were 85° ice and one rock section of M4. On the 10th we reached the summit at 7:30 a.m. We descended our route by rappelling from Abalakov ice anchors.

It took about six hours to reach 6,000m, after which it was faster to downclimb. The height of the face was 1,200m, and we were the first to climb the mountain from Nepal.

[*Editor's note: Gimmigela Chuli East was first climbed from Sikkim, in September 1993, by a large Japanese expedition that was attempting to reach the main (west) summit of Gimmigela Chuli via the east ridge. It was climbed again by the same route in October the following year, also by Japanese, who this time successfully continued west to the 7,350m main summit of Gimmigela Chuli.*]

– HANSJÖRG AUER, *AUSTRIA*

[Below] **The northwest face of Gimmigela Chuli East and the Austrian Route (2016).** *Elias Holzknecht*

CHINA

[Above] Kazuya Hiraide acclimatizing on the north-northwest spur of Loinbo Kangri (7,095m) before the first ascent of Loinbo Direct. *Kenro Nakajima* [Inset] Loinbo Direct and the Japanese bivouac site on the 1,400m north-northwest face of Loinbo Kangri. The two climbers descended by the north-northwest spur, partially visible on the left. *Kenro Nakajima*

TIBET / TRANS-HIMALAYA – GANGDISE RANGE

LOINBO KANGRI, NORTH-NORTHWEST FACE, LOINBO DIRECT

ON SEPTEMBER 8, Kazuya Hiraide and Kenro Nakajima arrived in Lhasa, and three days later they reached the village of Kajang by 4WD. Locals transported them by motorbikes to base camp, at 5,280m, in the valley northeast of Loinbo Kangri (7,095m). After this the two Japanese were on their own, without the usual trappings of Chinese cooks and base-camp staff.

The weather was good, and over the next five days the pair reconnoitered the north-northwest face and acclimatized by climbing the easier-angled north-northwest spur on the left side of the face. They reached a height of 6,750m on this spur, which they planned to use as their descent route, and slept one night at 6,250m.

They returned to base camp on the 18th, expecting to rest and wait for a good weather forecast. However, when they realized that a large storm predicted on the afternoon of the 20th might deposit snow that would take some days to consolidate, and as conditions on the mountain were currently very good, they decided to take only one rest day and make an attempt on September 20, despite some misgivings about their acclimatization.

They set off with food for two days, two 50m, 7.5mm ropes, a number of ice screws, and four snow stakes. Thin but solid névé overlying ice made for good but sustained frontpointing for much of the way, with protection from screws. A strong wind ensured the pair was frequently swept by spindrift. In late afternoon, at 6,760m, they spent two hours chopping a tent site. There was a large thunderstorm, and Nakajima, feeling the altitude, was unable to eat or drink.

Despite the overnight snowfall, the pair reached the summit early next morning, and from there descended the northeast ridge for a short distance before heading down the north-northwest spur. They reached base camp the same day. They were back in Japan by September 27, having completed a new route, Loinbo Direct (1,400m, WI5), on a 7,000-meter peak in less than three weeks away from home. 📷 ▶

— LINDSAY GRIFFIN, *WITH INFORMATION SUPPLIED BY* HIROSHI HAGIWARA, *ROCK AND SNOW, JAPAN*

THE LOINBO KANGRI GROUP: *Few climbers have visited the Loinbo Kangri Group, an area characterized by many sharp, granitic summits. The highest peak, Loinbo Kangri (7,095m), was first climbed in October 1996 by Koreans Bang Jung-hil, Cha Jing-choi, and You Seok-jae, via the northeast ridge (AAJ 1998). From 1998 to 2005, small British parties made four visits, climbing some of the lower summits; they suggested the best weather would be found in the post-monsoon season. In 2006 a multinational team enjoyed perfect weather throughout its stay and climbed a number of peaks, including the elegant Phola Kyung (6,530m), Gopalho (6,450m), and Kangbulu (6,655m), the second-highest mountain in the range. This team noted a good ice couloir on the north face of Loinbo Kangri—the one eventually climbed by the Japanese.*

TIBET / NYANCHEN TANGLHA WEST

POGOLHA (JANG TSANG GO), NORTHEAST FACE AND EAST RIDGE

IN SEPTEMBER, DOMEN Kastelic (Slovenia), Marcus Palm (Sweden), and I traveled to Tibet to attempt two peaks in the Qungmo Kangri group at the western end of Nyanchen Tanglha West. We believed both to be unclimbed. Delayed permits forced us to spend a week acclimatizing in the Siguniang area before flying to Lhasa. On September 13 we established base camp northwest of the Suge La (Xogu La, 5,430m) in the Pagolam Valley, east of Qungmo Kangri. We were accompanied by our guide Nima and cook Lhakpa.

After some acclimatization and reconnaissance trips, we trekked to the base of the northeast face of Peak 6,328m, erroneously named Tangmonja on the Chinese Mi Desheng and Polish Jerzy Wala maps *(see editor's note)*. This mountain rises above the glacier named Pagolha on the Deshing map.

Although the forecast promised four days of good weather, it continued to snow throughout the night and the next morning. We started climbing the northeast face in less than ideal weather, first following a series of gullies with bad ice, where we had to fight heavy spindrift. When the face opened up, we followed easier ground to the east ridge and moved onto the east face, where we bivouacked a few hundred meters below the summit. By next morning the skies had cleared, and we summited in the early afternoon on September 20. After an hour on top we descended via the north face, rappelling and downclimbing. We estimate the length of the climb to be 700m and the difficulties as AI4 M5. A local nomad in the valley referred to the mountain as Jang Tsang Go, which roughly translates as "the mountain in the wolf valley."

At base camp we packed our things to relocate to another valley at the far western end of the group, where we planned to attempt unclimbed Tanmonjen (a.k.a. Jamo Gangar, 6,373m). After driving over the Suge La we experienced more problems with our permit and ended up spending the night in a small mountain village. Unexpectedly, we walked by a bar where five young Tibetans were engaged in traditional dance. They invited us to join and we spent the night

[Top] **Domen Kastelic climbing steep snow and ice in the middle section of the northeast face of Pogolha/Jang Tsang Go (6,328m).** *Olov Isaksson*
[Bottom] **Pogolha/Jang Tsang Go (6,328m) from the northeast, showing the line of the Slovenian-Swedish Route (2016) and the bivouac site. The climbers descended the north face and the icefall to the right of the ascent route.** *Olov Isaksson*

dancing Tibetan disco with our new friends.

The next day we were allowed to continue our journey. Our satellite images were not up to date, and we discovered that a road was being constructed past our mountain. From a base camp at 4,600m, we were able to ride borrowed motorcycles to the foot of the peak at 5,350m, reducing the approach from one or two days to one hour. Unfortunately, the weather remained very bad and we could not get a proper view of our objective.

The area of our second base camp was inhabited by three friendly and helpful families. While the bad weather persisted, one of the families invited us to stay in their house. They seemed to enjoy our company, and the feeling was mutual. We spent the remainder of our time in the area playing with their children and enjoying local cuisine. *Editor's notes: Tragically, a little over a month after this expedition, Domen Kastelic was killed in an avalanche above the Monzino Hut in the Mont Blanc Massif. The online version of this report includes notes on the climbing history of this area and clarifies the nomenclature of the peaks. Search "Pogolha" at publications. americanalpineclub.org.*

– **OLOV ISAKSSON**, *SWEDEN*

LAPCHE KANG II, EAST SPUR AND SOUTHEAST FACE, ATTEMPT

LAPCHE KANG II (7,250m) lies in the northern Himalaya, about 35km northwest of Cho Oyu, in a massif variously called Labuche Himal, Pamari Himal, or Lapche Kang. The highest summit, Lapche Kang I (a.k.a. Choksam, 7,367m), was first climbed in 1987 by a Sino-Japanese expedition. (*American climber Joe Puryear died while attempting this peak in 2010.*) The pyramid of Lapche Kang III (7,072m, sometimes erroneously called Lapche Kang West or Lapche Kang II) was first climbed in 1995 by a Swiss expedition. Until 2016 no one had attempted Lapche Kang II.

Maciej Przebitkowski, Jakub Rybicki, Jarosław Żurawski, and I arrived in Kathmandu on September 6. Although we had all the necessary documents, we were delayed twice by the Chinese bureaucracy, first in Nepal and then in Tingri, Tibet, where we were told we would not be allowed to approach the mountain from the north, via the Choksam Glacier, but instead would have to come in from the east, up the East Lapche

[Above] The attempted route up the east spur and southeast face of Lapche Kang II. Main summit (7,250m) is to the left. *Krzysztof Mularski*

Glacier. We were driven to Cho Oyu base camp, and on the 23rd we started up the glacier.

An advanced base was established at 5,400m and Camp 1 at 5,500m. After fixing some rope up sections of WI2, we placed Camp 2 at 6,150m, below a rib leading to an upper terrace at 6,400m. This rib had sections of UIAA IV and snow to 60°. Camp 3 was placed a little above the terrace at 6,600m. From here, Jakub and I made a summit attempt on October 12, climbing a 65° snow/ice face to 6,907m (GPS), where we decided to retreat when we felt there was no chance of reaching the summit before nightfall. 🗐 📷 🔍

– KRZYSZTOF MULARSKI, *POZNAŃ MOUNTAINEERING SOCIETY, POLAND, SUPPLIED BY JANUSZ MAJER*

EVEREST, SPEED ATTEMPTS AND NEW LINE TO NORTH RIDGE

Spanish climber and mountain runner Kilian Jornet planned to attempt a record-breaking speed ascent and descent of the north side of Everest during the monsoon period. He was accompanied to Tibet by fellow Spaniard Jordi Tosas and French filmmakers and alpinists Vivian Bruchez (one of France's best skiers of steep terrain) and Sébastien Montaz-Rosset.

After acclimatizing in Langtang, the four arrived at Rongbuk on August 19, and over the ensuing days climbed several summits up to 6,500m. The team then set advanced base camp at about 6,050m, their yaks unable to reach the usual site at 6,500m.

On August 31, Jornet, Montaz-Rosset, and Tosas tried a new line up Everest on the far right side of the north-northeast face, not far from the north ridge. Their planned route was the shorter couloir to the right of the line followed during the February 1988 attempt on the face by Japanese Tsuneo Hasegawa and Kiyotaka Hoshino, which ended at 7,700m. (The Japanese followed a more significant couloir that eventually was climbed, in 1996, by Russians.) The goal was to climb the shorter couloir until it meets the north ridge at around 7,900m, from where they hoped to follow the Messner traverse and Norton Couloir to the summit.

Leaving the 6,100m camp on Everest's normal route, the three climbers crossed the bergschrund at 6,500m and climbed mainly snow (50°) with easy mixed sections to around 7,600m, where bad weather and snowfall made conditions too avalanche-prone. From there they traversed right to the north ridge, reaching it at approximately 7,680m, and descended via the North Col.

The round trip from camp was 15 hours, at an average rate of vertical gain—from bergschrund to 7,600m—of 180m/hour. They climbed unroped throughout and had no camps on the mountain. *The online version of this report details several more extremely fast climbs in the area completed by various expedition members.* 🗐 📷

– LINDSAY GRIFFIN, *WITH INFO FROM JORDI TOSAS, SPAIN, AND RODOLPHE POPIER, THE HIMALAYAN DATABASE*

BOBONUNG MASSIF, PHOTOGRAPHIC EXPEDITION

IN NOVEMBER, TSUYOSHI Nagai and AAC Honorary Member Tamotsu Nakamura (Japan) traveled to southern Tibet to photograph peaks along the Yarlung Tsangpo. This region is sensitive and currently strictly restricted, due to its proximity to the Indian border. No climbers would be allowed to travel in the area without special permits from the Public Security Bureau and the Chinese Liberation Army in charge of the Tibet Autonomous Region.

[Above] **The north aspect of unnamed and unclimbed 6,000m tops surrounding the Bobonung Glacier.** *Tamotsu Nakamura*

Nakamura photographed peaks of the Bobonung Massif, a north-facing cirque of peaks surrounding the Bobonung Glacier and facing Route 306, which runs beside the Yarlung Tsangpo. Four of the summits are above 6,000m, with the highest at 6,215m. The most westerly is Chipula (a.k.a. Qipula, 6,152m). He also photographed the rocky peaks Nyel Japo (6,152m) and Worde Kongge (5,998m), farther to the west. Some of these mountains were photographed by Nakamura during a similar expedition in 2014 (and are seen in his comprehensive book East of the Himalaya), but the new photos reveal considerably more detail. A PDF with a map and the photos can be found at the AAJ website: publications.americanalpineclub.org. 📷 🔍

– LINDSAY GRIFFIN

KYZYL ASKER, EAST-SOUTHEAST FACE, THE SPEAR

FROM JULY 19–24, the Siberian team of Oleg Khvostenko, Alexander Parfenov, and Vasiliy Terekhin climbed a new route up the center of the east-southeast wall of Kyzyl Asker (5,842m). In 2010, Khvostenko had planned a visit to Kyzyl Asker with Denis Prokofyev, but it didn't work out, so when Prokofyev decided to take a young team to the region in 2016 (see report below), Khvostenko opted to come along with his own team of Krasnoyarsk-based and Stolby-trained climbers. Despite very unstable weather, the team was able to add a Krasnoyarsk route along the iced-up cracks in the wall between the St. Petersburg route on the southeast pillar (Mikhailov-Odintsov-Ruchkin, 2007) and the Moscow route War and Peace (Golovchenko-Grigoryev-Nilov, 2014) on the right side of the east-southeast face.

During the seven days the three climbers spent on the face, they faced all four seasons: two days of fine summer weather, one day of autumnal rain and snow, one day of winter, and the other three a mixture, representing spring. However, the temperature never dropped below -5°C. The ice generally proved unstable for climbing, yet the conditions never allowed the team to don rock shoes.

The crux occurred at around 5,500m, on the fourth day, when Terekhin had to surmount a large roof decorated with two huge icicles. This section was A3; the remaining aid climbing on the route was around A2. That day it rained and both team and equipment got soaked, so on the following day, while the other two progressed the route, Terekhin took a rest at the portaledge and dried all the gear, chipping ice from the ropes and melting it from cams over the stove.

On the sixth day, Terekhin climbed a mixed pitch of rotten ice at M8 and the team finally emerged onto the summit ridge. They reached the high point atop the southeast pillar at 1:30 p.m., where they were rewarded with bright sunshine and a fine panoramic view. (The true summit of Kyzyl Asker is some 200m farther to the west.) By 2 p.m. on the 25th, after sitting through an electric storm early that morning, they were back at camp on the glacier, having rappelled the route. Since the line followed a dihedral to a pointed snow cornice high on the wall, they named their

[Above] **Vasiliy Terekhin on a small roof at the start of the fourth pitch of the Spear, the new Russian route on the east-southeast face of Kyzyl Asker.** *Oleg Khvostenko*

route the Spear (1,000m, 1,300m of climbing, 6B, UIAA V A3 M8). *See photo on next page.*

— **LINDSAY GRIFFIN**, *WITH INFO FROM ELENA DMITRENKO, RISK.RU, AND ANNA PIUNOVA, MOUNTAIN.RU*

GREAT WALLS OF CHINA, EAST FACE, TEARS OF THE DRAGON

FROM JULY 20–23, the Russian expedition of Olesya Babushkina, Marina Popova, Denis Prokofyev, and Vladimir Sysoev made the first ascent of the east face of the northern summit of the Great Walls of China. The team had planned to attempt a new line on Kyzyl Asker, but when they arrived on the unnamed glacier south of the peak, two weeks of bad weather had covered the big southeast face in unstable snow and ice. In contrast, the east face of the Great Walls was relatively clear, so they opted for a line attempted in 2013 by Vincent Perrin and Bas Visscher (Netherlands). These two had struggled with wet rock, difficult aid, and icefall before retreating from about one-quarter height on the wall.

The Russian team progressed up the wall with portaledge camps, finding the rock generally monolithic, with lots of overhanging sections and roofs. Once above the initial 200m section, which was subject to falling rock and ice, the steep wall made it safe from falling debris. When the sun was out, the team could climb in rock shoes for the first few hours of the morning, but from early afternoon on, water would stream down the wall, even though the sun had left it.

Above the dangerous first section, 600m of very steep rock, with a roof every 30m or so, led to a series of offwidths choked with ice. At one point here the team had to rappel 50m to reach another line farther right. On the fourth day of climbing, July 23, the four reached 45–60°

[Above] At left are the Great Walls of China. (1) Border Control (Robinson-Tressider, 2004). (2) Dutch attempt, 2013. (3) Dutch attempt, 2013. (4) Tears of the Dragon (2016). (A) Kyzyl Asker and (5) the 2016 Russian route (other routes not shown). (B) Panfilovski Division. (C) Pik Jerry Garcia. *Supplied by Denis Prokofyev*

snow and ice at the top of the wall and continued up the ridge above to gain the summit by evening. They returned to the portaledge that night and rappelled the route to the glacier on the following day. Bolts were left at 60m intervals.

The 810m route (1,150m of climbing) was named Tears of the Dragon (Russian 6B, A3 M5), the "tears" being the water constantly running down the wall in the afternoon and the "dragon" the symbol of China.

This formation, dubbed the Great Walls of China in 1997, has a high point of 5,186m at its northern end. This high point is near the middle of a long, almost horizontal summit ridge running northwest to southeast. In 2013, Vincent Perrin, Bas van der Smeed, and Bas Visscher climbed the north face to a 5,120m summit toward the northern end of this summit ridge. The summit reached by the Russians sits more toward the southern end of this ridge.

– LINDSAY GRIFFIN, *WITH INFO FROM ELENA DMITRENKO, RISK.RU, AND ANNA PIUNOVA, MOUNTAIN.RU*

QINGHAI

NYAINBO YUZE MASSIF, LE PETIT GÉANT AND JAOMA

INSPIRED BY AN article in AAJ 2014, Jessica Keil and I traveled to the Nyainbo Yuze range of Qinghai. In late September we flew to Chengdu and drove 10 hours to Jiuzhi, the nearest town to the range. Armed with only a crude Google Earth map, our severely perplexed Chinese driver—I couldn't blame him for wondering about dropping off two young American women in the middle of nowhere—ferried us into the range by way of dirt roads used by the local yak herders. Our driver faithfully continued until the muddy road became impassable. We helped unstick the car and waved good-bye.

We could now choose among three valleys. We were drawn to several rocky peaks in the northernmost valley, which to our knowledge had yet to be explored by climbers. Our camp

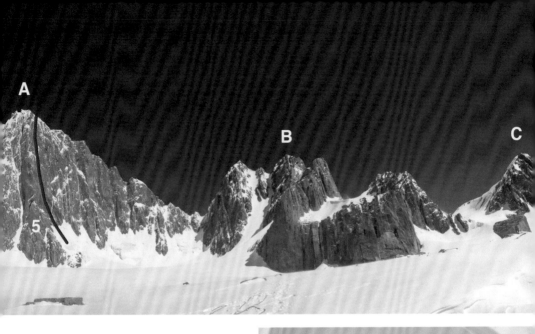

A

B

C

5

sat at 4,300m, above the outflow from a large lake, with most of our targeted peaks seemingly a short approach away.

Our first goal became a spire we later called Le Petit Géant, after the prominent feature above Chamonix's Vallée Blanche. We initially attempted its north face, which housed an aesthetic line, but after a battle with an ice-choked corner system we opted to revise tactics, hiking up and around to the sunny southeast aspect. There, a vegetated diagonal seam appeared to be the most feasible option. A pitch of gardening and horn lassoing on less than ideal rock led to two pitches of moderate free climbing and ultimately the summit (4,744m, 5.7 C2).

The following day we made our way to a peak the locals call Jaoma. We climbed two moderate pitches on the northeast ridge

[Above] **Looking southeast at Le Petit Géant, the prominent rock tower on the right, and Jaoma, the lower tower to the left, directly above the lake. Both ascent routes are hidden. Nyainbo Yuze (5,396m) is the large, snowy peak in the background, left of center.** *Tess Ferguson*

before reaching an impasse at a wide crack with poor rock. We opted to make a rappel onto the south face, where we found a pitch of excellent quality (5.8) leading to the 4,727m summit.

Back at camp we received a weather report showing precipitation for 10 days or more. Day after day of rain and snow completely coated the peaks in rime. On our 13th day in the range, we were awoken to the sound of yaks and soon discovered that two herders had moved their camp within 100m of our own. Over the next three days we spent much time with this couple, Matsu and Yaoushu. They spoke only Tibetan and we only English, but we managed to communicate. They fed us all sorts of interesting foods and let us warm by their yak-dung stove while the storm raged outside. Unfortunately, suitable climbing conditions never arrived, and after 18 days we had to begin our journey home. The herders ensured a safe and fast return to Jiuzhi, by way of their horses and their father's old station wagon, an incredible gesture on their part.

[Above] **Mark Smiley climbing the last mixed pitch on the first ascent of Lilliana Peak.** *Jason Wolfe*

Overall, the Nyainbo Yuze massif has the potential to be a mecca of moderate alpine rock climbing. While the peaks are relatively high, none of them boast huge vertical relief. The rock was of a reasonable quality in the valley that we visited, though we have heard lesser reviews of the valleys to the south. There are still countless rock lines to be had, and the potential for good ice, mixed, and ski lines is also promising. This expedition was funded in part by AAC Mountaineering Fellowship Grants. 📄 📷

— TESS FERGUSON, *USA*

SICHUAN / SHALULI SHAN

GANGGA RANGE, LILLIANA PEAK

IN SEPTEMBER, MARK Smiley and I decided to make a foray into the "West Sichuan Highlands," as Tom Nakamura describes the ranges on the eastern Tibetan frontier. Our plan was to travel overland to Ganzi, survey the area, and act opportunistically when we had a weather window.

We flew into Chengdu and continued with a two-day overland journey to Ganzi via the Sichuan-Tibet Highway. From here we traveled about 19km south along the well-constructed Ganbai road in the Zhuoda Qu (valley). Just before crossing Zhuodana Pass, we walked up a low ridge to ca 4,250m to see the mountains to the immediate west. These peaks are all referred to as the Gangga Range, despite there being a river valley, the Niyada Qu, between the range immediately west of the Zhuoda Qu and another range farther west containing the well-known Gangga I (5,688m). It wasn't clear if there would be better approaches to our peaks from the Niyada Qu, although Google Earth later showed this wasn't promising. After looking at our photos, we decided on a valley we could enter from the Zhuoda Qu, surrounded by three or four peaks in the 5,000–5,500m range. [*These lie in the same cluster of mountains as Asura*

Peak, climbed by an Australian, Japanese, and Scottish team in 2015 (AAJ 2016)].

We found a place to ford the river at what appeared to be a former gravel-mining site. With light packs, we followed a trail used by Tibetan farmers to a scree and boulder field. A small complex of rough stone buildings housing a Tibetan family appeared to be the only settlement in this valley. Rain was frequent and heavy, as it was much of the trip.

As we walked up the valley, we saw at least three potential climbs. Finding water and a campsite, we made our way back to the road, on the way stopping for tea with the Tibetans after they hailed us from a distance.

Next day we carried gear up to our campsite, where rain and sleet continued off and on for two more days before we received a window to climb. We headed west, up-valley, and decided on Peak 5,320m, to the north of camp. After booting up 35–40° snow slopes into a gully on the southwest face, we switched to crampons and ice tools and continued quickly and unroped on a 45° slope, eventually reaching a saddle between two rock peaks.

Initially we worked left, mostly on rock that was decidedly rotten in places. After 40–50m we reached an exposed ridge. Once there, it was obvious this was not the high point, so we rappelled to the saddle and started up the other side. Mark led up a snow and ice gully, winding toward the summit. After 60m of M2 we arrived on the summit (31°30'0.1"N, 99°57'16.9"E). Our peak had no known Tibetan name. We suggested Lilliana Peak, which the Sichuan Mountaineering Association has accepted. 📄 📷

– JASON WOLFE, *USA*

XIALONG REZHA, WEST FACE

IN EARLY NOVEMBER, Rob Baker, Mitch Murray, and I reached a point about 20m below the top of the previously undocumented Xialong Rezha (5,625m, based on two altimeter readings). The peak lies at 29.886444°N, 99.511519°E, to the west of the Genyen massif and to the southeast of the Yangmolong group. A quintessential Eastern Himalayan peak, Xialong Rezha is the closest mountain above 5,500m to the nearly completely closed border with Xizang (Tibet).

From the border town of Batang, a small road leads over a 5,000m pass that is almost unknown, even to locals. Xialong Rezha, which translates approximately as the "place of big-horned animals and large boulders," is clearly visible from a small hamlet at the end of this road, 25km from the

[Above] The west face of Xialong Rezha (5,625m) and the line of Standing Room Only. The top eight pitches are visible. The line stopped on the summit ridge, 20m below the highest point. *Rob Baker*

upper Yangtse River. With the aid of organizational legend Zhang Jiyue and of Alex Tang, who was instrumental in getting us to base camp, we planned to make our ascent with no additional support, a practice we have developed over many previous trips to western Sichuan and eastern Tibet. Our only limitations were the loads we could carry, acclimatization, and weather. With the latter we banked on a dependable early winter window, directly after the end of the last squall of the Asian monsoon and before the winter snows. We were not disappointed: There was an unbroken string of 15 days with no precipitation. We made base camp at 4,200m, a few kilometers above the hamlet, and then moved camp over marsh, boulders, and scree to 4,900m.

It was clear the prime route on the west face of Xialong Rezha was the offset central couloir. After climbing unroped up a 90m glacial snout to the cone below the couloir, we led in blocks, with the two seconders moving together for speed. Rob's run-out five pitches on decreasing-quality snow got us to the summit (north) ridge. I led a further half pitch along the ridge to a point where serious fall potential, with even worse snow on top of smooth slabs, offering no protection, deemed that we leave the bizarre summit formation unclimbed. We were always going to stop below the top anyway, out of respect for local Tibetan lore, so crossing the last bit of dangerous, low-angle terrain didn't seem worth it.

At 4 p.m. we began the many rappels that would get us back to camp by 10 p.m. On return to Batang we ate the hotel's entire supply of roast duck. We named our route to the high point Standing Room Only (650m of climbing, Scottish IV M4). The expedition was entirely self-funded, with no sponsors, no grants, no awards, and no film deals. 📷

– ED HANNAM, *AUSTRALIA*

GENYEN MASSIF, HUTSA, YAK ATTACK AND HOLOGRAPHIC JESUS; PEAK 5,912M, WEST FACE

ON SEPTEMBER 17 a multi-national team of three pairs—Tito Arosio and Luca Vallata (Italy), Peter Linney (Ireland) and James Monypenny (U.K.), and Tom Nichols (U.K.) and Rob Partridge (New Zealand)—assembled at Litang, the last outpost in the wild west of the Tibetan Plateau. Heather Swift (U.K.) was poised to join halfway through the trip. We were all linked through Monypenny, our expedition mastermind.

From Litang it took five hours by 4WD to reach the Rengo monastery, below the sacred peak of Genyen. Our hired horsemen arrived with 250cc "horses," strapped more than 60kgs to each motorbike, and drove up the narrow, rough, and sometimes steep valley path to establish our base camp at 4,200m.

[Below] Yak Attack on the west face of Hutsa. The arrows mark the striking steep couloir of Holographic Jesus. Farther right is a line attempted by Dave Anderson and partners. *James Monypenny*

That night we were woken by a magnitude 5.2 earthquake, filling camp with thoughts of being on an exposed section of a climb during an aftershock. We were now in the tail end of the monsoon season, so the weather was not ideal, but most days had a few hours of clear skies and sunshine.

Our main focus was Hutsa (5,863m, 29°54'2.96"N, 99°37'24.03"E), a peak attempted twice previously by

[Above] **Rob Partridge approaching difficult ice runnels on Yak Attack, west face of Hutsa.** *James Monypenny*

Dave Anderson and partners via a rock route from the south. Reconnaissance from advanced base revealed a steep ice line in a hidden couloir on the southwest face and some more approachable lines accessible from the tops of snow cones on the west face. We decided on the right-hand and steeper of two obvious options on the west face, leading directly to a snow slope that we hoped would take us to the summit ridge.

James, Peter, Tom, and I approached the first pitch as two pairs, but confidence waned in one of each pair, either due to a lack of recent mixed climbing or hypoglycemic compulsions, which had caused all the Snickers bars to be eaten before even tying in. With no real expectations of summiting, James and I pushed on. We swung leads, with sections of simul-climbing, up the 500m couloir. A snow ramp led to the summit ridge, where four long pitches with some interesting short, steep mixed sections led to the top. From here we could see many unclimbed granite peaks, all of which could only be climbed via steep mixed or rock lines. We rappelled the top four pitches, then a slightly more direct line back into the initial couloir, and returned to advanced base in a round trip of 17 hours. We named the line Yak Attack (800m, Scottish 6 / M5).

Returning to base camp, we rested and witnessed the change of seasons: At dawn on October 1 the monsoon was clearly over. The wind changed to the north, the summit of Genyen was visible for the rest of our time in the area, and the forecast was good. Now acclimatized, and with a better idea of conditions, the full team's psyche was restored, and we headed back to advanced base in our original pairs. Tom and I failed on our attempt to repeat the line that James and I climbed on Hutsa, but James and Peter made an incredible ascent of the steep ice line in the hidden couloir. They summited long after midnight, returning to camp after almost 30 hours, much to the relief of Heather, who had walked in to meet them. James and Pete gave the line WI6 M6 and named it Holographic Jesus, having purchased a holographic wall hanging of Jesus' Last Supper at the monastery shop.

Tito and Luca had reconnoitered an unclimbed 5,912m peak northeast of Hutsa, and from September 30 to October 2 they climbed the west face via a system of snowfields and ridges on the southern side of the wall. (Two bivouacs were needed due to uncertain weather on the first day.) Climbing through several crux rock bands, protected by pitons, they summited and then descended the northern part of the face. Difficulties were rated at D M4 70° snow.

Inspired by the splitter cracks in Dave Anderson's photos, and with a clear weather window for the remainder of the trip, James, Heather, and I repeated the south ridge of sharp-beaked Sachun (5,716m, Anderson-Huenien, 2006). Thirteen pitches brought us to the final spires, where, pulling all the tricks out of the bag, James climbed the final two pitches to à cheval the summit spire via some very bold climbing. 📖 📷

— ROB PARTRIDGE, *U.K. AND NEW ZEALAND*

YUNNAN

BALAGEZONG MASSIF: UNCLIMBED PEAKS AND OBSERVATIONS ON THE INFLUX OF TOURISM

IN JANUARY 2004 a letter arrived from William Bueler in Colorado (author of the Roof of the Rockies climbing history) with a brief description, maps, and pictures of his reconnaissance of Balagezong (5,545m) the previous year. I knew of this soaring peak, since I had seen it from afar in 1993, but to the best of my knowledge Bueler was the first to reconnoiter the massif with the intention of climbing there. Balagezong stayed in my mind thereafter, but it wasn't until May 2016 that I got the opportunity to visit.

The development of tourism in Yunnan and Sichuan is progressing at extraordinary speed, replacing traditional industry. New roads, bridges, and tunnels are being built through the mountains, visitors are appearing from every corner of China, and the Dagu Glacier Scenic Park now has a cable car to a 4,800m viewpoint. Thirteen years ago, it took Bueler eight days to trek on foot to Balagezong; now it is less than two hours' drive from Shangri La Airport to the village of Shuishuang (2,320m) at the mountain's base, where there are new four- and five-star hotels.

[Top] **The holy mountain of Balagezong (main summit on the left), viewed from Bala to the east.** [Middle] **Shangbala Stupa (Natural Stupa, ca 5,000m, left) and to its right (east) an unnamed rock peak of about 5,000m.** [Bottom] **Unnamed and unclimbed summit above 4,700m in the Balagezong massif.** *Tamotsu Nakamura*

As tourism progresses, controls over Tibetans have become tighter. Restrictions on foreigners entering East Tibet also have become much tighter. Two years ago, it was possible to drive across the border from Yunnan or Sichuan—not any more. Procedures for foreigners entering unopened areas

[Above] The Primitive Buttress in Laojunshan National Park in Liming, showing the approximate lines of (1) Lost World, (2) Back to the Primitive, and (3) Dawn Chimney. Each is about 8 pitches. The Lost World shows evidence of local people climbing the chimney at least 60 meters off the ground more than a century ago. *Mike Dobie*

have become very complex and time-consuming.

The Balagezong massif lies close to the meeting point of Tibet, Yunnan, and Sichuan. A shuttle bus leads from Shuishuang to the hamlet of Bala (17km) and then a further 23km to a pass at 4,250m, which provides a fine viewpoint of the mountains. Most of the mountains in this area are from 4,700m to 5,000m and form striking rock summits with large walls. All are unclimbed. A full report of this trip, with more information and photos, can be found at the AAJ website. 📷 🔍

— TAMOTSU NAKAMURA, *AAC HONORARY MEMBER, JAPAN*

LIMING, PRIMITIVE BUTTRESS, LOST WORLD AND DAWN CHIMNEY

ADAM PECAN AND I met in Liming (Li Ming) and spent October through early December, 2015, establishing free routes to the tops of impressive walls in the main valley described in AAJ 2012 and 2013. The highest wall in the area, at just over 200m, is dubbed the Primitive Buttress, after the first route to reach the top of the formation: Back to the Primitive (8 pitches, III 5.11 A0, Dobie-Rasmussen, 2012). We began work on a line left of Back to the Primitive known as the Lost World (5 pitches, III 5.11). More than 100 years ago, locals pecked holes into the chimney 60m above the ground, and then evidently bashed in sticks to create a ladder, probably to access honey. Modern climbers Eben Farnsworth and Sarah Rasmussen pushed the line past the locals' high point in 2012, but they retreated after a 35m run-out squeeze chimney. When Adam and I showed up, only pitch four remained unclimbed—the best on the route but also the hardest, at 5.11, with a 15cm (6") crack through a roof. Above this, the line joins Back to the Primitive, which it follows to the top.

Next up was a line started by the Chinese climber Griff, who called it Dawn Chimney. Acting on reports of loose rock in the flake system, Adam and I prepared the route from the top. The last two pitches were cleaned of enormous quantities of dirt and vegetation, exposing bomber rock. We also placed bolts to protect sections where natural gear might be suspect. On our first attempt we were successful in freeing what is now the tallest line in Liming: Dawn Chimney (8 pitches, IV 5.10+). 📷

— BRANDON GOTTUNG, *USA*

JAPAN

[Photo] Keita Kurakami sticks the 5.14a deadpoint after an eight-meter runout on pitch three of Senjitsu-no Ruri (250m, 5.14a R/X). *Satoru Hagiwara*

MT. MIZUGAKI, MOAI FACE, FIRST FREE ASCENT

THE MOAI FACE is a smooth wave of granite that rises out of the pines at Mt. Mizugaki, one of Japan's premier traditional rock climbing crags. The nearly blank, 110m headwall appeared to be stunning to climb but very hard to protect, and the traditional ethic is strong at Mt. Mizugaki. It was in this spirit that I began the quest for a ground-up ascent of the Moai Face with Yusuke Sato. However, I soon realized that going ground-up would require placing bolts to be safe. In order to maintain the traditional protection style, we changed tactics to a top-down, "headpoint" approach. With much practice over six months, we were able to climb each pitch free and discover the available protection—some pitches had as few as three pieces of gear.

On October 18, 2015, I attempted to lead the entire route. Some pitches required multiple attempts; however, I succeeded in making a clean redpoint lead of all seven pitches, using only cams, nuts, and skyhooks for protection. (I had placed bolts only for anchors at natural stances, a ledge-to-ledge strategy.) The crux pitches two through four are 5.13c, 5.14a, and 5.13d, respectively, all with substantial runouts. The hardest sequence, a 5.14a deadpoint move to a sloping hold, is 8m above the last gear. It took immense focus to execute these hard moves while exposed to big falls. The next day, Yusuke free climbed each pitch on lead as well. We were excited with this success, but the story of the route was not over. On April 23, 2016, we returned to the Moai Face to make a one-day continuous ascent from the ground, with no falls, climbing the route in the best style.

We named the route Senjitsu-no Ruri (250m, 5.14a R/X). Senjitsu-no literally means "thousand days" and "ruri" is the jewel lapis lazuli. I compared "thousand days jewel" to a thousand days of precious experiences through climbing. 📷 🔍

– KEITA KURAKAMI, *JAPAN*

THE KUROBE GOLDEN PILLAR
32 DAYS IN THE NORTHERN ALPS IN WINTER

BY HIROSHI HAGIWARA

TOP ALPINISTS HAVE two main "practice climbs" within Japan to prepare for the Himalaya. "Pachinko" involves a linkup of 200m to 600m walls and mixed ridge climbing in the Mt. Hotaka region. Pachinko means "pinball," and the climbs are so named because of their zigzagging nature. The other training climb is the Kurobe Traverse. Starting from the east side of the Northern Alps, climbers first ascend Mt. Kashima-yari (2,889m) and then continue west to the bottom of the Kurobe Valley and across the Kurobe River. They then traverse a precarious snow ridge to reach Mt. Tsurugi (2,999m), which can be ascended via various ridges. The Japanese Northern Alps are not particularly high, but winter conditions present formidable challenges. The proximity to the sea brings harsh winds laden with moisture, and nighttime snow accumulations of a meter or more are common. Completing the Kurobe Traverse in winter is like a graduation test for Japanese alpinists.

In February, Koji Itoh, Kimihiro Miyagi, and Yusuke Sato made the first ascent of the "Kurobe Golden Pillar" during a 32-day winter traverse of the Kurobe Valley. This steep 380m

[Top] The extremely rugged Kurobe River Gorge, with the 11-pitch line of the Golden Pillar in center and Mt. Tsurugi (2,999m) in the background. [Bottom] Yuke Sato makes his way across the Kurobe River en route to the first ascent of the Golden Pillar. *Expedition Photos*

formation is in the middle of the rugged traverse, near the Tsurugisawa waterfall. The name is a reference to the Golden Pillar of Spantik in the Karakoram, which Sato climbed in 2009.

Koji Itoh, a veteran climber with ascents of the north face of Kwangde (Nepal) in 2002 and a new route on the west face of Mt. Rishiri (Japan) in winter, had twice before done the Kurobe Traverse in winter. However, he was still hoping for the right conditions to attempt the Golden Pillar.

The team started on February 3 at Otanihara, on the east side of the Northern Alps. They reached the summit of Mt. Kashima-yari on February 5 and descended the Ushikubi Ridge toward the Kurobe River, waiting in a snow cave for avalanche conditions to improve. (In all, the climbers spent 19 nights in snow caves because of massive snowfalls.) They would need a three-day window of good weather to attempt the unclimbed Golden Pillar. When the time came, they stripped naked and swam the icy river, hauling their gear across in dry bags, and then approached the buttress through an avalanche-prone gorge. They began their climb at 3 p.m. on February 25, three weeks after leaving the road.

The Golden Pillar is a very steep mixed wall, yet brush-covered and laden with snow. Nine hanging belays were required. After climbing three pitches, they reached a small snow terrace, set up their tent, and continued climbing in order to fix two more pitches. The next day they pushed to the summit through deteriorating weather, completing the Kurobe Golden Pillar (380m, 11 pitches, IV ED2 V+ 80°). They descended by rappelling the route.

The team had seven days of food remaining, so they decided to go for the summit of Mt. Tsurugi. However, a spell of bad weather forced them to wait until March 4 to climb the peak, via a long ridge. The next day they descended the Hayatsuki Ridge to Banbajima and finished their 32-day expedition.

SUMMARY: First ascent of Kurobe Golden Pillar (380m, IV ED2 V+ 80°), during a 32-day winter traverse of the Northern Alps, by Koji Itoh, Kimihiro Miyagi, and Yusuke Sato, February 2016.

[Top] Yusuke Sato, Koji Itoh, and Kimihiro Miyagi (left to right) at the start of the Kurobe winter traverse. Each climber began the month-long expedition carrying, among other things, 11 kilograms of rice. [Bottom] Yusuke Sato leading steep snow- and brush-covered rock on the ninth pitch of the Kurobe Golden Pillar. *Expedition Photos*

AUSTRALASIA

MT. WILHELM, FIRST KNOWN ROCK CLIMBS

RISING TO 4,509m above the rainforests of Papua New Guinea, Mt. Wilhelm is the highest peak in the country. With a glaciated past, Mt. Wilhelm has scenic lakes and several steep rock faces—the latter *not* covered in the dense rainforest that smothers lower-elevation walls at this latitude. The mountain is a somewhat popular trekking destination, but locals and mountaineering databases all were in agreement: Technical rock climbing likely had never taken place there.

Gaby Lappe, Clemens Pischel, and I visited the area in July with rock climbing as our goal. After ascending from the village of Keglsugl to the beautiful Pindaunde Lakes, halfway up the mountain, we first established Muglo dude po (UIAA V+, "The Direct Ascent") on Point 4,054m. This subpeak is located just above the Mt. Wilhelm Track (trekking route), and the route involved three technical pitches (fully bolted) in addition to 60m of scrambling. We then moved on to Mt. Wilhelm, where we established Kammoro dumara (140m, UIAA VI+, "Where Earth Meets Sky") on the northeast wall. The route climbs four pitches (fully bolted) in a direct line to the summit. More information, including maps and topos, can be found at the AAJ website. 📷 🔍

– KAI MALUCK, *GERMANY*

[Top] Lukas Kirchner on the new route Thales, Mt. Aspiring. *Janette Heung* [Bottom] The northeast face of Mt. Wilhelm (4,509m). Kammoro dumara (140m, VI+) goes up the center of the wall. *Kai Maluck*

MT. ASPIRING, SOUTH FACE, THALES

KNOWN FOR ITS iconic pyramid shape, Mt. Aspiring is often called the "Matterhorn of the South," as it is the only peak above 3,000m outside of the Aoraki/Mt. Cook region and it towers above its surroundings, mesmerizing all who see it. In the days leading up my attempt, I was warmly welcomed by the local climbing community, who were generous with their advice. Allan Uren, a local climber, showed me what he thought could be an aesthetic and direct new line up Aspiring's south face. When a weather window emerged between September 9 and 11, I met up with Lukas

[Above] Janette Heung on Coxcomb Ridge, Mt. Aspiring. *Lukas Kirchner*

Kirchner, an experienced German alpinist and Kiwi transplant, to make an attempt.

We tramped (New Zealandese for "hiking") for a few hours to reach the Matukituki River, near which we spent the night, and then tramped up the French Ridge the next day to reach the base of Aspiring's southwest ridge, where we bivied in a snow cave on Bonar Glacier. We awoke to a calm morning sky, with Uren's proposed line up the 500m south face beckoning. After surmounting a bergschrund at the base, we simulclimbed moderate alpine ice that was, for the most part, in great condition. We began to swap leads in blocks, encountering occasional thinner, mixed sections, which added engaging variety to the long stretches of alpine ice.

After being in the shade all day on the south face, topping out onto the Coxcomb Ridge into the warm afternoon sun felt instantly rejuvenating. We safely reached the summit by late afternoon and carefully descended the northwest ridge. We named the route Thales, in honor of the ancient Greek philosopher's thoughts on fluidity and mindfulness. (750m climbing distance, which includes the 500m south face and part of the Coxcomb Ridge, NZ 5). [*Editor's note: The new line starts near Perspiring (2005) and Shooting Star (2014) and continues directly up toward the Coxcomb Ridge where those routes bear left.*] 📷

– JANETTE HEUNG, *USA*

FASTNESS PEAK, EAST FACE, SOLO WINTER ASCENT BY NEW ROUTE

FASTNESS PEAK (2,383M) dominates the skyline above Ruth Flat in the Mt. Aspiring region. The east face is a forbidding wall of compact schist streaked with ice runnels. The first winter ascent was made in 1997 by Clinton Beavan, Al Uren, and Al Wood, who established Storming the Barbican (16 pitches, VI 6) over two days. This face has been largely neglected since that climb, especially during the cold winter months; however, Guy McKinnon made a bold first solo ascent along the original 1990 Sveticic-Dickson Route (IV 5) in the austral summer of 2014.

My idea to make a solo winter attempt on the face didn't really take hold until I chatted with Al Uren in mid-July. Looking back, I should have paid more attention when he asked if I was planning to take skis or snowshoes for the approach up Rainbow Stream. At the time I laughed off the idea: I can't ski to save myself on the best of days, and the valley is only around 5km long. How hard could it be? After more than six hours of wading through knee- to waist-

[Above] The east face of Fastness Peak (2,383m). (1) Storming the Barbican (16 pitches, VI 6, Beavan-Uren-Wood, 1997). (2) Sveticic-Dickson Route (IV 5, 1990). (3) Dare Route (700m, VI 6, 2016). *Danilo Hegg*

deep snow, and one rather cold and unpleasant bivy, I had the answer! I had set out from Queenstown on August 5 with an improving weather forecast. In fact, it would snow almost continuously for the next two days, but the promise of improvement kept me going.

In the morning, as I dropped off the toe of the east ridge toward the foot of the face, fleeting glimpses through the swirling cloud revealed the lower face to be banked with loose snow. The main central gullies flowed with a continuous stream of spindrift, but broken ground to the right seemed to hold less snow. After a harrowing traverse, the conditions began to improve and the deep snow quickly turned to ice and rock. I had chosen a line right of center on the face, leading to the north ridge, to the right of the two existing routes. Climbing the first ice step, I slowly gained confidence. As the day progressed, I belayed myself through steep ice and mixed cruxes and free-soloed the rest. The climb was sustained, primarily on thin alpine ice and névé runnels that linked through a series of blank rock steps.

As dusk fell the persistent cloud cover slowly broke and I made my way through the final hurdle to gain the snow slopes below the upper north ridge. [*Editor's note: Dare's unnamed 700m route went at VI 6 or WI5 M5 A1.*] The weather was finally fulfilling the promise of the original forecast—a case of too little too late. Darkness overtook me as I labored through the deep snow, robbing me of the opportunity to enjoy the view from the ridge crest. A long, cold traverse over the foresummit, followed by an arduous descent of the east ridge into a swirling mist of wind-driven snow, reinforced how wild the New Zealand mountains can be. The climb pushed me close to my limits, and I had little left as I finally collapsed into my bivy at the head of Rainbow Stream. Never has a damp and partially frozen sleeping bag felt so warm and inviting.

The following afternoon I had a fortuitous meeting with Al Uren, and we discussed the merits of various approach tactics over cold beers at the historic Cardrona Hotel. We laughed at the struggles I had endured while breaking trail, discussed the hardships of solo climbs, and swapped stories about our experiences on the face. He recounted the adventures of its first winter ascent nearly two decades before, when he and his partners had shivered for a night without food or shelter before shaking off the numbing cold to tackle the crux ice pitch below the summit. Al and I had in some ways shared an adventure. Yet our climbs also stand apart in the unique memories that we each have, and this paradox will make the journey special to me.

Twenty years is a long time between visits, but it does cause the experience to become that much sweeter. I hope the face won't lie neglected for another 20 years.

– **BEN DARE**, *NEW ZEALAND*

SUMMARY OF 2016 NEW ROUTES

[Above] **Mt. Aspiring (3,033m) showing the first ascent of the northwest face (700m, Dare-Murphy-Skelton, 2016). The classic north buttress rises just to the left.** *Ben Dare*

THE MAJORITY OF new-route activity in New Zealand during 2016 occurred during the summer period, with a number of new alpine rock climbs. Starting in the Darran Mountains, in January, Conor Smith and I climbed the northeast face of Pyramid Peak (2,295m), covering 250m of new ground to the right of the 2002 Brown-Williams Route to reach the upper north ridge (grade 18/5.10a). I then paired up with Stephen Skelton for a new line on the northeast face of Marian Peak (2,102m), called End of the Earth, Top of the World (500m, 18/5.10a), and then to make the first ascent of the south face of Mt. Tuhawaiki (2,092m) via Bloody Jack (500m, IV, 4, 19/5.10b).

Farther north, on the main divide, Pete Harris and Alastair McDowell made the first ascent of the west ridge of Mt. Percy Smith (2,465m). Michael Eatson, Tawny Flagstaff, and Trev Ponting teamed up to climb a new route on the east face of Mt. Arrowsmith (2,723m): The Outlier (350m, IV, 4, 20/5.10c). And Steven Fortune and Kieran Parsons established Oma Rapeti (600m, IV, 4+, 17/5.9) on the southwest face of Mt. Huxley (2,505m). Finally, Stephen Skelton and I teamed up with Danny Murphy to make the first ascent of the northwest face of Mt. Aspiring (3,033m). We climbed 700m of new ground, at grade IV, 6, 19/5.10b, to join the upper north buttress just below the summit.

Moving into the winter season, Steven Fortune, Kieran Parsons, and Conor Smith made the most of thin conditions to put up a technical five-pitch mixed and ice line on the east face of Mt. Talbot (2,105m): Tears of Papatuanuku (IV, 7). I made the second winter ascent of the east face of Fastness Peak via a new 700m route, and Lukas Kirchner and Janette Heung established a new route on the south face of Mt. Aspiring (*see report above*). To round out the year, Richard Bassett-Smith and Stuart Hollaway made the first ascent of a new ice and mixed line on the Hidden Face of Mt. Tasman (3,497m) in mid-December: One Longer Day (VI, 5+). Unfortunately, this was to be Stu's last climb, as he was tragically killed, along with his partner, Dale Thistlethwaite, descending from Mt. Silberhorn later that month.

– **BEN DARE**, *NEW ZEALAND*

BOOK REVIEWS

EDITED BY **DAVID STEVENSON**

THE BOND: SURVIVAL ON DENALI AND MOUNT HUNTINGTON

SIMON MCCARTNEY. Mountaineers Books, 2016. Paperback, 304 pages, $19.95.

STANDING BENEATH THE north face of Alaska's Mt. Huntington, one cannot help but feel an overwhelming sense of awe. There is disbelief that such precarious seracs can cling to a wall so steep; disbelief that nature can produce something so beautifully sinister; disbelief that anyone was once mad enough to climb it; and, ultimately, disbelief that they survived. The 1978 climb of the Timeless Face, as it came to be known, remains one of the most legendary ascents in Alaskan climbing history. Yet, for more than three decades, almost nothing was known about it.

The brief but explosive partnership of Jack Roberts and Simon McCartney has been at the center of Alaska climbing lore, but other than a few *AAJ* entries, few details have ever emerged to separate truth from hearsay since their short marriage in the mountains. Certain accomplished alpinists doubted that Roberts and McCartney had actually climbed Huntington's north face at all. Perhaps to not give the doubters a stance, Roberts was reticent in his own defense. No one knew what happened to Simon McCartney. Many figured he had died.

When McCartney resurfaced nearly four decades later with his mountaineering memoir, I was elated to find the answers to such an astounding mountaineering mystery. Credible sources proved without a shadow of a doubt that Roberts and McCartney had indeed climbed the Timeless Face, and the ascent is chronicled here in terrifying detail. After his two monumental Alaska ascents (the other being Denali's southwest face) McCartney did the one thing that is perhaps hardest for an obsessive climber: He stepped away completely. Roberts continued climbing at a high level until his death in 2012, while McCartney moved to Australia and China and built a very successful lighting company. He did his best to put the life-changing experiences in Alaska as far in his past as possible. In the age before cell phones and email, he and Roberts lost touch.

As someone for whom alpinism is still the driving force in life, I've always wondered how one could suddenly walk away from it all. *The Bond* answered those questions for me. Simon McCartney knew he wanted to live life to the fullest, but the trajectory of his climbing most likely would have cut his life short. All of McCartney's emotions from his timeless adventures resurfaced in his late 50s, and the result is one of the most refreshing works of mountaineering literature to appear in the last few decades. To climb the futuristic routes that he and Roberts climbed took a strength and vision that I struggle to comprehend. To walk away at one's peak is a strength that I only now understand after reading *The Bond*, a magnificent account of partnership, indescribable trials, and one man knowing when he had reached the end of his rope. [*Editor's note: This book won the 2016 Boardman-Tasker Award.*]

– CLINT HELANDER

VALLEY WALLS: A MEMOIR OF CLIMBING AND LIVING IN YOSEMITE

Glen Denny. Yosemite Conservancy, 2016. Paperback, 240 pages, $18.95.

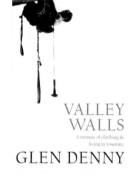

EVERY ONCE IN a while, a book poetically depicting the core essence of the climbing experience comes along—books carrying the reader to the grip of the moment, on a crux move on a demanding climb, say, while also painting an expansive awareness of the experience. Glen Denny's *Valley Walls* rings to the heart, offering a sharp and insightful translation of the oft-ephemeral big-wall experience to the written page. The book is a collection of snapshots, moments in time revealed in colorful light with words, and contrastingly complemented by Denny's soulful black and white images of the era.

Denny's stories softly and candidly describe his upbringing among the Valley masters, during the later-coined "Golden Age" of Yosemite big-wall climbing. He relates the means by which he integrated himself into the hierarchy of Valley denizens while absorbing the latest techniques of moving on the vertical. Throughout the book, one gains a glimpse of traditional skills that a rock climber had to master back in the day before moving onto more difficult climbs. Joining Denny on his exploration of Mt. Whitney, one gets a sense of his natural abilities in finding the best line through a sea of likely paths, a lost art in modern climbing. His tales of discovering winter challenges with the gear of the era on the steep, icy slabs of Glacier Point Apron boggle the mind.

One of my favorite vignettes is the short chapter "The Endless Night," about Denny's first night on a big wall, supporting Warren Harding and Chuck Pratt's first ascent of the east face of Washington's Column (now Astroman). He recollects his upward journey on prusiks in the dark: "Our voices sounded too loud in the still night air, like they might shake something loose."

The book also offers new glimpses into the well-known legends of the era: fresh insight on Harding's early climbing personality, for example, and firsthand insight on the enigmatic characters of the day, such as Denny's description of the contented smile on Chuck Pratt's sleeping face after a full day on the big stone ("The demon had been exorcised"). Dozens of climbers whose names hitherto might be only vaguely associated with a Valley climb or two are brought to light. The book ends with the third ascent of the Nose, with Steve Roper and Layton Kor, at a time when the climb was still assumed untouchable by mere mortals. Denny's hard work at perfecting his skills is now clear, despite his modest renditions in these stories.

A vivid depiction of the climbing life, the ceaseless struggle between confidence and doubt, and the intensity of the vertical world awaits the reader of *Valley Walls*. Highly recommended.

– JOHN MIDDENDORF

A PLACE IN WHICH TO SEARCH: SUMMERS IN THE WIND RIVERS

Joe Kelsey. Black Canyon Books, 2016. Paperback, 269 pages, $18.

IN AUGUST 1969, Joe Kelsey set out alone to hike eight dusty miles into the mountains from Big Sandy Opening. In this inaugural trip to the Wind River Range, Kelsey missed a switchback at Jackass Pass and wandered into a meadow of tumbled granite, not knowing he was lost. He soon regained the trail to Lonesome Lake, and next morning, he writes, "I woke up…knowing

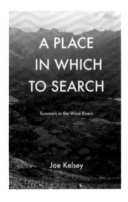

I had come home." Kelsey has spent every summer since then in the Wind Rivers, where he first encountered "a place in which to search." The title hearkens back to the records of a 16th-century Spanish expedition across the West: "They did not find the riches of which they had been told, they found a place in which to search for them…. Now when it is too late they enjoy telling about what they saw, and even of what they realize they lost."

During a hundred trips, Joe Kelsey established several first ascents in the Winds and published numerous articles about the range, as well as the beloved guidebook *Climbing and Hiking in the Wind River Mountains*. But there's little in the way of the blow-by-blow accounts of adventuresome first ascents in Kelsey's memoir.

Rather, *A Place in Which to Search* offers the reader a series of vignettes, rife with historical detail, poetic fragments, and philosophical notes about life and the quest to find meaning in the mountains. And yet the reader is left with the impression that Kelsey conceals as much as he reveals. Characters emerge and disappear, naked of context outside of their actions or role in a particular story. Tales of Vulgarian charades, a skittish golden retriever, an arrowhead on a fourth-class summit, and Bonneville's 1833 journey through the vague geography of a mythical West emerge to form a collection of Wind River portraits, with plenty of silence still hanging in the margins.

Don Mellor, in his history of climbing, *American Rock* (2001), notes that adventure is an essential element to any Wind River experience. "The Wind Rivers," he writes, is still "a range cherished for its secrets." Through various stories, Kelsey examines the fragile paradox of modern exploration: the desire for both mystery and understanding, and that the journey into the unknown eventually blots mystery out. In order to continue, the explorer must always seek new questions; the mountaineer, new heights. While Kelsey continues to find "meaning and pleasure…in the questing," at the same time he manages to avoid over-mythologizing his personal experience. At one point, while he and his partner navigate a precarious gully of ice, meltwater, and rock, Kelsey notes, "This is a classic mountaineering predicament but is not magical." To spend time in *A Place in Which to Search* is to meander through moments of lakeside musings and backcountry scrambling—to encounter the rough, bright fragments of a life spent searching in the wild.

— PAULA WRIGHT

ABOVE THE REICH

DAVID CHAUNDY-SMART. Imaginary Mountain Surveyors, 2016. Paperback, 231 pages, $19.95.

"THE NAZIS SAID war was the same as mountaineering. They lied." Thus speaks Lukas Eichel, orphan turned reluctant German soldier in World War II, in David Chaundy-Smart's debut novel. Lukas never embraces the Nazi climbing ethos that blazing up nordwands defeats, even "murders," a mountain.

Still, as a young man in the wrong country at the wrong time, Lukas' fate is intricately wound with the Nazi establishment, especially when his love of alpinism dovetails with the fascist party's desire for international fame. Hungry for a home after the bewildering power plays of a Munich orphanage, Lukas finds comfort in the Alps, in the driving of pitons or the straightforward escape of abseiling. As Nazi Germany rises around him, he savors alpine isolation, though it's his climbing partners who fuel the story. Lukas comes alive not on the battlefront but when he ties in on the mountain, belaying a series of colorful characters—an SS officer, an American, a mixed-race African—that goad him into camaraderie, action, and rebellion.

David Chaundy-Smart

Chaundy-Smart, the founding editor of Canadian climbing magazine *Gripped*, takes care to paint the Nazi characters with equal parts collective perversion and individual motivation. Lukas may not care much for the fascist philosophy, but there's claustrophobia in the fact that these are literally the only people he knows. While the regime's horrors are mostly alluded to, in oblique mentions of medical experiments and watchtower guards, Chaundy-Smart nails the stew of bravado and insecurity that powers the National Socialists; Lukas' childhood friend Dietrich is casually racist but goes apoplectic about anyone mocking his ascendant party.

Dietrich's fury takes national form with German failure in the Himalayan race, where the British held a stranglehold on Everest; Nanga Parbat became the German objective, more significant simply because it was *theirs*. In a move that efficiently distances the book from Heinrich Harrer and real events, Chaundy-Smart uses a Nanga Parbat stand-in, imagining a 7,348-meter Himalayan peak called Istighfar. Its bluish ice slopes and kilometer-high ice wall, littered with the remains of failed expeditions, make a convenient objective after Lukas and the novel have been worn down by the pernicious Reich.

Lukas' disinterest in fame or power makes him invulnerable to the macho Nazi climbing philosophy, and today the nationalistic concept of climbing solely for the homeland feels outdated. But Chaundry-Smart makes a more subtle argument: It isn't merely vanity that sours the Nazi outlook, but rather their irrational insistence on certainty: that Christian Germans are simply better, enemies are clearly evil, and to summit is to win. Lukas, having lost his family before he even understood it, embraces the open questions of mountaineering. He turns, he fails, he lets go of possessing much of anything. His first climb on the mighty Matterhorn is unremarkable, even ignoble. In the course of the novel, he's the only one who concedes to powers beyond his control and relies on partnerships forged on individual connection, not tribal affiliation. Wars are about beating someone else, but mountains aren't; it's that recognition of ambiguity that frees him. "As long as there is a centimeter of mountain left above me, nothing is decided," he says.

— ALLISON WILLIAMS

CONTINENTAL DIVIDE: A HISTORY OF AMERICAN MOUNTAINEERING

Maurice Isserman. Norton, 2016. Hardcover, 426 pages, $28.95.

Given climbers' obsession with meticulously chronicling ascents from 8,000 to 8 meters, it is odd to see how little actual history has been written on climbing in North America in recent decades. Local narratives such *Yankee Rock and Ice* or *Climb!* are important contributions, but they hardly synopsize the extraordinary developments that have occurred in climbing since its inception in this country in the later 19th century. The "classic" remains Chris Jones' *Climbing in North America*, which was published over 40 years ago, at a time of dramatic transformation of the sport. Jones' account was vividly written and accessible, retelling stories that, if perhaps too good to be true, were apparently too good not to be told. But was the book an actual history?

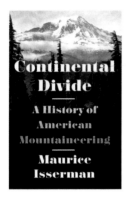

Even by the standards of 1976, the Jones book was a throwback to an idea of history as the account of the deeds of great men, mostly white, impressing their character upon a land ripe for conquest. Jones tended to avoid more sophisticated accounts of historical change rooted in theoretical contexts. A nod to changes in the post-WWII American economy or the counterculture movement of the 1960s or environmentalism, perhaps, but no deeper reading of the complex forces that shaped the sport over a period marked by extraordinary historical change.

Maurice Isserman, professor of history at Hamilton College and coauthor of *Fallen Giants*, a history of Himalayan climbing, has published a volume titled *Continental Divide: A History of American Mountaineering*, which is clearly intended to pick up to some degree where Jones left off. (At least methodologically—one of the odd commonalities of Isserman's book with its predecessor is that both authors omit any deep study of climbing after roughly 1970.) An interesting paradox found in comparing the two books is that the first is a history of climbing without much actual history, while the second could be considered a history of climbing without much actual climbing, taking, as it does, well over 100 pages to get to the point where we see genuine climbing discussed as opposed to hiking or scrambling.

The book's primary strengths start to show as Isserman discusses institutions such as the American Alpine Club and East Coast university outing clubs. It's in these contexts that the ideologies of modern climbing took form in this country, and Isserman's archival research is by far the most original and compelling portion of the book. Particularly interesting is a discussion of anti-Semitism and other forms of discrimination from very well-known figures in climbing, such as Robert Underhill. This makes an uncanny parallel with similar efforts in Austria and Germany to exclude Jews from associations such as the German Alpine Club.

In a sense, a historian of climbing has two distinct tasks. The first, which is relatively straightforward, is to narrate the events and personalities of climbing, while the second, anything but straightforward, is to answer the perennial question, "Why climb?" not merely in relation to individuals but to entire generations of individuals. We tell ourselves that climbing is a profoundly individualistic pursuit, but a good historian recognizes that many external factors affect our actions as climbers, including political ideologies such as nationalism, economic systems such as capitalism, and emergent technologies that enable access to climbing areas and climbing itself. Climbers are conflicted in exploring the implications of these seemingly abstract, impersonal, and anonymous forces, but a serious appraisal of the sport requires this effort, now more than ever. Isserman's book is a welcome step in that direction.

– PETER BEAL

THE PEN Y GWRYD HOTEL: TALES FROM THE SMOKE ROOM

Edited by Rob Goodfellow, Jonathan Copeland, and Peter O'NeilL. Gomer Press, Wales (U.K.), 2016. Hardcover, 278 pages, £14.99.

IMPOSSIBLE, YOU SAY! Could it be that the Beatles, George Mallory, Ed Hillary, Tenzing Norgay, John Hunt, Joe Brown, Don Whillans, Lionel Terray, Bill Tilman, Eric Shipton, Graham Chapman (*Monty Python*), and Anthony Hopkins (*Silence of the Lambs*) all walked through this very same front door? The answer is a resounding *Yes!*

The Pen Y Gwryd Hotel in Snowdonia, North Wales, is no ordinary wayfarer's inn. Founded in 1810 and known to climbers as the "PyG," this famed hostelry is justifiably renowned as "the home of British mountaineering." The inn was base camp for 19th-century alpinists—and for the 1953 Everest and 1954 Kanchenjunga expeditions. Both teams trained in Snowdonia and held reunions at the PyG for decades. The signatures of these illustrious mountaineers and others, plus assorted glitterati (think Roger Bannister, who broke the four-minute mile) grace the ceiling of the hotel's Everest Room.

Tales From the Smoke Room is an absolutely delightful and thoroughly varied compendium of short reminiscences about the hotel by over 60 individual contributors, among them 1953 Everest correspondent Jan Morris, Joe Brown, Sir Chris Bonington, Doug Scott, various environmentalists, former employees, historians, and even yours truly.

The "Smoke Room" of the title is the intimate sitting room housed directly behind the bar. (There's no smoking there these days, but for an idyllic setting to sip a fortifying pint, you could find no better.) Upon one wall of the Smoke Room is the glass-covered Everest Cabinet, with an assortment of "holy relics," including a piece of the rope that united Tenzing and Hillary on May 29, 1953. To fully experience the history of Himalayan and British mountaineering, and of Welsh rock climbing, a pilgrimage to the PyG in North Wales is required. Prepare yourself in advance by reading *Tales From the Smoke Room*, and then, after arriving, hoist your glass, make a heartfelt toast, and absorb not just the alcohol but also the unforgettable atmosphere of one of the world's greatest mountain inns.

— ED WEBSTER

ROCK QUEEN

CATHERINE DESTIVELLE. Hayloft Publishing, 2015. Paperback, 228 pages, £12.

CATHERINE DESTIVELLE'S MEMOIR *Rock Queen* spins the yarns of her most famous ascents—pioneering a solo new route on the Dru and soloing the north face of the Eiger in 17 hours, to name a couple—in palm-sweating detail. But just as fascinating are her vulnerable vignettes of life as one of the world's first female sponsored climbers. In a moment when female confidence is a hot topic in the media, Destivelle's raw combination of boldness and insecurities feels surprisingly fresh and timely.

Raised in Paris, Destivelle's first forays into climbing became a form of teenage rebellion. While her parents thought she was bouldering with the Alpine Club at Forêt de Fontainebleau, she was often sneaking off for weekends to race up classic routes in the Alps with an older (male) partner, feeding a growing addiction to pushing her limits. Her independence and audacity as a young person foreshadow her accomplishments as an adult—but the road to professional climbing wasn't a straight shot. Questions of motivation and ethics—and a gambling addiction—complicate the story.

Destivelle's anxiety and mixed feelings about competing in the first-ever international climbing competition in Italy—which she won—will resonate with any climber who's second-guessed his or her own motivations. And her open account of climbing in front of filmmaker Robert Nicod's camera, as well as the media and sponsorship flurry that followed, shed light on the complicated reality of climbing for money.

Destivelle's detailed telling of her 11-day solo quest up a new route on the west face of the Dru is at once riveting, humble, and accessible. After losing myself in the desperate and emotional moments of the climb, beginning to understand her deep personal need to climb, and empathizing with her embarrassment at receiving a helicopter ride down from the top (her hands were swollen with extremely painful, seeping wounds), I found myself amazed at the criticism she received regarding her motivations. Today we're used to seeing sponsors' logos and funded expeditions. But in 1991, Destivelle wasn't just pushing the limits of climbing, she was breaking new ground by cobbling together a living—having given up a career as a physiotherapist.

Destivelle comes across as a strong character, but she's not unaware of her faults, and one feels her mature throughout the book. I'm sure some subtleties in the writing are lost in translation from the French, but there are still notes of humor, and the reader is left with the sense of having met a woman who, despite insecurities, dreamed greatly of mountains and was unafraid to reach and risk for what she wanted.

— HILARY OLIVER

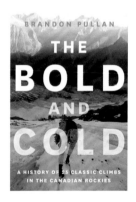

THE BOLD AND COLD: A HISTORY OF 25 CLASSIC CLIMBS IN THE CANADIAN ROCKIES

Brandon Pullan. Rocky Mountain Books (Canada), 2016. Hardcover, 264 pages, $45.

THE BOLD AND *Cold* is not a guidebook, nor a picture book, but it is essential reading and dreaming. In place on the shelf of old climbing magazines, where collectively is a repository scattered like gems amid choss, *The Bold and Cold* brings together an accounting of the Canadian Rockies in a manner that reveals a bright cord of courage, inspiration, and friendships running through the decades and stringing together the selected routes.

Pullan "inherited" this project from Urs Kallen, a longtime Rockies climber who compiled the original notes and list, and it runs from the CMC Wall on Yamnuska to the legendary north face of North Twin. This is not just the stories of the hard first ascents in the wilds of the Great White North, but a look at how these routes pushed standards and inspired those who would return to these same routes to measure themselves. As scoured rock can reveal the progress of a great glacier, so do these icy corners show how the epitome of the ideal has been advanced.

The overall experience of reading *The Bold and Cold* is of sitting around a low but hot campfire, surrounded by the cold night, hunched close, where the enthusiastic and awed voice of Pullan paints the mountains in your imagination. At each heavy pause he reclines into the circle of darkness while a different face leans in—the firelight throwing shadows upward on the lines that crease their life maps of determination and inner struggle—and another of the great climbers comes into the light, briefly, to tell a small part of the overall act. This method is mesmerizing. This is not an *accounting,* as in history; this is a necessity as in war story. And Pullan is the consummate host: never hogging the stage, merely facilitating others to tell the tale with their own humor and humanity.

Most of these routes may be out of reach of the average mountaineer, but the tales of their creation are the cave paintings and fire chants of our tribe, and their essence echoes far from their originating stone. And that is their true strength: to be the legends that are heard above the fear. For who could not be inspired when faltering on a lesser route to compare their own situation to the desperate commitment at the crux of a huge climb? This is a book that you carry within you and will return to, yet again, to run a calloused fingertip down the smooth words and try to find purchase on that elusive courage.

— JERRY AULD

SIXTY METERS TO ANYWHERE

Brendan Leonard. Mountaineers Books, 2016. Paperback, 176 pages, $16.95.

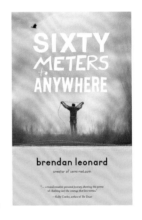

BRENDAN LEONARD IS a relentless machine. He blogs (semirad. com), designs T-shirts, posters, and memes, and he writes books about outdoor adventures. Much of this, one imagines, he does very quickly, and some of it is merely OK: mildly amusing, a quick blip in the infinite competition for 15 seconds of our attention. This book, however, is a serious, measured reflection worthy of every minute of our attention. The story is how an alcoholic Midwestern young man escapes his demons and finds focus and meaning in the climbing life.

When Leonard arrives in Missoula, Montana, for grad school at the age of 23 he had been sober for six months. He describes his intimidation at meeting his new colleagues, imagining his own self-introduction: "Hi, I'm a Small-Town Guy Who's Never Been Anywhere. I barely graduated from Public University in the Great Plains, and I just got out of jail." Most of the first 50 pages describe his "fight [against] a constant compulsion to drink alcohol."

As a recovery narrative, Leonard's is the exact opposite of James Frey's *A Million Little Pieces.* Frey's story was presented to the world as nonfiction when it was fiction, a highly exaggerated self-portrait in which the hero's flaws and triumphs are over-dramatized, with the apparent attempt to present the self as the ultimate badass (and make a lot of money). Leonard's self-presentation is calm and matter-of-fact; he's not the worst drunk we've known, nor the best climber. But he's very, very good at telling us what it's like to be human, and we believe his every word.

Fifty pages into the story, Leonard finally gets into the backcountry. It's not like the clouds open up and strike him with a divine calling. His epiphany, such as it is, comes in the form of questions: *"Could I come back here? What does it take to be a person who does this stuff? Can I be in the mountains again, and breathe the air, and feel small?"* The answers to these questions are yes, yes, and yes. Leonard is very good at describing actual climbing, but the climbs themselves (particularly their difficulty) are never central. I loved his description of an epic day on Mt. Hayden with a friend who was a beginner: "At the end, when you get to the car, or the tent, or just the bottom of the climb, your brain finally understands: I am not going to die today. There is no more doubt, no more fear, and you are warmed with a feeling of satisfaction, just enough so you start thinking, *Hey maybe I'd do that again. Not anytime soon, but what a day.*"

Leonard's nine-year relationship and marriage falls apart, he takes his parents climbing, and his beloved grandmother dies—none of these events is given short shrift here. Leonard may have thought he was simply telling us what it's like to be an alcoholic and a climber, but his story is larger: He shows us nothing less than what it is to be wholly human. I'm not an exceptional climber, he tells us, adding that he does, however, consider himself an "exceptional recovering addict." To that I would add: He is an exceptional writer as well.

– DAVID STEVENSON

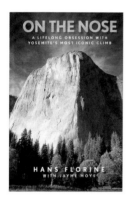

ON THE NOSE: A LIFELONG OBSESSION WITH YOSEMITE'S MOST ICONIC CLIMB

Hans Florine, with Jayme Moye. Falcon Guides, 2016. Hardcover, 240 pages, $25.

HANS FLORINE IS one of the great rock climbers of our generation, having reached that echelon primarily on the back of one climb: the Nose of El Capitan. He's had plenty of other gigs, with wins in climbing competitions around the world, but once he stepped foot on the Big Stone it would forever change his legacy. Undefeated for years in speed climbing, he became one of the first rock climbers known in the mainstream world, before Honnold came along and soloed his way to infamy.

Florine's *On The Nose*, coauthored with Jayme Moye, is a book that is filled with so much information that, at times, can feel like an over-explanation. The book is not just written for lifelong climbers but also for new climbers or even casual couch adventurers. As an experienced climber you'll rip through the pages and be swallowed by Florine's determination. There are few in the world who could tell you the exact second they finished a climb, and even fewer who would have calculated that finish to the second beforehand. This obsession seems at times a test of Florine's sanity as he struggles to shave seconds from a climb that begins to sound almost casual as he gains experience. When you remember that each event he relates is happening thousands of feet above the ground, then you know why your palms are sweating while reading. Each moment is told quickly, like it's another speed climb; the pages turn quickly as you work to keep up, and when you reach the end you'll be wishing for one more page.

– KELSEY GRAY

WARNINGS AGAINST MYSELF: MEDITATIONS ON A LIFE IN CLIMBING

David Stevenson. University of Washington Press, 2016. Hardcover, 248 pages, $29.95.

WE'RE ALL WELL-ACCUSTOMED to trip reports and lyrical, upbeat "finding myself" stories, among other variants, but in *Warnings Against Myself*, David Stevenson—purposefully or not—taps into a sort of Jungian collective unconscious of the mountaineering community and draws, from the smoldering embers of his yesterdays, a kind of mountaineer's dream. Thoughts about a climb, a person, a situation, a sunset are blended together—oftentimes with memories inserting themselves into other memories—at seemingly random times (the way in which real dreams happen), but with an acknowledgment that the dreams and memories relate to the event at hand. A simple outing with Steve Roper and Al Steck, for example, becomes the odd but fitting bookmarks of a memory about a car accident. Stories overlap too, just as in the subconscious. Stevenson's memory of getting a phone call about the death of Willi Unsoeld is presented twice, chapters apart, but in the author's layered style it fits, just as dreams and memories fold together into a greater understanding of existence.

The book is a retooled collection of literary pieces that Stevenson authored over several decades, all of which have appeared in journals and magazines. The title story, "Warnings Against Myself," is something of a sampler of the entire work, in which Stevenson learns about other climbers named Stevenson gaining attention for less-than-heroic acts, all the while lamenting the death of a friend—the pieces falling into place just as in a reverie. And it's in these ethereal interstices of the stories that Stevenson explores the heady themes we all experience, both in the mountains and back in our thinking chairs: isolation, solitude, joy, danger, pain, death. These lofty thoughts are peppered with reflections on the more base aspects of life—getting old and fat, having to pay bills, working too much, *familying* too little, commitments and constraints. He ties together these two worlds of the average Joe effortlessly.

Stevenson is gentle on the reader. There are few superlatives in his vocabulary, no shock attacks, and almost no foul language. His storytelling style is free of discursiveness and aggrandizement. In *Warnings* he gently, but completely, pulls the reader into a place we all know—whether we want to or not.

— CAMERON M. BURNS

NEW BOOKS IN BRIEF

The 9th Grade: 150 Years of Free Climbing, by David Chambre (Mountaineers Books, $50). A large-format, comprehensive history of free climbing; Eurocentric with terrific color photographs. **My Old Man and the Mountain, A Memoir, by Leif Whittaker** (Mountaineers, $24.95). The author retells the story of his father's famous ascent, interweaving their family lives and his own trips to Everest. **Night Naked: A Climber's Autobiography, by Erhard Loretan, with Jean Ammann.** (Mountaineers, $19.95). "One of the finest memoirs ever written by mountaineers," says David Roberts in his foreword. Enough said. **Alaska Range: Exploring the Last Great Wild, by Carl Battreall** (Mountaineers, $19.95). Spectacular alpine photography, with essays by Clint Helander, Roman Dial, Brian Okonek, Jeff Benowitz, and others. **Sherpa: The Memoir of Ang Tharkay, translated by Corrine McKay** (Mountaineers, $19.95). Appearing in English for the first time, the story the most renowned Sherpa who accompanied Shipton and Tillman and was sirdar for the 1950 French expedition to Annapurna. **Surviving Logan, by Eric Bjanason and Cathi Shaw** (Rocky Mountain Books, $28). Big storm, tent blown away. "We'll come back for you if we can." A classic mountain survival tale.

—DAVID STEVENSON

IN MEMORIAM

These articles have been edited for length. The complete tributes may be found at the AAJ website: publications.americanalpineclub.org. Here, readers also will find In Memoriam tributes to Hooman Aprin, Allen Frame Hill, Jim Detterline, John Filsinger, and Woodward Kingman.

SCOTT ADAMSON, 1981–2016

AN ADVENTURER AT an early age, Scott Adamson joined a group of kids who pushed each other to train, climb hard, and live life to the fullest, all under the motto NWS ("No Weak Shit!"). "NWS" adorned everything: their helmets, packs, clothing, and gear. This small group lived up to the saying, one winning the American Ninja Warrior TV game, others climbing 5.14 and developing some of Utah's hardest boulder problems, and Scott quickly becoming one of the best mixed climbers and alpinists in the state, and then the world.

Early on, Scott partnered with his younger brother, Tom. The two traveled through South America, slogging up snowy peaks and icy couloirs and faces, a few by possible first ascents. In 2005 they went to Kyrgyzstan for an early attempt on Kyzyl Asker. Later, Scott would do first ascents in Alaska, including new routes on the east face of the Mooses Tooth, two first ascents in the Rolwaling Himal of Nepal, and two attempts on the Ogre II in the Karakoram, the final attempt claiming his life and that of his partner, Kyle Dempster.

Everything seemed so effortless when Scott climbed, and I think he believed it should be the same for everyone else. That sentiment was mine and many others' secret weapon. Not only was I sure he could make it up anything, but, when climbing with Scott, so would we. He believed in his partners more than they believed in themselves, and you fought hard to not let him down.

He was in constant motion, climbing nonstop, researching the next big route, and establishing entire regions of ice climbing, including the world-class ice of Zion National Park, which he explored for several recent seasons. Yet he always seemed to be there for his friends and family when they needed him most. To the outside observer, Scott could seem aloof and distant, but those who took the time to talk to him quickly found out otherwise. Scott was gregarious, quick to instigate a party, and extremely generous toward his friends and family.

Once he found sponsorship, he often would place large orders before a trip. His sponsors, knowing how fast he destroyed gear, never questioned the need. Only later did some discover that he would purposely use gear that was in poor shape longer than he should have and then give the new gear to someone he thought was deserving of support.

Scott is survived by Angela VanWiemeersch, the love of his life, as well as his parents, Tom and Kathy, sisters Shayla, Andrea, and Sheresa, and his brother, Tom. His absence is felt strongly in the climbing community. Though we may never again see his wide smile and sparkling eyes behind that big bushy mustache, those who knew him will always aspire to his calm and his ability to enjoy life under the most difficult circumstances. NWS.

– NATHAN SMITH

WOLF BAUER, 1912–2016

Pioneering Northwest skier, climber, rescuer, kayaker, and conservationist Wolf Bauer died on January 23, a month shy of his 104th birthday. Born in Bavaria, Bauer immigrated to Seattle with his family in 1925. As a Boy Scout, he was awarded a free membership in the Mountaineers in 1929, beginning his long association with the club and the larger outdoor community.

An accomplished skier, Bauer competed in regional races in the 1930s and was one of 60 competitors who started from Camp Muir on Mt. Rainier during the legendary Silver Skis downhill race in 1934. In 1936, Wolf's three-man team won the Mountaineers Ski Patrol Race between Snoqualmie and Stampede passes in a time that was not bettered until 2016, a month after his death.

In 1935, Wolf organized and single-handedly taught the Mountaineers' first climbing course, importing modern climbing techniques from European experts. During the course, he teamed with students to complete first ascents of Ptarmigan Ridge on Mt. Rainier (1935) and Mt. Goode in the North Cascades (1936). Wolf's student Lloyd Anderson later founded Recreational Equipment Inc. to provide gear to the growing ranks of course graduates.

While traveling in Germany in 1948, Wolf learned about the Bavarian Bergwacht, a volunteer rescue group. He concluded that a similar organization was needed in the Northwest. With the help of veteran rescuer Ome Daiber, physician and mountaineer Otto Trott, and others, he founded the Mountain Rescue Council in Seattle and served for six years as its first chairman. Similar rescue councils were formed in other Northwest cities, and in 1959 the national Mountain Rescue Association was organized, largely through the work of Seattle council members.

Wolf's pioneering contributions were not limited to the mountains. With friends he kayaked and mapped dozens of rivers throughout the Northwest, as well as now-popular sea kayaking destinations on the coasts of Washington and British Columbia. This led to an interest in conservation of shorelines and free-flowing rivers, which spawned a new career as the Northwest's leading shore resource consultant. In 2010, Wolf published his autobiography, together with Lynn Hyde, entitled *Crags, Eddies & Riprap: The Sound Country Memoir of Wolf Bauer.*

— LOWELL SKOOG

NICHOLAS CLINCH, 1930–2016

Nicholas Bayard Clinch III was born in Evanston, Illinois, and grew up mainly in Dallas, with high school years at the New Mexico Military Institute in Roswell, influenced by his father's and grandfather's careers in the military. A number of Nick's preteen summers were spent at Cheley Camps near Estes Park, Colorado. There, as junior counselors, our lives intersected and our lifelong friendship began.

Nick received a B.A. in political science from Stanford University in 1952, followed by a law degree three years later. His education superseded classrooms, as his muse became the mountains that he shared with other members of the Stanford Mountaineering Club and the Sierra Club. Their playground ranged from the Sierra to the Coast Mountains of British Columbia and the Cordillera Blanca of Peru. After graduating from law school, Nick put in

a stint with the U.S. Air Force, based in Iceland; he retired to the reserves as a major in 1957, setting the stage for a future life of mountain exploration.

In 1958, Nick collected some friends and acquaintances to pull off the first ascent of Gasherbrum I (a.k.a. Hidden Peak, 8,068 meters) in the Karakoram, the only one of the 8,000-meter peaks first ascended by Americans (Kauffman and Schoening). With his appetite for expedition organizing whetted, Nick was back to the Karakoram in 1960, now, "having done the high one, to attempt the hard one." This was Masherbrum (7,821 meters). I was invited along as climber and doc, my first big expedition experience. With no lack of thrills and spills, Willi Unsoeld and George Bell pulled off Masherbrum's first ascent, followed a couple of days later by Nick and Pakistani teammate Jawed Akhter Khan in a 24-hour saga that tapped the depths of Nick's reserves. They topped out as the sun set on K2, then descended through a moonlit night. Nick was never a physically strong climber, but this climb is testimonial to uncommon tenacity and skill.

In 1966, the American Alpine Club asked Nick to fuse competing teams from the Pacific Northwest and the Northeast into a unified effort to attempt the first ascent of Antarctica's highest peak. The expedition not only made the first ascent of Mt. Vinson, it then proceeded to top off about everything else in sight, including the committing ascent of Mt. Tyree by Barry Corbet and John Evans.

Nick's expedition to Ulugh Muztagh, in 1985, was perhaps the most exotic of all his creations. He and Bob Bates consulted with Eric Shipton on the biggest unexplored blank left on Earth's maps. With Nixon's opening of communication with China, this expedition became the first joint Chinese-American mountaineering effort. Ulugh Muztagh (6,973 meters) is a mountain in the Kunlun Range, first spotted by St. George and Teresa Littledale in 1895 during their attempt to reach Lhasa. Five young Chinese, supported from the highest camp by Schoening and me, attained the summit. They opted for a night descent, and two of the climbers fell, sustaining moderate injuries and immoderate frostbite. The Americans then gave up their own summit aspirations to rescue the two injured climbers.

With Ulugh Muztagh, Nick and team had so endeared themselves to their Chinese hosts that they were pretty much given carte blanche to return, freed from the bureaucratic hassle faced by most expeditions. Nick had found a photo in a 1926 National Geographic depicting an alluring peak named Kangkarpo, rising above the Mekong River where it descends from the Tibetan Plateau, and in the late 1980s and early '90s he led four trips to the range. These were the final chapters of Nick's expedition-creating life.

Nick became a member of the American Alpine Club in 1954 and served as its president from 1968 to 1970. He was a visionary who saw the need for the AAC to transition from an exclusive club to a national organization and voice for American mountaineering. It took a decade of patient planning to finally open membership to all comers, during the term of his partner-in-change, Jim McCarthy, as president. Nick brought not only vision but also patient backroom plotting to this evolution; he was always working on ways to effect change in a way the old guard could accept. This was a role he loved to play, not only within the AAC but also during his terms as a board member at REI, and, I suspect, during his time as executive director of the Sierra Club Foundation.

Another outcome of Nick's vision and priceless negotiating skills was the creation of the Grand Teton Climbers' Ranch in 1970. It is fitting that the club opted at its annual meeting in 2017 to name the ranch's main building the Nicholas B. Clinch Historic Lodge.

Along with many expedition accounts and other writings, Nick was the author of two books, *A Walk in the Sky*, published 24 years after the ascent of Hidden Peak, and with his, wife Betsy, *Through a Land of Extremes: The Littledales of Central Asia*, published in 2008.

Nick died from an untreatable sarcoma of a leg. On November 30, in full dress uniform, he was buried at Arlington National Cemetery near his father and grandfather. Nick, among many other things, was a quiet patriot who believed in his country as well as its and the world's wild places.

— TOM HORNBEIN

SCOTT COSGROVE, 1964–2016

When you're 20 years old, living in Yosemite and climbing every day, the Earth seems to spin a bit slower. Time seems stretched out as you rope up with a friend on another big day. In 1984 I tied in with Scott Cosgrove for our first big climb together, Space Babble, a very bold route on Middle Cathedral Rock. There was no chalk, no string of bolts as on modern routes. We played the ground-up, onsight game and tried to play with no mistakes. I was nervous but confident in the Coz; he had the reach, the strong mind, and good footwork to get the job done. Our friendship was cemented that day and would continue for 32 years.

Scott was one hell of a climber, bold and tough as nails. He was the first American to establish a 5.14a (New Deal at Joshua Tree). He and Dave Schultz made the first free ascent of Half Dome's legendary Southern Belle (5.12c R/X). He climbed a new route on the Central Tower of Paine in Patagonia and on Mt. Proboscis in northern Canada. He guided throughout the world and was a world-class rigger, working on many films, including one for which his team won an Academy Award in 1985.

In the mid-1980s, his finger was crushed in a climbing accident and doctors said he would never climb again. A few years later, he was thrown from the back of a pickup truck, while asleep, at 80 miles an hour. His ankle was so shattered that the first two doctors he saw wanted to remove his foot. After two years of intense pain and physical therapy, he was back to guiding in Joshua Tree for Bob Gaines and climbing incredibly well.

In the winter of 1993 I was sitting in his living room with Greg Epperson, the yellow Valley guidebook open to page 62: the Muir Wall. We ended up spending about three months working on a free ascent, from the bottom up, following in the footsteps of TM Herbert and Yvon Chouinard, who did the route in 1965 with no fixed ropes or support. We wanted to find the same kind of adventure. In the end we managed to free all but 30 feet of the wall. And then a drama with the park service ensued. We had used a power drill to replace old anchors and add a handful of bolts to our variations. We got busted on the summit in an undercover sting operation, a surreal way to finish an epic wall.

I'll never forget sitting on the summit with Scott after the rangers left, depressed and bewildered by what had just happened. Scott was quick to remind me of what we'd done as a team and what we had just free climbed. "Man, we spent the times of our lives up there, sending perfect pitches of Yosemite granite and living the dream. Cheer up, man!"

It's sad to think he will be climbing with me no longer. Scott Cosgrove was a survivor, one of the toughest guys I know. In 2014 he was on a rigging job when I got a call from Jeff Constine: "Cosgrove is in the hospital, and he may not make it." I was stunned speechless, but deep down I knew the Coz had the will to live. He had proved doctors wrong many times before.

Scott slowly but surely crawled back from the brink. My son was born six months after his accident, and he was the first to reach out to congratulate me and offer his support. Milo was three months premature, and Scott's energy and support got me through some dark times that winter. We made plans to climb again, and he wanted to be there when Milo was tied into the rope for the first time.

I'm grateful to have grown up with Scott, spending hours with him in the boulder fields and chasing John Bachar around the Tuolumne solo circuit. Scott, you will never be forgotten in the annals of climbing. I know someday we will meet up with Bachar and continue that circuit from days long passed.

– KURT SMITH

GLEN DAWSON, 1912–2016

GLEN DAWSON was born in northeast Los Angeles on June 3, 1912. As a child, he was presented with a lifetime membership to the Sierra Club. Glen helped shape the Sierra Club's mountaineering and climbing exploits throughout the 1930s, and he would serve on the club's board from 1937 to 1951.

Glen and his close friend Jules Eichorn made the first ascents of what became Eichorn Pinnacle on Cathedral Peak and Eichorn Minaret. When Robert Underhill came to California to teach proper belayed climbing and the use of pitons, Glen, Eichorn, and other "students" made the first ascent of the last unclimbed California 14er, Thunderbolt Peak. They, Underhill, and Norman Clyde then headed south to attempt the untouched east face of Mt. Whitney. Seventy-four years later, Glen noted, "I've climbed in many parts of the world and published over 300 books. But of all the things of my life, that day in August in 1931—well, I still get a good deal of pleasure out of it."

Both Glen and Jules became members of the American Alpine Club in 1933—at 21, likely among the youngest. With Glen's support, the Sierra Club's Southern California Chapter was among the earliest to develop a rock climbing group; its Rock Climbing Section was formally established in 1934.

Shortly after graduation from UCLA in 1935, Glen began an around-the-globe trip. His exploits began in the Alps, with ascents in the Wetterstein and the Dolomites. A year later, Glen climbed in North Wales, the Caucasus, and the Japanese Alps. Returning home, he would write, "After having climbed in a dozen different countries, I can agree with John Muir and Clarence King that our own High Sierra is the finest and most friendly of all."

Glen and longtime climbing partner Dick Jones had a phenomenal year in 1937. With Bill Rice, they made their first climb of Higher Cathedral Spire. Glen and Dick, joined by brother Muir Dawson, Howard Koster, and Bob Brinton, then climbed directly up Whitney by its east buttress, a much more difficult route than the original east face. A month later, Glen and Dick completed a frightful Tahquitz route. Later named Mechanic's Route, it took 16 pitons, with Dick in the lead, plus a long, crackless run-out pitch. Years later this route would be hailed as the first 5.8 climb in North America.

Glen and Jones also did the first ascent of East Temple in Zion National Park, and in 1938 he assembled a strong team for the first LA/RCS Sierra Club foray into alpine Canada, focusing on the Bugaboos, where they climbed Bugaboo Spire.

Glen was married to Mary Helen Johnston for 62 years and they raised three children. He and his brother, Muir, succeeded their father as proprietors of Dawson's Book Shop in Los Angeles. Glen largely withdrew from climbing in 1942, following the death of his close friend Bill Rice on the Grand Teton. However, he remained active in AAC affairs and was the founding chair of the Southern California Section. During World War II he helped train ski troopers and was awarded a bronze star for his service in Italy with the 10th Mountain Division.

Starting in his late 70s—and then for nearly 30 years—Glen presented to or was featured in numerous programs for climbing audiences, where he would introduce himself as "a historical curiosity—a living fossil." We were privileged to have had him among us for 103 years.

– BILL OLIVER

KYLE DEMPSTER, 1983–2016

IT'S BEEN MONTHS since Kyle Dempster and Scott Adamson disappeared while attempting a new route on the Ogre II (Baintha Brakk II) in the Karakoram. The Utah climbing community is still reeling; two of our most promising climbers—but, more importantly, two of our most kind, humble, and supportive friends—are now gone. Many of us still catch ourselves including them in upcoming plans or picturing their faces when they hear of our latest successes or failures, only to be painfully reminded that they are gone.

Kyle was born in March 1983 to Terry and Tom Dempster. The Dempsters were not your average family. TV was shunned, and ball sports were not a part of daily life. Instead, the family introduced Kyle and his younger sister Molly to life in the outdoors: hiking, biking, camping, skiing. This is the venue where they learned cause and effect, the beauty of life, in all its forms, physical exhaustion, and other lessons. Kyle grew up encouraged to push himself, to embrace the unknown, and always choose adventure.

When he was 14, Kyle was introduced to climbing by his cousins, Drew and Erin Wilson and was instantly hooked. Having moved to Salt Lake City a few years earlier, his parents took him to Rockreation and he became a gym rat: sport climbing, bouldering, and spending hours pulling on plastic. In his 20s he added traditional climbing, big walling, mountaineering, and alpine and ice climbing to his skill set. His constant drive to better himself and push his personal boundaries led to a long list of accomplishments, including new routes in Canada, Venezuela, Alaska, and China. In Pakistan he did a new route on the Ogre (the third ascent of the legendary peak). He spent 24 days alone on the west face of 6,651-meter Tahu Rutum, coming up just short of the first ascent. He won Piolets d'Or twice, in 2010 and 2013. He biked solo across Kyrgyzstan, putting up first ascents and capturing footage of the journey that would be edited into the classic film *The Road From Karakol*.

While these accomplishments were all a big part of Kyle's life, in reality they were only a fraction of who Kyle was.

In college, as Kyle was talking with a group of friends, a newcomer joined the group and the conversation moved to climbing. Someone mentioned the route Arm and Hammer in Bells Canyon, a multi-pitch Wasatch classic. Ian, the newcomer blurted out, "Ah, man, I wanna do that thing!" Kyle looked at him and said, "You wanna do it right now?" Hours later, almost at midnight, the two returned to the car, a new friendship formed.

Kyle knew how experiences like this could affect others. He constantly challenged his friends and acquaintances to be better. To push deep into reserves that only he knew were there. Kyle's generosity and kindness were always out in the open. When you had a conversation with him, he made you feel as if you were the only person in the world. He'd deflect questions about his accomplishments and ask about your life, your accomplishments, dreams and desires. If possible, he helped make those dreams a reality.

Adventure was usually a big part of Kyle's travel plans, but just as important to him were the connections he made with those he met. You can see this in *The Road From Karakol*. His face fills with joy as he races a young boy on his bike. Over five expeditions to Pakistan, Kyle became extremely close with his base camp manager, Abdul Ghafoor. After Kyle's death, Ghafoor traveled to America to spend time with Kyle's family. He was there to comfort them as much as they were comforting him.

Kyle grew up with literature playing a strong role in his life, but writing wasn't always his strongest suit—until he decided he wanted to be better. He worked hard, pushing his mind in the same way he pushed his body in physical training. This led to many articles in *Alpinist* and other magazines—introspective, reflective, and insightful stories. He truly honed his literary voice and bared his soul to the world.

Kyle often hand-wrote letters to his family and friends. In one he sent to me, he stated, "I do hope that my deep passion for adventure burns bright and encourages others in the same way that you have encouraged me. Thank you my friend, the journey has been joyous." I can't think of a better way to end but to say to Kyle: Thank *you* my friend, the journey has been joyous.

– NATHAN SMITH

DON GORDON, 1931–2016

An intensely private man, Don Gordon passed away in April in the Capitol Hill neighborhood of Seattle, where he lived for over 50 years. Born Don Gordon Claunch in Ely, Nevada, he changed his name for personal reasons, according to longtime friend Ed Cooper.

Don Gordon joined the Seattle Mountaineers in the late 1940s. He soon displayed a knack for adventurous climbing, making first ascents of the Pyramid and East McMillan Spire in the Cascades' Picket Range in 1951. In 1953, with four companions, he climbed Mt. Robson in the Canadian Rockies by the south face, the first successful ascent of that peak since 1939. During the same year, with Fred Beckey, he climbed two new routes on Mt. Goode in the North Cascades.

Gordon's success on Robson laid the foundation for his greatest climb, the first ascent of Robson's Wishbone Arête, in 1955. The climb was made with Harvey Firestone and Mike Sherrick, who would later make the first ascent of Half Dome's northwest face. On Robson, Sherrick led the lower rock sections while Gordon tackled the summit ice gargoyles, which had repulsed a 1913 attempt led by Swiss guide Walter Schauffelberger. In 1956, with John Rupley, he climbed the north ridge of Mt. Stuart in the Cascades—a route that, along with Wishbone Arête, was later recognized as one of the "Fifty Classic Climbs in North America."

With Beckey, Cooper, and others, Gordon pioneered many routes in the Cascades, including the Mowich Face of Mt. Rainier (1957), north face of Mt. Maude (1957), west ridge of Prusik Peak (1957), direct east ridge of Forbidden Peak (1958), and south buttress of Cutthroat Peak (1958). Following many attempts, he succeeded with Cooper on one of the most difficult and protracted Cascade climbs of the era, the north face of Mt. Baring (1961). Gordon also helped open many low-elevation crags, including Castle Rock, Midnight Rock, Snow Creek Wall, Peshastin Pinnacles, and Stawamus Chief in British Columbia.

Ed Cooper recalled that Gordon always seemed to be on a spiritual journey whose nature varied over time. Among early Mountaineers, he was best known for his "all the way on foot" climbs in the Cascade foothills, starting and ending at his home in Seattle and not using any type of mechanical aid for travel. On a winter day in 1958, he walked some 35 miles from his home to Mt. Si, hiked to the summit, and made a good start on the return walk before lying down in wet roadside willows to sleep. Cooper believed that Gordon finally found his calling in the 1990s when he became a certified Reiki Master, specializing in energy healing and balancing.

— LOWELL SKOOG

JAMES F. HENRIOT, 1927–2016

JIM HENRIOT WILL be much missed by all who knew him, on or off the mountains. A distinguished attorney, an outstanding outdoorsman and mountaineer, a wise counselor, a loyal friend, a leader of consummate grace and style—he left his mark in all spheres of his long and active life.

Naturally sociable, Jim always had a sympathetic ear, good advice, a ready smile, and an encouraging word. But when needed he could also reveal a core of steely resolution, a quality that served him in both litigation and mountaineering. I well remember the last time I climbed with him in the North Cascades, where steeper snow slopes are best negotiated *de bonne heure*. He was amiable enough while the rest of us wasted valuable time chattering at breakfast, but when we finally were ready to leave, as if in rebuke, he led off at a breakneck

pace that soon absorbed any wind for chatter. Thanks largely to this corrective measure, our party was able to summit safely.

For most of his mature life, Jim was a partner in the eminent law firm of Eisenhower Carlson in Washington state, his specialty being employment and labor law, a field in which he gained national recognition. For many years he was general counsel to the University of Puget Sound, a post he enjoyed for the contact it gave him with higher education. He served on many committees of the bar—regional, national, and international.

At the AAC, he served on the board of directors and chaired the Expeditions Committee from 1974 to 1976, before becoming president in 1977. He also was a board member of a number of civic entities, including his alma mater, Seattle University, the Washington State Historical Society, Lowell Observatory, REI, and the Tacoma Mountaineers, of which he was several times president.

During his presidency—the first of a member from the Pacific Northwest—Jim induced the board to expand its meeting places to more Western locales, which aided in recruiting new and younger members. A quiet campaign added much-needed funds to the club's endowment. Perhaps most importantly, he worked with Bill Putnam to strengthen our ties with the UIAA and the international climbing fellowship. During his presidency, the AAC first hosted the UIAA General Assembly, in 1977, in Pinkham Notch, New Hampshire.

Jim took an active part in encouraging mountaineering exchanges, such as that between the Russian Mountaineering Federation and the AAC, which began with the participation of an American team in the International Pamirs Camp in 1974 and continued with visits from teams of Russian climbers in 1976 and 1977. Following his presidency, Jim remained chair of the Climbing Exchanges Committee for 14 years.

Jim was so modest that even good friends were often unaware of many of his exploits. In addition to climbing six out of the seven highest peaks on the continents, he once helped sail a brigantine from Hong Kong to the Philippines. His mountaineering philosophy is best summed up in his own words: "There's a personal satisfaction in reaching a summit; you get so close to nature and God. You are dependent on your companions and they are dependent on you, so you work together as a team." Isn't that what we all prize as climbers?

– T. C. PRICE ZIMMERMANN

RICHARD POWNALL, 1927–2016

ON MY FIRST trip to the Tetons, in 1955, I met three already iconic climbers: Dick Emerson, the climbing/rescue ranger, and Willi Unsoeld and Dick Pownall, both Exum guides. I never imagined the four of us would reconnect eight years later as members of the 1963 American Mount Everest Expedition.

Dick Pownall was born in West Branch, Iowa. He climbed on local trees and windmills, and in his teens he happened to read an article about climbing mountains and thus changed his venue. In 1947, Glen Exum offered him a job as a climbing guide and Dick made the first of some 150 ascents of the Grand, mostly while guiding.

During these years, he also pioneered a few dozen first ascents, including the first complete climb of the north face of the Grand, in 1949, with Ray Garner and Art Gilkey; Dick led the crux Pendulum Pitch in the dark, and they bivouacked on top. The next year, he and Mike Brewer pulled off a major enchainment in 14 hours: Nez Perce, Cloudveil Dome, South and Middle Teton, and the Grand, a big chunk of the link-up now known as the Grand Traverse. In 1959, Dick, fellow guide Willi Unsoeld,

and Pete Schoening pulled off the Cathedral Traverse: Teewinot, Mt. Owen, and the Grand. During this time, Dick met and married Nancy Flint, and together they raised two children, Betsy and David.

Dick's contributions to the 1963 Everest expedition exemplify Norman Dyhrenfurth's skill in assembling a compatible team of summit-motivated climbers who could subjugate their personal aspirations to the goal of getting one or two teammates to the top. He was profoundly challenged by the death of his rope mate Jake Breitenbach, who was buried beneath a falling serac in the Khumbu Icefall on the second day above base camp. Though, as Dick said, Jake's death "spoiled the expedition for me," he declared he would go through the Icefall twice more—once up, once down. He and Lute Jerstad were the first to reach the South Col, on April 16, and he was a member of the quartet that made the second summit attempt. As the first team was descending from Camp 6 after Jim Whittaker and Nawang Gombu summited on May 1, the second team, including Dick, unhesitatingly aborted their own summit plans to assist their exhausted companions down the mountain.

After Everest, Dick bid good-bye to Teton guiding and taught math and physical education in the western suburbs of Denver. He became a counselor, assistant principal, and a principal. For me, now living in Colorado, encountering his former students and hearing their unsolicited comments about how he touched their lives has been pure pleasure.

The Pownalls bought land in Vail, and Dick skied, taught skiing, and served on the Vail ski patrol for many years. He also started a mountaineering school in the nearby Gore Range. During this time, Dick and Nancy divorced, and in 1979 Dick and Mary Rheinberger married. After he retired in 1982, they moved full-time to Vail, where they became a vital part of the permanent community, officiating at ski races and contributing in many other ways. Dick had become one of the old-timers who imbued a place they cherished with a bit of their own persona.

Dick lived modestly with the fame he gained as a consequence of the 1963 Everest expedition, incorporating it into his mission to inspire and challenge young people, whom he taught not to be afraid to dream. He was fundamentally a teacher, whether as a guide on mountains, of young minds in Jefferson County classrooms, or on the steep, deep slopes at Vail. He was low-key and soft-spoken, causing one to listen when he talked. He did not pontificate, just exemplified.

At a 50th anniversary event for the Everest expedition in Jackson Hole, Dick's response to the question of what he took away from the experience was preciously put: "I'd like to think it gave me a sense for the importance of life, and friends, and activities that would contribute to a better life for everybody." And it did.

— TOM HORNBEIN, *WITH A BELAY FROM FRED WOLFE*

KIM SCHMITZ, 1946–2016

KIM SCHMITZ WAS a force of nature and life. I first met him in the Tetons, in 1979, during a trip to climb the east ridge of the Grand. He came roaring out of his tent cabin on the old Guides' Hill, with piercing steel-blue eyes, a jaw like Jack Palance's, and a towering physique. His presence was stunning.

I knew of his speed climbs and first ascents of Yosemite walls. His recent expeditions to Nepal and Pakistan were already legendary, including the first ascents of Great Trango Tower and Gaurishankar. On Uli Biaho Tower, he had completed what was probably the world's first Grade VII wall during an 11-day epic. Since I had only been climbing for six years, I looked at Kim as a kind of god; I could never imagine being that good and strong and accomplished. But he was viewed no differently by the other guides of Exum. Even Chuck Pratt knew he was the best of them all.

A few years later, in 1981, I went to China to attempt Mt. Siguniang with Kim, Jim Donini, and Jim Kanzler. Kim had broken his back in a fall a year earlier in China, on Minya Konka (Gongga Shan), but on Siguniang he was as strong and resolute as ever. Our expedition did not summit the unclimbed peak, but Kim and I became fast friends. The following summer I was invited to become an Exum guide, and Kim became my mentor. I lived in my parents' Sears and Roebuck family camping tent but shared Kim's cabin for meals. I cooked for both of us, and I soaked up Kim's knowledge of the range and his climbing acumen. He was fast and efficient and bold as a guide. All Kim did was guide and climb. I remember him telling me he had been on either a wall or an expedition on his birthday, in June, every year since he was 16.

In 1983, Kim's life changed forever because of an accident while guiding on Symmetry Spire. We'll never know for sure what happened, but as he was running the rope out on "easy ground," around the fourth pitch, he plummeted 80 feet onto a ledge next to his client, shattering both legs and severely breaking his back and teeth, with a 150-stitch head wound to boot. The Jenny Lake rangers saved his life through heroic and fast action. After 26 reconstructive surgeries and years of PT, he returned to guide at Exum for a short time later in the '80s, but it proved to be too painful.

The remaining years of Kim's life saw enormous growth of character and being as a result of the constant challenges he faced medically and psychologically. Climbing and guiding had been his whole life, and now he had to define himself in different ways. He had to deal with new health challenges, including prostate and colon cancer and MRSA. On his most recent birthday, last June, he had been in the hospital for eight to ten weeks with a blood infection. We spent the day together, and I sprung him from the hospital and took him out to eat.

I was struck that day with the realization that I had always looked up to the climber and the person that Kim had been. But what I realized was that I admired most the person he had become—gentle, thoughtful, and non-judgmental. He was the most well-read person I have ever known, enjoying a wide spectrum of books. He wasn't bitter and embraced what was good about each day. We should all take Kim's struggle and example to heart. Life's turns take us down new, unexpected paths. Kim's difficult path in life led him to a form of enlightenment that I could only hope to achieve myself someday.

– JACK TACKLE

LOWELL THOMAS JR., 1923 – 2016

Lowell Thomas Jr. had a long life filled with extraordinary adventures and accomplishments. He was born in London, where his father, world-renowned journalist Lowell Thomas, was embarking on his career as a war correspondent. Lowell Jr. grew up in New York State. In World War II he was a fighter-pilot flight instructor in the Army Air Corps, and flying came to play a central role in his life.

Lowell made his first trip to Alaska in 1940, as a teenager, when he was part of the team led by Bradford Washburn that made the first ascent of Mt. Bertha (10,204') in the Fairweather Range. Lowell and his father traveled to pre-communist Tibet in 1949, and were perhaps the last Westerners to meet the teen-age Dalai Lama before the Chinese invasion. Lowell wrote a bestselling book, *Out Of This World*, and later produced a movie by the same name, to raise awareness of the Tibetan people.

In 1954 and 1955, Lowell and his wife, Tay, flew their Cessna 180, "Charlie," around the world, from France to Morocco, across Africa and into the Middle East and Afghanistan, where a visit by private single-engine aircraft was nearly unheard of. In 1958, Lowell and his family flew their 180 from the East Coast to Alaska, and they decided to make Anchorage their home.

Lowell was elected to the Alaska State Senate in 1966 and became the prime sponsor and advocate of the bill that, in 1970, created Chugach State Park, Anchorage's spectacular, 495,000-acre "backyard." He was elected lieutenant governor in 1974, serving with Gov. Jay Hammond, perhaps the only time in U.S. history that bush pilots occupied the top two offices in any state.

After leaving politics, he obtained a commercial pilot license and purchased Talkeetna Air Taxi in 1981. He began flying climbers in and out of the Alaska Range in his trusty, ski-equipped Helio Courier, earning a reputation as the consummate Alaska climbing-support pilot, with a vast knowledge of Alaska's mountain weather and terrain. In Lowell's flying career he made a total of seven forced landings, but he never once even scratched his aircraft.

Lowell was also a winter mountaineer, particularly in the Tordrillo Mountains, across Cook Inlet from Anchorage. In addition to flying numerous climbing parties into this seldom-visited area, he made two first ascents: Mt. Gerdine (11,258'), in 1963, and Mt. Torbert (11,413'), in 1964. Lowell finally sold Talkeetna Air Taxi in 1994, at age 70, but he continued to fly, with less stress and for his own enjoyment, until age 86. In 2012, he donated his beloved Helio Courier to the Alaska Aviation Heritage Museum.

– TOM MEACHAM

NECROLOGY

In addition to those covered above, AAC members who passed away in 2016 included:

D.W. Baird	Jim Detterline	Everett Melancon
Lorraine Bonney	Laurel Fan	Woodward Kingman
Margaret Craighead	John Filsinger	Richard Vlamnyck
Mark Davisa	Alfred Kwok	

INDEX

COMPILED BY EVE TALLMAN & RALPH FERRARA

Mountains are listed by their official names. Ranges, geographic locations, and maps are also indexed. Unnamed peaks (eg. Peak 2,340) are listed under P. Abbreviations are used for the following: Cordillera: C.; Mountains: Mts.; National Park: Nat'l. Park; Obituary: obit. Indexed photographs are listed in bold type.